PIAGET,
EVOLUTION,
AND
DEVELOPMENT

The Jean Piaget Symposium Series
Available from LEA

OVERTON, W. F. (Ed.) • The Relationship Between Social and Cognitive Development

LIBEN, L. S. (Ed.) • Piaget and the Foundations of Knowledge

SCHOLNICK, E. K. (Ed.) • New Trends in Conceptual Representation: Challenges to Piaget's Theory?

NEIMARK, E. D., De LISI, R., & NEWMAN, J. L. (Eds.) • Moderators of Competence

BEARISON, D. J., & ZIMILES, H. (Eds.) • Thought and Emotion: Developmental Perspectives

LIBEN, L. S. (Ed.) • Development and Learning: Conflict or Congruence?

FORMAN, G., & PUFALL, P. B. (Eds.) • Constructivism in the Computer Age

OVERTON, W. F. (Ed.) • Reasoning, Necessity, and Logic: Developmental Perspectives

KEATING, D. P., & ROSEN, H. (Eds.) • Constructivist Perspectives on Developmental Psychopathology and Atypical Development

CAREY, S., & GELMAN, R. (Eds.) • The Epigenesis of Mind: Essays on Biology and Cognition

BEILIN, H., & PUFALL, P. (Eds.) • Piaget's Theory: Prospects and Possibilities

WOZNIAK, R. H., & FISCHER, K. W. (Eds.) • Development in Context: Acting and Thinking in Specific Environments

OVERTON, W. F., & PALERMO, D. S. (Eds.) • The Nature and Ontogenesis of Meaning

NOAM, G. G., & FISCHER, K. W. (Eds.) • Development and Vulnerability in Close Relationships

REED, E. S., TURIEL, E., & BROWN, T. (Eds.) • Values and Knowledge

AMSEL, E., & RENNINGER, K. A. (Eds.) • Change and Development: Issues of Theory, Method, and Application

LANGER, J., & KILLEN, M. (Eds.) • Piaget, Evolution, and Development

PIAGET, EVOLUTION, AND DEVELOPMENT

Edited by

Jonas Langer
University of California, Berkeley

Melanie Killen
University of Maryland, College Park

LEA LAWRENCE ERLBAUM ASSOCIATES, PUBLISHERS
1998   Mahwah, New Jersey   London

Lawrence Erlbaum Associates, Inc., Publishers
10 Industrial Avenue
Mahwah, New Jersey 07430

Cover design by Kathryn Houghtaling Lacey

Library of Congress Cataloging-in-Publication Data

Piaget, evolution, and development / edited by Jonas Langer, Melanie
Killen.
   p.   cm.
   Includes bibliographical references and indexes.
   ISBN 0-8058-2210-0 (alk. paper).
   1. Cognition. 2. Human information processing. 3. Thought and
thinking. 4. Psychology, Comparative. I. Langer, Jonas.
II. Killen, Melanie.
  BF311.P527 1998
  153—dc21   98-12663
                                                       CIP

Books published by Lawrence Erlbaum Associates are printed on acid-free paper,
and their bindings are chosen for strength and durability.

Printed in the United States of America
10 9 8 7 6 5 4 3 2 1

CONTENTS

PART II: SOCIAL DEVELOPMENT

PART III: CULTURAL DEVELOPMENT

PREFACE

This volume is a product of the 25th Anniversary Symposium of the *Jean Piaget Society: The Study of Knowledge and Development*, entitled "Piaget, Evolution, and Development," which met in Berkeley, California, June 1995. In planning the Symposium and the volume, we focused on three comparative mental developments for which there is increasing phylogenetic, ontogenetic, and historical data. Research on comparative cognitive, social, and cultural development is (we believe this is not an overstatement) undergoing a renaissance. This volume seeks to illuminate and nourish this rebirth.

Setting the recent historical stage for the volume, Langer and Killen point to the major landmarks along the path of this century's study of comparative mental development. They are proximate systematizations upon which contemporary efforts build in studying comparative cognitive (Part I), social (Part II), and cultural (Part III) development. Anchoring these wide-ranging research explorations on comparative mental development are, to begin with, McKinney on its biological evolution and, to conclude, Damerow on its prehistory plus Turiel on culture and mentation. In between, the focus is upon classical and fundamental categories and processes marking the phylogeny, ontogeny, and history of mental development. The categories comprise knowledge of logical classes by Langer, of physical objects by Doré and Goulet, of others as psychological objects by Whiten, and of the self as object by Parker. The processes comprise adaptive functions of imitation by Russon, Mitchell, Lefebvre, and Abravanel, of symbolization by Savage-Rumbaugh, of conflict resolution by Cords and Killen, and of enculturation by Tomasello.

The varied findings and approaches reported in this volume by these anthropologists, biologists, historians of science, paleontologists, and psychologists reveal that contemporary comparative research on mental development is in a phase of differentiation and integration (to borrow once again from Werner, 1948). Far from being global and fused, the comparative study of mental development is a flowering field of diverse disciplinary approaches, empirical phenomena, scholarly topics, and theoretical perspectives on its evolution, ontogeny, and history.

Thanks are extended to the *Jean Piaget Society: The Study of Knowledge and Development* for supporting the symposium and the volume, to Terry Brown and Michael Chandler as President and President-Elect of JPS in 1995, to Ellin Kofsky Scholnick as Series Editor, and to Connie Milbrath, Matthew Schlesinger, Daphne Anshel, and Jim Messinger for invaluable assistance in organizing the symposium.

Jonas Langer
Melanie Killen

1

THE COMPARATIVE STUDY
OF MENTAL DEVELOPMENT

Jonas Langer
University of California, Berkeley

Melanie Killen
University of Maryland, College Park

In the great majority of animals there are traces of psychical qualities or attitudes, which qualities are more markedly differentiated in the case of human beings. For just as we pointed out resemblances in the physical organs, so in a number of animals we observe gentleness or fierceness, mildness or cross temper, courage or timidity, fear or confidence, high spirit or low cunning, and, with regard to intelligence, something equivalent to sagacity. Some of these qualities in man, as compared with the corresponding qualities in animals, differ only quantitatively: that is to say, a man has more or less of this quality, and an animal has more or less of some other; other qualities in man are represented by analogous and not identical qualities: for instance, just as in man we find knowledge, wisdom, and sagacity, so in certain animals there exists some other natural potentiality akin to these. The truth of this statement will be the more clearly apprehended if we have regard to the phenomena of childhood: for in children may be observed the traces and seeds of what will one day be settled psychological habits, though psychologically a child hardly differs for the time being from an animal; so that one is quite justified in saying that, as regards man and animals, certain psychical qualities are identical with one another, whilst others resemble, and others are analogous to, each other.
—Aristotle. *Historia Animalium*. Book VIII, Chapter I.

The comparative approach to the evolution of mental development has a long and rich history reaching back to antiquity. Contemporary comparative approaches represented in this volume have their more proximate roots in the systematization Hobhouse (1901) pioneered at the turn of the century. Following Darwin's lead (see Gruber, 1974, on Darwin's efforts), Hobhouse compared the phylogeny and ontogeny of mental development.

Hobhouse systematized all mentation into six progressively evolving forms of activity that comprehend the direction of mental development in both phylogenesis and ontogenesis. The most primitive is stimulus-controlled reflex reactions. Three intermediate forms are progressively dependent on interaction: from trial-and-error learning (e.g., a paramecium may acquire habitual responses) to assimilatory behavioral adjustment (e.g., Lloyd Morgan's [1896] discovery that chicks learn to discriminate bitter from agreeable food) to practical judgments about concrete relations (e.g., Kohler's [1926] discovery that chimpanzees construct and use tools as means to obtain desired goals). The two most advanced forms are progressively independent of interaction: conceptual thought freed from perception by which knowledge, tradition and culture are learned and used; followed by analysis by rational systems of logicomathematical operations.

Not all species develop all six means of mentation. According to Hobhouse, only humans do: only humans develop conceptual thought and logical analysis. Only human cognition goes beyond the information given by interactive experience.

Comparing the extent to which species develop was central to Hobhouse's phylogenetic systematization and to subsequent efforts. It continues to be a key, formal feature of evolutionary analyses of mental development as is evident across the wide-ranging spectrum of behavioral research and theoretical perspectives represented in this volume. Indeed, it is a key consideration in every chapter but the last.

Determining the comparative extent of mental development is prerequisite to investigating the causes. One approach (represented in chapters 10 and 11, and considered in chapter 6), cultural history as cause of humans' uniquely extended mental development, was expressed early on by Vygotsky (1935/1978):

> It is my belief, based upon a dialectical materialist approach to the analysis of human history, that human behavior differs qualitatively from animal behavior to the extent that the adaptability and historical development of humans differ from the adaptability and development of animals. The psychological development of humans is part of the general historical development of our species and must be so understood. (p. 60)

Vygotsky grants humans "adaptability and historical development" while limiting all other species to "adaptability and development." As already found in Freud's (1915/1958) formulation, human historical development is embodied in its cultural heritage. Cultural heritage is a proximate cause of human's qualitative mental progress beyond that of other species. It is also our curse, according to Freud and other Romantic theorists, leading to human's unique development of neurosis.

Vygotsky's account of both the extent and cause of humans' mental development seems circular. It posits historical cultural heritage as the cause of humans' qualitative mental extension while, at the same time, positing that humans' qualitative mental extension is the cause of our cultural history. Apparently Vygotsky (1934/1962) tried to overcome this circular account of humans' extended mental progress by appealing to the distinction between the development of everyday, informal individual knowledge in ontogeny and the development of formal, cultural knowledge in history. Everyday knowledge develops spontaneously in ontogeny from the bottom up: from individuals' concrete familiar experience up toward abstract cultural concepts, such as scientific equations and legal principles. Formal knowledge does not develop spontaneously in ontogeny. Instead, it is taught from the top down: from culture's historical heritage of abstract generalizations down to individuals' everyday concrete knowledge. The dialectical interaction of these two antithetical ontogenetic and historical trajectories, Vygotsky speculated, synthesizes into humans' uniquely extended mental development.

The role of cultural history was anticipated in Baldwin's (1915) more comprehensive developmental model. Baldwin undertook the first major shift in and elaboration on the systematic comparative developmental approach initiated by Hobhouse. Although concurring in the importance of comparing phylogenetic and ontogenetic development, Baldwin also compared the ontogenesis and ethnogenesis (cultural history) of human mentation. By expanding the comparative developmental approach to include ethnogenesis, Baldwin prepared the way for its fullest elaboration so far, undertaken by Werner (1926/1948).

Baldwin's augmented comparative approach enabled him to found the discipline of genetic epistemology, brought to fruition by Piaget (1950/1973, 1950/1974). Piaget grounded genetic epistemology in experimental and historical research on the comparative origins, development, and structures of knowledge in the ontogeny and cultural history of ideas, respectively. In this, Piaget followed Baldwin's original conception—to study how thought or experience constructs reality by comparing the progressive stages of mentation that develop in ontogenesis and ethnogenesis. Baldwin's aim was to create a natural history of interpretation. While agreeing, Piaget sought to also make the study of genetic epistemology amenable to experimental as well as critical investigation.

Baldwin's comparative thesis was that the development of objective external organization of thought and values in ethnogenesis parallels its subjective internal development in ontogenesis. Moreover, he extended aspects of what has come to be known as the Baldwin Effect in biological evolution (Baldwin, 1896) to account for historical evolution. Accordingly, he hypothesized that ontogenesis gives ethnogenesis "its vital impulse and its progressive 'uplift'." Baldwin (1915, p. 34), unlike Vygotsky, attributed causal priority to ontogeny in extending human mental development beyond that of other species and to our cultural history of ideas. It is the comparative developmental perspective adopted by Piaget (1971) and those crediting ontogeny with primary causal roles in the evolution of mental development and cultural history (i.e., chapters 2, 3, 8 and 12, and considered in chapters 5 and 6).

Baldwin's natural history of interpretation comprised three progressive mental stages in the development of both human ontogenesis and ethnogenesis: the prelogical, logical, and hyperlogical. Ontogenesis begins with a stage of intuitive and quasidiscursive or quasililnguistic behavior. Thereby, children develop prelogical, pragmatic, and presentational knowledge. Their knowledge is egocentric, "a meaning of immediate presence and intuition" (Baldwin, 1915, p. 26). Children begin by accepting "the reality of the datum" of experience. They do not distinguish between subjective and objective experience. The intermediate, logical stage involves imaginative activity taking discursive or linguistic forms. Imaginative interpretations of experience are assumptions, proposals and hypotheses that "have the force of possibility and probability" such that "reality is embodied in all sorts of 'as if' constructions" (Baldwin, 1915, pp. 26–27). These constructions are tested by verification procedures to assess their validity. The results are logical processes of judgment, reasoning, and implication determining what is accepted as reality. Finally, at the highest interpretative stage, action becomes esthetic contemplation that "erects into postulates its ends, values, and goods" (Baldwin, 1915, p. 29). At this hyperlogical stage, "Consciousness achieves a freeing from logic as before she worked to secure the freeing of logic" (Baldwin, 1915, p. 28).

Baldwin (1915) hypothesized that mental ontogenesis feeds forward to and provides the initial impetus for the parallel development of three stages in ethnogenesis. Accordingly, the initial forms of the three stages of ethnogenesis are amplifications of the three stages of ontogenesis. Once established, the stages of ethnogenesis begin to feed back to the stages of ontogenesis. This hypothesis of reciprocal amplification between prior individual mental development and subsequent cultural history implies that both are progressively evolving open systems (cf. chapters 2 and 3).

Ethnogenesis, in Baldwin's view, is the progressive construction of objective societal embodiments of subjective individual interpretations into laws, rites, customs, theories, and so forth. Ethnogenesis, like ontogenesis, begins with a prelogical stage in which the group's interpretative behavior is mystical and takes mythical and religious forms. At the intermediate, the logical stage, it is speculative and takes scientific and critical forms. Finally, at the hyperlogical stage societal interpretative action becomes esthetic contemplation that creates advanced philosophical theory.

Werner (1926/1948, 1957) extended Baldwin's comparative approach into the most comprehensive program for ordering all lawful development. Werner's (1926/1948, p. 55) comparative program assumes that "... wherever there is life there is growth and development, that is formation in terms of systematic, orderly sequence." He therefore argued that general comparative laws of "mental life as a whole" must account for microgenesis (short-term local development) and pathogenesis (pathological development) as well as ontogenesis, phylogenesis, and ethnogenesis. Such laws should encompass the processes of mental development as well as the new organization of its structures at succeeding stages (Werner, 1937; Werner & Kaplan, 1963). This requires accounting for the genesis and structural organization of the original, most rudimentary (primitive) mentation; plus subsequent processes and derivative intermediate structures of mental development leading to the so far most advanced (final) mentation.

To these ends, Werner (1926/1948) proposed his orthogenetic principle (adapted from embryogenesis) as the most general law governing all forms of mental developmental in ontogenesis, phylogenesis, ethnogenesis, microgenesis, and pathogenesis. The principle asserts that progressive development is (a) a process of increasing differentiation and specification of initially relatively global mental organization, coupled with (b) a process of advancing centralization and hierarchic integration of the individuating mental structures, leading to (c) more powerful mental adaptation (cf. chapters 5, 6, 8, and 9).

Pathogenesis, of course, involves degenerative regressive forms of orthogenesis. Each type of genesis, then, has its own phenotypic material form of orthogenesis although some may share formal features, that is, comprise genetic parallels. To illustrate, both phylogenetic and ontogenetic development in the relationship between organisms and their Umwelt progresses from (1) initial stages of biophysical and biochemical, stereotyped tropistic and reflex reactions to stimuli; to (2) intermediate stages of species-specific and individually learned goal-directed sensorimotor actions upon signaled things; to (3) final stages of symbolic construction of contemplative knowledge about phenomena (Werner & Kaplan, 1963).

Piaget concurred in the search for general comparative laws of developmental processes (Piaget, 1971; Inhelder, Garcia, & Vonéche, 1977) and structures (Piaget, 1977). Indeed, Piaget (1971, 1977) formulated one of the truly novel evolutionary theories of the origins, transformation, and development of mentation. The theory is multifaceted but three elements are basic: (1) adaptive functions—accommodating, assimilating, and organizing—are invariant and continuous in phylogeny, ontogeny, and history; (2) initial psychological structures (e.g., object permanence schemes discussed in chapter 4 and symbol formation discussed in chapter 7) are constructed derivatives of biological functions; and (3) psychological as well as biological structures are variant, discontinuous, and progressively equilibrated in phylogeny, ontogeny, and history. The third element provided the theoretical basis for Piaget's uniquely comprehensive stage model of cognitive development from the sensorimotor to the formal operational. All three elements are theoretical bases for his genetic epistemology that compared the history and ontogeny of ideas (cf. chapters 2 and 11).

Focusing on the comparative phylogeny, ontogeny, and history of mentation—especially on the comparative onset and offset ages, velocity, extent, sequencing and organization of thought, symbol, and value development—this volume seeks further understanding of the mechanisms of mental development. As it has been throughout its history, the guiding purpose of this comparative research continues to be determining the possibilities that evolution opens up for the ontogenetic origins, development, and history of mentation; as well as the constraints that evolution imposes on mental development.

REFERENCES

Baldwin, J. M. (1896). A new factor in evolution. *American Naturalist, 30,* 441–451, 536–553.

Baldwin, J. M. (1915). *Genetic theory of reality.* New York: Putnam.

Freud, S. (1915/1958). Instincts and their vicissitudes. In *Collected Papers* (Vol. 14). London: Hogarth.

Gruber, H. E. (1974). *Darwin on man.* New York: Dutton.

Hobhouse, L. T. (1901). *Mind in evolution.* New York: Macmillan.

Inhelder, B., Garcia, R., & Vonéche, J. (Eds.). (1977). *Epistémologie génétique et équilibration.* Neuchâtel, Switzerland: Delachaux et Niestlé.

Kohler, W. (1926). *The mentality of apes.* New York: Harcourt Brace.

Morgan, C. L. (1896). *Habit and instinct.* London: Edward Arnold.

Piaget, J. (1950/1973). *Introduction à l'épistemologie génétique* (Vol. 1). *La pensée-mathé-matique.* Paris: PUF.

Piaget, J. (1950/1974). *Introduction à l'épistemologie génétique* (Vol. 2). *La pensée physique.* Paris: PUF.

Piaget, J. (1971). *Biology and knowledge.* Chicago: University of Chicago Press.

Piaget, J. (1977). *Equilibration of cognitive structures.* New York: Viking.

Vygotsky, L. S. (1935/1978). *Mind in society.* Cambridge, MA: Harvard University Press.

Vygotsky, L. S. (1934/1962). *Thought and language.* Cambridge, MA: MIT Press.

Werner, H. (1926/1948). *Comparative psychology of mental development.* New York: International Universities Press.

Werner, H. (1937). Process and achievement. *Harvard Educational Review, 7,* 353–368.

Werner, H. (1957). The concept of development from a comparative and organismic point of view. In D. B. Harris (Ed.), *The concept of development* (pp. 125–148). Minneapolis: University of Minnesota Press.

Werner, H., & Kaplan, B. (1963). *Symbol formation.* New York: Wiley.

COGNITIVE DEVELOPMENT

2

COGNITIVE EVOLUTION BY EXTENDING BRAIN DEVELOPMENT: ON RECAPITULATION, PROGRESS, AND OTHER HERESIES

Michael L. McKinney
University of Tennessee

Adult human beings share many features with infant apes . . . like Peter Pan, we never grow up.

—Gribbin, 1988

A philosophy of human growth and development that emphasizes the progressive appearance of new biological and behavioral traits is more satisfying empirically, and intellectually, than a view of development that emphasizes growth retardation and permanency of childhood.

—Bogin, 1988

Evolutionary biology is experiencing greatly renewed interest in development. As recently as 1988, Futuyma in his Presidential Address to the Society for the Study of Evolution noted that understanding how the dynamics of development influence evolutionary rates and direction is perhaps the most glaring deficiency in modern evolutionary theory. But after decades of focusing on the evolution of genes and adults, evolutionary biologists are once again beginning to acknowledge that it is individual development (i.e., ontogeny) that evolves, not genes or adults. Gene mutations may underlie such developmental evolution and modified adults are products of this. However, viewing evolution as adaptation through altered ontogeny provides many insights, as reviewed in a rapidly growing literature (e.g., Hall, 1992; McKinney & McNamara, 1991; McNamara, 1997; Raff, 1996).

Some of this developmental renaissance in evolutionary biology has much relevance to Piaget's ideas. There are two key areas of relevance that

I will focus on in this chapter: 1) progressive mental evolution via recapitulation, and 2) mechanisms of this mental evolution. These areas represent aspects of Piaget's ideas that have been widely criticized as being biologically unsound or inadequate but that current biological research, discussed later this chapter, supports Piaget. The first area reflects Piaget's interest in the evolutionary origins of human mental development (e.g., Piaget, 1971). Piaget (along with Freud, Gessell, Erikson, Kohlberg, and many others) was strongly influenced by *recapitulationism*, which holds that individual development (ontogeny) repeats the evolutionary history (phylogeny) of the individual's ancestry. As noted in chapter 1 of this volume, Piaget argued that such mental functions as accommodation, assimilation, and organization are invariant and continuous in phylogeny, ontogeny, and history.

Biologists have generally acknowledged since the early 20th century that strict Haeckelian recapitulation does not necessarily occur because development can evolve in many ways besides just terminal addition of traits at the end of development. Thus, Piaget (along with Freud and others as just noted) has been often and strongly criticized for his recapitulatory interpretations of mental evolution and development. But these criticisms, while often rich in historical detail (e.g., Morss, 1990), are themselves usually based on simplistic interpretations of obsolete evolutionary data as discussed later in this chapter.

I review well-documented biological evidence that conservation of early ontogenetic processes does in fact lead to observable recapitulatory patterns in the development of many species. Furthermore, this is especially true in the primate brain, which has an extremely constrained growth pattern. Organs with constrained patterns are the ones most likely to experience terminal developmental changes. These recapitulatory patterns in children do not perfectly repeat evolutionary events, but provide evidence that Piaget and many other psychologists of the developing mind are not totally erroneous in their evolutionary and functional interpretations. I suggest that this is of profound importance because so much of the foundation of developmental psychology, such as stage concepts and progressive change, requires that recapitulationistic processes are involved. Cells, tissues, organs like the brain, thoughts, and behaviors do not arise *ex nihilio*. They usually are developmental and evolutionary extensions assembled from pre-existing structures, although sometimes in nonadditive ways. The phrase *terminal extension* is thus often more accurate than *terminal addition*, as discussed next. Despite strident claims to the contrary (e.g., Gould 1996a), evolutionary progress does occur and terminal extension of development, especially brain development, has been a key process promoting it.

The second area where the developmental renaissance in evolutionary biology is relevant to Piaget is how it addresses biological mechanisms of cognition. A number of critics (e.g., Case, 1991) have noted that Piaget's acute observations on behavior and mentation generally lacked under-standing of the precise neurobiological processes that influence or cause cognitive development. Some of the rapidly growing evidence in neurobiol-ogy on the development and evolution of the brain is reviewed that relates terminal extension of brain maturation to terminal extension of cognitive development. This evidence is a necessary complement to the recapitula-tory ideas just discussed because Piaget's (and many others') inference of stage-like, progressive recapitulatory change in mental development (ontog-eny) and evolution (phylogeny) are more persuasive if the neurobiological details can be specified. Given that simple Haeckelian universal recapitula-tion does not occur in evolution, we must specify exactly what is being developed and recapitulated: which cells, which organs, which behaviors, which cognitive skills, and so on.

RECAPITULATIONISM: BIRTH AND DEATH

Recapitulationism originally peaked with the 19th century discovery that natural selection acts throughout individual development, from fertilization through death. As reviewed in Gould (1977), McKinney and McNamara (1991), and Raff (1996), the basic mechanism originally proposed to produce evo-lutionary recapitulation in the individual was terminal addition, sometimes called overdevelopment. Proponents of this argued that gene mutations that affect early ontogeny cannot be favored by selection because they have so many cascading impacts on later development that the organism dies. The only successful mutations (so goes the logic) are therefore those that add on to existing developmental patterns such as extended morphological and mental growth.

Two distinct abuses of this early brand of extreme recapitulationism caused its downfall. One was ideological and the other was scientific. The ideological abuse, documented by Gould (1977) and Richards (1992), was the application of recapitulationist interpretations of human evolution to rank some humans as racially inferior and therefore justified subjugation and even genocide. Recapitulation essentially provided the evolutionary mechanism to rationalize the Scale of Nature that placed Europeans at the top of the evolutionary ladder during European age of imperialism. Europe-ans, being more developed (e.g., larger brains via extended growth), were also more evolved (see especially Gould, 1977, 1981). The ultimate extension of this logic was by Hitler, who used it to explain the superiority of Aryan, northern Europeans. The tragic genocidal culmination of Hitler's racial ideas produced such social revulsion that recapitulationism, as an ideology, be-came in a sense guilty by association. Indeed, the larger notion of evolution-ary progress (with or without recapitulationistic causes) continues to be widely disfavored by many evolutionary biologists (e.g., Ruse, 1993).

The scientific abuse of recapitulationism involves the extreme and simplistic manner that it was originally used to explain everything. As noted, Haeckel's notion that all evolution occurred only via terminal addition of traits to development was long ago discredited (Gould, 1977; Raff, 1996; Richards, 1992). An early problem was the relianceof terminal addition on Lamarckian inheritance of acquired traits, an idea that Piaget unfortunately never completely shed. But even more sophisticated versions of terminal addition, which replaced Lamarckian inheritance with late-acting genetic mutations, were clearly wrong in their assertions that all evolution involved only terminal additions to developmental pathways. Even by the late 1800s, it was clear that many kinds of developmental changes had occurred during the evolution of species. Examples include terminal subtractions, nonterminal insertions, and even some early embryonic alterations that are seen in evolution (Gould, 1977; McKinney & McNamara, 1991; Raff, 1996).

By the middle 20th century, these ideological and scientific abuses had combined to make recapitulation a thoroughly unpopular notion in both scientific and social circles. This general neglect of development in evolution lasted approximately from the 1930s to the 1970s (Hall, 1992). Furthermore, even the relatively little work that was published during this period was often influenced by an antirecapitulationist bias. The swing of opinion against recapitulation led to increasing interest in other forms of developmental changes besides terminal addition (overdevelopment). Of special interest was the opposite kind of change, that of terminal subtraction, or underdevelopment (also called juvenilization as noted later because descendant ontogenies never become fully developed or adultified). Thus, the work of Huxley and especially deBeer (1958) often focused on the greater evolutionary flexibility of underdevelopment (juvenilization) as a way of removing burdensome developmental pathways that had been sequentially added on by terminal addition.

Humans as Juvenilized Apes

In keeping with the milieu of the 1930s through the 1970s, work in human evolution also generally ignored the issue of development and especially the likelihood of recapitulatory overdevelopment as a mode of human evolution. As reviewed by Gould (1977) and especially Montagu (1981), most anthropologists during this period (when they considered ontogenetic evolution at all) perceived humans as having evolved as underdeveloped or juvenilized apes. Montagu's (1981) book *Growing Young* is perhaps the most extreme testimony to this view, attributing not only physical traits such as hairlessness and head shape to this, but many behavioral traits ranging from curiosity to dancing, singing, humor, and many others. Gould (1977) was more restrained in his attributions, reviewing evidence that humans are neither fully underdeveloped nor overdeveloped apes, but show a mosaic of developmental changes compared to the ancestral condition. Some traits, such as reduced body hair, are states of underdevelopment (more similar to ancestral juveniles), whereas other traits such as larger body size are from overdevelopment (i.e., prolonged growth) compared to ancestors. But Gould (1977) did infer that the major trend in human evolution was juvenilization (Shea, 1989). As early as 1979, this view was being questioned by Parker and Gibson (1979), who proposed that human evolution was more generally characterized by overdevelopment. Since then, a growing number of workers, discussed next, have also argued the case for overdevelopment especially for mental evolution. Despite this growing evidence against human juvenilization, discussed next, Gould (1996b) continued to argue for it. One reason may be his extreme dislike of the idea of evolutionary progress (Gould, 1996a), which is historically linked to recapitulation via overdevelopment, as noted previously.

A NEW LOOK: EVOLUTION BY TERMINAL EXTENSION

The current rebirth of interest in development in evolution is often demarcated as beginning with Gould's (1977) widely cited *Ontogeny and Phylogeny* (Hall, 1992; McKinney & McNamara, 1991). Although Gould placed considerable emphasis on the role of juvenilization, he also provided detailed discussions of overdevelopment and allowed the possibility that it has been important in the history of life. Since then, during the 1980s and 1990s, a growing literature has sought to understand the role of development in evolution (e.g., most recently, Raff, 1996). A significant proportion of this literature has produced evidence that terminal modifications to ontogeny, including overdevelopment, have indeed played a major role in the evolution of life and humans. It is probably not coincidental that this rebirth of interest in recapitulatory notions has occurred after sufficient time has passed to allow the past ideological and scientific excesses to fade from recent memory.

I now review evidence in this growing evolutionary and anthropological literature for the importance of terminal developmental change. Given the past excesses of recapitulatory ideas, I want to be very explicit at the outset that this recent interest in evolution by terminal extension makes fewer sweeping assertions than the universal recapitulationism postulated by 19th century theorists. Specifically, the current thinking acknowledges the following two key limitations compared to past assertions.

1. Rather than viewing terminal addition as a deterministic process that is the only mechanism by which ontogenies evolve, the current view recognizes that terminal addition is only one of many mechanisms. Different traits may have distinct ontogenetic trajectories that are altered in different ways.

2. The phrase *terminal addition* is itself problematic because *addition* implies a linear process of simple addition of brain cells and cognitive functions. In reality, development (especially of the brain) is a highly complex, non-linear process characterized by many kinds of tissue interactions and shape changes even when development pathways are simply extended or truncated. The term *terminal extension* is thus more appropriate because it indicates that extension of a complexly interacting developmental process is not simply additive.

Current thinking incorporates these limitations and is based on the empirical observation that terminal extensions are statistically more common in evolution than other kinds of ontogenetic changes. As discussed later in this chapter, this is especially true of highly constrained growth systems such as the brain, where terminal extensions are the easiest kinds of developmental changes to carry out.

DEVELOPMENT AS A CONSTRAINT ON EVOLUTION

The logic used by Piaget and others to infer recapitulation and evolutionary progress has traditionally been based on the fact that development is highly constrained by contingencies of interaction: Early ontogenetic changes cannot occur because they have cascading effects so that terminal stages of ontogeny are most easily modified by evolution. This produces developmental constraints. *Developmental constraint* means that a species may not freely adapt to an environmental change because development limits available morphological and behavioral variation. In an ideal world, species could freely alter their morphology and behavior in order to adapt to unexpected change. But instead, to use the famous metaphor of Monod (1970), natural selection is restricted to tinkering with existing species in order to produce new ones. Developmental constraints are a major category of constraints because natural selection can only tinker with the limited variety of developmental trajectories that are in existence at any given time. Environmental change produces evolution only to the degree that developmental variation is available for selection to act on. As a result, development strongly influences both the rate and direction of evolution (e.g., Hall, 1992; McKinney & McNamara, 1991; McNamara, 1997).

Furthermore, the constraining influence of development has increased over evolutionary time as developmental processes have become less flexible. McKinney and McNamara (1991), Hall (1992) and Raff (1996) are among those who review the considerable developmental and paleontological evidence that the defining traits found in the basic body plans of all life on

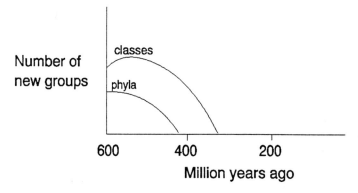

FIG. 2.1.   Generalized schematic illustrating the early origination of new phyla and classes in geological time. (Redrawn and modified from McKinney & McNamara, 1991.)

Earth have gradually congealed after an initial period of relative plasticity. Figure 2.1 shows that higher taxonomic levels such as phyla and orders, representing the most novel ontogenetic and evolutionary variations, are overwhelmingly clustered in the early history of life. This asymmetrical pattern of origination of basic morphologies is attributable to less con-strained ontogenies in early Paleozoic multicellular life (Levinton, 1988; McKinney & McNamara, 1991; Raff, 1996). Furthermore, this pattern is also found in individual taxonomic groups. Detailed studies of fossil marine gastropods exemplify this pattern of increasing developmental constraint since the early Paleozoic Era (Wagner, 1995).

Data from living organisms reveal similar findings. The defining traits that are characteristic of higher taxonomic groups (e.g., phyla and classes) alive today tend to appear early in ontogeny and show reduced levels of variation compared to traits that appear later in ontogeny (Hall, 1992). Stearns (1992) views modern constraints on evolution as the result of early adaptations that have become embedded in developmental pathways. Similarly, phylo-genetic analysis documents how more closely related taxa tend to have more similar traits and more similar ontogenies. These follow the predicted pattern of nested evolutionary change arising from nested developmental modifications (McKinney & Gittleman, 1995).

Ontogenetic conservativism is also becoming evident at the genetic and cell level. A recent review of homeotic genes (Carroll, 1995) shows a striking degree of conservatism throughout such disparate groups as arthropods and vertebrates. These early-acting genes sculpt the basic body plan of these animals. Recent evidence shows that the entire course of evolution in arthropods and vertebrates has largely involved regulatory changes in expression of highly conserved arrays of homeotic genes and the many developmental genes that they regulate (Carroll, 1995).

Causes of Increasing Constraint

Explanations for ontogenetic congealing or hardening have emphasized that, because development is a highly orchestrated process of interacting parts, the earlier interactions are less amenable to alteration. Alteration of early interactions would tend to have cascading effects on too many later inter-actions. As a result, developmental evolution has tended to involve mainly alterations of late ontogeny while early developmental interactions have become progressively entrenched, or canalized, through stabilizing selection (Hall, 1992).

Very general theoretical substantiation for this pattern of increasing con-straint include models by Kauffman (1993), which show that even randomly interacting parts will quickly congeal into patterns of nonrandomness. More specific explanations have focused on the various kinds of interactions that occur in early ontogeny. Levinton (1988) reviewed the concepts of genetic and epigenetic burdens that originate from the interdependency of genetic and tissue interactions, respectively, during early ontogeny. Hall (1992) reviewed these and still other constraints that can limit variation in early development, including structural, cellular, and functional constraints. The limitations that such ontogenetic constraints place on evolutionary change have received a variety of names, for example, burden, epigenetic traps, epigenetic cascades, generative entrenchment, and gene nets at the genetic level (reviews in Hall, 1992; McKinney & McNamara, 1991; Raff, 1996).

EVOLUTION BY EXTENDING DEVELOPMENT

These increasing constraints on alteration of early ontogeny have meant that mutations altering later development have been favored. This does not mean that terminal addition to development is the only way that evolution has occurred. I emphasize that many other kinds of developmental changes can also occur. For example, terminal subtraction, which removes traits at the end of development, is relatively common (Hall, 1992). Also, nonterminal changes can occur, including early changes in development (Raff, 1996). Furthermore, different changes can affect different traits in different ways in an evolving lineage. This is often called *mosaic evolution* and is well-documented in fossils (Levinton, 1988). One trait may thus exhibit terminal subtraction during evolution, whereas another may show terminal addition. Evolution of the human body is a such a mosaic hodgepodge of develop-mental changes (Shea, 1989).

A key point is that universal terminal addition, whereby all traits always evolve by addition to their development, is simply wrong. This of course also means that universal recapitulation, wherein all aspects of ontogeny perfectly repeat all aspects of the individual's evolution, is wrong.

But I caution against throwing the baby out with the bathwater. The many lines of evidence previously noted in favor of increasing developmental constraint over evolutionary time implies that terminal developmental changes (terminal subtractions, additions, and substitutions) are likely the most common type of evolution (Hall, 1992; Levinton, 1988; McKinney & McNamara, 1991; Raff, 1996). Direct evidence for this includes Mabee's (1993) thorough phylogenetic study of living species that finds that terminal addition may account for up to 51.9% of character state evolution in centrarchid fishes. She also showed that when other terminal changes (such as terminal subtractions and substitutions) are included, up to 75% of change is accounted for. Similarly, Sordino, Hoeven, and Duboule (1995) have shown how terminal changes in limb appendages (via minor regulatory gene change) can explain the evolutionary origin of fingers and toes from fish fins, by unequal proliferation of cells.

I emphasize that this is a statistical and not a deterministic process: Early changes in ontogeny do still occur (Raff, 1996), but are less likely than late-acting changes. This also implies that recapitulatory patterns may be expected as a common statistical tendency in that more closely related species will share more similar ontogenies. The more closely related are species, then the more likely that their ontogenies will not differ until later (terminal) stages of development. This agrees with Mayr (1994, p. 231) who, in citing agreement with Gould (1977), noted that "recapitulation, properly understood, is simply a fact."

Finally, terminal changes leading to a larger, more complex brain are, in many ways, the ultimate evolutionary response to increasing developmental constraint. As discussed later, increasing plasticity of behavior is an extremely adaptive solution to the problem of reduced plasticity of morphology. This has traditionally been implicitly acknowledged by the recognition by many evolutionists that increased behavioral plasticity is correlated with higher grades of evolution (Bonner, 1988).

What Is Overdevelopment?

Given that terminal changes are the commonest way to modify development, what kind of terminal changes can occur? The most commonly observed terminal changes involve alterations of developmental timing, called *heterochrony* (McKinney & McNamara, 1991; McNamara, 1997). These can produce either: 1) overdevelopment, where the developmental trajectory is extended; or 2) underdevelopment, where the trajectory is truncated.

For example, adults of a later descendant species may closely resemble juveniles of its ancestral species. In such a case, we might infer that the new species arose through some kind of underdevelopment, or juvenilization, process. Juvenilization thus produces individuals that are adults in being sexually mature, but otherwise retain the ancestral juvenile's morphology and behavior. Many domesticated pets, such as cats and dogs, are juvenilized relative to their wild ancestors. This is because humans have selectively favored smaller, cuter (more juvenilized) morphologies and more playful behaviors (Morey, 1994).

Conversely, if all aspects of the individual's development are terminally extended, then the juvenile continues to develop beyond the developmental point at which the ancestral adult stopped so that the descendant adult is overdeveloped. Terminal extension of development may therefore involve much more than simply adding on new cells or tissues. Terminal extension of the same trajectory can produce morphological, behavioral, or cognitive traits that are not simple linear extrapolations of ancestral traits. Terminal extension of the complex neuronal interactions during brain growth has produced neuronal interconnections in the human brain, for example, that are much more complex than would be produced from strictly additive processes. This, in turn, has resulted in a rich repertoire of behavioral and cognitive skills.

In human evolution, there is a general theme of sequential terminal extension of developmental stages: Terminal extension of prenatal brain growth is followed by sequential extension of postnatal stages of body and brain growth and maturation (McKinney & McNamara, 1991; McNamara, 1997). See also chapter 3 this volume. In the case of human brain evolution, I discuss next how sequential stages in brain and cognitive development throughout the human lifespan are ultimately traceable to a relatively simple root cause: prolongation of fetal development that has cascading effects throughout later human development.

OUR OVERDEVELOPED BRAIN: EXTENDING BRAIN GROWTH

Given the often complex developmental origins of many evolutionary changes (McKinney & McNamara, 1991; Raff, 1996), it is perhaps ironic that evolution of the life's most complex organ, the human brain, has a comparatively simple basis. Production of cortical neurons in mammals is limited to early prenatal development (Deacon, 1990; Finlay & Darlington, 1995). Mitotic rates of neuron creation in mammals are relatively constrained, perhaps reflecting a ceiling on neuron mitosis in the prenatal environment (Sacher & Staffeldt, 1974). Thus, as discussed by Finlay and Darlington (1995), it is developmentally easier to produce a larger brain by extending prenatal brain growth rather than altering rate of growth. In the case of modern humans, this fetal brain growth phase is extended about 25 days compared to living monkeys (Deacon, 1990; Gibson, 1990, 1991).

As discussed next, this delay in fetal brain growth has profound cascading consequences that underlie nearly all later major brain and cognitive developmental delays and complexity increase. Specifically, this fetal growth delay causes the following key traits that characterize brain overdevelopment in humans.

High Brain/Body Ratio

Relative to other primates, humans have an enormous brain compared to our body size. This is produced by the positive brain/body allometry of extended fetal growth, that is, the brain grows faster than the body during the fetal phase producing a high brain/body ratio (Shea, 1989). After this phase, especially postnatally, brain growth is much slower than body growth so that a lower brain/body ratio could result if body growth were accelerated as in the relatively fast-growing gorilla (McKinney & McNamara, 1991). Instead, human postnatal body growth is relatively slow, so that our bodies stay relatively small. Thus, as seen in Fig. 2.2, modern humans have a brain size that would be predicted for a much larger primate (Deacon, 1990).

This high brain/body ratio has sometimes been used as evidence for juvenilization in human evolution (Gould, 1977). We see here however that it results from a brain that is overdeveloped in both absolute and relative (brain/body) terms. Thus, as Deacon (1990) noted, "Paedomorphism (juvenilization) of human brain/body proportions ... is an artificial correlate of brain size evolution ... The fact that humans exhibit paedomorphic brain/stature proportions with respect to other apes ... in no way implies any corresponding arrest of brain differentiation" (p. 27).

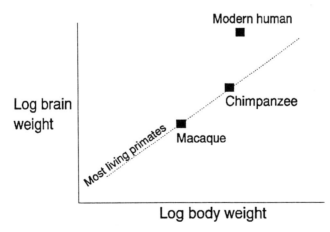

FIG. 2.2. If human brain/body ratio were equivalent to other primates, it would fall on the regression line of most living primates. Instead, humans have a much larger brain for their body size. (Redrawn and modified from Deacon, 1990.)

More Neural Complexity

Having a relatively large brain is obviously a main component of cognition, but brain size alone is a very coarse way to define overdevelopment. A finer view would also note that the large number of neurons produced during prolonged fetal growth also undergo a prolonged period of postnatal growth and maturation. Delay in offset of infancy and juvenile stages of development leads to a more complex brain as dendritic growth in the cortex is extended to 20 years or more in humans (Gibson, 1991). Similarly, glial cell growth and synaptogenesis are all also prolonged, and thus go through, and extend beyond, ancestral developmental patterns (Gibson 1990, 1991). This extension of dendritic and synaptic growth is why neurons in the human brain have many more dendritic and synaptic interconnections with each other than other primates (Purves, 1988). Stanley (1996) discussed how such interconnections are essential for intelligence.

In addition, brain myelination is prolonged in humans. As it promotes more effective nerve transmission, myelination plays a large role in maturing memory, intelligence, and language skills (Case, 1992; Gibson, 1991). Myelination is highly canalized, following the same specific sequence among primates so the regional delays are readily seen in humans. In both monkeys and humans, myelination begins in the brainstem, proceeds through subcortical areas, with neocortex and especially prefrontal cortex being among the last to myelinate (Gibson, 1991). But rhesus monkeys show myelination only up to about 3½ years whereas in humans myelination continues until well over 12 years of age (Gibson, 1991). Even regressive events such as neural pruning are delayed in humans. Dendritic complexity in the human brain peaks at about 2 years of age and begins to decline thereafter as pruning begins (Edelman, 1987). In contrast, in apes and monkeys, dendritic pruning begins well before 2 years old (Purves, 1988).

More Neocortex and Prefrontal Cortex

Finlay and Darlington (1995) provided an excellent illustration of the constraints on mammalian brain development. They showed that increase in brain size, from shrews to primates, accounts for an enormous amount of variation (over 96%) in size of individual brain regions. Of special relevance to humans is that the order of neurogenesis is phylogenetically highly conserved so that evolutionary brain size increase occurs by disproportionately more growth in late-generated structures such as the neocortex (Finlay & Darlington, 1995). In terms of behavior and cognition, they note that the neocortex (or isocortex) is a general-purpose integrator, so that increasing neocortical size produces an increasing capacity to process information of all kinds. Tool use, language, and social behavior may all increase in complexity as the neocortex increases because, as Gibson (1993) reviewed, they all share common neocortical substrates that promote mental constructional skills.

It has long been held that an area of the neocortex that is crucial for cognitive function is the prefrontal cortex (Stanley, 1996). In particular, it is the center for short-term memory (central executive system) where information is temporarily stored and manipulated (Case, 1992). This has been confirmed by magnetic resonance imaging showing prefrontal brain activation during various cognitive tasks (D'Esposito et al., 1995). How has prolonged fetal growth affected this key area of the neocortex? Deacon (1990) calculated the relative size of the prefrontal area in modern humans as 202% the size of the prefrontal area in an anthropoid ape of our body size. This is much greater than the percentage increase in any other area of the brain. Some areas even decrease in relative proportion compared to apes, especially the sensory and motor systems: olfaction (32%), vision (60%), and motor (35%). Neurons in the prefrontal cortex are mainly connected to other neurons so that neural interconnections there are established during cognitive development (Case, 1992).

On the basis of such evidence, Gibson (1991, p. 51) concluded that "on neurological grounds . . . there is nothing [juvenilized] about the adult human brain." In direct contrast to the infant primate, adult human brains are "large, highly fissurated and myelinated with complex synaptic morphology."

Our Overdeveloped Cognitive Skills: Prolonged Acceleration

Human mental development follows the same general pattern as that of the brain: prolongation with no reduction in rate of development to ultimately produce a cognitively overdeveloped adult. In fact, humans prolong a period of accelerated cognitive development.

Comparison of cognitive stages indicates that humans, apes, and (with some exceptions) monkeys follow the same general sequence of cognitive development (Parker, 1996; Langer, chapter 3, this volume). However, there is a clear developmental difference between monkeys, apes, and humans in terms of: 1) rate and 2) ultimate level of terminal cognitive development. Figure 2.3 summarizes decades of work by Parker on comparative cognitive development in primates (review in Parker, 1996). Monkeys have the lowest rate and ultimate level, whereas humans have the highest rate and ultimate level, indicating a correlation between rate and level of cognitive attainment (just the opposite of that predicted by juvenilization).

Figure 2.3 shows that monkeys (macaques) do not complete the Sensorimotor Period. The highest levels achieved by monkeys is about equal to that of 2-year-old children in the Piagetian Late Sensorimotor Period. Apes do complete the Sensorimotor Period at about 3 years of age, and go on to

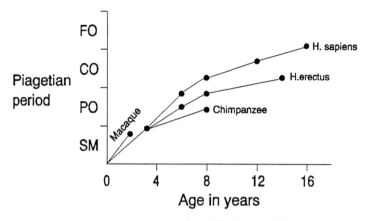

FIG. 2.3. Age of attainment of Piagetian Cognitive Periods differs among these primates. SM = Sensorimotor Period, PO = Preoperations Period, CO = Concrete Operations Period, FO = Formal Operations Period. (Redrawn and modified from Parker, 1996.)

complete the first subperiod of Preoperations, terminating cognitive development at a level approximating that of 4-year-old children (Parker, 1996). Human cognitive development goes beyond that of other primates by development of additional modalities and increased number and complexity of schemes. It is also accelerated because the same stages are attained at a younger age in humans (Fig. 2.3).

The adult ancestor of all hominids apparently attained the cognitive level of 2- to 4- year-old children (Parker, 1996). Thereafter, human ancestors, from australopithecines to *H. erectus* progressively evolved through a sequence of cognitive developmental stages intermediate to apes and modern humans (Parker, 1996). This implies prolongation and acceleration of cognitive development during human evolution. Figure 2.3 shows an intermediate cognitive development for *H. erectus*.

CAUSES OF COGNITIVE OVERDEVELOPMENT

Causes of developmental evolution can be described at many levels, ranging from genetic to behavioral (Raff, 1996). At a coarse level, we might attribute the evolution of our cognitive overdevelopment as being caused by the combination of accelerated learning plus the prolongation of childhood and our life history in general. Accelerated cognition is ultimately attributable to having a larger endowment of neurons, dendrites, and synapses that allows storing and manipulating information at a faster rate, especially in the prefrontal area. Another important control is myelination rate, which occurs 3 to 4 times faster in humans. Again, maturation of the prefrontal area is important in determining abilities on Piagetian tasks (Case, 1992).

But we can trace this accelerated and prolonged learning ability back one step further, to the prolongation of fetal growth that extends the duration of neuron mitosis (Finlay & Darlington, 1995). This not only produces the large number of cortical neurons characteristic of the human brain but also seems to have cascading effects on neuron complexity by prolonging development of individual neurons. This allows more complex dendritic and synaptic outgrowths and connections.

Furthermore, many aspects of brain complexity seem to originate as cascading effects that ultimately derive from prolongation of fetal brain growth. As Deacon (1990) noted:

> In all the major indicators of mammalian brain development and maturation, including the level of differentiation of brain structures, the morphological maturation of neurons, the level of myelination of axons, the rates and specificity of neurotransmitter synthesis, . . . as well as many other measures, the adult human brain has at least achieved the level of . . . mature mammalian brains and typically has carried these trends much further. (p. 270)

That many aspects of brain size and complexity are overdeveloped at so many scales from the cellular to that of gross tissue morphology is indicative of a highly integrated system. This agrees with the highly covariant, constrained patterns found by Finlay and Darlington (1995) in mammalian brain evolution. In such highly integrated systems, we might expect, for example, that prolonged duration of axon growth causes not only longer axons but increased myelination of those axons as needed for effective nerve transmission.

Can we take the sequence of causation back one step further and specify what causes the prolongation of fetal brain growth? It is tempting to ascribe the cause to a resetting of a global, heterochronic clock that governs rate and duration of brain mitosis. Evidence for such a global clock is discussed by Finlay and Darlington (1995). Unfortunately, the exact genetic and cellular mechanisms that would control such a hypothetical clock are as yet unknown. Interestingly, Deacon (1997) suggested that the prolonged fetal brain growth occurs because of changes in segmentation in very early embryonic development. Changes in homeotic gene expression may alter the initial proportion of late-maturing embryonic stem (parent) neurons. If so, then the ultimate heterochrony underlying human brain evolution would be traceable to mutations in homeotic genes that produce *predisplacement*, the heterochronic term referring to starting off with more (McKinney & McNamara, 1991).

WHAT, EXACTLY, IS BEING RECAPITULATED?

To summarize, human cognition is, in many ways, overdeveloped compared to ancestral primate patterns. This is ultimately due to a larger endowment of neurons, dendrites, and synapses that allows storing and manipulating information, especially in the prefrontal area. We attain higher levels of cognitive development as we prolong each stage of our life history, and we learn faster, accelerating cognitive development during each stage (Langer, chapter 3, this volume).

It may be tempting to interpret this pattern as one of developmental terminal addition that produces evolutionary recapitulation in modern human ontogeny. There are at least two key reasons why this is not a valid interpretation. One is that this is not a process of terminal addition. The second reason is that, although general aspects of brain and cognitive evolution are likely recapitulated, there are likely to be deviations from it. We must therefore specify exactly what is being recapitulated.

Terminal Extension, Not Terminal Addition

Our cognitive overdevelopment has been largely produced by prolonged fetal brain growth. This produces more than simply the addition of more neurons at the end of brain growth. Instead, as noted previously, this produces overdevelopment in many aspects of brain (and cognitive) development such as neuron, dendritic, and synaptic complexity and connectedness. For this reason, the term *terminal extension* is more accurate than *terminal addition* because it better describes the process whereby many aspects of the developmental trajectory, from cellular to brain morphology to behavior, are extended.

The Triune Brain: Phylotypic Embedding

MacLean's (1990) triune brain hypothesis is the most popularized view of our overdeveloped brain (e.g., Sagan, 1977). The triune brain refers to the three grades of brain evolution represented by the protoreptilian (R-complex), the paleomammalian (limbic system), and the neomammalian (neocortex) structures (MacLean, 1990). This hypothesis has been strongly criticized as being too simplistic (e.g., Deacon, 1990) and is no longer accepted as textbook dogma (Shepherd, 1994). But the idea that human brain ontogeny follows this three-fold sequence continues to have a very strong hold. Many popular books (e.g., Damasio, 1994) discuss how the evolutionarily oldest part of the brain, especially the basal ganglia that handles biological regulation and develops first. This is followed by emotional (limbic) development and, lastly, the cognitive (neocortex) as the evolutionarily youngest part.

This apparent contradiction in current thinking may be explained in terms of developmental constraints, previously discussed. Specifically, we can refer to phylotypic embedding, a concept used by Raff (1996) to describe how basic ontogenetic traits become entrenched among higher taxa: Traits that develop late in ontogeny are modularized and can be independently modified by selection. Traits that develop earlier than this, during organogenesis, are less liable for modification because modularization has not yet occurred. In this light, the triune brain appears to describe phylogenetic embedding representing reptilian, early mammal, and late mammal brain evolution, respectively.

Phylotypic embedding implies recapitulation only in a general sense. General aspects of development among higher taxa tend to repeat the evolutionary history of those taxa. This does not require that the development of each species repeats each evolutionary detail.

General Brain and Cognitive Recapitulation?

For humans, phylotypic embedding may help explain why the topic of recapitulation in our mental evolution keeps resurfacing. That the development of children may repeat the mental development of early humans was an idea favored by Darwin (1871) himself and many early psychologists such as Baldwin and G. Stanley Hall (Morss, 1990). It is a theme in the writings of Freud (1913) and Piaget (1971) and continues to be proposed today (e.g., Ekstig, 1994).

The evidence just discussed thus indicates that the order of both origination and maturation (e.g., myelination) of various areas of the brain roughly correspond to the order of evolutionary appearance. Konner (1991), for example, discussed how smiling and other ritualized motor displays also found in reptiles are the first to appear in infants due to maturation of the basal ganglia. This is followed by bonding, attachment, and other more complex emotional behaviors evoked by maturation of the limbic system. Finally, maturation of neocortical areas initiates cognition, a maturation process that lasts through adolescence (Gibson, 1991). Damasio (1994) noted that this sequence does not mean that neocortical areas control earlier-appearing emotional areas. Rather, in the brain, all areas interact as an integrated whole as each one matures.

Konner's (1991) scenario of recapitulation is very general indeed. It mainly focuses on the fact that humans are recent mammals and thus developmentally repeat the mammalian sequence of mental evolution, with neocortical areas being the last to originate and mature. Also, in a general way, the growth of our large neocortex recapitulates the evolutionary enlargement of neocortex in the human lineage (Finlay & Darlington, 1995). Do the finer details of development of areas in the human neocortex recapitulate our evolution? Unfortunately, we cannot be sure. I noted, for example, that human cognition rests largely on the prefrontal area that has increased about 202% relative to an average living anthropoid. But we do not know the exact evolutionary sequence that produced that increase because fossil crania do not preserve the details of neocortical structure. We can speculate however that the steadily increasing brain size of human evolution largely translated into steadily increasing prefrontal area. Fossil crania, for instance, show disproportionate increase of the prefrontal cavity during human evolution (Stanley, 1996).

So far, I have focused on general recapitulation in brain structure. What about brain function? Cognitive abilities are related to neocortical size and complexity that permit increasingly complex mental constructions (Gibson 1990, 1991). This allows increasingly complex combinations of objects, words, and, ultimately, ideas to be created and manipulated (Gibson, 1993). We might thus infer that, as our complex brain matures (e.g., myelination), our general ability to think by manipulating ideas (and objects and words) recapitulates that ability of our ancestors. This is especially true of maturation of our prefrontal area (Case, 1992). At a finer level, this is reflected by our increasing ability to perform Piagetian tasks, to produce the cognitive recapitulation in Fig. 2.3.

HUMAN COGNITION AS EVOLUTIONARY PROGRESS

Perhaps the British paleontologist Simon Conway Morris (1995) said it best when he recently noted that "it is now distinctly unfashionable to talk about evolutionary progress" (p. 290). Yet there are many paleontologists (including Morris) who acknowledge that evolutionary progress is real, depending on how it is defined (Ruse, 1993). In particular, there is a clear overall trend in the history of life toward increasing complexity, as documented by Bonner (1988) and Valentine, Collins, and Meyer (1993). This increase in complexity is certainly not a deterministic, irreversible march toward perfection or improvement, as was visualized by 19th century theorists (Richards, 1992). Rather, it is a statistical evolutionary increase, replete with reversals and episodic tempo, much like terminal developmental extension that is the mechanism that drives this upward complexity trend.

Given the strident arguments against evolutionary progress based on the concept of chance (e.g., Gould, 1996a), it is very important to clarify the badly misunderstood terms of *chance* and *randomness*. Gould's usage of *chance* has always been very nonrigorous and informal (e.g., Gould, 1996a). As Raup (1977) noted, random patterns do not reflect a lack of causation. Rather, they indicate that all the processes causing the patterns are unknown and often involve many complex interactions that preclude our having full knowledge of them.

In other words, perceived randomness or chance is nothing more than a confession of ignorance by the observer (McKinney, 1990). Our perception of chance says nothing about the true forces driving evolutionary patterns.

It means that all the variables determining evolution, including terminal extension, cannot be entirely specified. Furthermore, there are many causes that can be specified. In the case of brain evolution, there has been an obvious tendency to favor larger brains and increased intelligence, probably for a variety of adaptive advantages (see Bonner, 1988; Dennett, 1995, for a detailed critique of Gould's arguments against progress).

Cognitive Complexity as Freedom
From Morphological Constraint

There is perhaps no better illustration of how natural selection produces progressive complexity increases than the human brain. Figure 2.4 shows that morphological complexity has increased during geological time, but this increase has tended to steadily slow down. In Fig. 2.4, morphological complexity can be measured in many ways. But the most common is maximum number of cell types that evolved in multicellular organisms during geological time. When Bonner (1988) and Valentine et al. (1993) did this, they found the pattern of morphological change shown in Fig. 2.4.

This is because virtually all complexity trends reach an upper limit. Statistical patterns of the evolution of complexity in hundreds of psychological, social, and technological phenomena showed S-shaped curves (Casti, 1995). The reason is that any novelty or innovation initially shows a

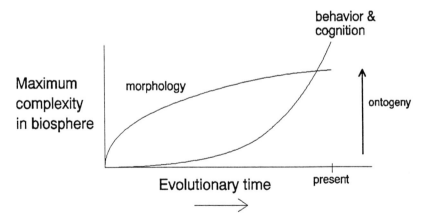

FIG. 2.4.   Terminal extension of ontogeny has increased maximum complexity of the morphology in the biosphere through evolutionary time. But morphological complexification has leveled off because of intrinsic constructional, functional, and other constraints. Complexification of cognition and behavior via terminal extension of brain development is an evolutionary solution of natural selection in response to these constraints on morphology. Behavioral and cognitive complexification, as yet, show no signs of slowing down.

period of rapid exponential growth but eventual (and inevitable) limitations eventually cause a reduction of the complexity trend (McKinney & Gittleman, 1995). Such limitations usually reflect some ultimate structural (engineering) constraint on the phenomenon. As a machine, for example, becomes extremely complex (and large), it becomes more prone to malfunction because there are more things that can go wrong. The only way to circumvent such diminishing returns are to innovate and create a fundamentally new kind of device (Casti, 1995).

We see in Fig. 2.4 that this S-shape pattern is found in biological evolution when the upper limit of ontogenetic complexity in the biosphere is measured by cell type. As cells are the basis of tissue and organ complexity, Fig. 2.4 may approximate morphological complexity evolution. This same S-shape pattern of Fig. 2.4 is also seen when the upper limit of morphological complexity is estimated by body size (Bonner, 1988) and by genomic complexity (Brooks & Wiley, 1988).

Figure 2.4 shows why the study of behavior and brain function (cognition) is so important to evolutionary biology. A basic premise of Darwinian selection is that it favors new ways of doing things, as this reduces competition and exploits new resources; becoming more complex is one way of doing something new (McKinney, 1990). In the case of morphological complexity, complexity evolution via terminal extension seems to have encountered the kind of structural limitations referred to, as shown by the S-shaped patterns observed. In contrast, behavioral and cognitive evolution shows a pattern of increasing complexity (e.g., discussions by Bonner, 1988, and Dennett, 1995).

As previously noted, the only way to overcome the structural constraints intrinsic to an engine or any designed functioning entity is to create a fundamentally new design. We might thus infer that behavior and cognition represent a fundamentally new design to overcome the structural constraints inherent in the morphological (cellular) assembly of an individual (McKinney & Gittleman, 1995). Enhanced learning ability, for instance, allows the organism to overcome morphological limitations such as by the use of tools. Complex behavior represents new ways of utilizing the morphological variation of the biosphere because behavior is what one does with one's morphological traits.

It is thus my contention that terminal extension of brain and cognitive ontogeny is a major mechanism of overcoming limitations on morphological complexity evolution (see also McKinney & Gittleman, 1995). In the perpetual struggle to find new ways of surviving in the evolving biotic environment, increased brain and behavioral complexity has many advantages, given physical limitations on evolving morphological complexity and the generally slower pace of morphological evolution. Empirical evidence for this is that, in general, relative brain size in mammals has increased throughout most of the Cenozoic (Bonner, 1988).

Prospects for Cognitive Evolution

Speculations about the future must consider the dynamics of the past. Future patterns of complex phenomena, whether stock markets or evolutionary trends, are rarely simple extrapolations of the past. But the past does provide measurable clues about the probability of events. In this case, even though the dynamics of the biosphere (e.g., speciation and extinction) are enormously complex, the long-term sum of these dynamics produces a nonrandom statistical pattern at the very coarse scale of geological time. There is a tendency for life on Earth to become more complex. Furthermore, we can identify a main driving force of this complexity evolution as that of development: Ontogenies evolve (not genes or adults) so that late-acting developmental traits are often favored. Terminal extension of morphological development has been a common trend because of this.

A simple extrapolation of the cognitive trend of Fig. 2.4 would imply that cognitive complexity will continue its exponential increase. Wills (1993), for example, speculated that the current human population probably contains a substantial number of genes that would promote prolongation of the human life span and, presumably, prolonged gestation, childhood, and so on. But although genes for longer gestation (and thus greater neuron proliferation) do likely exist, infants with larger brains would produce even greater stress for the mother's birth canal, which is already near its apparent maximum (Wills, 1993). This would seem to represent the biological design limitation for human cognitive evolution and one might be tempted to predict an S-shaped leveling off of the cognitive curve in Fig. 2.4. But the fact that humans now have the ability to exceed biological designs in a variety of ways (e.g., recombinant DNA, Caesarian and potentially even extra-uterine births), it would seem that no immediate constraint on cognition is clearly visible. This view is bolstered even more when one includes the potential interactions with computers. Donald (1991), among many others, described how future cognitive complexity evolution will involve the use of computers and other nonbiological information storage devices.

ACKNOWLEDGMENTS

I am very grateful to Jonas Langer and Melanie Killen for inviting me to the Piaget Symposium, and for their support and editorship. Funding by the National Science Foundation during the writing of this chapter is gratefully acknowledged.

REFERENCES

Bogin, B. (1988). *Patterns of human growth*. Cambridge, England: Cambridge University Press.
Bonner, J. T. (1988). *The evolution of complexity by means of natural selection*. Princeton, NJ: Princeton University Press.

Brooks, D. R., & Wiley, E. O. (1988). *Evolution as entropy*. Chicago: University of Chicago Press.

Carroll, S. B. (1995). Homeotic genes and the evolution of arthopods and chordates. *Nature, 376*, 479–485.

Case, R. (1991). *The mind's staircase*. Hillsdale, NJ: Lawrence Erlbaum Associates.

Case, R. (1992). The role of the frontal lobes in the regulation of cognitive development. *Brain and Cognition, 20*, 51–73.

Casti, J. L. (1995). *Complexification*. New York: Harper & Row.

Damasio, A. R. (1994). *Descartes' error*. New York: Putnam.

Deacon, T. W. (1990). Problems of ontogeny and phylogeny in brain size evolution. *International Journal of Primatology, 11*, 237–282.

Deacon, T. W. (1997). *The symbolic species*. New York: Norton.

deBeer, G. (1958). *Embryos and ancestors*. Oxford, England: Oxford University Press.

Dennett, D. C. (1995). *Darwin's dangerous idea*. New York: Simon & Schuster.

D'Esposito, M., Detre, J., Alsop, D., Shin, R., Atlas, S., & Grossman, M. (1995). The neural basis of the central executive system of working memory. *Science, 378*, 279–281.

Donald, M. (1991). *Origins of the modern mind*. Cambridge, MA: Harvard University Press.

Edelman, G. (1987). *Neural Darwinism*. New York: Basic Books.

Ekstig, B. (1994). Condensation of developmental stages and evolution. *Bioscience, 44*, 158–164.

Finlay, B. L., & Darlington, R. B. (1995). Linked regularities in the development and evolution of mammalian brains. *Science, 268*, 1578–1584.

Freud, S. (1913). *Totem and taboo*. London: Hogarth Press.

Futuyma, D. (1988). Sturm and Drang and the evolutionary synthesis. *Evolution, 42*, 217–226.

Gibson, K. R. (1990). New perspectives on instincts and intelligence: Brain size and the emergence of hierarchical mental construction skills. In S. Parker & K. Gibson (Eds.), *"Language" and intelligence in monkeys and apes* (pp. 97–128). Cambridge, England: Cambridge University Press.

Gibson, K. R. (1991). Myelination and behavioral development: A comparative perspective on questions of neoteny, altriciality and intelligence. In K. Gibson & A. Petersen (Eds.), *Brain maturation and cognitive development* (pp. 29–64). New York: deGruyter.

Gibson, K. R. (1993). Tool use, language and social behavior in relationship to information processing capacities. In K. Gibson & T. Ingold (Eds.), *Tools, language, and cognition in human evolution* (pp. 251–270). Cambridge, England: Cambridge University Press.

Gould, S. J. (1977). *Ontogeny and phylogeny*. Cambridge, MA: Harvard University Press.

Gould, S. J. (1981). *The mismeasure of man*. New York: Norton.

Gould, S. J. (1996a). *Full house*. New York: Harmony Books.

Gould, S. J. (1996b). Creating the creators. *Discover, 17*, 42–57.

Gribbin, J. M. (1988). *The one percent advantage*. New York: Blackwell.

Hall, B. K. (1992). *Evolutionary developmental biology*. London: Chapman & Hall.

Kauffman, S. (1993). *Origins of order*. Oxford, England: Oxford University Press.

Konner, M. (1991). Universals of behavioral development in relation to brain myelination. In K. Gibson & A. Petersen (Eds.), *Brain maturation and cognitive development* (pp. 181–224). New York: deGruyter.

Levinton, J. S. (1988). *Genetics, paleontology, and macroevolution*. Cambridge, England: Cambridge University Press.

Mabee, P. M. (1993). Phylogenetic interpretation of ontogenetic change: Sorting out the actual and artefactual in an empirical case study of centrarchid fishes. *Zoological Journal of the Linnean Society, 107*, 175–291.

MacLean, P. D. (1990). *The triune brain in evolution*. New York: Plenum.

Mayr, E. (1994). Recapitulation reinterpreted: The somatic program. *Quarterly Review of Biology, 69*, 223–232.

McKinney, M. L. (1990). Classifying and analyzing evolutionary trends. In K. McNamara (Ed.), *Evolutionary trends* (pp. 28–58). Tucson: University of Arizona Press.

McKinney, M. L., & Gittleman, J. G. (1995). Ontogeny and phylogeny: Tinkering with covariation in life history, behavior, and morphology. In K. McNamara (Ed.), *Evolutionary change through heterochrony* (pp. 15–31). New York: Wiley.

McKinney, M. L., & McNamara, K. J. (1991). *Heterochrony: The evolution of ontogeny.* New York: Plenum.

McNamara, K. J. (1997). *Shapes of time.* Baltimore: Johns Hopkins University Press.

Monod, J. (1970). *Chance and necessity.* Paris: Le Seuil.

Montagu, A. (1981). *Growing young.* New York: McGraw-Hill.

Morey, D. F. (1994). The early evolution of the domestic dog. *American Scientist, 82,* 336–347.

Morris, S. C. (1995). Ecology in deep time. *Trends in Ecology and Evolution, 10,* 290–294.

Morss, J. (1990). *The biologizing of childhood.* Hillsdale, NJ: Lawrence Erlbaum Associates.

Parker, S. T. (1996). Using cladistic analysis of comparative data to reconstruct the evolution of cognitive development in hominids. In E. Martins (Ed.), *Phylogenies and the comparative method* (pp. 361–398). Oxford, England: Oxford University Press.

Parker, S. T., & Gibson, K. (1979). A developmental model for the evolution of language and intelligence in early hominids. *Journal of Human Evolution, 2,* 367–408.

Piaget, J. (1971). *Biology and knowledge.* Chicago: University of Chicago Press.

Purves, D. (1988). *Body and brain: A trophic theory of neural connections.* Cambridge, MA: Harvard University Press.

Raff, R. A. (1996). *The shape of life.* Chicago: University of Chicago Press.

Raup, D. M. (1977). Stochastic models in evolutionary paleontology. In A. Hallam (Ed.), *Patterns of evolution* (pp. 59–78). Amsterdam: Elsevier.

Richards, R. (1992). *The meaning of evolution.* Chicago: University of Chicago Press.

Ruse, M. (1993). Evolution and progress. *Trends in Ecology and Evolution, 8,* 55–59.

Sacher, G. A., & Staffeldt, E. (1974). Relation of gestation time to brain weight for placental mammals. *American Naturalist, 108,* 593–615.

Sagan, C. (1977). *The dragons of Eden.* New York: Random House.

Shea, B. T. (1989). Heterochrony in human evolution: The case for neoteny reconsidered. *Yearbook of Physical Anthropology, 32,* 69–101.

Shepherd, G. M. (1994). *Neurobiology.* Oxford, England: Oxford University Press.

Sordino, P., Hoeven, F., & Duboule, D. (1995). Hox gene expression in teleost fins and the origin of vertebrate digits. *Nature, 375,* 678–681.

Stanley, S. M. (1996). *Children of the ice age.* New York: Basic Books.

Stearns, S. C. (1992). *The evolution of life histories.* Oxford, England: Oxford University Press.

Valentine, J. W., Collins, A., & Meyer, C. (1993). Morphological complexity increase in metazoans. *Paleobiology, 20,* 131–142.

Wagner, P. J. (1995). Testing evolutionary constraint hypotheses for early gastropods. *Paleobiology, 21,* 248–272.

Wills, C. (1993). *The runaway brain.* New York: Basic Books.

3

PHYLOGENETIC AND ONTOGENETIC ORIGINS OF COGNITION: CLASSIFICATION

Jonas Langer

University of California at Berkeley

Cognition is a product of evolutionary and developmental processes. Like other natural biological phenomena, cognitions' roots are phylogenetic as well as ontogenetic. Unlike other natural biological phenomena, however, cognition generates cultural historical trajectories. How and at what stages of evolution and development remain subjects of much debate (as evidenced, for example, in the Damerow, Savage-Rumbaugh, Tomasello, and Turiel chapters, this volume).

Primates' sensorimotor interactions with their physical and social environments construct elementary preformal cognition. All primate species develop some logical cognition (e.g., classificatory categorizing discussed in this chapter), arithmetic cognition (e.g., numerical ordering reported in Antinucci, 1989, Poti', 1997, and Poti', Langer, & Savage-Rumbaugh, 1996), physical cognition (e.g., object permanence discussed by Doré & Goulet, this volume), and social cognition (e.g., of self by Parker; of others by Cords & Killen, by Tomasello, and by Whiten; and of imitation by Russon, Mitchell, Lefebvre & Abravanel in this volume). In this foundational sense, primate species' cognitive development converges. Cognitive ontogeny concords with its phylogeny. This is reflected well in the origins and initial development of logical classifying that we have found in monkeys, chimpanzees, and humans. Because classifying is also key to cognition, I have therefore targeted it as my focal illustrative data set discussed in the first part of this chapter.

As important as the convergences are, we also see illustrated with respect to logical classifying that we have found much variation in the onset and offset ages, velocity, extent, and organization of monkeys', chimpanzees', and humans' cognitive development. We have even discovered a significant exception to the law of invariant developmental sequencing in primates that I summarize in the first part of this chapter. In this foundational sense, primates species' cognitive development diverges. Even elementary cognitive ontogeny does not simply recapitulate its phylogeny. Nor for that matter does biological ontogeny as has, of course, long been recognized (see Gould, 1977, Mayr, 1994, and McKinney, this volume, for historical analyses of recapitulation and its relation to heterochrony).

Instead, the findings of cross-species converging and diverging cognitive development indicate heterochronic mechanisms (of temporal displacements as discussed by McKinney, this volume) of its evolution that I consider in this chapter. This requires enlarging our scope beyond logical classifying to our other cross-species findings of converging and diverging elementary cognitive development; and then further enlarging our scope beyond cognitive development to the converging and diverging noncognitive behavioral development and physiological maturation of primate species. From evolution I turn to history and propose some implications of the phylogeny and ontogeny of elementary cognition for its formalization in cultural history of ideas.

THE ORIGINS OF CLASSIFYING: COMPOSING
SINGLE CATEGORIES BY GROUPING OBJECTS

All five primate species tested so far (i.e., two monkey, two chimpanzee, and human) construct single categories when presented with random arrays of objects embodying two or more classes (e.g., blue and red, triangular and cross rings). They do this by spontaneously composing objects in space by grouping them together; no problems are posed nor are any instructions, training, feedback, reward, reinforcement, and so forth given (see Antinucci, 1989, and Langer, 1980, 1986, for details). Thereby, all primates eventually and spontaneously construct single sets of identical objects (e.g., two blue triangular rings) and similar objects (e.g., a red and a blue triangular ring or a blue triangular and a blue cross ring).

The developmental trajectories of constructing single category classifying by young humans (Langer, 1980) and common chimpanzees, *Pan troglodytes*, (Spinozzi, 1993) follow similar sequences. They comprise four stages in both species: first, and surprisingly, consistently grouping different objects into sets (e.g., a blue triangular and a red cross ring); second, random or inconsistent object grouping; third, consistently grouping identical objects into sets; and fourth, consistently grouping similar objects into sets. On the other hand, other major features of their developmental trajectories diverge. The onset and offset ages of single category classifying are much later in common chimpanzees; and their developmental velocity is slower (see Langer, in press-a, for details). The origins of classifying are both precocious and greatly accelerated in young humans. These differences are not attributable to the assessment methods because they were essentially the same nonverbal and nondirective procedures for all five primate species in our research.

Although the stage sequence is similar in humans and common chimpanzees, it diverges in the monkey species tested so far, cebus (*Cebus apella*), and macaques (*Macaca fascicularis*) (Spinozzi & Natale, 1989). Moreover, it differs between these two monkey species as well as from that of humans and of common chimpanzees. For instance, the developmental trajectory found in juvenile cebus is first, mainly random or inconsistent object grouping; second, consistently grouping different objects into sets; and third, consistently grouping identical objects into sets and grouping similar objects into sets.

In comparison to the development in young humans, then, monkeys' development of classificatory categorizing is not only delayed like common chimpanzees (i.e., later onset and offset ages plus slower velocity) but unlike common chimpanzees, its path (i.e., stage sequence) also diverges (i.e., follows a different developmental trajectory). Nevertheless, it should be reiterated that all primate species tested so far eventually construct at least single categories of identical objects and of similar objects. This includes bonobo chimpanzees (*Pan paniscus*) as well, but for whom we do not yet have ontogenetic data on onset and offset ages, velocity and sequence (Spinozzi, Natale, Langer, & Savage-Rumbaugh, 1996).

Overall, these data disconfirm the theory that cognitive ontogeny simply recapitulates its cognitive phylogeny. Diverging ontogenetic onset and offset ages, velocity, and even sequence (although not between humans and common chimpanzees) marks the primate phylogeny of the origins of classifying. At the same time, the data confirm the theory that cognitive ontogeny concords with its cognitive phylogeny (Langer, in press-a). The ontogenetic end of the origins of classifying in primate phylogeny is the same in all species tested so far: spontaneously constructing single categories of identical objects and of similar objects. Directional progress marks its primate phylogeny, even if it is probabilistic and not deterministic (see McKinney, this volume, for a general discussion of directionality in evolution and development). I return to the issue of directional progress in the concluding section of this chapter when considering the transformation from preformal to formal cognition.

THE ORIGINS OF CLASSIFYING: COMPOSING SINGLE CATEGORIES BY MANIPULATING OBJECTS

The origins of composing classes does not hinge on grouping objects into sets. Manipulating objects at the same time suffices, even when not grouping them together (e.g., holding an object in one hand while pushing another object with the other hand). Composing classes of objects requires forming some minimal binary relation, but the relation need not be spatial (Langer, 1980). The supporting evidence, so far, comes from its origins in both young humans (Langer, Schlesinger, Spinozzi, & Natale, in press) and common chimpanzees (Spinozzi, Natale, Langer, & Schlesinger, in press). Both species' ontogenetic trajectories of composing single categories by manipulating objects simultaneously but separately parallels their trajectories of composing single categories by grouping objects together into sets.

Human infants develop from serial to parallel manipulation of objects. At age 6 months, infants' acts predominantly comprise serial one-at-a-time manipulations of objects. The objects are consistently different when they manipulate two or more objects at the same time, even when not grouped into sets. By age 12 months, infants' acts change markedly. They shift to becoming predominantly parallel two-at-a-time manipulations of objects. The objects are consistently identical when they manipulate two or more objects simultaneously, even when not grouped into sets.

The developmental shift during human infancy from doing single things in series to doing two things in parallel, I proposed (Langer, 1980), manifests infants' progressive ability to split their transformational attention. Whether and how developing manipulatory attention when classifying objects is related to infants' developing nontransformational perceptual attention when categorizing objects (e.g., Madole, Oakes, & Cohen, 1993; Ruff, 1982, 1984), is a subject of ongoing research (Schlesinger & Langer, 1993) to which I return in this chapter. When young infants begin to split their manipulatory attention by doing two things at a time (e.g., picking up an object with one hand while shoving another object with the other hand), the acts are usually restricted to two different parallel transformations. By age 18 months, about half their parallel manipulatory transformations become identical or reciprocal.

Transforming objects identically by manipulating them in the same way affords infants a means to begin constructing functional equivalence classes even when the objects are different, as proposed a long time ago by Piaget (1952). For example, throwing a stick and a toy turns them both into throwables. Similarly, we have suggested that transforming objects by manipulating them in reciprocal ways affords infants a means to begin constructing functional complementary or dependent classes even when the objects do not belong to the same logical class hierarchy (Langer, Schlesinger, Spinozzi, & Natale, in press). For example, using a stick to retrieve a toy makes them complements of event hierarchies such as getting. On these hypotheses, infants' parallel manipulatory transformations begin to compose functional equivalence and complementary classes by age 18 months.

Composing functional equivalence and complementary classes are preceded ontogenetically by human infants' transformational manipulations beginning to compose predicate identity classes by age 12 months. To compose equivalence and complementary classes, infants assimilate objects to their action schemes while disregarding the objects' actual class properties. Conversely, to compose identity classes, infants accommodate their action schemes to objects' actual class properties while disregarding their functional affordances. Accommodating by attending to objects' properties to compose predicate identity classes seems to precede assimilating by attending to objects' affordances to compose functional equivalence and complementary classes in human infants' developing cognition. These findings suggest that neither (Piagetian) assimilation nor (Gibsonian) affordances have ontogenetic priority in the origins of constructive classification; (Piagetian) accommodation has priority.

Like human infants, with age, young common chimpanzees' manipulations progress from serial one-at-a-time acts to parallel two-at-a-time acts. So too, their parallel manipulations develop from predominantly different acts to predominantly identical or reciprocal acts. And, their acts also shift from manipulating different objects to manipulating identical or similar objects.

In these respects, then, the ontogeny of classificatory cognition converges with its phylogeny. In other respects, however, it diverges. The onset age for composing manipulatory identity classes by chimpanzees is the beginning of their third year, twice the chronological age for humans (and about four times the maturational age if we take into account the life history span of each species as detailed in Langer, in press-a, and illustrated in Fig. 3.1). Moreover, at this age, chimpanzees just begin to do two things at the same time. Only 20% of their behavior comprises parallel two-at-a-time manipulations. In comparison, when human infants shift to composing manipulatory identity classes at age 12 months, 60% of their acts already comprise parallel manipulations. It is not until their fifth year that half of chimpanzees' acts comprise parallel two-at-a-time manipulations. So, too, it is not until their fifth year that more than half of their manipulations become identical or reciprocal transformations.

The trajectories of human infants' developing spontaneous classifying and their manipulatory behavior that constructs it are synchronous. Their switch to consistently classifying objects by identity co-occurs with their switch to primarily performing parallel manipulations that are becoming identical or reciprocal with each other. Classifying objects is produced by relatively complex transformations. For instance, infants begin to combine serial one-at-a-time and parallel two-at-a-time manipulations to form hierarchical routines (Langer, 1986). To illustrate, by age 15 months, infants begin to collect all objects belonging to one class by serial one-at-a-time identical transformations (e.g., gathering three forks in one hand in succession) and then combine some with objects belonging to another class by parallel two-at-a-time reciprocal transformations (e.g., uprighting and holding a cup

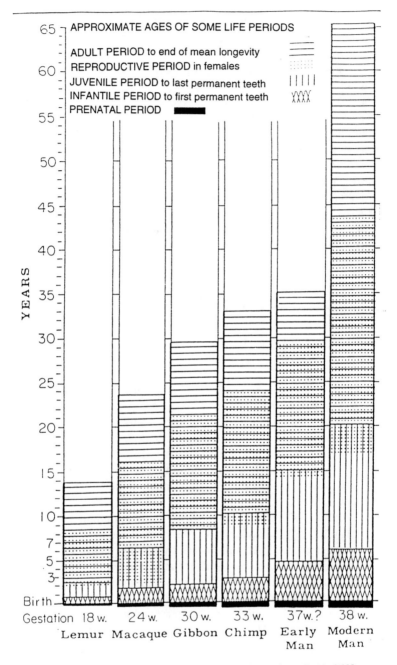

FIG. 3.1. Maturational periods of primate life histories from Smith (1992, p. 136).

with the second hand while the first hand repeatedly inserts and takes out some of the forks it has gathered).

In comparison, the trajectories of developing spontaneous classifying and manipulatory transformations are asynchronous in young common chimpanzees. Serial one-at-a-time manipulations still predominate when they switch to classifying objects by identity and similarity by age 2 years. Thus, categorizing objects is initially produced by serial manipulations that are not structurally complex.

The divergence between the development of logical cognition by young chimpanzees and humans cascades as the difference in the complexity ratio of their manipulations increases. Comparative asynchrony, temporal retardation, and structural simplicity of chimpanzees' manipulatory transformations account for or are proximal causes of their minimal further development of cognition. In the next section, we see how this plays out for classificatory development by young primates.

FURTHER DEVELOPMENT OF CLASSIFYING

The extent to which logical cognition develops varies immensely in primate phylogeny. Up to at least age 4 years, effectively their adolescence, cebus and macaques monkeys are limited to composing single categories of no more than three objects (Spinozzi & Natale, 1989). In general, they seem to be locked into developing nothing more than very simple first-order logical cognitions (Poti' & Antinucci, 1989).

Common chimpanzees develop elementary two-category (that is, second-order) classifying, but not until their fifth year (Spinozzi, 1993). To illustrate, presented with a random mix of red and yellow cups, chimpanzees begin to pick up red cups in one hand and yellow cups in the other hand at this age. In comparison, humans begin to by age 1½ years (Langer, 1986; Nelson, 1973; Riccuiti, 1965; Starkey, 1981; and Sugarman, 1983). Thus, the developmental velocity is greatly accelerated in humans (see Langer, in press-a, for details).

The fifth year, when common chimpanzees begin to construct two-category classifying, is also the age when most of their object manipulations begin to be generated in parallel (i.e., two-at-a-time acts) as we just saw. At this age, chimpanzees begin to simultaneously manipulate objects belonging to two classes (e.g., concurrently pushing two rings and two cups apart). Parallel manipulations seem to promote their elementary second-order cognitive development. The products of these manipulations, including elementary two-category classifying, are similar to those of 1½-year-old human infants.

The manipulatory transformations by which common chimpanzees compose two categories, however, are extremely limited in comparison to human infants. Common chimpanzees' object compositions remain largely inseparable from their manipulations. They do not combine or integrate their manipulations to transform or integrate their second-order compositions. As long as their coordination of their parallel transformations does not become more structurally complex, common chimpanzees' development of logical cognition remains limited.

Indeed, we are finding that common chimpanzees' classifying development does not progress with age beyond its elementary second-order level (Spinozzi, Natale, Langer, & Savage-Rumbaugh, 1996). Adult common chimpanzees' classifying does not advance beyond the two-category level they already achieve by their fifth year. Moreover, nor do the two bonobos (*Pan paniscus*) that we have tested extensively develop beyond the two-category level (Panbanisha age 6 years and Kanzi age 11 years). These results suggest that the developmental extent of spontaneous classifying does not vary as a function of chimpanzees' species. The highest level we have found in both bonobo and common chimpanzees is elementary second-order categorizing.

Previous findings indicated that the chronological onset age of spontaneous classifying is later in chimpanzees (Spinozzi, 1993) than in humans (Langer, 1980; see Langer, in press-a for details). Our current findings (Spinozzi, Natale, Langer, & Savage-Rumbaugh, 1996) indicate that the developmental offset age is also much earlier in chimpanzees, their fifth or sixth year. In humans, the development of classification develops through early adolescence at least (e.g., Inhelder & Piaget, 1964, and Markman, 1978; see Langer, 1994b, for a recent review). Comparatively, then, chimpanzees have an extremely brief ontogenetic window of cognitive development.

Whereas chimpanzees are constrained to constructing no more than two-category classifying, humans already begin to develop three-category classifying during early childhood (Langer, in preparation). To illustrate, presented with a random mix of different colored cups, young children begin to group them into three separate sets by color. This is a vital difference. It determines whether hierarchically integrated cognition becomes possible. Three-category classifying opens up the possibility of hierarchization, whereas two-category classifying permits nothing more than linear cognition. Minimally, hierarchic inclusion requires two complementary subordinate classes integrated by one superordinate class. Thus, young human children already open up the possibility of hierarchization of nested classes forming a genealogical tree structure (Langer, 1994a). Even adult chimpanzees do not. They remain limited to linear cognition of classes.

THE ROLE OF LANGUAGE

Cognition and language are dissociated in phylogeny until human ontogeny. Cognition without language is the rule. Thus, in primates, we have seen, single-category classifying develops without the benefit of any language in young monkeys and chimpanzees. Young chimpanzees, we have also seen, develop even further, to two-category classifying without the benefit of any language. Thus, language is not necessary for the origins of classifying in primate phylogeny. Nor is it necessary for its initial development in primate phylogeny. The foundations of concept formation are unrelated to language acquisition in evolution and development; even if two-category classifying is correlated with a naming burst in American human infants (Gopnik & Meltzoff, 1992; Mervis & Bertrand, 1994; but see Gershkoff-Stowe, Smith, & Namy, 1992, for a nonreplication).

Further, we are finding that language-trained bonobo and common chimpanzees reared by humans do not develop three-category classifying (Spinozzi, Natale, Langer, & Savage-Rumbaugh, 1996). In this regard, they do not differ from nonlanguage-trained chimpanzees reared by their mothers. They all develop two-category classifying, but no further. Thus, language training and human rearing does not seem to be a sufficient condition for the development of three-category classifying by chimpanzees. Three-category classifying, I argued in the previous section, is essential to the formation of hierarchic cognition. It begins to develop in humans during early childhood.

In phylogeny, language does not originate until around the end of the first year of human ontogeny with the onset of the one-word stage (Brown, 1973). By then, we have seen, human infants have developed first-order cognitions such as single-category classifying (Langer, 1980) and are in transition to second-order cognitions such as two-category classifying (Langer, 1986). So, the ontogenetic onset and initial developmental stages of human cognition precede the onset of language by about a year. On the other hand, the developmental offset of language precedes the offset of human cognition by decades. Cognitive development continues until at least ages 25 to 30 years in humans and the acquisition of formal reasoning (Kuhn, Langer, Kohlberg, & Haan, 1977). Extended cognitive development in humans is consistent with our prolonged brain maturation up to young adulthood, including in glial cell growth, myelination, synaptogenesis, and especially dendritic growth in the cortex (Gibson, 1990, 1991; Purves, 1988). Language development only continues to between age 5 years and puberty (depending on the measure). Thus, cognition and language develop asynchronically.

In both phylogeny and ontogeny, then, cognition originates and develops prior to and without language. Conversely, language does not originate prior to and without cognition in both phylogeny and ontogeny. The phylogenetic dissociation and ontogenetic asynchrony proves that language is not a necessary condition for the origins of cognition and for its development up to at least second-order cognition. It has long been recognized that language is not necessary for the origins and early development of physical cognition, such as object permanence and causal instrumentality by human (e.g., Piaget, 1954) and nonhuman (e.g., Kohler, 1926; Vygotsky, 1962) primates. Our research is showing that language is also not necessary (a) for the origins of logical cognition, such as single-category classifying, by monkeys, chimpanzees, and humans; and (b) for its subsequent initial development, such as two-category classifying, by chimpanzees.

Because language development lags behind cognitive development during most of human infancy, it cannot inform cognition. As language catches up with cognition around early childhood, the influences between cognition and language may become more mutual. Because cognition precedes language during human infancy, the predominant potential influence is from cognition to language.

I have therefore proposed that second-order cognition is a necessary condition for human infants to produce and comprehend arbitrary but conventional rules by which symbols stand for and communicate referents in grammatical forms (Langer, 1986, 1993, in press-b) . Second-order cognitions may well be axiomatic to grammatical formations in which linguistic elements are progressively combinable and interchangeable yet meaningful. For example, this is not possible without the second-order operation of substituting elements in and between two compositions (or sets) that develops toward the end of infants' second year (Langer, 1986). The hypothesis is that second-order operations (of composing, decomposing, matching, commuting, substituting, etc.) provide the rewrite rules without which grammatical constructions are not possible.

On the present view, cebus and macaques monkeys, who develop first-order but not second-order cognition, have only evolved the cognitive structures necessary for signalling. Cebus and macaques have not evolved the recursive hierarchical cognitive structures necessary for grammatical language that human infants begin to develop in their third year (for related discussions see Bickerton, 1990; Lieberman, 1991). At most, signal systems are rudimentary symbolic systems. They are very poor systems for generating new phenomena for cognitive consideration.

If, as seems to be the case, cebus and macaques are limited to signalling, then their symbolizing can only play a minor role in expanding their cognitive development. In comparison, when human infants begin to develop advanced language, their symbolizing can play a progressive role in fostering their continuing cognitive development. With continuing symbolic development, most especially in mathematical expressivity in childhood and adolescence, new and ever more powerful possibilities are increasingly opened up for cognitive development.

Second-order cognition, I have been hypothesizing, is a necessary condition for developing grammatical language by humans. It is also, I have hypothesized, a necessary condition for learning protogrammatical lan-

guage by chimpanzees (Langer, 1996). Although requiring much more research, support for the learning hypothesis is provided by findings on the
development of symbolic indexing (Savage-Rumbaugh, this volume) and
the acquisition of protogrammatical language by chimpanzees (Greenfield & Savage-Rumbaugh, 1990; Savage-Rumbaugh et al., 1993) who develop second-order cognition (Poti', 1997; Poti', Langer, & Savage-Rumbaugh, 1996) but not by monkeys who only develop first-order cognition
(Poti' & Antinucci, 1989).

THE ROLE OF PERCEPTION

A classical proposal is that perception is prerequisite to concept formation
(e.g., Wertheimer, 1945). A recent application of this hypothesis to the formation of class concepts by human infants is that it requires perceptual analysis
of objects' features at an early age (e.g., Mandler, 1992, 1993). A related
information processing version of this hypothesis is that perceptual categorizing (manifested by habituation/dishabituation techniques, e.g., Cohen &
Younger, 1983; Columbo, O'Brein, Mitchell, D. W. Roberts, & Horowitz, 1987)
is prerequisite to conceptual classifying. It is difficult, however, to see how
either version can account for why young humans and chimpanzees' manipulatory transformations first consistently compose different objects and with
increasing age switch to consistently composing identical objects in forming
their single-category classifying (as detailed previously).

Perceiving is undoubtedly a rich source of acquiring and processing
information. As yet, however, the relations between receptive perception and
constructive sensorimotor acting in the development of cognition remain
undetermined. To begin analyzing this problem requires examining phenomena that have apparent counterparts in receptive perception and constructive
activity. Human infants' developing cognition of classes, number, and causality serve as especially good exemplars and is therefore the focus of most of
this discussion. They are fundamental categories of knowledge and they come
with relatively well-documented databases on human infants' developing
receptive perceptions and constructive activity (but see Bogartz, Shinskey, &
Speaker, 1997; and Fischer & Bidell, 1991, for critiques of the data on receptive
perception). Less is known in this regard for nonhuman primates.

The findings on constructive activity, we have been seeing, are based on
measures of subjects' manipulatory transformations of objects. In contrast,
the findings on receptive perception are based on measures of subjects'
perceptual dishabituation or preferential attending to stimulus displays. The
crucial difference is that constructive activity transforms the objects of their
attention, whereas receptive perception does not.

Human infants' developing perceptual categorizing (see Bornstein, 1981,
1984; Cohen & Younger, 1983; Quinn & Eimas, 1986; and Reznick & Kagan,

1983, for extensive reviews) is an apparent receptive counterpart to their constructive composing of classes. Using a habituation preparation, infants can be familiarized with a variety of single categories of similar stimuli (e.g., triangles) by about age 4 months and two categories of contrasting stimuli (e.g., triangles and squares) sometime between ages 4 months (Quinn, 1987) and 10 months (Husaim & Cohen, 1981). Up to two categories, then, receptive perception seems to develop more rapidly than constructive composition.

This comparative ontogenetic picture raises fundamental questions about the foundational cognitive and developmental relations between receptive and constructive categorizing. These include whether perceptual categorizing merely antedates composing classes or whether they facilitate each other's development. Of course, given that perceptual categorizing seems to antedate composing classes, one might well expect the primary influence during this age period to be from perception to action.

To investigate these questions we tested infants age 6, 10, and 12 months (Schlesinger & Langer, 1993). The experiments sought to determine whether prior perceptual categorizing (induced by a standard habituation preparation) influences subsequent composing classes (by sensorimotor activity); and whether prior composing classes (by sensorimotor activity) influences subsequent perceptual categorizing (in a standard habituation preparation). With some local exceptions, the overall main findings are negative. During this age period, infants' perceptual categorizing and sensorimotor composing classes do not influence each other. They seem to follow independent developmental trajectories with little if any information flow between them.

The comparative ontogenetic picture on young infants developing causal cognition is the converse. Composing causal relations seems to antedate its receptive perception. Neonates' sensorimotor activity already constructs two primitives of causal cognition (i.e., efficacy and phenomenalism) at or shortly after birth (e.g., hand sucking; Piaget, 1954). The youngest reported age for perceiving causal phenomena is sometime between ages 3 and 10 months (e.g., Ball, 1973; Borton, 1979; Leslie & Keeble, 1987; and Oakes & Cohen, 1990).

Here, too, we have therefore been doing experiments to determine whether prior causal activity (e.g., using a tool correctly to retrieve a goal object) influences subsequent causal perception (e.g., discriminating between displays of possible and impossible use of a tool to retrieve a goal object); and vice versa (Schlesinger, 1995; Schlesinger & Langer, 1994). Here too, the overall main findings are negative. With some local exceptions, they seem to follow independent and noninteractive developmental trajectories.

So far, then, our findings point to predominant dissociation between perception and action during early infant cognitive development. Not only do they develop asynchronously, but in the main they seem to be modular cognitive processes that do not inform each other's knowledge. Perceptual cognition sometimes develops more precociously and sometimes less precociously than cognition in action during early human infancy.

Regardless of which turns out to be the case for particular domains of knowledge, the comparative extent of perceptual cognitive development remains extremely limited for all domains of knowledge. The reach of perceptual cognitive development is extremely limited for a variety of reasons. Most importantly, perception is reactive, not transformative. Further, perception has a very restricted spatiotemporal span of attention; it can only encompass minimal stimuli in any given fixation. Although this holds true for all cognitive domains, it is simplest to illustrate for numerical phenomena. Throughout ontogeny, including adulthood, there is little further development in the perception of numerosity beyond the minimal detection and discrimination of up to 3 or 4 elements by infants, as the subitizing data show (Starkey & Cooper, 1995). So too, the apparent perception of numerical addition and substraction is limited to no more that 3 or 4 elements from infancy (e.g., Wynn, 1992; but see Rivera & Wakeley, 1997, for nonreplications) through early childhood (e.g., Starkey, 1992).

In comparison, the extent of number cognition in action is fairly far-reaching. To appreciate its more extended development, it is only necessary to recall one finding (Langer, 1986). By age 24 months, infants begin to construct quantitative equivalence upon equivalence by composing two numerically corresponding sets of objects and then substituting equal numbers of objects between them. This is not to deny many limitations to the numerical cognition that can be constructed by manipulatory composing; for example, it is limited to operating on pragmatic (i.e., concrete, present, and finite) elements (see Langer, 1980, 1986, for other limitations).

The phyletic evidence on numerosity perception is sufficient to suggest that the level attained by humans is matched and even exceeded by some other species (see, e.g., the Klein & Starkey, 1987, review). For example, in birds, Koehler (1951) found discriminating numerosities up to 5 or 6 elements by pigeons, 6 elements by jackdaws, and 7 elements by ravens and parrots. Even though their capacity for numerosity perception exceeds that of human subitizing, these avian species do not develop a number system comparable to that developed by humans, which at a minimum comprises a closed system of arithmetic operations and necessary numerical products (Klein & Langer, 1987). Clearly, then, numerosity perception is far from a sufficient condition for developing advanced numerical cognition.

Is numerosity perception even one of several necessary conditions? For instance, does it partially prefigure and/or help get the development of advanced numerical cognition going? The evidence is not yet in on this question. We do know, however, that individuals born with multiple perceptual handicaps (such as Helen Keller) nevertheless develop advanced numerical cognition. So we cannot rule out the possibility that numerosity perception is an inessential peripheral process or encapsulted module that is not even a necessary condition for the development of advanced numerical cognition.

If numerosity perception is neither a necessary nor a sufficient condition for developing advanced numerical cognition, then we may well wonder what its role is in the evolution of intelligence. The presence of numerosity perception in avian species that do not develop an advanced number system of arithmetic operations and necessary products, as well as in humans who do, suggests that numerosity perception may play a very limited evolutionary role. Two hypotheses recommend themselves.

One hypothesis is that numerosity perception serves a transitory function. In human ontogeny, it enables infants to make minimal receptive judgments about quantitative equality and inequality. As such, it complements infants' initial constructive abilities to compose minimal quantitative equality and inequality. Numerosity perception is rapidly outstripped by children's developing constructive operations as they grow older (e.g., as already noted, even older infants already construct equivalences upon equivalences by mapping substitution operations upon correspondence mappings). Then numerosity perception basically ceases to develop in power and play any further evolutionary or developmental role. This would account for the insubstantial difference in humans between infant and adult subitizing and between infant and early childhood perception of addition and subtraction.

The other hypothesis is that numerosity perception is a cognitive analogue to an evolutionary appendix. Like an appendix, it may have served an as-yet-unknown function in the phylogeny of intelligence; but it no longer does so in human cognitive ontogeny. Unlike an appendix, it retains its function of discriminating between minimal numerosities. Accordingly, numerosity perception does not develop beyond its primitive infantile stage, whereas numerical cognition continues to develop far beyond its primitive beginnings in human ontogeny. Numerosity perception may well be an evolutionary dead-end as far as human cognitive development is concerned (but see Mayr, 1994, for a speculative proposal, his somatic program, of the evolutionary function of vestigal biological structures that may apply to vestigal behavioral structures as well).

THE HETEROCHRONIC EVOLUTION OF COGNITIVE DEVELOPMENT

Divergent primate ontogeny of logical classification illustrates the temporal displacements in the structural development of cognition during phylogeny. These dissociations are key to its heterochronic evolution. Crucially, the ontogenetic window of opportunity for logicomathematical cognitive development is constricted temporally in nonhuman primates and expands greatly in humans. The reasons, we have seen, are threefold: late onset age and early offset age plus decelerated developmental velocity in nonhuman primates; coupled with early onset age and late offset age plus accelerated developmental velocity in humans.

The findings so far support our heterochronic hypothesis that the ontogenetic window of opportunity for cognitive development expands exponentially in the primate lineage (Langer, 1989, 1993, 1996, in press-a). Its duration is briefest in the two monkey species we have studied, perhaps doubled in chimpanzees, and then multiplied about another six to seven times in humans. Obviously, these estimates can only be approximations until much more data on many more primates species are gathered. The data we have already gathered are sufficient to be fairly confident that the divergences between human and nonhuman primates' cognitive ontogenies include onset age, offset age, and developmental velocity. Whether all three factors contribute to the differences between nonhuman species' cognitive development is yet to be determined.

To grasp the significance of these temporal displacements in primate species' ontogenetic windows of opportunity for heterochronic evolutionary mechanisms of cognitive development requires placing them in their proper contexts. These include primate species' physiological maturation, noncognitive behavioral development, and cognitive behavioral development that is not logicomathematical. So, I briefly review each in turn, keeping to those features that are most relevant to my proposals about heterochronic mechanisms.

With one crucial exception, physiological maturation tends to be delayed or hypermorphic in primate evolution (see Fig. 3.1). The onset and offset ages are progressively retarded and the maturational velocity is decelerated in descendant primate species. Obviously, this is the opposite trend from that we find in the primate evolution of logicomathematical cognition. It is not delayed. Instead, it is precocial or progenetic (see Langer, in press-a, for details and McKinney & McNamara, 1991, for comprehensive discussions and definitions of hypermorphosis and progenesis).

The crucial exception to humans' delayed physiological maturation is brain maturation (see Fig. 3.2). The rate of brain maturation in humans is in the average range for primates; but it is prolonged in humans (Gibson, 1990, 1991). The offset age is later. A result, evident in Figs. 3.2 and 3.3, is great expansion of the modern human brain (as measured by the EQ, or encephalization quotient, that represents the fraction of a body's mass devoted to brains), most probably in the neocortex (Deacon, in press; Finlay & Darlington, 1995). Prolonged ontogenetic expansion of the modern human brain, on this hypothesis, underpins terminal expansion of human cognition,

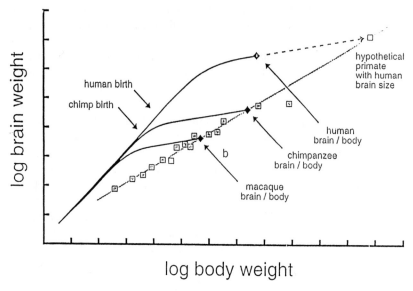

FIG. 3.2. Primate trend in ontogeny of brain/body (EQ) growth from Deacon (in press).

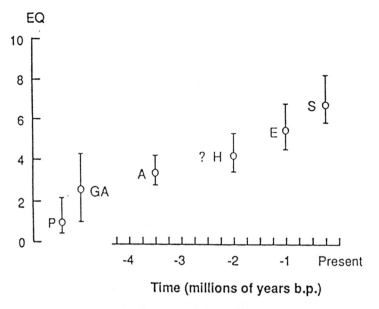

FIG. 3.3. Evolution of EQ means and approximate ranges for prosimians (P), great apes (GA), australopithecines (A), *Homo habilis* (H), *Homo erectus* (E), and *Homo sapiens* (S) from Deacon (in press).

including logicomathematical cognition (Gibson, 1990, 1991; Langer, in press-a).

A consequence of progressively delayed nonbrain physiological maturation in the primate lineage, illustrated in Fig. 3.1, is progressive deceleration of noncognitive behavioral development such as locomotion and self-reliance. Comparatively, then, noncognitive behavior develops more slowly in human than nonhuman primates. Accelerating cognitive development is progressively coupled with decelerating noncognitive behavioral development in the primate lineage.

Comparatively accelerated nonbrain physiological maturation and noncognitive behavioral development covary with decelerated cognitive development in nonhuman primates. These covariations increasingly decouple and recouple in primate evolution producing inverse covariations in humans. Comparatively decelerated nonbrain physiological maturation and noncognitive behavioral development covary with accelerated cognitive development in humans.

So far, my discussion of the primate evolution of cognitive development has focused mainly on the logicomathematical domain, including importantly its progressively accelerating velocity and expanding temporal window of opportunity. A more complete picture requires taking account of the two other major domains, developing physical knowledge such as causal reasoning and developing social knowledge such as moral reasoning. Although it is becoming increasingly clear that the same general trend holds for the primate evolution of social cognitive development, such as terminal extension and later offset age, the available comparative developmental data are relatively sparse (see Langer, in press-a, and Parker & McKinney, in preparation, for further details). So I only consider the primate evolution of physical cognitive development for which there is comparable data to that on logicomathematical cognition (see Parker & McKinney, in preparation, for a comprehensive review).

The ontogenetic window of opportunity for developing physical knowlege is constricted temporally in nonhuman primates and greatly expands in humans. In general, then, the evolutionary trend is similar to that of logicomathematical cognitive development. However, the temporal factors involved vary somewhat (see Langer, in press-a, for details). The onset age of physical cognition is during the neonatal period in all primate species studied so far. Thus, there is no fundamental divergence in onset age as, we have seen, there is for logicomathematical cognition. Instead, we find even earlier offset ages in physical than logicomathematical cognition in nonhuman primates. The emerging comparative picture is predominantly out-of-phase development of physical and logicomathematical cognition in monkeys, shifting to partially in-phase development in chimpanzees and completely in-phase development in humans.

These comparative findings led me to propose that a key heterochronic mechanism of cognitive evolution has been progressive temporal displacement in the primate lineage from asychronic to synchronic development of physical and logicomathematical cognition. On this proposal, the fundamental consequence is increasing probability of maximizing information flow between cognitive domains generating cascading cognitive possibilities and necessities. For example, constructing a logic of experimentation or a history of ideas becomes increasingly probable. They are, of course, not determined consequences, as I elaborate next.

An orchestrated suite of displaced covariations marks the heterochronic evolution of cognitive development. Expanding ontogenetic windows of cognitive opportunity and of their underlying brain maturation, accelerating cognitive development, decelerating noncognitve behavioral developments and of their underlying nonbrain physiological maturation, and progressively synchronizing cognitive domains are its prime covarying constituents. Primate intellectual evolution is marked by increasing duration, velocity, and synchrony generating cascading cognitive developmental progress. These heterochronic mechanisms provide humans with more developmental duration, velocity, and structural synchrony for intellectual growth.

FROM PREFORMAL TO FORMAL
COGNITIVE PROGRESS

Foundational elements of cognition, on the present view and empirical findings, are universal. Basic cognitive elements develop in all anthropoid primates. The extent to which these elements develop varies among primate species, as does their developmental velocity. The sequence in which the elements of physical cognition develop does not seem to vary among primate species. Probably, this has much (perhaps, most) to do with the constraints imposed by the laws of physics on both (a) the evolution of primate species and (b) what it is possible to know at elementary preformal levels about physical phenomena. On the other hand, we have discovered that the sequence in which classifying, a central component of logicomathematical cognition, develops varies among primate species.

Archaeology is just beginning to provide us with some empirical data, if still necessarily reconstructive empirical data, on the prehistory of hominids' cognitive development. Although limited to the archaeology of preformal spatial competence, the findings have strong paradigmatic potential. Thus, Wynn (1989) found a similar sequence in the hominid evolution of preformal spatial cognition (initially proposed by Parker & Gibson, 1979) as Piaget and Inhelder (1967) found in human ontogeny.

The sequence in childrens' development is from topological to projective to Euclidean constructions. Similarly, the sequence of stone knapping began in the hominid lineage at least 1.8 million years ago with the construction of Oldowan tools marked by topological features of proximity, separation, and order. Wynn (1989) pointed out that these artifacts resemble the tool constructing level of modern chimpanzees. The overlap in their EQ ranges (see Fig. 3.3) suggests that developing to similar levels of spatial cognition by early hominids and modern great apes is plausible. By 1.2 million years ago, early *Homo erectus'* stone knapping progressed to constructing tools involving projective interval and symmetry. This is beyond the apparent spatial competence of great apes and concords with the nonoverlap between their EQ range and that of *Homo erectus* (see Fig. 3.3). According to Wynn, this prehistoric sequence culminated before 300,000 years ago in later *Homo erectus* creating tools marked by Euclidean features of bilateral symmetry, congruence and, perhaps, external frames of reference or perspectives.

It is imperative not to overlook the fact that the parallelism between the ontogeny of *Homo sapiens* and its evolution in the hominid lineage is limited to preformal spatial cognition. As already noted by Piaget and Inhelder (1967), the history of formal spatial cognition followed the opposite course. It began with Euclidean geometry and progressed to projective and eventually topological geometry.

These comparative data on the prehistory and ontogeny of preformal spatial cognition plus the history of formal spatial cognition lead me to the following proposition. The evolutionary and developmental direction of preformal cognitive change, or if you will progress, does not constrain the direction of formal cognitive change, whether in ontogeny or history. The trajectory of preformal cognition does not determine the trajectory of formal cognition even though preformal cognition is the elementary structure on which it is built. Instead, preformal cognition is a foundation that opens up exponential multiplication of possible formal progress in ontogeny and history. Thus, change is progressively open; and, thus, the permanent possibility for formal cognitive evolution, development, and history.

REFERENCES

Antinucci, F. (Ed.). (1989). *Cognitive structure and development of nonhuman primates*. Hillsdale, NJ: Lawrence Erlbaum Associates.

Ball, W. A. (1973, April). *The perception of casuality in the infant.* Paper presented at the Society for Research in Child Development meetings, Philadelphia.

Bickerton, D. (1990). *Language and species*. Chicago: University of Chicago Press.

Bogartz, R. S., Shinskey, J. L., & Speaker, C. (1997). Interpreting infant looking. *Developmental Psychology, 33*, 408–422.

Bornstein, M. (1981). Two kinds of perceptual organization near the beginning of life. In A. Collins (Ed.), *Minnesota symposium on child psychology* (Vol. 14, pp. 39–91). Hillsdale, NJ: Lawrence Erlbaum Associates.

Bornstein, M. (1984). A descriptive taxonomy of psychological categories used by infants. In C. Sophian (Ed.), *Origins of cognitive skills* (pp. 313–338). Hillsdale, NJ: Lawrence Erlbaum Associates.

Borton, R. W. (1979, April). *The perception of casuality in infants.* Paper presented at the Society for Research in Child Development meetings, Denver.

Brown, R. A. (1973). *A first language: The early stages.* Cambridge, MA: Harvard University Press.

Cohen, L. B., & Younger, B. A. (1983). Perceptual categorization in infants. In E. K. Scholnick (Ed.), *New trends in conceptual representation* (pp. 197–219). Hillsdale, NJ: Lawrence Erlbaum Associates.

Columbo, J., O'Brein, M., Mitchell, D. W., Roberts, K., & Horowitz, F. D. (1987). A lower boundary for category formation in preverbal infants. *Journal of Child Language, 14,* 383–385.

Deacon, T. W. (in press). How flexible is the neurodevelopmental clock. In S. T. Parker, M. L. McKinney, & J. Langer (Eds.), *The evolution of development: Biology, brain and behavior.* Santa Fe, NM: School of American Research Press.

Finlay, B. L., & Darlington, R. B. (1995). Linked regularities in the development and evolution of mammalian brains. *Science, 268,* 1578–1584.

Fischer, K. W., & Bidell, T. (1991). Constraining nativist inferences about cognitive capacities. In S. Carey & R. Gelman (Eds.), *The epigenesis of mind* (pp. 199–236). Hillsdale, NJ: Lawrence Erlbaum Associates.

Gershkoff-Stowe, L., Smith, L. B., & Namy, L. L. (1992, May). *A further look at the relationship between categorizing and naming in the second year.* Paper presented at the Meeting of the International Society of Infant Studies, Miami.

Gibson, K. R. (1990). New perspectives on instincts and intelligence: Brain size and the emergence of hierarchical mental construction skills. In S. T. Parker & K. R. Gibson (Eds.), *"Language" and intelligence in monkeys and apes* (pp. 97–128). Cambridge, England: Cambridge University Press.

Gibson, K. R. (1991). Myelination and behavioral development: A comparative perspective on questions of neoteny, altriciality and intelligence. In K. R. Gibson & A. C. Petersen (Eds.), *Brain maturation and cognitive development* (pp. 29–63). New York: deGruyter.

Gopnik, A., & Meltzoff, A. N. (1992). Categorization and naming: Basic level sorting in eighteen-month-olds and its relation to language. *Child Development, 63,* 1091–1103.

Gould, S. J. (1977). *Ontogeny and phylogeny.* Cambridge, MA: Harvard University Press.

Greenfield, P. M., & Savage-Rumbaugh, E. S. (1990). Grammatical combination in Pan paniscus. In S. T. Parker & K. R. Gibson (Eds.), *Language and intelligence in monkeys and apes* (pp. 540–578). Cambridge, England: Cambridge University Press.

Husaim, J. S., & Cohen, L. B. (1981). Infant learning of ill-defined categories. *Merrill-Palmer Quarterly, 27,* 443–456.

Inhelder, B., & Piaget, J. (1964). *Early growth of logic in the child: Classification and seriation.* New York: Harper & Row.

Klein, A., & Langer, J. (1987, April). *Elementary numerical constructions by toddlers.* Paper presented at the Society for Research in Child Development meeting, Baltimore.

Klein, A., & Starkey, P. (1987). The origins and development of numerical cognition: A comparative analysis. In J. Sloboda & D. Rogers (Eds.), *Cognitive processes in mathematics* (pp. 1–25). Oxford, England: Oxford University Press.

Kohler, W. (1926). *The mentality of apes.* NY: Harcourt Brace.

Koehler, O. (1951). The ability of birds to count. *Bulletin of Animal Behavior, 9,* 41–45.

Kuhn, D., Langer, J., Kohlberg, L., & Haan, N. S. (1977). The development of formal operations in logical and moral judgment. *Genetic Psychology Monographs, 95,* 97–188.

Langer, J. (1980). *The origins of logic: Six to twelve months.* New York: Academic Press.

Langer, J. (1986). *The origins of logic: One to two years.* New York: Academic Press.

Langer, J. (1989). Comparison with the human child. In F. Antinucci (Ed.), *Cognitive structure and development of nonhuman primates* (pp. 229–242). Hillsdale, NJ: Lawrence Erlbaum Associates.

Langer, J. (1993). Comparative cognitive development. In K. Gibson & T. Ingold (Eds.), *Tools, language and cognition in human evolution* (pp. 300–313). New York: Cambridge University Press.

Langer, J. (1994a). From acting to understanding: The comparative development of meaning. In W. F. Overton & D. Palermo (Eds.), *The nature and ontogenesis of meaning* (pp. 191–213). Hillsdale, NJ: Lawrence Erlbaum Associates.

Langer, J. (1994b). Logic. In V. S. Ramachandren (Ed.), *Encyclopedia of human behavior* (Vol. 3, pp. 83–91). San Diego: Academic Press.

Langer, J. (1996). Heterochrony and the evolution of primate cognitive development. In A. Russon, K. A. Bard, & S. T. Parker (Eds.), *Reaching into thought: The minds of the great apes* (pp. 257–277). Cambridge, England: Cambridge University Press.

Langer, J. (in press-a). The heterochronic evolution of primate cognitive development. In S. T. Parker, M. L. McKinney, & J. Langer (Eds.), *The evolution of development: Biology, brain and behavior*. Santa Fe, NM: School of American Research Press.

Langer, J. (in press-b). The mosaic evolution of cognitive and linguistic ontogeny. In M. Bowerman & S. Levinson (Eds.), *Conceptual development and language acquisition*. Cambridge, England: Cambridge University Press.

Langer, J. (in preparation). *The origins and early development of cognition in comparative perspective*.

Langer, J., Schlesinger, M., Spinozzi, G., & Natale, F. (in press). Developing classification in action: I. Human infants. *Human Evolution*.

Leslie, A. M., & Keeble, S. (1987). Do six-month-old infants perceive causality? *Cognition, 25,* 265–288.

Lieberman, P. (1991). *Uniquely human*. Cambridge, MA: Harvard University Press.

Madole, K. L., Oakes, L. M., & Cohen, L. B. (1993). Developmental changes in infants' attention to function and form-function correlations. *Cognitive Development, 8,* 189–209.

Mandler, J. M. (1992). How to build a baby: II. Conceptual primitives. *Psychological Review, 99,* 587–604.

Mandler, J. M. (1993). On concepts. *Cognitive Development, 8,* 141–148.

Markman, E. M. (1978). Empirical versus logical solutions to part-whole comparison problems concerning classes and collections. *Child Development, 49,* 168–177.

Mayr, E. (1994). Recapitulation reinterpreted: The somatic program. *Quarterly Review of Biology, 69,* 223–232.

McKinney, M. L., & McNamara, J. K. (1991). *Heterochrony: The Evolution of ontogeny*. New York: Plenum.

Mervis, C. B., & Bertrand, J. (1994). Acquisition of the novel name—nameless category (N3C) principle. *Child Development, 65,* 1646–1662.

Nelson, K. (1973). Some evidence for the primacy of categorization and its functional basis. *Merrill-Palmer Quarterly, 19,* 21–39.

Oakes, L. M., & Cohen, L. B. (1990). Infant perception of a causal event. *Cognitive Development, 5,* 193–207.

Parker, S. T., & Gibson, K. R. (1979). A developmental model for the evolution of language and intelligence in early hominids. *Behavioral and Brain Sciences, 2,* 367–408.

Parker, S. T., & McKinney, M. L. (in preparation). *Childhood's end*.

Piaget, J. (1952). *The origins of intelligence in children*. New York: International Universities Press.

Piaget, J. (1954). *The construction of reality in the child*. New York: Basic Books.

Piaget, J., & Inhelder, B. (1967). *The child's conception of space*. New York: Norton.

Poti', P. (1997). Logical structures of young chimpanzees' spontaneous object grouping. *International Journal of Primatology, 18,* 33–59.

Poti', P., & Antinucci, F. (1989). Logical operations. In F. Antinucci (Ed.), *Cognitive structure and development of nonhuman primates* (pp. 189–228). Hillsdale, NJ: Lawrence Erlbaum Associates.

Poti', P., Langer, J., & Savage-Rumbaugh, S. (1996, September). *The development of logical operations in monkeys and chimpanzees.* Paper presented at the symposium on "Piagetian approaches to the evolution of intelligence," Congress on The Growing Mind, Geneva, Switzerland.

Purves, D. (1988). *Body and brain: A trophic theory of neural connections.* Cambridge, MA: Harvard University Press.

Quinn, P. C. (1987). The categorized representation of visual pattern information by very young infants. *Cognition, 27,* 145–179.

Quinn, P. C., & Eimas, P. D. (1986). On categorization in early infancy. *Merrill-Palmer Quarterly, 32,* 331–363.

Reznick, J. S., & Kagan, J. (1983). Category detection in infancy. In L. P. Lipsitt (Ed.), *Advances in infancy research* (Vol. 2, pp. 79–111). Norwood, NJ: Ablex.

Riccuiti, H. N. (1965). Object grouping and selective ordering behavior in infants 12 to 24 months. *Merrill-Palmer Quarterly, 11,* 129–148.

Rivera, S., & Wakeley, A. (1997, April). *Determining the parameters of infants' ability to add and subtract.* Poster presented at the Society for Research in Child Development meetings, Washington, DC.

Ruff, H. A. (1982). Role of manipulation in infants' responses to invariant properties of objects. *Developmental Psychology, 18,* 682–691.

Ruff, H. A. (1984). Infants' manipulative exploration of objects: Effects of age and object characteristics. *Developmental Psychology, 20,* 9–20.

Savage-Rumbaugh, E. S., Murphy, J., Sevcik, R. A., Brakke, K. E., Williams, S. L., & Rumbaugh, D. M. (1993). Language comprehension in ape and child. *Monographs of the Society for Research in Child Development, 58,* nos, 3–4.

Schlesinger, M. (1995). *Infants' developing knowledge about causality: Perception, action, and perception-action relations.* Unpublished doctoral dissertation, University of California at Berkeley.

Schlesinger, M., & Langer, J. (1993, March). *The developmental relations between sensorimotor classification and perceptual categorization in early infancy.* Paper presented at the Meeting of the Society for Research in Child Development, Chicago.

Schlesinger, M., & Langer, J. (1994, June). *Perceptual and sensorimotor causality in 10-month-old infants.* Poster presented at the Jean Piaget Society meeting, Philadelphia.

Smith, H. (1992). Life history and the evolution of human maturation. *Evolutionary Anthropology, 1,* 134–142.

Spinozzi, G. (1993). The development of spontaneous classificatory behavior in chimpanzees (*Pan troglodytes*). *Journal of Comparative Psychology, 107,* 193–200.

Spinozzi, G., Natale, F., Langer, J., & Savage-Rumbaugh, E. S. (1996, September). *The development of classification in monkeys and chimpanzees.* Paper presented at the symposium on "Piagetian approaches to the evolution of intelligence," Congress on The Growing Mind, Geneva, Switzerland.

Spinozzi, G., & Natale, F. (1989). Classification. In F. Antinucci (Ed.), *Cognitive structure and development of nonhuman primates* (pp. 163–188). Hillsdale, NJ: Lawrence Erlbaum Associates.

Spinozzi, G., Natale, F., Langer, J., & Schlesinger, M. (in press). Developing classification in action: II. Young chimpanzees (*Pan troglodytes*). *Human Evolution.*

Starkey, D. (1981). The origins of concept formation: Object sorting and object preference in early infancy. *Child Development, 52,* 489–497.

Starkey, P. (1992). The early development of numerical reasoning. *Cognition, 43,* 93–126.

Starkey, P., & Cooper, R. G. (1995). The development of subitizing in young children. *British Journal of Developmental Psychology, 13,* 399–420.

Sugarman, S. (1983). *Children's early thought: Developments in classification.* New York: Cambridge University Press.

Vygotsky, L. S. (1962). *Thought and language.* Cambridge, MA: MIT Press.

Wertheimer, M. (1945). *Productive thinking.* New York: Harper.

Wynn, T. (1989). *The evolution of spatial competence.* Urbana: University of Illinois Press.

Wynn, K. (1992). Addition and subtraction by human infants. *Nature, 358,* 749–750.

4

THE COMPARATIVE ANALYSIS
OF OBJECT KNOWLEDGE

François Y. Doré
Sonia Goulet
Ecole de psychologie, Université Laval, Québec, Canada

Gibson (1990) proposed a new perspective on the evolution and development of cognitive capacities that combines a reformulation of Jerison's (1973, 1985) theory of brain evolution, parallel distributed models of information processing (Rumelhart & McClelland, 1986), and Piagetian (Piaget, 1967/1971) and neo-Piagetian (Case, 1985; Langer, 1986) developmental theories of intelligence. In this perspective, intellectual differences between humans and animals, as well as between animal species, reflect brain-size-mediated expansions of mental constructional skills. In animals with small brains or poorly interconnected perceptual and motor systems, mental constructions are minimal. Objects are recognized on the basis of simple key stimuli, behavior consists mainly of modal action patterns (Barlow, 1968), and stimulus-response associations are automatic. In species that have evolved expanded brain size and rich neural networks, more perceptual, motor, and conceptual units can be held and processed simultaneously. The discrete units are combined and recombined to produce fine perceptual discriminations and to construct object images, object-object relationships, and flexible and hierarchically organized behavioral patterns.

Infantile developmental patterns also play a crucial role in the level of constructional abilities reached by a given species. For example, although there are many similarities between human and primate ontogeny, the human infant possesses species-typical behavior patterns lacking in most primates: imitation of simple facial expressions, manipulation of objects manually prior to developing mature locomotor patterns, repetitive actions on objects (secondary circular reactions), experimentation with object-object and object-force interactions (tertiary circular reactions). These species-typical, minimally constructed infantile behaviors channel human neural, cognitive, and behavioral development in specific directions (linguistic and tool-using domains) that are different from those in which primate adult development is channeled.

In Gibson's (1990) perspective, feeding behavior would be especially instrumental in channeling animal evolution and ontogeny toward greater information-processing capacity and mental constructional skills. According to her, the largest-brained mammals can be divided into two groups. One group, which includes many monkeys and great apes, comprises omnivorous or frugivorous extractive foragers. These animals have to construct cognitive maps of their environment to locate widely dispersed food; they must recognize that one object may lie inside another; and they must possess the manipulative skills to peel fruits, crack shells, and so forth. The other group consists of dolphins, sea lions, otters, and some carnivores that actively pursue prey and in some cases hunt cooperatively. Feeding is probably a very important selective pressure in the evolution of cognitive capacities and a determining element in the channeling of development. This activity as well as other activities, like avoiding predators or sustaining an interaction with a social partner, sometimes involve finding an object that has disappeared momentarily. Etienne (1973, 1984) suggested that animals' reactions to the disappearance of physical and social objects can be classified into three kinds or degrees that correspond, in Gibson's (1990) framework, to different levels of mental constructional skills.

The first kind is observed in predatory species of various phyla (insects, spiders, and some lower vertebrates) that have developed special devices and stereotyped movements or postures to increase the probability of further contact with a prey that has disappeared. These reactions last for a limited time and exclusively concern objects that have an immediate survival value. The second kind of reaction is displayed by some birds such as the domestic chicken and by some mammals such as the rabbit. They are unconditional or learned responses to perceptual cues that are adaptive but empirically determined. The third kind of reaction, which according to Etienne (1973) is an attribute of birds of the Corvidae family, some mammalian carnivores, and primates, consists of spontaneous and active search behavior. These reactions are characterized by plasticity and generality and result from the action of an integrated cognitive structure, object permanence.

Piaget (1937/1967) defined object permanence as the understanding that objects continue to exist when they are no longer available to immediate perception. As pointed out by Etienne (1984), not all species are fully capable of such an understanding. Evolution has several ways of ensuring the organism's survival, albeit the most effective and flexible of all is the cognitive capacity of object permanence. Being able to mentally prolong the existence of an object confers more behavioral freedom and is far less susceptible to accidental disruption than any other devices. It is indeed one of the most useful tools an organism can possess to feed, mate, protect its territory, and escape predators.

Object permanence is not an all-or-none phenomenon (Piaget, 1937/1967). In human infants, for instance, this cognitive capacity develops gradually during the sensorimotor period (0 to 24 months) and has been divided by Piaget into six stages. This development can also be viewed as consisting of four major successive levels of object knowledge. Each level is in fact a reorganization of the acquisitions made at the prior level and confers more flexibility and objectivity to the infant's interactions with the world.

At the first level (Stages 1, 2, and 3), perceptual and motor prerequisites to search behavior are acquired. For example, by the end of Stage 3, infants are able to retrieve an invisible whole from a visible fraction of it. However, if the object leaves the perceptual field, infants quit searching. Therefore, infants are not yet capable of object permanence per se. At the second level or Stage 4, actions previously made toward partially visible objects are now applied to objects that move and disappear. An object can be hidden and discovered in a place (A) several times consecutively. On the other hand, if the object is concealed in a different place (B), the infant will still search for it at its initial hiding location (A). This is the well-known Stage 4 or A-not-B error. According to Piaget (1937/1967), the infant, instead of relying on what he/she sees, repeats a previously successful behavior because objects are not separate entities and exist only as far as the subject acts on them.

At the third level or Stage 5, search behavior reflects an increasing separation of objects from the subject. Infants now rely on immediate perception instead of on the result of their previous actions and thus, the A-not-B error is no longer committed. Moreover, when an object is successively hidden in a number of places (successive visible displacements), they search for it where it last disappeared. Still, objects and their movements are not totally independent from the subject because their existence is linked to direct perception. If some movements of an object have not been perceived, infants are not able to infer them from indirect cues. These invisible displacement problems are solved only at the fourth level, or Stage 6, when complete object permanence is achieved with the appearance of what Piaget (1937/1967) called symbolic representation. Objects are now totally dissociated from the subject. The radical egocentrism of the newborn has been gradually replaced by the understanding that objects exist beyond the scope of action or direct perception. The parallel emergence of language will provide the child with new ways to refer to and sustain the existence of unperceived objects. Although the developmental sequence described by Piaget and his interpretations have been challenged (Baillargeon, 1995; Cornell, 1978; Harris, 1983; Spelke, Vishton, & von Hofsten, 1995), the theories of object permanence have played and still play a central role in the study of infant cognition.

The aforementioned levels—no active search of hidden objects followed by active search based on action, perception, and representation—have all been investigated in human infants, but Stage 4 has generated the most extensive research (e.g. Bjork & Cummings, 1984; Bremner, 1978; Butterworth, 1977; Harris, 1983; Wellman, Cross, & Bartsch, 1986).

Several reasons might explain the attention given to this specific level. First, Stage 4 marks the very beginning of active search. Secondly, the A-not-B error is a striking and robust phenomenon that defies adult logical sense. Thirdly, there are many alternative interpretations of this error and of the further acquisitions necessary to overcome it. The factors responsible for the errors made at Stage 5 have received much less attention. This stage may appear as a natural, not so significant, transition between active search and complete object permanence that all normal human infants achieve. However, the transition between Stage 5 and Stage 6 involves a major cognitive reorganization that radically changes the way the world is understood and represented from that point on.

In this chapter, we expose and defend the idea that Stage 6 organisms, because they possess symbolic representation, are able to recall past events whereas Stage 5 organisms are only capable of recognizing events as they re-occur. This idea has several implications for theories of animal and human cognition. It means that (1) Stage 5 organisms cannot generate internal substitutes, including mental images, to stand for absent objects or events; (2) when they have to search for a hidden object, they do not represent this object but rather respond to an environmental cue that was associated with the object at the time of its disappearance; (3) they are confined to their immediate perception, that is, their memories of the past and their anticipation of the future depend entirely on the presence of relevant cues in the environment.

First, we briefly review the animal literature on object permanence and show that most species already studied display Stage 5 search behavior. Then, we analyze the behavior of some of these animals on the basis of criteria defined by Piaget (1937/1967) as typical of Stage 5 human infants. Studying animals that live their whole adult life at this stage will hopefully throw a new light on the adaptative value of these constructional skills and on the challenges that Stage 5 human infants have to face before they acquire symbolic representation.

SEARCH BEHAVIOR AND OBJECT PERMANENCE
IN ANIMALS

There are only three longitudinal studies where spontaneous search behavior was observed (Dumas & Doré, 1991; Mathieu & Bergeron, 1981; Parker, 1977) and a limited number of longitudinal or cross-sectional studies where human analog tests of object permanence were administered (Dumas & Doré, 1989; Gagnon & Doré, 1994; Gruber, Girgus, & Banuazizi, 1971; Redshaw, 1978; Wood, Moriarty, Gardner, & Gardner, 1980). In most animal studies, standardized tests were administered to adult subjects.

The object permanence tests were adapted to the sensory, motor, and motivational characteristics of each species. The animal is faced with a row of 2 to 5 identical screens under or behind which an object can be hidden. In some experiments, a piece of food is the target object but an incentive object (toy or secondarily reinforced object) is frequently used in order to avoid olfactory cues. In invisible displacement tests, the target object is first hidden in a container and then, the container is moved to a hiding screen. In some studies, the experimenter's hand is used as a container but more generally, the container is a small mobile box. Both the target object and the container are usually displaced with a manipulandum (stick or thread). In primate studies, the hiding screens are in the reach of the subject and can be lifted to uncover the target object. With other animals, the subject has to walk toward the screens, choose one, and touch the target object.

In the stump-tail macaque, the chimpanzee, and the gorilla, the developmental sequence is very similar to the one described in human infants and includes the A-not-B error. In cats and in dogs, the sequence is roughly similar but there are some differences. Stages 4 and 5 are acquired very rapidly, in only 1 or 2 weeks instead of 4 to 5 months in human infants, and the A-not-B error is not observed, probably as a result of early locomotion in these animals.

Of all the species that have been studied yet, only chimpanzees (Mathieu, Bouchard, Granger, & Herscovitch, 1976; Wood, Moriarty, Gardner, & Gardner, 1980), gorillas (Natale, Antinucci, Spinozzi, & Poti', 1986; Redshaw, 1978), and maybe psittacine birds (Pepperberg & Funk, 1990; Pepperberg & Kozak, 1986; but see Gagnon & Doré, 1992, for a critical analysis of these data) seem to truly understand invisible displacements. Some monkeys have also been reported to achieve Stage 6 of object permanence but these results were not conclusive because of methodological problems (see Antinucci, 1989; Doré & Dumas, 1987) or they were not replicated in recent studies (De Blois & Novak, 1994; Dumas & Brunet, 1994). Experiments on dogs suggested that they are able to solve invisible displacement problems (Gagnon & Doré, 1992, 1993, 1994; Triana & Pasnak, 1981). However, the latest results revealed that although they can reach a moderate level of success in these problems, dogs do not fully understand invisible displacements (Doré, Fiset, Goulet,

Dumas, & Gagnon, 1996). As for cats, a few studies (Dumas, 1992; Triana & Pasnak, 1981) concluded that they succeed in invisible displacement tests of object permanence but overwhelming evidence shows that they do not (Doré, 1986, 1990; Doré et al., 1996; Dumas & Doré, 1989; Goulet, Doré, & Rousseau, 1994; Pasnak, Kurkjian, & Triana, 1988).

In summary, comparative studies on animals indicate that among mammals, only chimpanzees and gorillas reach Stage 6 of object permanence. These apes are thus able to find an object that was invisibly transferred from a container to a screen. Different species of monkeys as well as cats and dogs display search behavior that corresponds to Stage 5. One study (Doré, Goulet, & Herman, 1991) with one juvenile and one adult dolphin suggests that dolphins would also achieve Stage 5 of object permanence. These species fail invisible displacement problems but can retrieve an object that was visibly moved in a succession of screens. As already mentioned, the difference between Stage 5 and Stage 6 search behavior has major implications in terms of mental constructional skills.

In his description and discussion of Stage 5 and Stage 6 object permanence, Piaget (1937/1967, 1967/1971) raised three main issues that can be summarized as the nature, content, and limitations of representation. These three issues orient our analysis of cognitive functioning at Stage 5. Because the most detailed studies have been done with cats and dogs, the following discussion of Stage 5 cognitive functioning focuses mainly on these two species.

THE NATURE OF REPRESENTATION

Since the *The Origins of Intelligence* (1936/1974), Piaget always made a clear distinction between two forms of representation. Both allow an organism to acquire and to structure knowledge about its environment and to regulate its interaction with the world. However, one form, primitive representation, uses external substitutes to stand for absent objects or events whereas the other form, symbolic representation, uses internal substitutes (mental images, words, etc.) for the same purpose. The former characterizes the sensorimotor period and the latter, the subsequent periods of human development. In *Biology and Knowledge*, Piaget (1967/1971) related these two forms of representation to the contemporary concepts of cognitive psychology, recognition and recall.

At Stage 6, an organism would be capable of recall whereas before this stage, it would be capable of recognition only. In recall, the organism has a mental image of the object and can therefore represent the object behind the screen. In recognition, the memory of an object is retrieved only by the reappearance of this object; external cues associated with this object at the time of its disappearance guide search behavior. In other words, in object permanence tasks, a Stage 5 organism would not have a mental image of the object hidden behind the screen. When it searches for the object, the subject recognizes either the screen that was associated with the object's disappearance or the spatial location of this screen. Results from studies on cats tend to support this assumption. These studies used three different manipulations: standard Piagetian invisible displacement tests, invisible displacements with a transparent container, and a new invisible displacement procedure without a container.

In standard Piagetian invisible displacements (Fig. 4.1), the target object is first hidden in an opaque container, which is immediately moved behind a screen. While the container is still behind the screen, the object is removed from it and is concealed behind the screen. Finally, the container is removed

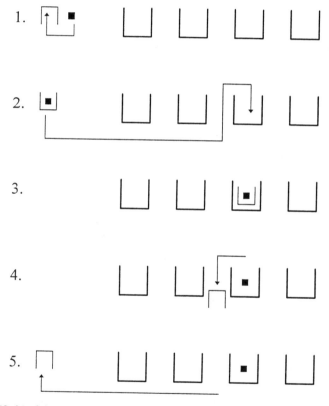

FIG. 4.1. Schematic representation of a standard Piagetian invisible displacement. (1) The target object (a cube) is moved in the open container. (2) The container and the invisible object are moved behind the target screen. (3) The object is removed from the container and left behind the target screen. (4) The empty container is shown to the subject. (5) The container is moved to its final position, which is the same as its initial position, as in this example, or opposite to its initial position. The container is left open as shown in this figure or is rotated and left closed at the end of the manipulation.

from the target screen and is shown to be empty to the subject before being moved to its final position. Seeing the empty container is an indirect cue that the object was transferred from the container to the target screen. In some studies, the container is left open at the end of the manipulation and in others, it is left closed.

Naive cats submitted to these tests have a stronger tendency to search for the object at the container than at the target screen, whether it is left open or closed at the end of the manipulation (Doré, 1986). Even though it is obviously empty, the container becomes the target of search behavior. This is a first indication that Stage 5 animals do not represent the hidden object. Because the container is the only element associated with the object at the time of the object's disappearance (the container but not the object itself was associated with the target screen), the container guides search behavior. Cats can overcome this tendency only if they have acquired experience with the potential hiding locations through visible displacement problems. Still, the container exerts a strong influence on search behavior as revealed by the concentration of search attempts made at the screen nearest the container (Doré, 1986, 1990).

Exactly the same invisible displacement procedure was used by Goulet et al. (1994), but with a transparent container. Although it may appear as a contradiction in terms, this procedure indeed involves an invisible displace-ment. The object is moved behind the transparent container from its starting position to the target screen but it is transferred from the container to the target screen while both the object and the container are concealed by the screen. In this procedure, cats make as many search attempts at the screen nearest the transparent container as at the target screen. Therefore, their search behavior is clearly guided by two elements of the environment. In fact, the object was seen moving behind the container and was then seen disappearing, through the container, behind the target screen. This distri-bution of search attempts toward both the container and the target screen is a second indication that Stage 5 animals recognize elements associated with the object instead of recalling the hidden object.

The basic requirements of the new procedure developed by Goulet et al. (1994) are similar to the ones in the invisible displacements with a transpar-ent container but no container is used (Fig. 4.2). The object is first visibly moved behind a screen and is invisibly removed from there; a few seconds later, the front panel of another screen is briefly lifted to show the object at this new location; then, the front panel is closed and the object disap-pears. A cue that the object was moved from the first to the second screen was given by simulating the movement, the noise, or both that cats had learned to associate with a visible displacement of the object. Cats saw the object disappear at two successive locations but did not see the transfer of

FIG. 4.2. Schematic representation of Goulet et al.'s (1994) new procedure of invisible displacement. (1) The object is visibly moved toward the first screen. (2) The object is hidden behind the first screen. (3) The object is invisibly removed from the first screen and the movement toward the second (or target) screen is simulated. (4) The front panel of the target screen is lifted and the object is shown to the subject at this second location. (5) The front panel of the target screen is closed and the object disappears. In another variant of the procedure, the displacement and disappearance at the first screen are identical to those occurring at the target screen. The displacement toward the first screen is simulated, the front panel of the first screen is lifted, the object is shown to the subject, and the front panel of the first screen is closed. The results with this variant are identical to the ones observed with the manipulation illustrated in this figure.

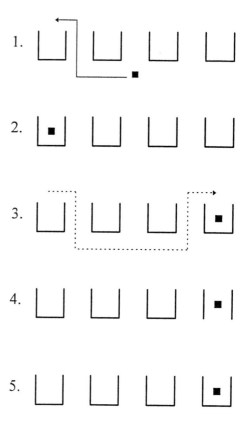

the object from one location to the other. As in the transparent analog of invisible displacements, subjects searched for the object equally often at the two successive locations.

In another experiment using the same procedure, Goulet et al. (1994) attempted to reduce the influence of the first hiding screen on search behavior. Immediately after the object's disappearance at this location, the object was invisibly removed from there and the front panel of the screen was briefly lifted to show that this location was now empty. Then, the displacement of the object toward another screen was simulated, the front panel of this second screen was lifted, and the object was shown to the subject before lowering the front panel. Although it was clear that the object was not to be found behind the first hiding location, cats' search attempts were still equally distributed between the two successive locations. Showing the first screen empty did not change subjects' search behavior and again, this result strongly suggests that Stage 5 animals do not represent the object behind its hiding screen.

THE CONTENT OF REPRESENTATION

The data reported in the preceding section argue against the idea that Stage 5 organisms recall the invisible object. Instead, they recognize the object only once they find it. They also recognize cues associated with the object at the time of its disappearance and these cues guide their search behavior. In Piaget's theoretical framework, it is not clear whether subjects recognize the hiding screen itself or its spatial location. In *The Construction of Reality in the Child* (1937/1967), he referred indifferently to both. Studies on cats and dogs show that these animals do not use the visual features of the screens and solve the problem by encoding spatial information.

Fiset and Doré (1990) compared the performance of four groups of cats in single visible displacement tests. The control group was presented with identical screens as in standard tests of object permanence. The three other groups were presented with visual cues that could help in encoding and recognizing the target screen. In one group, each screen could be discriminated from the others by its intrinsic features, that is, visual patterns displayed on its front panel. In another group, the screens were identical as in the control group but they could be discriminated on the basis of local cues. The area surrounding each screen was delimited by a specific visual pattern. In still another group, both intrinsic features and local cues were available. Because the performances of the four groups did not significantly differ, it can be concluded that cats did not use those visual features to identify the target screen and that they relied on spatial information.

In standard tests of object permanence, the position of a screen can be encoded either egocentrically or allocentrically. Egocentric encoding is possible because the relationship between the subject's position and the screens remains the same from the beginning of a trial to the subject's response. Using the intrinsic features of the screens or local cues would be more relevant in situations where searching can be successful only if the position of the target screen is encoded allocentrically. A detour task is one of these situations because the relationship between the subject's position and the screens is modified between encoding and searching.

Fiset and Doré (1992) combined an object permanence task with a detour task. In one condition, the screens were identical whereas in the other condition, they differed by their sizes (height and width) and by the visual patterns presented on their front panels. At the beginning of a trial, cats were confined in a holding box and saw in front of them an object move and disappear behind a screen. When released, one of the doors on each side of the holding box was opened and subjects had to walk through an opaque tunnel parallel to the row of screens. As they arrived at the end of the tunnel 2 or 3 seconds later, cats were facing the screens from a new angle. Again in this situation, the performances in the two conditions did not differ significantly and it seems that the problem was solved by encoding spatial cues rather than the intrinsic features of the screens.

One could argue that because the problem presented in the preceding tasks was in the cognitive capacities of Stage 5 animals, the absence of a significant difference between groups or conditions can be explained by a ceiling effect. In other words, cats would already be so successful with identical screens that the use of intrinsic features or local cues would not improve their performance significantly. According to this interpretation, encoding of these discriminative stimuli would be better assessed in problems that are beyond Stage 5 cognitive capacity. In fact, cats' behavior in invisible displacement problems seems to support this hypothesis. As already mentioned, they have a strong tendency to search for the object at or near the container, which is visually different from the screens. The following experiments have addressed this specific issue.

In one of Doré's (1990) experiments, cats were presented with five screens. The two screens at each end of the array as well as the center screen were white and the other two screens were black. Two groups of subjects were first trained in visible displacement tests. For one group, the object was always hidden under the white screens at each end of the array (and never under the center screen) whereas for the other group, it was hidden under the black screens. Following this training, both were submitted to the same invisible displacement task in which the object was first moved in a container and then behind one of the two white screens at each end of the array. Whether the subjects had been previously trained with spatially and visually relevant (white) or irrelevant (black) screens, they failed the invisible displacement test and the performances of the two groups did not differ. Consequently, training cats to recognize the visual features of the future hiding screens did not make them succeed. Cats' search behavior was still strongly influenced by the container. The container was the only potential hiding screen that moved and this attribute could be the one that was discriminated by the subjects and that determined their search behavior. The next experiments investigated this possibility and showed that cats and dogs recognize a spatial location rather than an attribute of a screen.

These experiments (Doré et al., 1996) used a testing procedure that was based on a methodology initially developed by Sophian (1985) with human infants. In this procedure, called invisible transposition problems, an object is visibly moved and hidden behind a screen and then this screen is visibly moved to a new position. Like in Piagetian invisible tests of object permanence, the object is invisibly moved from one location to another. On the other hand, the problem is simpler because the object always remains behind the screen where it disappeared and this screen always remains in subjects' full view.

One group of subjects was tested with identical screens whereas another group was tested with screens that differed by their sizes and the visual features displayed on their front panels. There were four different types of invisible transposition. In two types of transposition, the initial position of the target screen was left empty after the manipulation. In the other two types, the initial position of the target screen was filled by an empty screen. Cats and dogs were highly successful in the former condition but had serious difficulties when an empty screen replaced the target screen. This result was the same without regard to the presence or absence of visual cues on the screens.

Moreover, cats' and dogs' search behavior was not determined by the mobility of the screens. In one type of control trials, the target screen never moved but an empty screen was switched to another position after the object's disappearance. Subjects were as successful in these control trials as in another type of control trials where none of the screens moved. Taken together, these results confirmed that search behavior of Stage 5 organisms is not determined by any visual features of the screens themselves or by some other characteristics like mobility. Instead, they recognize a spatial location.

This conclusion was further reinforced by a series of experiments conducted by Fiset and Doré (1996). These experiments revealed that cats can efficiently use egocentric or allocentric spatial encoding depending on the task demands. They also examined four sources of spatial information that subjects could encode in a detour task where they had to rely on an allocentric strategy. The location of the target screen could be identified by referring to a specific landmark in the environment. In this procedure, the position of the experimenter placed behind the screen array was the only identifiable landmark in an otherwise homogeneous room. Another source of spatial information, which is at the core of dead reckoning or path integration (for a review, see Gallistel, 1990), is inertial information. The animal could find the hiding location by computing the direction changes that it had to make during the detour and by adjusting its trajectory accordingly. The other two sources are the relative and the absolute positions of the target screen. The relative position is defined as the position of the target screen in the array of screens. The absolute position is the coordinates of the target screen in the general frame of reference provided by the room. Results indicated that cats encode this last source of information in searching for a hidden object in single visible displacements.

REPRESENTATIONAL LIMITATIONS

One important issue that was addressed by Piaget (1937/1967) concerns the cause of errors made by Stage 5 human infants when confronted with invisible displacement problems. As already mentioned, instead of retrieving the object behind the target screen, infants at this stage persevere in searching at the container. This error can be interpreted in two ways. The interpretation sustained by Piaget is that it results from a representational limitation. Because the infant is unable to represent or recall the hidden object and to infer its invisible transfer from the container to the target screen, his/her search behavior is guided by the association of the object with the last location where it was seen disappearing. The other interpretation, which was discarded by Piaget, is that the Stage 5 error results from a limitation in memory storage or retrieval. An invisible displacement comprises a number of successive events and the tendency to search at the container would reflect a difficulty in storing or retrieving the sequence of events. According to Piaget, although it seems that memory fails to order properly the events in time, the problem has more to do with the nature of one of these events (the invisible transfer of the object) than with their temporal sequence. Research on cats supports Piaget's viewpoint.

In invisible displacement problems, there are two major successive events: the disappearance behind the container followed shortly by the disappearance behind the target screen. However, in a double visible displacement, there are also two successive events: the disappearance behind the first screen and the disappearance behind the target screen. In this last task, subjects search for the object at its final hiding location. One could argue that they easily solve this problem by remembering only the most recent event. Goulet et al. (1994) analyzed search behavior in double visible as well as in invisible displacements. In invisible displacements, most search attempts were made near the container, but the remaining search attempts were biased toward the target screen. In double visible displacements, almost all search attempts were made at the target screen and the majority of errors were biased toward the first hiding location. Therefore, in both cases, cats clearly remembered the two successive hiding locations of the object. It would be very unlikely that cats would be able to remember the temporal sequence of events in double visible but not in invisible displacement problems.

In Goulet et al.'s (1994) new procedure (Fig. 4.2), the invisible displacement task is highly similar to a double visible displacement. Subjects see the object disappear at two locations and the only difference with double visible displacements is that cats cannot see the object being moved from one location to the other. In this new procedure, events are as easy to order in time as they are in double visible displacements. Consequently, according to the memory storage or retrieval hypothesis, cats should have no problem in remembering which event happened last and in finding the object behind the target screen. Results confirmed that in double visible displacements, cats were highly successful and most of their search attempts were made at the final location. In invisible displacements, they did not behave as predicted by the memory hypothesis. Their search attempts were equally distributed between the initial and the final locations. These results support Piaget's (1937/1967) interpretation that Stage 5 behavior in Stage 6 tasks reflects a representational rather than a storage or retrieval limitation. Indeed, memory seems to fail only when an invisible displacement of the object is involved.

CONCLUSION

In the Piagetian theory, object permanence is not the sole concept on which achievement of Stage 6 and symbolic representation are assessed. Causality, space, time, and means-end coordination are other indications of cognitive functioning. Studies of these notions in apes (Antinucci, 1989; Chevalier-Skolnikoff, 1989; Parker & Gibson, 1990) do not allow definite conclusions, but their results are generally consistent with behavior exhibited in object permanence tests. Piagetian comparative research concurs with studies of language learning (see Savage-Rumbaugh, this volume) to show that apes have evolved the capacity to refer to absent objects by using internal substitutes and symbolic representation.

Monkeys and some carnivore mammals display Stage 5 of object permanence. Although this implies that their representation is primitive rather than symbolic (Piaget, 1936/1974), their reactions to disappearing objects belong to the third kind of reactions defined by Etienne (1973, 1984). Search behavior in these organisms is not based on special behavioral devices or on any form of elementary learning. Even though they associate the disappearing object with an external substitute, these associations do not result from repeated exposures to the same events but from only one presentation. In Stage 5 object permanence tests, the hiding location varies from trial to trial and sometimes in a trial as in successive displacements. Therefore, the associations have to be constantly updated and reflect a fair degree of mental constructional skills.

The analysis presented in this chapter has focused mainly on cats and dogs because object permanence has not been investigated as thoroughly in other mammals and primates. As it stands, we have to assume that cats and dogs are representative of Stage 5 organisms. Our analysis confirmed Piaget's assumption that the problem of these organisms in Stage 6 tasks is of a representational rather than mnemonic nature. Because they cannot use internal substitutes for absent objects, they cannot recall the hidden object and instead recognize an environmental cue that was associated with it at the time of its disappearance. That such a statement also applies to Stage 5 human infants may appear to some a distant possibility. It is extremely difficult for human adults to imagine what it is like to function without recall because we constantly evoke memories with no apparent priming cues in the environment. Functioning without explicit or conscious recognition and recall is difficult to imagine as well. Yet, the literature in clinical neuropsychology has clearly shown that amnesic patients can improve from day to day in a variety of procedural or nondeclarative tasks and they have no explicit recollection of even being submitted to these tasks (Squire & Knowlton, 1995).

From our analysis, we also concluded that Stage 5 organisms encode the absolute position of the external substitute of the object rather than its intrinsic features or some other properties like mobility. In object permanence tasks, cats and dogs may notice the intrinsic features of the screens but they do not rely on them to search for the object. We can assume that in the natural environment, intrinsic features or local cues are not as reliable as a position in a spatial frame of reference. In many cases, the animal will visit a location infrequently, leaving enough time for radical changes in intrinsic features or local cues to occur and to make them unrecognizable. By contrast, the spatial frame of reference comprises many different elements that are more static and less likely to change altogether. Encoding of the absolute position in object permanence problems does not imply that Stage 5 organisms would not be able in other contexts to encode and use nonspatial information if it was crucial for adapted behavior.

In human infant development, object permanence is not an all-or-none capacity that appears at a given stage. It is rather a gradual construction based on preliminary acquisitions and interactions with the environment. Similarly, among the species that have evolved object permanence, different levels can be observed. Gibson (1990) identified a correlation between mental constructional skills and the relative size of the brain. She also suggested that species-typical, minimally constructed behaviors channel the ontogenetic development in specific directions. Similarly, we must assume that some behaviors have been submitted to special selective pressures that have channeled evolution toward different levels of object permanence.

Gibson (1990) suggested that cooperative hunting is a determining factor in the evolution of sophisticated constructional skills. Canids that are in nature cooperative hunters exhibit, in fact, relatively high constructional skills. But cats reach the same level of object permanence as dogs even though they and most felids are solitary hunters. Therefore, it seems that cooperation in the sole domain of feeding is not sufficient to evolve the representational capacity displayed by apes. Such an evolution requires either cooperation in a variety of social activities or special challenges in the individual realm.

REFERENCES

Antinucci, F. (1989). *Cognitive structure and development in nonhuman primates*. Hillsdale, NJ: Lawrence Erlbaum Associates.

Baillargeon, R. (1995). Physical reasoning in infancy. In M. S. Gazzaniga (Ed.), *The cognitive neurosciences* (pp. 181–204). Cambridge, MA: MIT Press.

Barlow, G. W. (1968). Ethological units of behavior. In D. Ingle (Ed.), *The central nervous system and fish behavior* (pp. 217–232). Chicago: Chicago University Press.

Bjork, E. L., & Cummings, E. M. (1984). Infant search errors: Stage concept development or stage memory development. *Memory & Cognition, 12*, 1–19.

Bremner, J. G. (1978). Spatial errors made by infants: Inadequate spatial cues or evidence of egocentrism. *British Journal of Psychology, 69*, 77–84.

Butterworth, G. (1977). Object disappearance error in Piaget's stage IV task. *Journal of Experimental Child Psychology, 23*, 391–401.

Case, R. (1985). *Intellectual development. Birth to adulthood*. New York: Academic Press.

Chevalier-Skolnikoff, S. (1989). Spontaneous tool use and sensorimotor intelligence in *Cebus* compared to other monkeys and apes. *Behavioral and Brain Sciences, 12*, 561–627.

Cornell, E. H. (1978). Learning to find things: A reinterpretation of object permanence studies. In L. S. Siegel & C. J. Brainerd (Eds.), *Alternatives to Piaget: Critical essays on the theory* (pp. 1–10). New York: Academic Press.

De Blois, S. T., & Novak, M. A. (1995). Object permanence in rhesus monkeys (*Macaca mulatta*). *Journal of Comparative Psychology, 108*, 318–327.

Doré, F. Y. (1986). Object permanence in adult cats (*Felis catus*). *Journal of Comparative Psychology, 100*, 340–347.

Doré, F. Y. (1990). Search behavior of cats (*Felis catus*) in an Invisible Displacement Test: Cognition and experience. *Canadian Journal of Psychology, 44*, 359–370.

Doré, F. Y., & Dumas, C. (1987). Psychology of animal cognition: Piagetian studies. *Psychological Bulletin, 102*, 219–233.

Doré, F. Y., Fiset, S., Goulet, S., Dumas, M. C., & Gagnon, S. (1996). Search behavior in cats and dogs: Interspecific differences in spatial cognition. *Animal Learning & Behavior, 24*, 142–149.

Doré, F. Y., Goulet, S., & Herman, L. M. (1991, September). *Permanence de l'objet chez deux dauphins (Tursiops truncatus)* (Object permanence in two dolphins). Paper presented at the XXIIIème Journées d'étude de l'Association de Psychologie Scientifique de Langue Française, Rome.

Dumas, C. (1992). Object permanence in cats (*Felis catus*): An ecological approach to the study of invisible displacements. *Journal of Comparative Psychology, 106*, 404–410.

Dumas, C., & Brunet, C. (1994). Permanence de l'objet chez le singe capucin (*Cebus apella*): Etude des déplacements invisibles (Object permanence in capuchins monkeys (*Cebus apella*): A study of invisible displacements). *Canadian Journal of Psychology, 48*, 341–357.

Dumas, C., & Doré, F. Y. (1989). Cognitive development in kittens (*Felis catus*): A cross-sectional study of object permanence. *Journal of Comparative Psychology, 103*, 191–200.

Dumas, C., & Doré, F. Y. (1991). Cognitive development in kittens (*Felis catus*): An observational study of object permanence and sensorimotor intelligence. *Journal of Comparative Psychology, 105*, 357–365.

Etienne, A. S. (1973). Developmental stages and cognitive structures as determinants of what is learned. In R. A. Hinde & J. Stevenson-Hinde (Eds.), *Constraints on learning: Limitations and predispositions* (pp. 317–395). New York: Academic Press.

Etienne, A. S. (1984). The meaning of object concept at different zoological levels. *Human Development, 27*, 309–320.

Fiset, S., & Doré, F. Y. (1990, October). *Encodage égocentrique chez le chat domestique (Felis catus) (Egocentric spatial encoding in cats)*. Paper presented at the meeting of the Société Québécoise pour la Recherche en Psychologie, Montréal, Canada.

Fiset, S., & Doré, F. Y. (1992, June). *Cats' spatial encoding in a detour task*. Paper presented at the meeting of the Canadian Society for Brain, Behavior and Cognitive Sciences, Québec, Canada.

Fiset, S., & Doré, F. Y. (1996). Spatial encoding in domestic cats (*Felis catus*). *Journal of Experimental Psychology: Animal Behavior Processes, 22*, 420–437.

Gagnon, S., & Doré, F. Y. (1992). Search behavior in various breeds of adult dogs (*Canis familiaris*): Object permanence and olfactory cues. *Journal of Comparative Psychology, 106,* 58–68.

Gagnon, S., & Doré, F. Y. (1993). Search behavior of dogs (*Canis familiaris*) in invisible displacement problems. *Animal Learning & Behavior, 21,* 246–254.

Gagnon, S., & Doré, F. Y. (1994). A cross-sectional analysis of object permanence development in dogs (*Canis familiaris*). *Journal of Comparative Psychology, 108,* 220–232.

Gallistel, C. R. (1990). *The organization of learning.* Cambridge, MA: MIT Press.

Gibson, K. R. (1990). New perspectives on instincts and intelligence: Brain size and the emergence of hierarchical mental constructional skills. In S. T. Parker & K. R. Gibson (Eds.), *"Language" and intelligence in monkeys and apes* (pp. 97–128). Cambridge, England: Cambridge University Press.

Goulet, S., Doré, F. Y., & Rousseau, R. (1994). Object permanence and working memory in cats. *Journal of Experimental Psychology: Animal Behavior Processes, 20,* 347–365.

Gruber, H. E., Girgus, J. S., & Banuazizi, A. (1971). The development of object permanence in the cat. *Developmental Psychology, 4,* 9–15.

Harris, P. L. (1983). Infant cognition. In P. H. Mussen (Ed.), M. M. Haith, & J. J. Campos (Vol. Eds.), *Handbook of child psychology, 4th ed. Vol. 2: Infancy and developmental psychobiology* (pp. 689–792). New York: Wiley.

Jerison, H. J. (1973). *Evolution of the brain and intelligence.* New York: Academic Press.

Jerison, H. J. (1985). Animal intelligence as encephalization. *Philosophical Transactions of the Royal Society of London, B308,* 21–35.

Langer, J. (1986). *The origins of logic: One to two years.* New York: Academic Press.

Mathieu, M., & Bergeron, G. (1981). Piagetian assessment of cognitive development in chimpanzees (*Pan troglodytes*). In A. B. Chiarelli & R. S. Corruccini (Eds.), *Primate behavior and sociobiology* (pp. 142–147). Berlin: Springer-Verlag.

Mathieu, M., Bouchard, M. A., Granger, L., & Herscovitch, J. (1976). Piagetian object-permanence in *Cebus capucinus, Lagothrica flavicauda* and *Pan troglodytes. Animal Behaviour, 24,* 585–588.

Natale, F., Antinucci, F., Spinozzi, G., & Poti', P. (1986). Stage 6 object permanence in nonhuman primate cognition: A comparison between gorilla (*Gorilla gorilla gorilla*) and Japanese macaque (*Macaca fuscata*). *Journal of Comparative Psychology, 100,* 335–339.

Parker, S. T. (1977). Piaget's sensorimotor series in an infant macaque: A model for comparing unstereotyped behavior and intelligence in human and nonhuman primates. In S. Chevalier-Skolnikoff & F. E. Poirier (Eds.), *Primate bio-social development: Biological, social, and ecological determinants* (pp. 43–112). New York: Garland.

Parker, S. T., & Gibson, K. R. (1990). *"Language" and intelligence in monkeys and apes. Comparative developmental perspectives.* Cambridge, MA: Cambridge University Press.

Pasnak, R., Kurkjian, M., & Triana, E. (1988). Assessment of Stage 6 object permanence. *Bulletin of the Psychonomic Society, 26,* 368–370.

Pepperberg, I. M., & Funk, M. S. (1990). Object permanence in four species of psittacine birds: An African grey parrot (*Psittacus erithacus*), an Illiger mini macaw (*Ara maracana*), a parakeet (*Melopsittacus undulatus*), and a cockatiel (*Nymphicus hollandicus*). *Animal Learning & Behavior, 18,* 97–108.

Pepperberg, I. M., & Kozak, F. A. (1986). Object permanence in the African grey parrot (*Psittacus erithacus*). *Animal Learning & Behavior, 14,* 322–330.

Piaget, J. (1936/1974). *La naissance de l'intelligence* (The origins of intelligence). Neuchâtel, Switzerland: Delachaux et Niestlé.

Piaget, J. (1937/1967). *La construction du réel* (The construction of reality in the child). Neuchâtel, Switzerland: Delachaux et Niestlé.

Piaget, J. (1967/1971). *Biologie et connaissance* (Biology and knowledge). Paris: Gallimard.

Redshaw, M. (1978). Cognitive development in human and gorilla infants. *Journal of Human Evolution, 7,* 133–141.

Rumelhart, D., & McClelland, J. (1986). *Parallel distributed processing. Volume 1. Foundations*. Cambridge, MA: MIT Press

Sophian, C. (1985). Understanding the movements of objects: Early developments in spatial cognition. *British Journal of Developmental Psychology, 3*, 321–333.

Spelke, E. S., Vishton, P., & von Hofsten, C. (1995). Object perception, object-directed action, and physical knowledge in infancy. In M. S. Gazzaniga (Ed.), *The cognitive neurosciences* (pp. 165–180). Cambridge, MA: MIT Press.

Squire, L. R., & Knowlton, B. J. (1995). Memory, hippocampus, and brain systems. In M. S. Gazzaniga (Ed.), *The cognitive neurosciences* (pp. 825–838). Cambridge, MA: MIT Press.

Triana, E., & Pasnak, R. (1981). Object permanence in cats and dogs. *Animal Learning & Behavior, 9*, 135–139.

Wellman, H. M., Cross, D., & Bartsch, K. (1986). Infant search and object permanence: A meta-analysis of the A-not-B error. *Monographs of the Society of Research in Child Development, 51* (Serial No. 214).

Wood, S., Moriarty, K. M., Gardner, B. T., & Gardner, R. A. (1980). Object permanence in child and chimpanzee. *Animal Learning & Behavior, 8*, 3–9.

5

EVOLUTIONARY AND DEVELOPMENTAL ORIGINS OF THE MINDREADING SYSTEM

Andrew Whiten
University of St. Andrews

An immense flowering of research in the last decade has explored what we can now see, in retrospect, to have been a largely uncharted continent in the child's mind—a territory concerned with an appreciation of the properties of the mind itself, both in oneself and others. This appreciation has been referred to in different ways—as a theory of mind, a mindreading system, mentalism, natural psychology, or mental simulation, to name a few (Whiten, 1994). Interest in the child's developing understanding of mental phenomena has a long history, perhaps most famously including Piaget and Inhelder's (1948/1956) three mountains experiments, in which the developing child's ability to construct the visual perspective of others was first investigated. But in the last decade, theory of mind has become such a growth area in developmental psychology that it has sometimes seemed to threaten to swamp all the rest, apparently reflecting a rapid and overdue realization about just how much we have still to learn about this subject. What a human being comes to understand about the mind may ultimately be limited largely by the nature of the to-be-understood mind itself, and as professional psychologists as well as everyday folk psychologists, we have some inkling of what a gigantic project the young mindreader is therefore embarked on (although only an inkling—by contrast with what has been learned about the child's mindreading in recent years, the full nature of the adult mindreading system has remained largely the province of philosophers of mind (e.g. Dennett, 1987; Gordon, 1986), and empirically understudied (see d'Andrade, 1987; Heelas & Lock, 1981).

As with the case of language acquisition, commentators have surmised that the facility with which the young child comes to discriminate states of mind in others, and rapidly proceeds to become a sophisticated reader and manipulator of mind, must depend on a high degree of innate preparedness (Fodor, 1992; Leslie, 1991). This means that we have at least two genesis stories to trace—a developmental or ontogenetic one in the lifetime of the individual, and a phylogenetic one spanning evolutionary timescales of millions of years. As Piaget and Baldwin appreciated long ago, these developmental and evolutionary accounts must ultimately be interwoven (Baldwin, 1902; Piaget, 1967, 1974, 1976). Evolution has molded development, although the evolutionary legacy is not simply read out at some arbitrary early point in development—instead, there is an unfolding interaction between genetic and other information from the evolutionary past, the current cognitive state of the organism and information from the environment. But what happens in ontogenetic development has in turn molded evolution: Evolutionary change is itself shaped by repeated passes through the complex, interactive, developmental cycle. Thus, in order to understand our development, we need to understand what has happened in evolution, and conversely our evolution is the story of change through an almost unimaginably long string of progressively modified ontogenetic cycles.

In theory of mind research, the bulk of the effort to date has been developmental rather than evolutionary. In the late 1980s and early 1990s, the core of this work was concerned with what came to be described as a watershed in the development of a theory of mind, when the child comes to recognize that others may hold beliefs about the world which can be false and different from their own. In what has become a standard test for the attribution of false beliefs, the child subject watches a scenario in which Sally hides a prized possession in one container, leaves, and then returns to search for it only when Anne has moved it to a different container in Sally's absence. (Baron-Cohen, Leslie, & Frith, 1985; Wimmer & Perner, 1983). Many studies replicated the finding that 4-year-olds would usually be able to correctly predict that Sally will first search in the container where she (falsely) believes the possession to be, whereas 3-year-olds would typically fail to do so, suggesting instead that Sally will look in the container where the child now knows the possession to be. Such egocentrism in the younger subjects was one of the principal themes for which Piaget's (e.g., Piaget & Inhelder, 1948/1956) developmental psychology became famous, but the new research showed that in the Sally-Anne test, children go beyond such egocentrism in an important respect, earlier than the 6 to 7 years indicated by Piaget. Perner (1991) argued that the importance of the 4-year watershed is that in attributing false beliefs, children are grasping the important principle that the mind represents (and so can misrepresent) the world. They are thus capable of second-order representation or metarepresentation (they can mentally represent the mental representations of others). The watershed sees the emergence of a suite of abilties including deliberate deception (the creation of false beliefs) and discrimination between appearance and reality.

As the new theory of mind research has matured, a more truly developmental approach has emerged, which attempts to trace the origins of the remarkable abilities identified in the 4-year watershed. This work has focused on the younger child's ability to discriminate other states of mind, including desire, attention, and pretense. Some of this research is discussed in this chapter, although the sheer bulk of work in this area means I must be selective. Readers wishing to pursue more comprehensive treatment of our current state of knowledge, including the principal outstanding controversies, are advised to first consult the collections of Baron-Cohen, Tager-Flusberg, and Cohen (1993), Lewis and Mitchell (1994), Davies and Stone (1995a, 1995b) and Carruthers and Smith (1996).

The study of theory of mind in developmental psychology has thus been enormously productive. However, the beginnings of this modern era of theory-of-mind research are typically traced back to a study not in developmental, but in comparative psychology: Premack and Woodruff's (1978) classic "Does the chimpanzee have a theory of mind?" Recent attempts to appraise the progress of theory-of-mind research have consistently incorporated a complement of papers covering the evolutionary perspective, typically utilising comparative primate research for empirical input (Baron-Cohen et al., 1993; Carruthers & Smith, 1996; Lewis & Mitchell, 1994; Povinelli & Eddy, 1996a; Tooby & Cosmides, 1995; see also Whiten, 1991a). In this chapter, I aim to describe recent developments in these evolutionary perspectives, with particular emphasis on those that should be of most interest and relevance to related progress in developmental psychology.

THE BEGINNINGS OF AN EVOLUTIONARY APPROACH TO MINDREADING

Why should an ability to mentalize—to discriminate states of mind—ever have evolved? To many developmental psychologists, the functional significance of mentalism has perhaps seemed self-evident, at least in general terms: Because a mentalist folk psychology seems so natural to us humans, it must simply be the best way to make sense of and predict the actions of others. Austistic individuals typically are deficient or drastically delayed in both theory of mind—they will often fail the Sally-Anne test for false belief attribution at mental ages well beyond 4 years—as well as in social competencies such as communication and cooperation (Baron-Cohen, Leslie, & Frith, 1985, 1986; Frith, 1989). This has been interpreted as supporting the basic idea that the function of mentalism is to make sense of human action in some quite general way, and that indeed it is pretty much the only way for our species effectively to acheive this. Lacking a theory of mind, the world of the autist has been portrayed as lacking meaning, such that it may even be frightening (Happe, 1994). Baron-Cohen (1995) quoted Alison Gopnik's vision of mindblindness:

> Around me bags of skin are draped over chairs, and stuffed into pieces of cloth, they shift and protrude in unexpected ways.... Two dark spots near the top of them swivel restlessly back and forth. A hole beneath the spots fills with food and from it comes a stream of noises. Imagine that the noisy skin-bags suddenly moved towards you, and their noises grew loud, and you had no idea why, no way of explaining them or predicting what they would do next. (p. 5)

Baron-Cohen commented that, "Gopnik hints at how terrifying if would be to be mindblind. I think she must be right—I certainly would not want to be without the ability to read behavior in terms of mental states" (p. 5).

Yet a common working assumption in the child development literature is that most, or perhaps all, nonhuman animals share this predicament—they too lack a theory of mind. They are seen as making distinctions between others' behaviors, rather than between their states of mind. But this suggests something of a paradox in relation to the hypothesis noted, that it is lack of a theory of mind that radically disables the social functioning of children with autism. Monkeys and apes, by contrast, repeatedly and succesfully interpret the various different signals and social actions of their companions (Cheney & Seyfarth, 1990); they form alliances, sexual relationships and friendships with others (Harcourt & de Waal, 1992; Smuts, 1985); and they socially manipulate and deceive others (Whiten & Byrne, 1988a): In short, they are far from socially autistic—to the contrary, they are socially adept (Byrne & Whiten, 1988). If they are able to manage all this with no theory of mind, why should lack of a theory of mind be so crippling for autists, as suggested in the previous citations?

One answer we might suggest is that the communicative repertoire of most species is quite limited, such that the alternative meanings are innately specified in the species, or alternatively constitute an easily learned, limited set: By contrast, humans can generate an infinite variety of meanings (particularly through language) that are difficult to read without mentalistic assumptions, such as what the individual is trying to say.

However, in the late 1970s and 1980s, several ethologists pointed out that animal communication is not really so simple. Dawkins and Krebs (1978) for example, took issue with the then-prevailing assumption that animal communication signals are molded by natural selection to transmit good information about the internal state of a signaler—an individual's motivation to attack, for example. Such an assumption implies that the behavior will be shaped to benefit others, whereas in fact behavior is selected when it preferentially favors the reproductive output of the individual actually performing the behavior. Accordingly, behavior would be more likely selected to manipulate others to the self's advantage, including the sending of signals that mislead others about the self's true intent: for example, signaling nonchalance or even friendliness when truly the motivation is to mount a (surpise) attack. But this then creates a selection pressure for other animals to see through the misleading acts to the true state of mind of the actor: in short, to mindread (Krebs & Dawkins, 1984). This thus suggests that straightforward behavior-reading is too simplistic an assumption in animal behavior generally, and it highlights one particular evolutionary context—deception—in which animals might be expected to begin to discriminate the true state of mind (intent) of a protagonist from thier surface behavior.

At about the same time, Humphrey (1981, 1986) drew attention to a particular group of animals in which what he called natural psychology might be expected to become a profitable way of interpreting the actions of others. In 1976, Humphrey had been instrumental in developing the Social Intelligence Hypothesis, that intellect has evolved in human and nonhuman primates not so much to solve the kinds of physical, object-related problems beloved of the laboratory-animal psychologist, but rather to handle unusual levels of complexity that characterize primate societies (see also Jolly, 1966; Whiten & Byrne, 1988a). It has since become well established that in the primates we do indeed find cognitively challenging social contexts, aptly described as political because of fluid coalitions and alliances that often fluctuate rapidly (Byrne & Whiten, 1988; Whiten & Byrne, 1997). For, example, situations have been described in which the balance of power among top-ranking male chimpanzees is held by a third individual acting as kingmaker, in both captive and wild chimpanzees (de Waal, 1982; Nishida, 1983). Not only do such individuals shift their allegiance, exploiting their influence over the ranks of their superiors to gain benefits for themselves such as being permitted some mating opportunities, but the high rankers seek to influence them in turn, through tactics ranging from friendly gestures like grooming to the breakup of liaisons with potential enemies. This allegiance fickleness in political primates (Nishida, 1983) and the associated aspects of social maneuvering might be expected to put a premium on tracking the true state of mind of one's often shifty companions.

These speculations of Krebs and Dawkins and Humphrey set the stage for a different approach to Premack and Woodruff's (1978) attempt to experimentally test for primate theory of mind, which had been followed by a 10-year fallow period in primate theory of mind research. The new emphasis was on the social behavior of wild primates—the context suggested as a likely hotbed for the evolutionary roots of mindreading. Following our own

observations of deceptive behavior among wild baboons, Richard Byrne and
I collated further records of deception in primates made by different observers to search for common functional patterns (Whiten & Byrne, 1988a).
Our rationale was that deception, by its nature, was likely to be subtle and
infrequent: for it to become accessible to scientific scrutiny, pooling of data
would likely be required. As we collated the records, we realized that a
significant subset of them included the kinds of behavior we would expect
to see if elementary forms of mindreading were at work. In other words, if
we were to ask, "what would their behavior look like if primates are the
kinds of mindreaders Humphrey and others proposed?" then here, in natural
animal societies, we seemed to be seeing candidate actions, as well as the
kinds of functional contexts in which mindreading might be selected for in
the first place.

For example, one major functional category involved primates concealing
something from others. In some cases, this involved hiding the whole body.
In other cases, it involved just one offending body part, such as the hands
surreptitiously grooming another individual, or the covering of an erect
penis that would otherwise betray sexual arousal to a rival male. A nice
example of concealment is de Waal's (1982) description of a male chimpanzee who:

> sitting with his back to his challenger, showed a (fear) grin on hearing hooting
> signs. He quickly used his fingers to push his lips back over his teeth again.
> The manipulation occurred three times before the grin ceased to appear. After
> that, the male turned around to bluff back at this rival. (record No. 205 in
> Byrne & Whiten, 1990)

The way in which such concealment is done suggested an ability to rather
sensitively compute just what another individual would be likely to see, and
act on (and thus implicitly to know of).

In other cases, apes clearly noticed half-hidden food items, but then
witheld their visual attention to these attractions until a rival had departed,
suggesting some appreciation of the attentional powers of the rival, including the rival's propensity to attend to the visual attention of the deceiver.
On other occasions, primates would manipulate others' attention by various
techniques of distraction, such as looking away intently into the distance
as if at a (nonexistent) predator (Whiten & Byrne, 1988c).

Some of the most striking episodes involved not only deception, but
counter-deception. Deception itself is of obvious interest with respect to the
question of mindreading, because intentional deception implies an appreciation of the possibility of creating false beliefs. However, recall that our
classification was based only on functional deception. That is to say, on the
behaviors having the useful consequence of misleading another, leaving

open the question of whether this was intentional or caused in some other way. In uncontrolled field conditions, even where an episode strikes the experienced observer as quite novel, it is typically impossible to rule out the explanation that the animal has learned to perform the act because, perhaps originally by accident, it had once had the beneficial effect of misleading another individual. Where both an initial deceptive act and a counterdeceptive retaliation appear novel, the likelihood of alternative explanations becomes less credible. Thus, for example, episodes in which an individual would react to an attempt at concealment by appearing not to attend only until the deceiver let down their guard, or in which an attempt at distraction was followed by retaliatory aggression, suggest just the kind of ability envisaged in Krebs and Dawkins' (1984) model of mindreading, in which the mindreader recognizes some distinction between the true intent of the would-be deceiver and the apparent intent indicated by the surface behavior (for full accounts of these episodes see Byrne & Whiten, 1991, Whiten & Byrne, 1988a).

Of course, such observations provide far from a firm demonstration of primate mindreading: By their nature, they are not able to do this. What they did do was to suggest what mindreading could look like and usefully achieve in the natural social lives of these animals. The catalogue also provided a valid jumping-off point for more systematic experimentation. And after the long fallow period in the decade following Premack and Woodruff's (1978) pioneering study, such experimentation began again in earnest as reported in the publications of Cheney and Seyfarth (1990, 1991) on macaque monkeys and Povinelli, Nelson, and Boysen (1990) on chimpanzees. The 1990s has seen this effort swell to a small but substantial literature that is beyond detailed description here. Accordingly, Table 5.1 summarizes the principal claims made to date. Reviews of these studies can be found in Whiten (1993, in press) and Povinelli (1996).

Consistent with the picture created by the deception studies, the subsequent experiments have provided some evidence in the case of chimpanzees for abilities to recognize the intentions of others, and to discriminate between states of ignorance versus knowledge. Experiments with monkeys, by contrast, have to date produced only negative results, even when an attempt was made to match procedures to those that produced positive results for chimpanzees (Povinelli, Parks, & Novak, 1992a). This is also consistent with the conclusions drawn from the deception studies insofar as evidence from the latter for monkeys was limited to simple visual perspective-taking—the ability to judge what others might be able to see—and the evidence for deeper mindreading based on counter-deception was limited to apes, and then mainly to chimpanzees (see Table 5.1).

This led to the working hypothesis that in our evolutionary history a cognitive progression may have occurred, beginning with a capacity for

TABLE 5.1
The Study of Mindreading in Animals: A Summary History
(Modified and extended after Whiten, 1996, 1997. Italicized
phrases summarize the claims made by the authors.)

Early speculations on the possibility of animal mindreading
* Thorndike 1911
* Lloyd–Morgan 1930

Theoretical analyses of the functional plausibility of animal mindreading
* Humphrey 1981
  - *skilled social gamesmanship would be enhanced by natural psychology*
* Krebs & Dawkins 1984
  - *communication should evolve to be manipulative and in turn select for mindreading*

Empirical studies
* Premack & Woodruff 1978
  - *chimpanzee attributes wants, intentions*
*Savage–Rumbaugh 1986
  - *chimpanzees recognize ignorance (need for information)*
* Whiten & Byrne 1988a, 1988b
  - *chimpanzees distinguish true and apparent intention; baboons discriminate what others can see*
* Premack 1988
  - *chimpanzees recognize seeing-knowing linkage, fail to attribute false belief*
* Cheney & Seyfarth 1990
  - *macaque monkeys do not discriminate knowledge versus ignorance*
* Byrne & Whiten 1990, 1991, 1992
  - *great apes distinguish true and apparent intention; baboons, macaques discriminate what others can see*
* Boesch 1991
  - *chimpanzee recognizes need for information*
* Gòmez 1991
  - *gorilla understands perception-action linkage*
* Povinelli et al. 1990, 1992
  - *chimpanzees and 4-year-olds discriminate knowledge and ignorance; macaques and 3-year-olds do not*
* Povinelli 1991
  - *chimpanzee discriminates intentional from accidental acts*
* Povinelli, Parks, & Novak 1992a, 1992b
  - *chimpanzees show empathy in role reversal; macaques do not*
* Gòmez & Teixidor 1992 (see also Gòmez 1996)
  - *orangutan recognizes ignorance*
* Povinelli, Rulf, & Bierschwale 1994
  - *young chimpanzees fail to discriminate knowledge (through seeing) and ignorance*
* Call & Tomasello 1994
  - *enculturated orangutan (but not nonenculturated one) signals when recipient's eyes open*
* Gòmez, Teixidor, & Laa (see Gòmez 1995, 1996)
  - *enculturated chimpanzees attract attention if others' gaze is diverted or occluded*
* Povinelli & Eddy 1996a
  - *young chimpanzees fail to discriminate all but the crudest aspects of seeing; fail to understand seeing as the mental state of attention*
* Povinelli & Eddy 1996b
  - *chimpanzee gaze-following shows understanding of visual occlusion by opaque barrier*
* Whiten 1997
  - *language-trained chimpanzees label objects a human questioner visually attends to*

visual perspective-taking in the common ancestor of monkeys and apes about 30 million years ago, to be followed in the more recent common ancestor we shared with chimpanzees about 6 million years ago by deeper mindreading of epistemic states and intentions. In this way the phylogeny of mindreading would be following a course similar to that observed in human ontogeny (Whiten, 1991b). This is not to suggest that ontogeny is merely recapitulating phylogeny (see McKinney, this volume), but rather, as envisaged by Piaget, certain cognitive constructions might follow natural, logical sequences of elaboration through both ontogenetic or evolutionary time. This, however, must be regarded as a tentative proposal, for several reasons. First, the deception database, as noted, is suggestive only and further research is required to clarify the extent of mindreading involved. Even the conclusion that monkeys can compute the visual perspective of others remains to be experimentally verified, for example. The most recent experimental studies have produced many more negative results even in the case of the chimpanzee (Povinelli & Eddy, 1996a; Povinelli, Rulf, & Bierschwale, 1994), and several reviews have concluded that the case for any real theory of mind remains weak, other than in humans (Heyes, 1993; Povinelli, 1996; Tomasello & Call, 1994, 1997; Whiten, 1993, 1997). Some of the most important reasons for this are discussed later in this chapter.

THE ROOTS OF MINDREADING IN EVOLUTION AND DEVELOPMENT

What does seem clear is that in some primates—particulary those more closely related to us—we see abilities that are somewhere close to the transition between what we may think of as mindreading on the one hand, and on the other hand rather sophisticated reading of behavioral and environmental configurations like gaze patterns and goal-directed movements, which are thought to become critical sources of input to the representational theory of mind that develops in humans (Baron-Cohen, 1995). In developmental psychology, there has been increasing interest paid to abilities that are on the edge of mindreading, or that are putative precursors to the sophisticated mindreading of the 5-year-old child who can attribute false beliefs (Lewis & Mitchell, 1994). In the following sections, I examine three of these in turn: pretense, reading visual attention, and imitation. I choose these because (1) theoretical analyses in both developmental and evolutionary psychology have focused on putative links between these abilities and mature theory of mind; and (2) two of the abilities (imitation and reading attention) have been the focus of a flurry of recent research generating important new results. The rationale for linking each ability with theory of mind is explained in the relevant following sections. Having discussed each in some detail, I then suggest what cognitive operations they all share, which may explain their co-occurrence in evolutionary and developmental pathways.

Pretense, Mindreading, and Second-Order Representation

One of the earliest attempts to trace the origins of theory of mind abilities was Leslie's (1987) analysis of metarepresentation. A theory of mind, by its very nature, involves second-order representations. The mind of the mindreader mentally represents the mental representations of the individual whose mind is read: thus, the mind of the mindreader holds nested representations (*A* thinks *B* thinks ...), or second-order representations, which Leslie called metarepresentations. Leslie suggested that one of the earliest signs of this underlying metarepresentational ability is to be observed in pretend play, which becomes quite elaborate in the child's second year. This proposal at first sounds rather odd because in the case of a child playing just by itself, there is no other mind to represent and the rationale for considering the pretense metarepresentational may thus appear far fetched. Leslie's reasoning was that, to take his now-famous example of a child pretending a banana is a telephone, the initial suggestion we might make to the effect that the child is simply representing the object as a telephone cannot be right. If the child does that, its primary representation of the world will be immediately corrupted—bananas and telephones will be confused. To prevent this representational abuse, the child must retain the basic function of the primary representational system, which is to represent the world as it is, with as much fidelity as possible (the banana as banana), but derive from this a secondary representation that can exist in parallel, of the banana as pretend telephone.

For evidence that both pretense and theory of mind rest on this same metarepresentational cognitive substrate, Leslie turned first to the sequence of normal development and argued that the first evidence of theory of mind, notably talking about mental states (Bretherton & Beeghly, 1982), occurs soon after evidence of pretend play, late in the second year of childhood. To me this represents only weak support: Different authorities claim various mindreading achievements from infancy through to the claimed 4-year watershed (contrast, for example, Chandler & Hala, 1994; Reddy, 1991), so that any could be picked as a correlate of another ability like pretense at many different stages of development—but this does not automatically show they are causally related. More powerful to Leslie's argument is the double deficit observed in autistic children, who are not only delayed in theory of mind as noted earlier, but who are also well known for deficits in pretend play— one of the principal criteria of diagnosis (Frith, 1989). This seems stronger support insofar as the theory suddenly makes sense of what would otherwise appear as two unrelated deficits in autism.

Turning this line of thinking toward the comparative and evolutionary data, Whiten and Byrne (1991) suggested that, if chimpanzees have taken significant steps toward a theory of mind that monkeys have not, then these apes, but not monkeys, might offer evidence of pretend play of the character Leslie's theory demands. In fact, the necessary criteria for such pretend play are quite severe. What is required is for the play to be elaborated as it progresses to make appropriate allowance for the logical implications of novel events: If a child is pretending to be boating and falls overboard, that it is fully in a pretend mode is clearly shown by further actions consistent with being wet. Remarkably, there are just a handful of well-described episodes in which chimpanzees' pretense appears this elaborate. In one, the young home-reared chimpanzee Viki was seen to play with what appeared to be a pull-along string toy, the critical observations of novel implications emerging when she acted out catching the string on a plumbing knob, eventually tugging it free and setting off again (Hayes, 1951—see Whiten & Byrne, 1991). In a second case, Savage-Rumbaugh and McDonald (1988—see Whiten & Byrne, 1991) describe the language-trained bonobo Kanzi pretending to have a nonexistent apple and elaborating on this by taking a bite and signing "bad".

It might be objected that, if apes are consistently capable of pretend play in the same way as are human children, such observations should be commonplace in both captivity and in the wild, whereas in fact such behavior is rarely remarked on in the now-extensive literature of field observations: Even when it is, the interpretation is admitted to be quite speculative (Goodall, 1986). The methodological problem is that if apes indulge in such pretend play in the wild, this is unlikely to be recognized as pretense in the same way as for the home-raised apes just described because all we see is variations on what wild apes naturally do. In the case of human-raised apes like Viki and Kanzi, the novelty of what they do with human artifacts can be sufficiently improbable to generate evidence of pretense like the previous accounts.

What of the evidence from deception on this issue? After all, any case of deception in which the perpetrator knows that its behavior is false is engaged in an act of pretense, and where this has a novel adaptive component, it could meet Leslie's criterion. In fact, although our deception database is now quite extensive, taking up 101 pages of a journal (Byrne & Whiten, 1990), each episode is relatively brief and novel elaboration is either not occasioned or not possible to verify. Perhaps the closest case comes again from Kanzi, described by Savage-Rumbaugh and McDonald (1988) as acting out rather fully the implications of a tool for opening his door being lost:

> I searched the entire enclosure while Kanzi watched me very patiently and with a most innocent expression on his face. I asked him if he had seen the

opening tool and he did not respond. I then asked him to help me look for it, and he began to act as if he was diligently helping me search for it. I did not find it. Finally, after satisfying myself that the opening tool could not possibly be there I walked out and turned my back on Kanzi for a moment to attend to the younger chimpanzees. Within 30 seconds after I had taken my eyes off him, Kanzi produced the tool from nowhere and let himself out. (p. 30)

Although admittedly encouraged to do so by Savage-Rumbaugh, Kanzi appeared to elaborate on acting as if searching for an object, the real location of which he knew well.

In sum then, the evidence for true pretense is anecdotal and quite minimal, but as far as it goes, it is consistent with the hypothesis that some kind of secondary representation of the kind envisaged by Leslie is possible. In the case of both pretend play and mindreading, the chimpanzee offers some evidence of going beyond primary or literal representation of the world as it is directly perceived, to secondary or nonliteral representation of how it may be to others (in the case of mindreading) or how it might be imagined to be (in the case of pretense). By contrast, an extensive trawl of the literature for other primates, including home-reared monkeys, failed to find evidence of elaborated pretend play (Whiten & Byrne, 1991). Such cognitive capacities, if they are confirmed by further research, therefore appear to be evolutionarily quite recent. Morevoer, they suggest that some kind of coupling of capacities for mindreading and pretense are detectable across some quite different contrasts: ontogenetically, in the comparison of toddlers with infants; clinically, in the comparison of normal children with autistic children; and phylogenetically in the comparison of chimpanzees (and by inference the ancestor we share with them) with our more distant relatives amongst the monkeys (and, therefore, with our more distant ancestors). If such coupling of capacities is confirmed by future research, some fundamental cognitive operation may be suspected to underly them (Whiten, 1996b). To be sure, the primate element in this speculation currently rests on fragile evidence, but the possible existence of such broad ranging cognitive patterns is intriguing and a spur to future research.

Reading Visual Attention

Another proposal for the child's early entry into the world of mentalism is also based partly on the delay in theory of mind suffered in the case of autism. Baron-Cohen (1991) noted that autistic children are able to say what another individual can see on the basis of their gaze orientation—in other words, they are capable of a simple form of visual perspective taking, based on the surface cues of eye and head orientation. When it comes to deeper, mentalistic aspects of seeing—in particular, visual attention—they have more difficulty. This is shown graphically by the difference in occurrence of two modes of pointing. Autistic subjects were shown to use what has been called proto-imperative pointing, in which the point is used to demand an object, but not proto-declarative pointing, where the aim is only to interest another individual in an object, or share attention with them on this focus. Baron-Cohen (1995) reviewed other findings supporting this general deficit, and accordingly developed a model of the development of the human mindreading system that incorporates a modular mechanism for shared attention, which is the earliest site of damage identifiable in autism. This already has practical applications, being used for screening young children for early signs of autism (Baron-Cohen, Allen, & Gillberg, 1992).

That reading visual attention might also be the mindreading entry-level of some nonhuman primates is an interesting hypothesis for several reasons. One is that, as in the case of the child's early theory of mind, the perception of attention may be mapped quite directly from overt signs like eye gaze, which as noted earlier, we have reason to believe primates are very sensitive to. A second reason is that, as suggested by the autism data, attention is nevertheless a mentalistic construct. It is therefore of interest that several lines of evidence in the deception database bear on the question of reading attention. At the most basic level, Whiten and Byrne (1988c) noted that not only were 7 of their 13 principal functional categories of deception concerned with the monitoring and manipulation of visual attention, but this was also true for the majority of all cases of deception classified. In short, visual attention is the primary medium through which much of primates' most sophisticated social maneuvering takes place. And as noted earlier, some specific types of deception appear to go beyond relatively surface features of visual behavior, as in those cases (restricted to apes) in which visual attention to choice half-hidden food items is witheld, signifying a recognition about what would be of potential interest to a rival.

Several recent experimental studies have now focused on visual attention, generating mixed conclusions on the prospects for mindreading in nonhuman primates. Povinelli and Eddy (1996a) have conducted a long, multiple series of tests of chimpanzees' understanding of seeing. Young chimpanzees would choose between two human helpers by making a begging gesture to one of them through an appropriate porthole in order to be fed. The helpers differed in their attentional stance vis-à-vis the ape subject. In the crudest contrast, one faced the ape and the other faced away. Not surprisingly, the subjects showed a clear preference for gesturing toward the person facing them. However, more subtle differences were not discriminated, including a blindfold over the eyes versus over the mouth, and the eyes closed versus open. In other tests, the chimpanzees were shown to track readily the gaze of a human to a novel object, yet when given the choice of begging from a person distractedly looking away in this fashion, as opposed to looking straight ahead toward the chimpanzee, subjects expressed no significant preference. This led Povinelli and Eddy to conclude that:

> even though young chimpanzee subjects spontaneously attend to and follow the visual gaze of others, they simultaneously appear oblivious to the attentional significance of that gaze. Thus, young chimpanzees possess and learn rules about visual perception, but these rules do not necessarily incorporate the notion that seeing is "about" something. (p. vi)

That chimpanzees might be insensitive to the deeper nature of attention in the same way as autistic children is reinforced by the fact that they have not been observed spontaneously to point in the wild. Wild chimpanzees simply do not point out interesting sights to each other.

Other experiments have drawn a rather different picture, indicating relatively sophisticated aspects of the way chimpanzees read the visual attention of others. In a separate series of experiments, Povinelli and Eddy (1996b) had chimpanzee and human subjects face each other through an open window in an otherwise opaque wall. When the human looked intently at a mark on their own side of the frame that surrounded the window, the chimpanzee attempted to peer around the frame toward the mark, rather than turning to look at another mark that had been placed behind the chimpanzee where the human's gaze would have terminated if the opaque frame were not preventing this. This shows that the chimpanzee subjects appreciated this aspect of visual occlusion to which others are subject. In addition, together with the demonstration that these ape subjects can track another's gaze to locii behind themselves (i.e., into space not visible to them at the commencment of their tracking, as achieved by 18-month-old human infants; Butterworth, 1991) the effort to see what the other sees (i.e., to peer around the frame to see what the human is looking at) can be interpreted as indicating that the chimpanzees expect the human's intent gaze to be *about* something—in other words, they may be said to read its intentionality in this respect.

A recent experiment (Whiten, 1997) was directly concerned with this issue. The design was derived from work by Baldwin (1993), which showed that by 18 months of age, human infants will learn the name of a new object that is looked at intently by a parent who is naming it. This is a sophisticated achievement on the infant's part, so much so that some developmental psychologists interpret it as the beginnings of mentalism. Baldwin and Moses (1994, p. 134), for example, suggested that such findings indicate that "by the middle of the second year, infants understand that other people's attentional cues (e.g. line of regard, gestures and so on) reflect their mental focus and referential intentions"—or how else would the infant connect together the utterance of the parent and its referent out there in the world?

Baldwin and Moses (1994, p. 151) thus talked of "a fledgling understanding of attention as something like a psychological spotlight that can be intentionally directed at external objects and events."

To come as close to this paradigm as possible, I have worked with apes who have for many years used a keyboard of symbols to talk about the world (Savage-Rumbaugh, 1986). Nowadays they can instead use a joystick to move a cursor around a computer screen containing 30 of these symbols at a time: When the cursor is moved to a new symbol, the computer records that choice and speaks the word in English (or if an appropriate symbol is selected, a new screen will open (there are screens for foods and objects, for example). The apes use this ability in two main ways: first, to request foods, objects, and activities; and second to respond to a question like, "Sherman, what is this?" when an object is held up in front of them, additionally being perhaps tapped or thrust toward them. Their facility in this two-way usage of the symbols makes it appropriate to talk of their activity as naming (see Savage-Rumbaugh, 1986, for experiments demonstrating the apes' grasp of the way in which the symbols stand for the objects they denote).

The basic attention-reading experiment was very simple, and exploited the fact that the apes are routinely asked about the names of things by holding them up or physically indicating them, typically by tapping them. Instead, an array of well-known objects was created between the ape and human experimenter, who sat facing each other (Fig. 5.1). The experimenter established eye contact with the subject, then turned head and eyes to gaze intently at one object, saying, "[name of subject], what's that?" The initial research question was simple—would this make any sense at all to the ape? Why should it, unless the ape reads this act as the kind of psychological spotlight to which Baldwin and Moses (1994) referred in the case of human infants acquiring language, and thus takes the object along the line of the experimenter's gaze as the referent of their question, "what's that?" Interestingly, those who work with these apes regularly were not able to make definite predictions about how they would respond.

In fact, the results were quite clear-cut. Both of the two apes tested to date achieved near-perfect, and thus statistically significant, accuracy of naming in the first two sets of trials, each of which incorporated four objects. Subjects received rewards only at the end of each trial, so were not shaped to respond appropriately on an item-by-item basis. Instead, their natural response appeared to be to read the intentionality of the experimenter's acts, suggesting that they perceive visual attention as likely to be about something in the world that they can themselves then attend to. This is consistent with the finding of Povinelli and Eddy (1996b) previously described, that chimpanzees tried to see what the experimenter's gaze was about on the occluding screen.

FIG. 5.1. Configuration of attention-reading experiment. The experimenter faces the chimpanzee subject, who has manual access to a joystick which moves a cursor over a computer screen of lexigrams. Several objects (string, keys, blanket, TV) are arranged between experimenter and subject: here, the experimenter looks up (see mirror) at the blanket, asking the chimpanzee Sherman "Sherman, what's that?" See text for further details.

Given that apes do not naturally acquire language, why should they spontaneously respond in this way? I suggest a two-part answer: first, that reading visual attention is an important part of chimpanzees' natural social behavior in the wild, as exemplified in the tactical deception database; but second, that reading attention as a state akin to a psychological spotlight is the most socially useful way to do this. For the Machiavellian primate, the advantage of perceiving attention as typically about things could lead to more sophisticated strategies to search for objects of another's attention, or attempt to control or shift it from one locus to another more to one's advantage (Whiten, 1997); for similar reasons, it could be beneficial in cooperative contexts such as group hunting (Boesch, 1994).

Using a somewhat different paradigm to that of Povinelli and Eddy, Gòmez, Teixidor, and Laa (reported by Gòmez, 1995; see also Gòmez, 1996[1]) offered evidence that chimpanzees can be more discriminating than the results of Povinelli and Eddy, suggested with respect to different levels of attention in others. In the experiments of Gòmez et al., the chimpanzee subject faced just one human experimenter from whom they could beg for food, but the human showed different conditions of (or lack of) attention. In the case of three chimpanzees who had experienced a long period of interactions with humans, attention-getting behavior like touching and vocalizing toward the human was scarcely shown when the human was looking at the chimpanzee, but such actions became common when the human looked to the side (82%), looked up (100%), had eyes closed (60%), or looked at an object (75%). Call and Tomasello (1994) also found that one orangutan who had been involved in intensive interactions with humans discriminated between whether a person's eyes were open or closed when using pointing to direct their attention, whereas another who lacked this experience only discriminated the cruder contrast between the person looking toward them or facing away.

Chimpanzees' reading of visual attention is thus beginning to be systematically charted. What is clearly needed is more comparative work extending to other ape and monkey species, to test whether the suggestion of greater sophistication of chimpanzees in reading attention in naturalistic deception contexts represents a real advance in this ability.

Imitation and Mindreading: Translating Between Self's and Other's Perspectives

I have suggested that the evidence on mindreading and pretense already reviewed can be interpreted as falling into some intriguing patterns when we shift back and forth between the ontogenetic, clinical, and phylogenetic perspectives, looking at contrasts between younger and older children, between autistic and nonautistic children, and between monkeys and apes. Speculating on the basis for such patterns, Whiten and Byrne (1991) suggested that a third capacity might also be correlated: imitation. There were two basic reasons for suggesting this from the phylogenetic perspective.

---

[1]Preliminary data reported in Gòmez (1996) differ slightly from the final figures described by Gòmez (1995, personal communication).

One is the recent reassessment suggesting that, despite their reputation, monkeys have not actually provided us with evidence they can truly imitate, whereas apes have (Byrne, 1995; Visalberghi & Fragaszy, 1990; Whiten & Ham, 1992; and see Russon, this volume; Tomasello, this volume). The second reason is that imitation and mindreading clearly share at least one fundamental operation, of translating between the perspective of another and oneself. This is not merely a change in visual perspective—in mindreading it is by definition a translation in mental perspective, and in imitation there is a requirement not merely to see the other's act from one's own perspective, but to construct the plan or program to execute it (Whiten & Byrne, 1991; Whiten & Ham, 1992). Just how much of a mental translation is involved in certain kinds of imitation—how much it is inherently mindreading—is a matter of debate, to which we shall return.

What of the link between this phylogenetic analysis and the ontogenetic and clinical ones? Whiten and Byrne (1991) suggested that, if primate imitation is correlated with the other patterns in pretense and mindreading, one might expect deficits in imitation to accompany the mindreading and pretense deficits in autism. Coincidentally at the same time, autism research workers Rogers and Pennington (1991) reviewed the scattered literature on this topic and concluded that there was in fact significant evidence for deficits in imitation in autistic samples. On this basis, Rogers and Pennington offered a new theory of the ontogenesis of theory of mind in normal and autistic individuals. By contrast with the prevailing theories at the time, they suggested that a fundamental capacity for "self-other perspective translation" is damaged in autism, leading to deficits first in imitation in infancy, and then further developmental consequencies including delayed theory of mind and distortions of related domains like pretense.

Studies by our research group have permitted some direct comparisons of the imitative behavior of primates and various samples of autistic and normal children. Some of the primate studies have been based on observational learning about how to open an artificial fruit, designed as an analog for the processing of food by these animals in the wild. Each part of the shell of the fruit can be removed using different, alternative methods, only one of which is demonstrated to each subject: The question then becomes whether subjects show significant biases toward adopting the particular method they saw. Experiments with primates have provided evidence consistent with the ape/monkey contrast alluded to, with 2-, 3-, and 4-year old children and chimpanzees showing imitation, but capuchin monkeys showing little or none (Whiten & Custance, 1996; Whiten, Custance, Gòmez, Teixidor, & Bard, 1996; but see Tomasello, this volume).

Studies with autistic children and adults faced with the same demonstrations confirmed imitation in preschool child control groups of similar mental age to the chronologically older autistic samples: but the latter failed to show a significant tendency to adopt the shelling method they had witnessed (Brown, 1996). This is consistent with the speculations of Whiten and Byrne (1991) and Rogers and Pennington (1991) summarized earlier. However, other approaches we took to the imitative capacity of the austistic samples painted a different picture, for when prompted to imitate an extensive battery of gestures and object-directed actions, the autistic samples performed at levels approaching those recorded for the young normal children. It thus appears that although autisitic subjects may well not imitate spontaneously in the way young children do, imitation may be within their grasp, at least once they have attained the chronological and/or mental age of our samples (CA mean = 12 years; VMA mean = 6.9 years).

One possible way of reconciling such results with the model of Rogers and Pennington (1991) begins by recognising that autism is a developmental disorder (Baron-Cohen, 1989). Although our results conflict with the idea of a generalized deficit in imitative capacity in autism, it could still be the case that there is an imitative deficit at an early point in development that has adverse developmental consequences for theory of mind, but that an imitative capacity nevertheless matures, at a slower pace than normal. Meltzoff and Gopnik (1993) and Gopnik and Meltzoff (1994) have outlined how imitation in infancy could play a key part in the developmental origins of mentalism because in imitation, the infant has to map from how actions look when performed (by others), to sensations and motor plans (its own) corresponding to those same actions. If the infant indeed learns something important about the mental correlates of observed acts in this way, then early imitation games—in which both infant and caretaker may imitate the other—must be functionally important in the normal development of theory of mind. Absence of imitation would have profound effects, consistent with Rogers and Pennington's model. Thus, even if the results of our autism studies represent the slow maturation of an imitative capacity, the finding that spontaneous imitation remains largely dormant could mean that an important early learning experience is lost in autism with respect to the genesis of mindreading.

Other findings in children and nonhuman species are consistent with the proposition that imitation is linked to pretense and mindreading more by way of being a precursor than a coincident capacity. In human infants, imitation of actions on objects appears in the first year (Meltzoff, 1988), whereas pretense and signs of mindreading in joint attention are characteristic of the latter half of the second year (Leslie, 1987).

In animal studies, the picture is currently quite complicated because despite the apparent lack of imitation in monkeys, there are now reports of simple imitative matching acts in rats (Heyes, Dawson, & Nokes, 1992) and pigeons (Zentall, Sutton, & Sherburne, 1996), and quite complex imitation in a parrot (Moore, 1992). It can be argued that these achievements do not compare with the kind of imitation observed in apes and children, however, for a variety of reasons (see Tomasello, this volume; Russon, this volume). Two arguments may be particularly important with respect to a link between imitation and mindreading (Whiten, 1992). The first relates to the hypothesis that certain forms of imitation are akin to mindreading in that they depend on an understanding of the means-ends structure of the models' actions—reading what they are trying to do (see Meltzoff, 1995, for an attempt to test this interpretation in human infants). Some of the nonprimate cases can be argued to lack such an appreciation, thus being relegated to a class of mere mimicking (Tomasello, 1996). The second way in which imitation might rest on cognitive abilities related to mindreading concerns the need, in the case of acquiring a new action pattern, to map the model's behavior, as seen from the imitator's point of view, into a motor plan executed from the imitator's own perspective. As Whiten and Ham (1992) observed, the imitator has in effect to reconstruct the model's action program—and again the putative link with mindreading is clear. Again, some of the nonprimate cases may make little cognitive demand in this respect, either because of the simplicity of the action or its similarity to actions already in the animal's repertoire.

Thus, it remains possible that imitation in apes is of a special character, correlated with capacities for mindreading and pretense. However, it begins to look as if some forms of imitation are more widespread in the animal kingdom than these latter abilities. Together with the early emergence of imitation in human infancy, this would suggest that we should not necessarily expect the co-emergence of imitation, pretense, and mindreading as correlated capacities. Instead, imitation becomes a candidate cognitive foundation for mindreading and pretense, such that where the latter emerge in ontogeny or evolution, we would expect to see an imitative capacity already in place.

SUMMARY AND DISCUSSION

In recent years, several hypotheses have been offered about the developmental origins of the human mindreading system, and corresponding questions about their evolutionary origins have been considered for three of them: pretense, attention-reading, and imitation. None of these are entirely new features of the human system, despite the fact that in each domain, the human child eventually goes far beyond anything observable in nonhumans.

With respect to the evolutionary origins of the kind of pretend play that emerges in children in the middle of their second year, we have noted there is evidence of dissembling (deception) in primates that is consistent with the possibility the animals are pretending. However, it is only in a handful of observations of chimpanzees that novel elaborations have been recorded that suggest that the animal's mind itself discriminates the pretense as pretense. The coincidence of this with the accumulation of the strongest evidence for animal mindreading in the same species has suggested that the common ancestor we shared with chimpanzees 5 to 7 million years ago (and perhaps other great ape ancestors 7 to 16 million years ago) was cognitively more advanced than the ancestors we shared with monkeys about 30 million years ago. The reading of visual attention, argued to be an early sign of mentalism in human ontogeny, is in some similar respects well-developed in chimpanzees: Chimpanzees will track the gaze of others with expectation that visual attention is likely to be about some object or event, appreciate aspects of visual occlusion to which others will be subject, and in some observations appear to anticipate the ability of others to notice certain objects of mutual interest

What pretense and mindreading appear to share is a capacity to go beyond primary or literal mental representation of the world as it is, to secondary, nonliteral representations of the world from the other's perspective (in the case of mindreading) or as it can be imagined to be (in the case of pretense). The evidence reviewed suggests that chimpanzees may share with 2-year-old children some capacity to operate at this nonliteral level, leading us to infer this kind of psychological operation in our common ancestor. However, this speculation must remain tentative because it is at present based on a small and fragile set of observations and experiments on apes, which is modest by contrast with the documentation of similar phenomena in human children.

What of earlier evolutionary foundations? As noted, observations of deception in modern-day monkeys suggests at least a basic capacity to track another individual's gaze, although this awaits experimental testing. This would suggest an ability with a much longer ancestry, shared more widely with both monkeys and apes, and a foundation on which more sophisticated analysis of other's visual attention could be built in more recent ancestors we share with chimpanzees or other apes.

Imitation of complex, novel, object-directed actions may also be limited to chimpanzees and/or other great apes and may fit the formulation of a secondary, nonliteral representational process insofar as it rests on appreciating the intentions of the model, or (re)constructing their action plan. However, simpler forms of imitation are both more widespread in animals and occur prior to pretense and mindreading in human ontogeny, consistent with the hypothesis that the cognitive foundations of imitation are not coincident with mindreading and pretense but can provide important foundations for them.

In this chapter, I have focused on a triad of competencies and possible links between them. Although there have been quite profound discussions in developmental psychology about potential cognitive links between mindreading and pretence (Harris, 1991; Leslie, 1987) and between mindreading and imitation (Meltzoff & Gopnik, 1993; Rogers & Pennington, 1991), the same does not appear to be true of the third arm of the triangle—the imitation-pretense link. This is despite the fact that there is a quite fundamental *a priori* similarity in the two processes: To pretend to be doing X is inherently to imitate the real counterpart of doing X; conversely in imitating the acts of another individual, there is a sense in which one acts as if pretending to be the original model. Both processes involve a crucial element of simulation.

Of course, there was one famous, early treatment of the developmental patterning of pretence and imitation: Piaget's (1945) *La Formation du Symbole*. Piaget remarked on the co-occurence in the final period of the sensori-motor stage during the second year, of both true imitation of relatively novel actions, and creative pretend play. He also made use of comparisons with the latest experimental findings on ape behavior, to argue that because chimpanzees also achieve symbolic psychological functioning, the human infant's parallel achievements are unlikely to be due to the emergence of language at this point in ontogeny (Piaget, 1945/1951). However, Piaget did not draw out the similarities between pretense and imitation other than a brief discussion of the representational level achieved concurrently in the two domains. He preferred to dwell on the difference between the two abilities, suggesting that imitation was an extreme case of mental accommo-dation to the requirements of reality, pretense an extreme case of assimila-tion of reality to the requirements of the mental process concerned. It is intriguing to contemplate where Piagetian theory might have led if instead of this fixation on the constructs of accommodation and assimilation, the weight of Piaget's intellect had explored the commonalities between imita-tion, pretense, and those mindreading abilities that take the child beyond the egocentrism Piaget emphasised so much.

Foundations of the mindreading system other than the triad of this chap-ter have been proposed, but not discussed here. Prominent amongst these putative foundations are the reading of emotions (Hobson, 1993), agency (Premack, 1990) and volitional states of various kinds, from goal-directed movements in one-year olds (Gergeley, Nádasdy, Csibra, & Bíró, 1995) to simple desire psychology in 2-year-olds (Wellman, 1991). Related abilities may well exist in nonhuman primates, in whom a range of emotional states has arisen, with associated abilties to read such states and for whom others' goals and intentions appear so important (Whiten, 1997). However, these domains remain virtually virgin research territory in nonhuman primates, just as they did in human infants a few years ago. It is to be hoped that in the coming years, the evolutionary roots of these will begin to be mapped and an account of the construction of the mindreading system more bal-anced in its ontogenetic and phylogenetic elements will become possible.

ACKNOWLEDGMENTS

I am grateful to Juan-Carlos Gòmez, Danny Povinelli, Mike Tomasello, and the editors of this volume for commentary on earlier drafts of this work.

REFERENCES

Baldwin, D. A. (1993). Infants' ability to consult the speaker for clues to word reference. *Journal of Child Language, 20,* 395–418.

Baldwin, D. A., & Moses, L. J. (1994). Early understanding of referential intent and attentional focus: Evidence from language and emotion. In C. Lewis & P. Mitchell (Eds.), *Children's early understanding of mind* (pp. 133–156). Hillsdale, NJ: Lawrence Erlbaum Associates.

Baldwin, J. M. (1902/1914). *Development and evolution.* New York: MacMillan.

Baron-Cohen, S. (1989). The autistic child's theory of mind: A case of specific developmental delay. *Journal of Child Psychology and Psychiatry, 30,* 285–298.

Baron-Cohen, S. (1991). Precursors to a theory of mind: Understanding attention in others. In A. Whiten (Ed.), *Natural theories of mind* (pp. 233–251). Oxford, England: Basil Blackwell.

Baron-Cohen, S. (1995). *Mindblindness: An essay on autism and theory of mind.* Cambridge, MA: Bradford/MIT Press.

Baron-Cohen, S., Allen, J., & Gillberg, C. (1992). Can autism be detected at 18 months? The needle, the haystack and the CHAT. *British Journal of Developmental Psychology, 161,* 839–843.

Baron-Cohen, S., Leslie, A. M., & Frith, U. (1985). Does the autistic child have a 'theory of mind'? *Cognition, 21,* 37–46.

Baron-Cohen, S., Leslie, A. M., & Frith, U. (1986). Mechanical, behavioral and intentional understanding of picture stories in autistic children. *British Journal of Developmental Psychology, 4,* 113–125.

Baron-Cohen, S., Tager-Flusberg, H., & Cohen, J. D. (Ed.). (1993). *Understanding other minds: Perspectives from autism.* Oxford: Oxford University Press.

Boesch, C. (1991). Teaching among wild chimpanzees. *Animal Behaviour, 41,* 530–532.

Boesch, C. (1994). Cooperative hunting in wild chimpanzees. *Animal Behaviour, 48,* 653–667.

Bretherton, I., & Beeghly, M. (1982). Talking about internal states: The acquisition of an explicit theory of mind. *Developmental Psychology, 18* 906–921.

Brown, J. (1996). Imitation, play and theory of mind in autism: An observational and experimental study. Doctoral dissertation, University of St. Andrews.

Butterworth, G. (1991). The ontogeny and phylogeny of joint visual attention. In A. Whiten (Ed.), *Natural theories of mind* (pp. 223–232). Oxford, England: Basil Blackwell.

Byrne, R. W. (1995). *The thinking ape.* Oxford: Oxford University Press.

Byrne, R. W., & Whiten, A. (1988). *Machiavellian intelligence: Social expertise and the evolution of intellect in monkeys, apes and humans.* Oxford: Oxford University Press.

Byrne, R. W., & Whiten, A. (1990). Tactical deception in primates: The 1990 database. *Primate Report, 27,* 1–101.

Byrne, R. W., & Whiten, A. (1991). Computation and mindreading in primate tactical deception. In A. Whiten (Ed.), *Natural theories of mind* (pp. 127–141). Oxford, England: Basil Blackwell.

Byrne, R. W., & Whiten, A. (1992). Cognitive evolution in primates: Evidence from tactical deception. *Man, 27,* 609–627.

Call, J., & Tomasello, M. (1994). Production and comprehension of referential pointing by orangutans (*Pongo pygmaeus*). *Journal of Comparative Psychology, 108*(4), 307–317.

Carruthers, P., & Smith, P. K. (1996). *Theories of theories of mind.* Cambridge, England: Cambridge University Press.

Chandler, M., & Hala, S. (1994). The role of personal involvement in the assessment of early false belief skills. In C. Lewis & P. Mitchell (Eds.), *Children's early understanding of mind* (pp. 403–425). Hove, UK: Lawrence Erlbaum Associates.

Cheney, D. L., & Seyfarth, R. M. (1990). *How monkeys see the world.* Chicago: University of Chicago Press.

Cheney, D. L., & Seyfarth, R. M. (1991). Reading minds or reading behaviour? Tests for a theory of mind in monkeys. In A. Whiten (Ed.), *Natural theories of mind* (pp. 175–194). Oxford, England: Basil Blackwell.

d'Andrade, R. G. (1987). A folk model of the mind. In D. Holland & N. Quinn (Eds.), *Cultural models in language and thought* (pp. 112–148). Cambridge, England: Cambridge University Press.

Davies, M., & Stone, T. (1995a). *Folk psychology: The theory of mind debate.* Oxford, England: Basil Blackwell.

Davies, M., & Stone, T. (1995b). *Mental simulation. Evaluation and applications.* Oxford, England: Basil Blackwell.

Dawkins, R., & Krebs, J. R. (1978). Animal signals: Information or manipulation? In J. R. Krebs & N. B. Davies (Eds.), *Behavoural ecology: An evolutionary approach* (pp. 282–314). Oxford, England: Blackwell.

Dennett, D. C. (1987). *The intentional stance.* Cambridge, MA: MIT Press.

de Waal, F. B. M. (1982). *Chimpanzee politics.* London: Jonathan Cape.

Fodor, J. (1992). A theory of the child's theory of mind. *Cognition, 44,* 283–96.

Frith, U. (1989). *Autism: Explaining the enigma.* Oxford, England: Oxford University Press.

Gòmez, J. C. (1991). Visual behaviour as a window for reading the mind of others in primates. In A. Whiten (Ed.), *Natural theories of mind* (pp. 145–207). Oxford, England: Basil Blackwell.

Gòmez, J. C. (1995, June). *Eye gaze, attention, and the evolution of theory of mind in primates.* Paper presented at the Annual Conference of the Jean Piaget Society ("Piaget, Evolution and Development"), Berkeley, CA.

Gòmez, J. C. (1996). Nonhuman primate theories of (nonhuman primate) minds: Some issues concerning the origins of mindreading. In P. Carruthers & P. K. Smith (Eds.), *Theories of theories of mind* (pp. 330–343). Cambridge, England: Cambridge University Press.

Gòmez, J. C., & Teixidor, P. (1992, August). *Theory of mind in an orangutan: A nonverbal test of false-belief appreciation?* Paper presented at the XIV Congress of the International Primatological Society, Strasbourg.

Goodall, J. (1986). *The chimpanzees of Gombe: Patterns of behaviour.* Cambridge, MA: Harvard University Press.

Gopnik, A., & Meltzoff, A. N. (1994). Minds, bodies and persons: Young childrens' understanding of the self and others as reflected in imitation and theory of mind research. In S. T. Parker, R. W. Mitchell, & M. L. Boccia (Eds.), *Self-awareness in animals and humans* (pp. 166–186). Cambridge, England: Cambridge University Press.

Gordon, R. M. (1986). Folk psychology as simulation. *Mind and Language, 1,* 158–171.

Happe, F. (1994). *Autism.* London: UCL Press.

Harcourt, A. H., & deWaal, F. B. (1992). *Coalitions and alliances in humans and other animals.* Oxford, England: Oxford University Press.

Harris, P. L. (1991). The work of the imagination. In A. Whiten (Ed.), *Natural theories of mind* (pp. 283–304). Oxford, England: Basil Blackwell.

Hayes, C. (1951). *The ape in our house.* New York: Harper & Row.

Heelas, P., & Lock, A. (Eds.). (1981). *Indigenous psychologies.* London: Academic Press.

Heyes, C. M. (1993). Anecdotes, training, trapping and triangulating: Do animals attribute mental states? *Animal Behaviour, 46,* 177–188.

Heyes, C. M., Dawson, G. R., & Nokes, T. (1992). Imitation in rats: Initial responding and transfer evidence. *Quarterly Journal of Experimental Psychology, 45b*, 59–71.

Hobson, P. (1993). *Autism and the development of the mind.* Hove: Lawrence Erlbaum Associates.

Humphrey, N. K. (1981). Nature's psychologists. In B. Josephson & V. Ramachandran (Eds.), *Consciousness and the physical world* (pp. 57–80). Oxford: Pergamon.

Humphrey, N. K. (1986). *The inner eye.* London: Faber & Faber.

Jolly, A. (1966). Lemur social behaviour and primate intelligence. *Science, 153*, 501–506.

Krebs, J. R., & Dawkins, R. (1984). Animal signals: Mind reading and manipulation. In J. R. Krebs & N. B. Davies (Eds.), *Behavioural ecology: An evolutionary approach* (pp. 380–401). Oxford, England: Blackwell.

Leslie, A. M. (1987). Pretense and representation in infancy: The origins of "theory of mind." *Psychological Review, 94*, 412–426.

Leslie, A. M. (1991). The theory of mind impairment in autism: Evidence for a modular mechanism of development? In A. Whiten (Ed.), *Natural theories of mind* (pp. 63–78). Oxford, England: Basil Blackwell.

Lewis, C., & Mitchell, P. (1994). *Origins of an understanding of mind.* Hove, UK: Lawrence Erlbaum Associates.

Lloyd-Morgan, C. (1930). *The animal mind.* London: Edward Arnold.

Meltzoff, A. N. (1988). Infant imitation and memory: Nine-month-olds in immediate and deferred tests. *Child Development, 59*, 217–225.

Meltzoff, A. N. (1995). Understanding the intentions of others: Re-enactment of intended acts by 18-month-old children. *Developmental Psychology, 31*(5), 838–850.

Meltzoff, A. N., & Gopnik, A. (1993). The role of imitation in understanding persons and developing a theory of mind. In S. Baron-Cohen, H. Tager-Flusberg, & D. J. Cohen (Eds.), *Understanding other minds: Perspectives from autism* (pp. 335–366). Oxford, England: Oxford University Press.

Moore, B. R. (1992). Avian movement imitation and a new form of mimicry: Tracing the evolution of a complex form of learning. *Behaviour, 122*, 231–263.

Nishida, T. (1983). Alpha status and agonistic alliance in wild chimpanzees. *Primates, 24*, 318–336.

Perner, J. (1991). *Understanding the representational mind.* Cambridge, MA: Bradford/MIT.

Piaget, J. (1951). *La Formation du Symbole.* Translated as *Play, dreams, and imitation in childhood.* New York: Norton. (Originally published 1945)

Piaget, J. (1967). *Biology and knowledge.* Edinburgh, Scotland: Edinburgh University Press.

Piaget, J. (1974). *Adaptation and intelligence: Organic selection and phenocopy.* Chicago: University of Chicago Press.

Piaget, J. (1976). *Behaviour and evolution.* London: Routledge & Kegan Paul.

Piaget, J., & Inhelder, B. (1956). *The child's conception of space.* London: Routledge & Kegan Paul. (Originally published 1948)

Povinelli, D. J. (1991). *Social intelligence in monkeys and apes.* Unpublished doctoral dissertation, Yale University, New Haven, Connecticut.

Povinelli, D. J. (1996). Chimpanzee theory of mind: The long road to strong inference. In P. Carruthers & P. K. Smith (Eds.), *Theories of theories of mind* (pp. 243–329). Cambridge, England: Cambridge University Press.

Povinelli, D. J., & Eddy, T. J. (1996a). What young chimpanzees know about seeing. *Monographs of the Society for Research in Child Development* (Vol. 61, No. 2, Serial No. 247).

Povinelli, D. J., & Eddy, T. J. (1996b). Chimpanzees: Joint visual attention. *Psychological Science, 7*, 129–135.

Povinelli, D. J., Nelson, K. E., & Boysen, S. T. (1990). Inferences about guessing and knowing by chimpanzees (*Pan troglodytes*). *Journal of Comparative Psychology, 104*, 203–210.

Povinelli, D. J., Nelson, K. E., & Boysen, S. T. (1992). Comprehension of role reversal in chimpanzees: Evidence of empathy? *Animal Behaviour, 43*, 633–640.

Povinelli, D. J., Parks, K. A., & Novak, M. A. (1992a). Do rhesus monkeys (*Macaca mulatta*) attribute knowledge and ignorance to others? *Journal of Comparative Psychology, 105*, 318–325.

Povinelli, D. J., Parks, K. A., & Novak, M. A. (1992b). Role reversal by rhesus monkeys: But no evidence of empathy. *Animal Behaviour, 44*, 269–281.

Povinelli, D. J., Rulf, A. B., & Bierschwale, D. T. (1994). Absence of knowledge attribution and self-recognition in young chimpanzees (*Pan troglodytes*). *Journal of Comparative Psychology, 108*, 74–80.

Premack, D. (1988). Does the chimpanzee have a theory of mind? revisited. In R. W. Byrne & A. Whiten (Eds.), *Machiavellian intelligence: Social expertise and the evolution of intellect in monkeys, apes and humans* (pp. 160–179). Oxford, England: Oxford University Press.

Premack, D. (1990). Do infants have a theory of self-propelled objects? *Cognition, 36*, 1–16.

Premack, D., & Woodruff, G. (1978). Does the chimpanzee have a theory of mind? *The Behavioral and Brain Sciences, 1*, 515–526.

Reddy, V. (1991). Playing with other's expectations?: Teasing and mucking about in the first year. In A. Whiten (Ed.), *Natural theories of mind* (pp. 143–158). Oxford, England: Basil Blackwell.

Rogers, S. J., & Pennington, B. F. (1991). A theoretical approach to the deficits in infantile autism. *Development and Psychopathology, 3*, 137–162.

Savage-Rumbaugh, E. S. (1986). *Ape language: From conditioned response to symbol.* New York: Columbia University Press.

Savage-Rumbaugh, S., & McDonald, K. (1988). Deception and social manipulation in symbol-using apes. In R. W. Byrne & A. Whiten (Eds.), *Machiavellian intelligence: Social expertise and the evoution of intellect in monkeys, apes and humans* (pp. 224–237). Oxford, England: Oxford University Press.

Smuts, B. (1985). *Sex and friendship in baboons.* New York: Aldine Publishing Company.

Thorndike, E. L. (1911). *Animal intelligence.* New York: Macmillan.

Tomasello, M. (1996). Do apes ape? In C. M. Heyes & B. G. Galef, Jr. (Eds.), *Social learning in animals: The roots of culture* (pp. 319–346). London: Academic Press.

Tomasello, M., & Call, J. (1994). The social cognition of monkeys and apes. *Yearbook of Physical Anthropology, 37*, 273–305.

Tomasello, M., & Call, J. (1997). *Primate cognition.* Oxford, England: Oxford University Press.

Tooby, J., & Cosmides, L. (1995). Foreword. In S. Baron–Cohen, *Mindblindness* (pp. xi–xviii). Cambridge, MA: MIT Press.

Visalberghi, E., & Fragaszy, D. (1990). Do monkeys ape? In S. Parker & K. Gibson (Eds.), *Language and intelligence in monkeys and apes: Comparative developmental perspectives* (pp. 247–273). Cambridge, England: Cambridge University Press.

Wellman, H. M. (1991). From desires to beliefs: Acquisition of a theory of mind. In A. Whiten (Ed.), *Natural theories of mind: Evolution, development and simulation of everyday mindreading* (pp. 19–38). Oxford, England: Basil Blackwell.

Whiten, A. (Ed.). (1991a). *Natural theories of mind: Evolution, development and simulation of everyday mindreading.* Oxford, England: Basil Blackwell.

Whiten, A. (1991b). The emergence of mindreading: Steps towards an interdisciplinary enterprise. In A. Whiten (Ed.), *Natural theories of mind: Evolution, development and stimulation of everyday mindreading.* Oxford, England: Basil Blackwell.

Whiten, A. (1992). Mindreading, pretense and imitation in monkeys and apes. *The Behavioral and Brain Sciences, 15*, 170–171.

Whiten, A. (1993). Evolving a theory of mind: The nature of non-verbal mentalism in other primates. In S. Baron–Cohen, H. Tager–Flusberg, & D. J. Cohen (Eds.), *Understanding other minds* (pp. 367–396). Oxford, England: Oxford University Press.

Whiten, A. (1994). Grades of mindreading. In C. Lewis & P. Mitchell (Eds.), *Origins of an understanding of mind* (pp. 47–70). Hove, UK: Lawrence Erlbaum Associates.

Whiten, A. (1996). Imitation, pretence and mindreading: Secondary representation in comparative primatology and developmental psychology? In A. E. Russon, K. A. Bard, & S. T. Parker (Eds.), *Reaching into thought: The minds of the great apes* (pp. 300–324). Cambridge, England: Cambridge University Press.

Whiten, A. (1997). The Machiavellian mindreader. In A. Whiten & R. W. Byrne (Eds.), *Machiavellian intelligence II* (pp. 144–173). Cambridge, England: Cambridge University Press.

Whiten, A. (1997). *What do chimpanzees see in visual attention?* Unpublished manuscript, University of St. Andrews.

Whiten, A., & Byrne, R. W. (1988a). Tactical deception in primates. *Behavioural and Brain Sciences, 11,* 233–273.

Whiten, A., & Byrne, R. W. (1988b). The Machiavellian intellect hypotheses. In R. W. Byrne & A. Whiten (Eds.), *Machiavellian intelligence: Social expertise and the evolution of intellect in monkeys, apes and humans* (pp. 1–9). Oxford, England: Oxford University Press.

Whiten, A., & Byrne, R. W. (1988c). The manipulation of attention in primate tactical deception. In R. W. Byrne & A. Whiten (Eds.), *Machiavellian intelligence: Social expertise and the evolution of intellect in monkeys, apes and humans.* Oxford, England: Oxford University Press.

Whiten, A., & Byrne, R. W. (1991). The emergence of metarepresentation in human ontogeny and primate phylogeny. In A. Whiten (Ed.), *Natural theories of mind: Evolution, development and simulation of everyday mindreading* (pp. 267–281). Oxford, England: Basil Blackwell.

Whiten, A., & Byrne, R. W. (1997). *Machiavellian intelligence II: Extensions and evaluations.* Cambridge, England: Cambridge University Press.

Whiten, A., & Custance, D. M. (1996). Studies of imitation in chimpanzees and children. In B. G. Galef & C. M. Heyes (Eds.), *Social learning in animals: The roots of culture* (pp. 291–318). London: Academic Press.

Whiten, A., Custance, D. M., Gòmez, J. C., Teixidor, P., & Bard, K. A. (1996). Imitative learning of artificial fruit processing in children (*Homo sapiens*) and chimpanzees (*Pan troglodytes*). *Journal of Comparative Psychology, 110,* 3–14.

Whiten, A., & Ham, R. (1992). On the nature and evolution of imitation in the animal kingdom: Reappraisal of a century of research. In P. J. B. Slater, J. S. Rosenblatt, C. Beer, & M. Milinski (Eds.), *Advances in the study of behavior* (pp. 239–283). San Diego: Academic Press.

Wimmer, H., & Perner, J. (1983). Beliefs about beliefs: Representation and constraining function of wrong beliefs in children's understanding of deception. *Cognition, 13,* 103–128.

Zentall, T. R., Sutton, J., & Sherburne, L. M. (1996). True imitative learning in pigeons. *Psychological Science, 7,* 343–346.

II

SOCIAL DEVELOPMENT

6

THE COMPARATIVE EVOLUTION
OF IMITATION

Anne E. Russon
Glendon College

Robert W. Mitchell
E. Kentucky University

Louis Lefebvre
McGill University

Eugene Abravanel
George Washington University

Looking into the evolution of imitation opens a veritable Pandora's box, given the wealth of phenomena that imitation encompasses, the widespread occurrence of imitation in the living world, the plethora of processes that can create imitations, and the lengthy history of scholarly interest. Baldwin (1894) once considered every aspect of life to have an essentially imitative quality, in that a certain replication of previous states is always involved. Imitation has played a central role in evolutionary debates since Darwin's 1871 publication of *The Descent of Man and Selection in Relation to Sex* because it was seen as one of the keys to unravelling the evolutionary origins of higher human mental faculties. It remains a perennial focus of study in psychology, perhaps because many of the original questions remain unanswered (e.g., Galef, 1988; Mitchell, 1987; Whiten & Ham, 1992). This chapter discusses some recent attempts to shed light on the subject.

THE FACES OF IMITATION

Problematic from the outset is that what scholars have included under the umbrella of imitation is not a unified phenomenon. Innocuous butterflies are said to imitate the form and color of toxic ones; some bird species imitate the songs of others; photocopies and portraits imitate their originals; and pretending to be mommy imitates mommy's behavior. To encompass all the uses of the last 100 years, imitation comes down to recognizing and creating resemblances:

> Imitation occurs when something C (the copy) is produced by an organism and/or machine, where C is similar to something else M (the model); registration of M is necessary for the production of C; and C is designed to be similar to M. (Mitchell, 1987, pp. 183–184)

Copies can be manifest in morphology, behavior, or artifacts; similarity must be taken as an undefined primitive (Mitchell, 1987, 1994a; Quine, 1969).

Imitations nonetheless differ in important dimensions. Interest in the mental faculties governing imitation narrows attention to behavioral rather than morphological imitation, but even behavioral imitation reflects a diversity of mental processes (e.g., Baldwin, 1894; Morgan, 1900; Thorndike, 1898). Those interested in the evolutionary origins of the modern human mind singled out types of behavioral imitation considered to reflect mental processes found in humans but not other species—true imitation and early infant imitation. Other types of behavioral imitation, those based on triggering existing responses or resemblances generated by fortuitous experience, have received little attention in the study of the evolution of imitation because they are seen as common and intellectually unsophisticated.

True Imitation

Three premises stand out as having significantly influenced conceptions of true imitation in psychology. Two of these stem from the behaviorist paradigm embraced by mainstream psychology early in the 20th century. Comparative psychology, the branch concerned with the evolution of mentality through the study of nonhuman species, followed suit. First, it abandoned Darwin's view of evolutionary continuity in favor of the dominant Western tradition of sharp, qualitative mental boundaries between humans and nonhumans. The watershed between human and nonhuman mental processes was presumed to be the capacity for symbolic versus sensorimotor reasoning, a view that can be traced to Aristotle (e.g., French, 1994; Gibson, 1993a). The premise was institutionalized in Morgan's Canon, which required attribution of nonhuman behavior to simple mental processes unless otherwise proven, whereas human behavior was normally attributed to higher processes (Morgan, 1894). Correspondingly, true imitation was construed as imitation governed by symbolic processes. Comparative psychology also focused its study of mentality on learning processes and so presumed that learning theory provided a suitable frame for true imitation. It emerged as imitative learning, or learning to do a novel act by merely seeing it done.

The third premise appeared in developmental psychology, which had a stake because of turn-of-the-century views that linked evolutionary with developmental processes (i.e., ontogeny recapitulates phylogeny). Early developmental models of Morgan, Baldwin, Guillaume, and Piaget saw imitation as classifiable into levels according to its governing mental processes. Higher levels of imitation resulted from more advanced mental processing, and these levels were presumed to be paralleled in developmental stages. The idea apparently behind this transformation through stages was that imitation derives from some general biological and/or psychological capacities that can be modified to create more advanced or complex capacities (Mitchell, 1995a). Levels then emerged, to lower or higher degrees, in human and nonhuman individual development; the developmental progression was read to reflect evolutionary change. This perspective saw true imitation as the level of creating resemblances that transcended and emerged out of rudimentary precursors achieved by nonhuman species: This was Baldwin's (internal) persistent imitation, Guillaume's symbolic imitation, Morgan's reflective imitation, and Piaget's stage 6 imitation (for details see Mitchell, 1987).

These conceptualizations have generated a list of specifications for true imitation as diverse as the five blind men's descriptions of the elephant. A few of those taken as essential are: True imitation copies the form of modeled behavior, not simply its aim or its consequences; it is goal-directed; it can generate new behavior for which the learner has no instinctive tendency; in true imitation, observation is both necessary and sufficient to copy novel behavior; the performance of imitative behavior can be temporally deferred, or delayed, from the mental process of true imitation; and true imitation is a generalized ability applicable across problems (e.g., Galef, 1988; Mitchell, 1987; Thorpe, 1963; Visalberghi & Fragaszy, 1990; Whiten & Ham, 1992). Creating resemblances across sensorimotor modalities is seen as one of its important fortes; a classic example is imitating invisible facial expressions, which involves translating visual into kinesthetic schemes (e.g., Abravanel, Levan-Goldschmidt, & Stevenson, 1976; Anisfeld, 1991; Piaget, 1945/1962; Stern, 1924/1975).

Similar threads run through these three conceptualizations of true imitation but it is not yet clear whether they represent different views of one phenomenon or of related but distinct phenomena. It is also significant that these conceptualizations specify threshold qualities of true imitation; until recently, relatively little consideration was given to the qualities of imitation that lie beyond.

Early Infant Imitation

The second imitative phenomenon promoted as significant in evolution is early infant imitation. This is matching behavior by human infants before they achieve true imitation, under about 7 or 8 months of age and perhaps as neonates. Meltzoff (1988b) suggested it shows that humans are *Homo imitans,* the most imitative of living species. It includes copying invisible facial gestures, suggesting that cross-modal imitation is possible from near birth in humans, not just at advanced stages.

Scholars had identified this phenomenon by the turn of the 20th century, but their studies led them to conclude that it was not imitation—it did not represent the recognition or creation of resemblances—but rather associative learning or innate behavioral dispositions (see Anisfeld, 1991, for a review). Some considered that it played little role in the true imitation that emerged later—at most, as a possible precursor (Piaget, 1945/1962). These views held until a series of studies by Meltzoff and Moore, the first published in 1977, reported reliable matching of gestures in very young infants and neonates. The last 20 years have seen considerable effort devoted to dissecting this phenomenon.

Some investigators maintain that recent studies show that young infants' abilities to match are not generalized and that early matching is restricted to a single action, tongue protrusion; their copies are not produced reliably; and their matching may be elicited by the cuing rather than the modeling function of the demonstrator (e.g., Anisfeld, 1991). Abravanel & Sigafoos (1984), for instance, modeled various gestures for infants 4 to 20 weeks old. The only gesture infants reliably matched was tongue protrusion; their copies were only approximate; and only 4- to 6-week-olds matched it reliably—older subjects failed to match even tongue protrusions. Those taking this stance reaffirm that this is not imitation but rather the product of associative learning, innate behavioral dispositions like contagion or fixed action patterns, or even methodological artifacts (e.g., Abravanel & Sigafoos, 1984; Anisfeld, 1991; Kaitz, Meschulach-Sarfaty, Auerbach, & Eidelman, 1988). Others consider recent findings to show young infants reliably match a range of vocalizations and facial and manual gestures in ways that qualify as imitation (e.g., Meltzoff, 1996); some attribute active intermodal matching (Meltzoff & Moore, 1992, 1994) and others, a constrained, unidirectional, visual to kinesthetic matching (Mitchell, 1994b).

Beyond this debate, the evolutionary significance of early infant matching is being challenged on another front, that it may not be unique to humans. Bard (1996) and Myoma (1996) have offered evidence, respectively, for similar neonatal and early infant matching in chimpanzees. From this comes an important realization, that early infant matching has not been systematically investigated in other species so we have little empirical basis for reconstructing its evolution.

IDENTIFYING TRUE IMITATION

Equally problematic is the methodology for studying true imitation. Methodological procedures create the filters controlling what phenomena are elicited and reported, so they importantly delimit what evidence is admitted into evolutionary debates. They create bottlenecks in the study of true imitation because there is still no consensus on which methods elicit true imitation accurately and conclusively. One difficulty is that true imitation comprises covert processes; they produce an observable trace, imitative behavior, but only sometimes; and so can, and do, many other processes. Further, true imitation is commonly one of a mix of processes generating imitative behavior, so its contribution to imitative behavior is nonexclusive and it is confounded (e.g., Aronfreed, 1969; Galef, 1988; Russon, 1996; Whiten & Ham, 1992; Yando, Seitz, & Zigler, 1978). Extensive effort has been spent on designing methods for sifting true imitation out.

In comparative research, most energy has been devoted to experimental tests of imitative learning. These focus on controlling for the intrusion of processes other than imitative learning in the generation of imitative behavior, primarily through procedures that preclude their use. Several procedures and criteria are currently in use (see Table 6.1). Scholars remain divided in their assessments of all these procedures: Each has its advocates, but each has also been doomed with those most ominous of words, "simpler explanations are possible," and all are susceptible to the charge of low ecological validity (e.g., Byrne, 1994; Byrne & Tomasello, 1995; Galef, 1988; Mitchell, 1995b; Moore, 1992; Whiten & Ham, 1992).

The alternative is systematic observation. Early procedures concentrated on identifying behavioral traditions, imitative behaviors that were prevalent in a group and transmitted socially; classic examples are the precultural traditions of Japanese macaques (e.g., Itani & Nishimura, 1973). Criticisms focused on lack of control over confounding processes (e.g., Green, 1975) so recent methods incorporate the identification of conditions that render processes other than true imitation implausible—the imitative behavior is arbitrary or improbable, it is novel and rapidly acquired, it was not tutored, etc. (Boesch, 1996; Hauser, 1988; Moore, 1992; Russon, 1996). Moore (1992), for example, argued that his Grey parrot imitatively learned his leaving gesture, a peculiar double wave, because the gesture was improbable, novel, and not tutored. Russon and Galdikas (1993) offered similar evidence for rehabilitant orangutans who copied peculiar local techniques for tying hammocks to trees, siphoning fuel, and making fires. Even the most recent observations, however, tend to represent small numbers of subjects (Mitchell, 1995b). Most experimenters still consider observational evidence as suggestive at best, lacking the power to demonstrate true imitation conclusively because generating processes are hopelessly confounded (e.g., Galef, 1988; Visalberghi & Fragaszy, 1990).

When study requires cross-species comparisons, the problem of confounding variables is even more sensitive. Potential behavioral confounds can be motivational or procedural (e.g., MacPhail, 1982): Different species, for instance, respond to food deprivation, task and social stimuli, and so

TABLE 6.1
Experimental Tests of True Imitation

Name	Procedure	Criterion for Imitative Learning
DAWSON-FOSS (Dawson & Foss, 1965)	Naive subjects observe one of several tutors solve a novel task. Different tutors using different behavioral techniques to solve the task (e.g., bird tutors pull a string to get food: tutor A—with a foot, tutor B—with the beak).	Subjects use the same technique as their own tutor.
HEYES (Heyes & Dawson, 1990; Heyes et al., 1992)	Naive subjects observe a tutor receive food reinforcement for pushing a vertical bar in one direction (left or right). Subjects observe through a window, from the front and facing the tutor, so they see movement in the opposite direction. The tutor is removed and the vertical bar is moved to another location in the chamber to remove spatial cues like its position relative to particular features of the chamber (Dawson & Foss variant)	Subjects push the vertical bar in the same direction with respect to their own body as their tutor did with respect to its own body.
PALAMETA (Palameta, 1989; Lefebvre et al., 1996)	Subjects are first trained in one of several techniques to solve a feeding task (e.g., peck down on the cap of a tube containing seed; lift a stopper blocking a hole containing seed by grabbing a metal ring in the beak). Once subjects have mastered their technique, they observe a tutor solve the same task: half observe tutor A (using the same technique) and the other half observe tutor B (using a new technique) (e.g., for the cap, pull it toward oneself; for the hole, rotate the metal ring downward to reveal a second hole containing seed). All subjects are given a task that can be solved only with tutor B's technique.	Subjects who observed tutor B (the new, effective technique) solve the new task faster than those who observed tutor A (the original, now ineffective technique).
HAYES' "DO-AS-I-DO" (Hayes & Hayes, 1952)	Subjects are trained to copy predetermined actions until they grasp the game rule, copy the action demonstrated.	Subjects correctly imitate many novel actions that are then demonstrated.

forth in different ways. Unless such confounds are removed, cross-species comparisons are invalid. Evolutionary biologists adjust for confounds in cross-species comparisons of morphological traits like brains or tail feathers; both covary with body size, so the effects of body size must be removed statistically to give relative indices of brain or feather size that are legitimately comparable. Comparative ecological predictions can also be tested this way; predictions about the role of the hippocampus in storing versus nonstoring birds, for instance, are tested by comparing relative hippocampal size after body and/or brain size has been removed. Similar standards have not yet been developed for handling species differences that can confound responses to tests of true imitation, like opportunism, tolerance for humans, social preferences, or level of neophobia (Greenberg, 1984, 1989). Pigeons, for instance, are urbanized, approach humans readily, and adapt quickly to new foods and feeding situations (Lefebvre, 1996; Lefebvre & Giraldeau, 1996). These are likely to affect true imitation tests that compare pigeons with species that avoid humans or that adapt less readily to capture by humans or to change in their normal habitat (Lefebvre, Palameta, & Hatch, 1996). Failure to control for species differences in sociality is recognized as confounding many of the experimental tests of true imitation in primates (Boesch, 1993a, 1993b; Russon & Galdikas, 1995).

The upshot is that we are in no way confident that we have the appropriate evidence in hand to establish the evolution of even one phenomenon, true imitation. With these conceptual and methodological caveats in mind, we consider what comparative evidence exists relevant to evolutionary reconstructions.

APING IMITATION? TRUE IMITATION
IN THE PRIMATES

If there are nonhuman species capable of true imitation, the primates are likely candidates owing to their close evolutionary relationship to humans. Great apes are at the center of attention. Their intelligence is exceptionally sophisticated, they ape, and their close genealogical relations to humans make them the species most likely to imitate in ways similar to humans. If true imitation has an ecological function—for example, contributing to learning how to forage—great apes should also show a marked need for this ability owing to their specialization as extractive foragers and the corresponding need to acquire complex food processing techniques (e.g., Byrne, 1995; Parker, 1996; Parker & Gibson, 1979). Accordingly, great apes figure prominently in comparative research on true imitation, primarily in the form of imitative learning.

Imitative Learning

Through much of the latter half of the 20th century, opinion quietly accepted earlier scholars' conclusions that great apes are capable of imitative learning (e.g., Hayes & Hayes, 1952; Kohler, 1927). The late 1980s saw an abrupt about face based on standard methodological criticisms and new evidence that great apes can learn independently the very routines touted as imitatively learned (e.g., Paquette, 1992). New empirical work ensued, using improved observational and experimental procedures; it is again generating evidence that great apes can learn imitatively (e.g., Custance & Bard, 1994; Custance, Whiten, & Bard, 1994, 1995; Meinel & Russon, 1996; Miles, Mitchell, & Harper, 1996; Russon & Galdikas, 1993, 1995; Tomasello, Savage-Rumbaugh, & Kruger, 1993; Visalberghi & Limongelli, 1996; Whiten, Custance, Gòmez, Texidor, & Bard, 1996).

Parallel studies on other nonhuman primates have, in contrast, found no evidence for this capacity (e.g., Anderson, 1996; Visalberghi & Fragaszy, 1990; Visalberghi & Limongelli, 1996; Whiten & Ham, 1992) despite substantial evidence for socially transmitted behavioral traditions in monkeys (e.g., Itani & Nishimura, 1973; Nishida, 1987). Some maintain, however, that the jury is still out on the capacity for imitative learning in monkeys (e.g., Anderson, 1996). There are several suggestive cases, like this one: A free-ranging female rhesus monkey was following a rhesus mother-infant pair, holding half a coconut shell in the same position as the mother held the infant; when the mother shifted the infant to a different position, the follower shifted her coconut shell to match (Breuggeman, 1973).

Despite reaffirmation of great apes' capacity for true imitation, there remain puzzling patterns. Their imitative learning is persistently fragile and weak—it remains difficult to elicit and of minor benefit to learning (Custance et al., 1994, 1995; Kohler, 1927). What great apes acquire imitatively is not clear—something about the demonstration's outcomes, motor actions, or program. Perhaps most glaring is the huge gulf between the impoverished imitative learning that experimenters elicit in the laboratory and the complex behavior that field researchers are convinced owes to imitative learning. For example, Meinel and Russon (1996) experimentally demonstrated joining infants' snap beads into a necklace to an adult female orangutan; when given the beads, she joined only two together. In contrast, cases of spontaneous imitation suggest great apes can learn very complex routines imitatively (e.g., Byrne & Byrne, 1991, 1993; Miles et al., 1996; Russon & Galdikas, 1993, 1995). A rehabilitant orangutan, for instance, imitatively learned to siphon fuel: She brought a gerry can and hose to a fuel drum, removed the caps from both containers, inserted one end of the hose into the drum, then sucked the other end and inserted it into the gerry can.

Because of such puzzling patterns, how and what great apes learn imitatively are becoming key issues. Answers are important because they delimit the phenomena considered in evolutionary reconstructions of higher imitative capacities. Some clues are just now emerging, as exemplified in findings like those of Tomasello and his colleagues (e.g., Call & Tomasello, 1994; Nagell, Olguin, & Tomasello, 1993; Tomasello, this volume). In their experiments, food was visible to great ape subjects out of reach, but there was a rake tool they could use to retrieve it. In one condition, a demonstrator picked up the rake tool by its handle, flipped it over, then raked in the food with the rake's edge. Subjects that observed this did use the rake tool to bring in food, but many did not first flip it over so they raked by catching the food in the rake's tines. Puzzling is their using a technique that is less effective and more difficult than the one demonstrated. The main interpretation of this puzzling performance is that the apes are learning about the outcomes demonstrated, not the behavior itself (Kohler, 1927; Tomasello, 1990; Whiten & Ham, 1992). Tomasello (1990) classified this as emulation (after Wood, 1989), not imitative learning, because the behavioral strategy itself was not learned.

An alternative that may better explain these and similar findings is that the apes learned the relational manipulations demonstrated (i.e., putting the tool into a rake rather than, e.g., a poke or hit relationship with the food), a possibility that has been raised but not pursued extensively (e.g., Tomasello, Davis-Dasilva, Camak, & Bard, 1987; Whiten & Ham, 1992; but see Visalberghi, 1993). In its favor, the concept of a tool is in essence a relational one—it rightfully refers to objects only when they are put into particular kinds of relationships with other objects (e.g., Beck, 1980; Reynolds, 1982).

We have some understanding of the cognitive processes and behavioral strategies for manipulating relationships from research on early child cognitive development at the level of simple physical relations like in-ness or through-ness (e.g., Case, 1985; Greenfield, 1991). Behavioral strategies for manipulating relationships involve sequences of actions, not single actions (e.g., sweeping, catching, and pulling are coordinated to effect raking). Such sequences are hierarchically integrated to form unified, higher level relational routines (e.g., we enact raking rather than a chain of sweeping, catching, and pulling actions). Relational routines can themselves be combined as subroutines to create even more complex multirelational routines (e.g., rake in a hammer, then hammer open a nut). Other key properties of such relational manipulations are (1) component actions or subroutines become subordinate to the higher level routine—they become behavioral details that are flexible and adjustable by design (e.g., in raking, sweeping actions may be modified or repeated to catch the target) and (2) the organization of actions in relational routines surpasses chaining to incorporate iteration, substitution, online error correction, and handling interruptions.

This suggests what relational level imitative learning should look like, recalling that even in humans, it depends on what observers understand

and encode from demonstrations (e.g., Abravanel, 1991; Abravanel, Ferguson, & Vourlekis, 1993; Moerk, 1989). If observers understand relational manipulations in demonstrated behavioral strategies, they can match these relational manipulations (e.g., if demonstrators rake with a tool, imitators also rake with a tool rather than throw or poke with it); they may fail to match lower or higher level components—lower ones, because they are flexible by design (e.g., in raking, a left-hand hold could be substituted for a right-hand one, or the rake's tines for its back edge; see also Byrne, 1994) and higher ones, because of incomprehension (e.g., organization may be fragmented or flawed, as in trying to insert a siphon into a fuel drum before opening the drum's cap). Such relational level imitation appears in human children 1 to 2 years old; they too imitate relational patterns proficiently but tend to ignore behavioral detail (Abravanel & Gingold, 1985; Gibson, 1993c).

Relational level imitative learning is plausible in great apes. Great apes can understand simple physical relations, both causal and logical ones (e.g., Langer, 1996; Visalberghi & Limongelli, 1996). Evidence is accumulating that their learned behavior is hierarchically constructed (e.g., Byrne, 1994; Langer, 1996; Reynolds, 1982) and that they can understand and construct multirelational routines (Matsuzawa, 1994; Russon, 1995; Russon & Galdikas, 1993). Some West African chimpanzees combine stone anvil and hammer relations to crack open nuts and place a third stone under the anvil, in a wedge relation, to level it (Matsuzawa, 1994).

Relational level imitative learning is also evident in great apes' responses in experimental tests. In the rake experiments, imitators did imitate the raking relational routine they observed: They raked, missing only one lower level component, orienting the rake on its back edge. They also showed the predicted flexibility in lower level component actions; they self-corrected, for instance, when food slipped between the rake's tines (Call, personal communication). The juvenile chimpanzee whose mother demonstrated an improved nut-cracking technique likewise imitated the hammer-nut relation demonstrated, but not most motor details (Boesch, 1991, 1993b; Gibson, 1993b). A juvenile female rehabilitant orangutan, Daidai, also acquired multirelational routines imitatively (Russon, 1995). One demonstration was inserting a jackfruit seed (like a huge lima bean) into a hole in the center of a 2-cm length of garden hose then setting the seed-in-hose ensemble onto a coconut shell dish. On receiving these items, Daidai immediately inserted the seed into the hose hole; she pushed it into the hole repeatedly (it tended to slip out), once retrieving it from the ground after it slipped out then pushing it in again. This accomplished, she carefully carried her seed-in-hole ensemble to the coconut shell dish. The seed slipped out on the way and she did not retrieve it (she either did not notice or was intent on the final phase), so she in fact placed an empty hose onto the dish. She nonetheless reproduced the causal sequence and the individual relational manipulations demonstrated; and she added and corrected lower level components, as needed, to carry out the overall strategy (corrected ineffective insertion by pushing, added picking up the fallen seed). Chimpanzees make similar smart mistakes (Kohler, 1927).

Great apes may then be parsing demonstrations into behavioral units at any of the levels they understand—motor actions, relational routines, or multirelational routines. In this, they are much like human children 2 to 3 years of age (e.g., Abravanel & Gingold, 1985; Abravanel et al., 1976). To return to the original issues—what and how great apes learn imitatively—they may learn behavioral strategies at higher cognitive levels than we have expected. They may achieve this by encoding demonstrations at the level of the physical relations involved, so their copies match relational (Russon & Galdikas, 1994) and program-level (Byrne & Byrne, 1991) patterns but generate motor details independently.

There remain differences between great ape and human imitative learning; other findings suggest why. (1) Great apes have fewer cognitive building blocks for parsing and recreating demonstrations, partly because their cognitive development advances more slowly and in fewer modalities—for instance, they appear to achieve true imitation later than humans do, about 3 to 4 years versus 14 months of age (Dore & Dumas, 1987; Mitchell, 1991, 1994a; Parker, 1977, 1996). Their understanding is correspondingly reduced. (2) Great apes may tend to combine fewer components in any one routine. For example, after training a juvenile female orangutan to imitate touching one forefinger to one eye, a new action was demonstrated, touching each forefinger to each eye; she responded by touching with both forefingers, but to only one eye (Russon, personal observation). Other apes have done similar things (e.g., Custance & Bard, 1994; Miles et al., 1996). (3) Great apes' encoding may be limited to undifferentiated relations; human children initially do the same (e.g., Abravenel & Gingold, 1985). For example, a demonstrator joined interlocking sticks by inserting then twisting, but the orangutan joined them by merely butting their ends together, in undifferentiated contact, then twisting (Meinel & Russon, 1996). (4) Great apes' schemes may be less modifiable (e.g., Parker & Russon, 1996). After training a juvenile female orangutan to imitate touching a forefinger to the center of her other palm, a new action was demonstrated, touching the forefinger to the tip of the other forefinger; she watched then touched the forefinger to her other palm at the base of the forefinger rather than the center of the palm or at the tip of the forefinger (Russon, personal observation). In each case, there are examples beyond the ones offered here.

These constraints are consistent with two long-standing views—that great apes achieve limited gains from a few demonstrations or attempts at imitative learning (e.g., Kohler, 1927) and the imitation found in free-ranging apes stems from years of observation and many imitative attempts (e.g., Lawick-

Goodall, 1973; McGrew, 1992). If great apes are constrained in the range of behavior they can understand, the number of components they can combine at once, the depth and precision of their encoding, and the rate at which they accommodate change, they will need many imitative drafts to generate a close copy of a demonstration. It must be kept in mind, however, that great apes do not normally enjoy the same intense cognitive scaffolding that humans do, such as intense and repetitive imitative practice, making their task relatively much more difficult.

Relational level understanding may offer a neat explanation for how great apes learn some problem-solving strategies imitatively. It is consistent with our knowledge of the cognitive levels they achieve and their rudimentary hierarchical cognition; it accounts for some of their puzzling mistakes; and it allows for a form of program level imitation that aims at general behavioral strategies rather than detailed techniques. If this is so, despite the constraints sketched, great apes are expressing sophisticated rather than impoverished imitative learning (Call & Tomasello, 1994; Nagell et al., 1993; Tomasello, 1990, this volume) that surpasses the symbolic divide long positioned between human and nonhuman mentality.

Higher Level True Imitation

Scholars interested in comparative research on true imitation are coming to recognize that the versions traditionally targeted (e.g., imitative learning, Piaget's stage 6 imitation) are only some of its manifestations. Others include self-recognition, pretense, and planning. The traditional versions are the first to emerge developmentally so they may represent threshold forms upon which others are constructed (e.g., Gopnik & Meltzoff, 1994; Hart & Fegley, 1994; Mitchell, 1991, 1993a, 1994a; Parker, 1991, 1996; Parker, Mitchell, & Boccia, 1994; Piaget, 1945/1962; Whiten, 1996). Great apes are demonstrating capacities for these higher level imitative abilities as well.

Mirror self-recognition may build on true imitation of motor actions: Both appear to require recognizing a resemblance between kinesthetic and visual images of one's own body (Mitchell, 1993a, 1993b; Parker, 1991) and in human children, imitating bodily actions becomes elaborated developmentally just prior to recognizing themselves in mirrors (Gopnik & Meltzoff, 1994; Hart & Fegley, 1994). At least some individuals in all great ape species, but no other nonhuman primates, come to recognize themselves in mirrors (for reviews see Anderson, 1996; Parker et al., 1994). Great apes, like humans, seem to recognize a visual (mirror) image of their own body and its actions as a copy; from the kinesthetic feel of their movements, they can apparently construct a visual-like image of their actions; and they can match the two.

Pretense incorporates a form of imitation in which the outcome seems relatively benign, at least in relation to the original demonstration (Mitchell,

1990). Typically in pretense, imitators copy the actions in demonstrations but not the results; for example, an individual who pretends to enact a model's feeding behavior does not in fact eat. Pretense may be built upon true imitation because it emerges later in human development, about 12 versus 9 months (Meltzoff, 1988a, 1988b; Mitchell, 1994a, 1994b). Many examples of great ape imitation are suggestive of pretense; those from great apes who have interacted extensively with humans can reach elaborate proportions surprisingly like human pretense (Mitchell, 1990, 1994a). The chimpanzee Viki, for instance, acted as if dragging a nonexistent pull toy that got caught then waited for her human caretaker to free it before moving along (Hayes, 1951). Their capacity for pretense appears limited to activities that recur in their daily lives and/or for which the functional relevance of imitation is apparent or interesting, like maternal behavior, locomotion, eating, and aggressive displays (e.g., Hayes, 1951; Miles et al., 1996; Mitchell, 1994a; and see Tanner, 1985).

Planning follows on pretense in human development, where a plan is a pretend scenario in which a sequence of behavior occurs in an individual's mind (Mitchell, 1994a). The imaginer recognizes that the scenario is imagined but that it resembles behavior that could, or will be, enacted. In humans, the capacity for planning is extensive and elaborate. It becomes evident in the pretend play of 2-year-olds and perhaps even earlier, in nonplay activities (e.g., Gopnik, 1982). Planning seems evident in some great apes' activities. Individual chimpanzees and orangutans have discovered food and waited until no others were around to obtain it—sometimes for hours and deliberately moving away from the food until others had left (e.g., de Waal, 1982; Goodall, 1986; Menzel, 1973; Russon, personal observation). At least in chimpanzees, plans may involve tools: West African chimpanzees who use stone hammer-anvil tool sets sometimes find hammer rocks far from anvil sites and transport them to the sites (e.g., Boesch & Boesch, 1984). Although interpretations of these incidents are disputed, that great apes plan for the immediate future is considered obvious by many who study them in the field.

This comparative work on higher level imitation buttresses the view that great apes are capable of true imitation well beyond rudimentary levels. Their higher achievements are particularly important in establishing the evolutionary platform from which human imitative capacities diverged.

TRUE IMITATION IN NONPRIMATES

Given the widespread occurrence of imitative behavior in the living world, nonhuman species other than primates are important to broader evolutionary questions. They are especially prominent in debates that portray the cognitive underpinnings of imitation as a key to establishing whether so-phisticated human intelligence represents evolutionary continuity or dis-continuity, that is, a product of the modification of rudimentary precursors or a unique creation unparalleled by other mental phenomena. In principle, the distribution of true imitation across all nonhuman species is of concern; in fact, research has focused on a limited number of species, some for their acknowledged intelligence or imitative propensities (e.g., avian mimids, ce-taceans), others for their convenience (e.g., rats and other rodents), and others still for their feeding ecology (e.g., pigeons, doves, and grackles).

Recent reviews have surveyed the available evidence on true imitation in non-primates (e.g., Galef, 1988; Mitchell, 1992, 1994a; Moore, 1992; Whiten & Ham, 1992). They tend to agree on four points. (1) Despite few reports, some cetaceans like bottlenose dolphins (*Tursiops truncatus*) are probably capable of true imitation (Herman, 1980; Norris, 1974; Pryor, 1975; Tayler & Saayman, 1973). Tayler and Saayman described a captive bottlenose dol-phin's trying to remove algae from an underwater window with a sea gull feather, in imitation of a human diver who regularly cleaned the window; while cleaning, it produced sounds like the diver's regulator demand valve along with a stream of bubbles like the air expelled by the diver. (2) Despite humans' extensive casual contact with carnivores (canids and felids), there is little convincing evidence that they are capable of true imitation. (3) There is no consensus in the literature that rodents, whose extensive contact with humans has been experimental rather than convivial, have demonstrated true imitation. (4) Avian species offer little evidence of visually guided motor imitation, and what exists is not convincing. New work on dolphins, rodents, and several avian species has appeared since these reviews.

Dolphins

Two studies have offered formal evidence of mirror self-recognition in bot-tlenose dolphins (Marino, Reiss, & Gallup, 1994; Marten & Psarakos, 1994). If mirror self-recognition builds on true imitation of motor actions, this evidence automatically constitutes evidence for true imitation. Others have offered observational evidence implying the imitative acquisition of signa-ture whistles (Sayigh, Tyack, & Wells, 1993) and of ring- and helix-bubble blowing (Marten, Shariff, Psarakos, & White, 1996) in bottlenose dolphins.

Rodents

Heyes and her colleagues (Heyes & Dawson, 1990; Heyes, Dawson, & Nokes, 1992; Heyes, Jaldow, Dawson, & Nokes, 1994) reported showing that rats can learn imitatively, using Heyes' procedure (Table 6.1). These studies have garnered much attention, partly due to their intriguing demonstration that observers orient their behavior with respect to their demonstrator's point of view, not their own (Heyes & Dawson, 1990) and can then transpose this orientation to a new spatial position (Heyes et al., 1992). The ensuing conclusion, however, that rats can learn imitatively, has been challenged. Some critics argue that the purported imitative behavior, pushing a vertical bar, is neither novel nor improbable; the procedure does not test behavior but only its outcome (direction of bar displacement); and simpler explanations are possible (e.g., Byrne & Tomasello, 1995; Mitchell, 1995b; Moore, 1992; Whiten & Ham, 1992).

The Birds

Avian species have been peripheral in comparative debates on true imitation because their forte, vocal imitation, is considered distinct from visually guided motor imitation (e.g., Galef, 1988; Whiten & Ham, 1992). Several researchers have recently tested visually guided motor imitation in avian species, to find surprisingly sophisticated imitation that challenges views that avian talents lie with vocal imitation alone. Their results also challenge views of imitative learning of motor behavior as a fixed species characteristic.

Moore (1992) conducted a 5-year experiment on imitation in one African Grey parrot (*Psittacus erithacus*). He gave the parrot several 3 to 10 minute demonstrations daily of various complex, novel, and improbable motor actions, each accompanied by a unique vocal pattern. Any motor imitation was then signaled and distinguished from the surrounding stream of behavior by its accompanying vocalization. By covertly photographing and videotaping the parrot's behavior, Moore captured a wide variety of motor imitations. For instance, the parrot reproduced (with its feet) Moore's routine for leaving the room—saying *ciao* along with a full wave of one hand (as he opened the door with his second hand) then a half wave of the second hand (as he closed the door with his first hand). Moore argued that a number of these motor imitations qualify as true imitation by Thorpe's criteria (1963), that they are novel and improbable for the species. These findings are impressive and suggestive, but they have not escaped criticism (e.g., the imitated actions are not improbable but in fact quite common in Grey parrots, and coding and reliability schemes are not clear; Mitchell, 1995b).

Lefebvre and his colleagues study nonmimid avian species combining controlled experiments with field observations. They have been exploring ecological factors that may correlate with imitative learning. In one suite of studies on Carib grackles (*Quiscalus lugubris*) and Zenaida doves (*Zenaida aurita*), Lefebvre and his colleagues (Lefebvre et al., 1996; Lefebvre, Koelle, Brown, & Templeton, 1997) considered the role of feeding competition strategies in imitative learning. In Barbados, the grackles forage in small flocks in opportunistic mixed-species aggregations that can include Zenaida doves. In these aggregations they mainly use one strategy, scramble competition, to compete for food, where speed (getting food into your stomach faster than your neighbor does) rather than aggression is the major determinant of success. The Zenaida doves experience varied social and physical living conditions that correlate with different feeding strategies. They are predominantly territorial across Barbados, but there are a few gregarious populations. The territorial doves use interference competition (aggression) against conspecific neighbors other than their mate, but scramble competition against grackles. The gregarious doves use scramble competition against conspecific neighbors; they encounter few grackles. Territorial Zenaida doves learn poorly from conspecific tutors but readily from grackle tutors; in contrast, gregarious Zenaida doves learn more readily from conspecifics than they do from grackles (Dolman, Templeton, & Lefebvre, 1996). This suggests that social learning, and perhaps imitative learning, may be favored by scramble competition.

If social, and possibly imitative, learning is linked with scramble competition, Carib grackles should learn as readily from grackles as they do from dove tutors. To test this, grackle tutors were trained to remove the stopper on an opaque food container using either the typical feeding technique of Zenaida doves (peck with closed beak) or of grackles (pry with open beak). Naive grackle subjects then observed a tutor remove the stopper—a trained grackle using one of the two techniques or an untrained dove using its typical technique—then had the opportunity to try themselves. Grackle subjects learned as quickly from grackles as they did from dove tutors and those that observed grackle tutors tended to use their particular tutor's technique. It can be argued that grackles did learn imitatively insofar as they acquired a novel feeding technique by observation, in a pattern consistent with the hypothesis that imitative learning is associated with feeding competition strategies.

THE EVOLUTION OF TRUE IMITATION

The patchiness of the evidence notwithstanding, the distribution of true imitation is essential to reconstructing its evolution. Current evidence suggests this level imitative capacity occurs in humans, the great apes, some cetaceans, and possibly some avian species. Evolutionary reconstructions consider processes that could account for this distribution. Study has focused on plausible evolutionary changes to ontogenetic and proximal factors—primarily cognitive and perceptual—as well as the selection pressures, social and ecological, that could have shaped them.

Proximal Mechanisms and Ontogeny

Cognition. With true imitation traditionally cast as a key mental ability, interest has fixed most prominently on cognitive mechanisms associated with its evolution. The distribution of true imitation is partly consonant with its portrayal as an advanced achievement in an evolutionary line characterized by increasingly sophisticated cognitive mechanisms. Great apes, bottlenose dolphins, and gray parrots share neurological and intellectual sophistication (e.g., Byrne, 1995; Herman, 1980; Morgane, Jacobs, & Galaburda, 1986; Pepperberg, 1988; Russon, Bard, & Parker, 1996).

These species are not closely related so most consider that their shared capacity for true imitation is analogous rather than homologous and that true imitation must have evolved at least three times independently. Primates offer the only potential homologues to human true imitation. Knowledge of the distribution of cognitive mechanisms linked with true imitation in cetaceans is extremely limited, leaving it difficult to speculate on what may have been involved, cognitively, in its evolution. The more extensive knowledge available on avian species offers greater scope. Moore (1992), for example, argued that the parrot's ability for true imitation is consistent with an evolutionary path in avian species characterized by increasingly sophisticated mimetic learning capacities. Vocal mimicry occurs only in the subset of avian species that learn their songs; nonvocal mimicry, copying sounds by movement rather than vocalizing (e.g., banging objects with the beak to mimic percussive sounds), occurs in two species that are among the best vocal mimics, gray parrots and starlings; and true imitation occurs in the more talented of the two, the gray parrot. This scenario does not, however, incorporate findings like those of Lefebvre and his colleagues (Dolman et al., 1996; Lefebvre et al., 1996, 1997) so its viability is uncertain. Given currently available evidence, the best opportunity for tracing an evolutionary line of cognitive changes leading to true imitation may lie with the primates.

The straightforward evolutionary interpretation of evidence on primate imitation is some form of terminal addition to cognition. Living primates readily show imitative behavior attributable to cognitive mechanisms simpler than true imitation; only the most recently evolved primates, the great apes and humans, share the cognitive capacity that affords true imitation; great ape and human true imitation appears to derive from progressive developmental changes to cognition achieved at the end of their infancy, and their earlier imitative behaviors appear to be governed by simpler cognitive mechanisms; and true imitation seems to tax the upper reaches of great ape cognitive capacity. This suggests that true imitation owes to cognitive mechanisms added at the end of a developmental, and phyletic, line.

Recent analyses of the cognitive mechanisms associated with true imitation are, however, suggesting a more complicated picture. Great apes and humans also share higher level imitative abilities and other advanced abilities that are linked with true imitation developmentally. This suggests that the evolutionary changes to cognition were powerful enough to carry true imitation beyond the mere brink of symbolic thought and to affect a broader range of abilities than true imitation alone. Views are still divided on whether these cognitive changes constituted a generalized mechanism (and single evolutionary change), an aggregate of independent ones, or something in between. This issue is highly charged, given long-standing debates on the modularity versus generality of human mentality itself.

Arguments are beginning to favor the view that the cognitive changes involved generalized or at least interconnected mechanisms. These are based on the shared clusters of abilities that co-occur or are interdependent with true imitation. We earlier discussed self-recognition, pretense, and planning as a shared cluster representing higher level imitative abilities, for which threshold level true imitation is both a developmental precursor and a prerequisite. Parker (1996) pointed to co-occurrence and interdependencies among true imitation, self-awareness, demonstration teaching, and intelligent tool use (see also Mitchell, 1994a) and suggested this represents an integrated complex of social and ecological cognitive abilities that constitute an apprenticeship system. Demonstration teaching relies on learners' abilities for imitative learning, and involves greater cognitive and motivational complexity than true imitation, so Parker argued that it probably emerges developmentally and phylogenetically out of high level imitative abilities of true imitation, pretense, and complementary role-taking. Others (Gallup, 1982; Whiten & Byrne, 1991) link a modified cluster with true imitation, primarily comprised of social cognitive abilities—pretense, mindreading, and more tentatively, complex tool use, self-recognition, and insight.

These are among the first attempts to consider the cognitive mechanisms underlying primate true imitation in view of ability clusters. Given that the cluster of abilities linked with true imitation extends beyond those currently specified in any one model and it may well expand, further efforts along these lines promise important insights. At this point, they suggest that the cognitive evolution that afforded true imitation involved some larger package. This moves discussion to the broader arena of the evolution of primate cognition itself and changes the question to what sorts of evolutionary changes to cognition are entailed by the shared cognitive package—one that spans a broad range of abilities and multiple levels of cognitive complexity.

Before even touching on any such enterprise as it concerns true imitation, several limitations to narrowly cognitive reconstructions should be addressed. First, cognition may not be the master key to understanding the evolution of true imitation that has been presumed. True imitation may occur in species not noted for their intellect, such as nonmimid avians, and it can depend on mechanisms other than cognition like affect, motivation, social relations, memory, and perception. Psychology's focus on the cognitive processes of imitation has channeled attention away from these other mechanisms, although the evolution of true imitation could have been equally critically affected by changes to them. Second, several scenarios for the cognitive evolution of true imitation have been proposed and choosing among them may require weighing other evidence, like the selection pressures that could have given rise to true imitation or the role of noncognitive processes. Consideration of key selection pressures is also important in broader comparative perspective. If the capacity for true imitation is analogous rather than homologous across species, understanding its evolution likely lies with similarities in ecological and/or social selection pressures. Third, some emphasize that cognitive development is grounded in experience, with true imitation especially bound up in social practices of enculturation (e.g., Miles et al., 1996; Tomasello, Kruger, & Ratner, 1993). In light of these concerns, we consider three other factors potentially involved in the evolution of true imitation—perception, then social and ecological selection pressures—before returning to the issue of cognitive evolution.

Perception. If cognitive mechanisms appear to have been subject to important evolutionary modification, so do perceptual ones (e.g., Mitchell, 1994a). Perceptual products form the basis on which cognitive processes act, so evolutionary modifications to them may underpin changed cognition.

The extent to which perceptual processes may underlie the species distribution of imitative abilities is a relatively neglected issue. There are hints to their significance in the developmental patterns of human imitation (e.g., Guillaume, 1926/1971; Piaget, 1945/1962). Piaget's notion of decalage, for instance, points to the potential for cognitive structures associated with different perceptual, or sensorimotor, modalities to develop at different rates; in imitating, children may be competent in imitating motor activities at an earlier age than vocalizations (Piaget, 1945/1962). The phenomenon of neonatal matching is also significant. Although much disputed, arguments that humans show cross-modal matching as neonates have garnered considerable support. If they hold up, they imply that precognitive mechanisms that afford cross-modal matching are in place prior to the cognitive abilities commonly considered necessary to effect cross-modal matching.

Variability in imitative sophistication associated with perceptual modality is more pronounced in nonhuman species. For instance, compared with humans, nonhuman primate auditory imitation is either absent or less well developed, whereas (at least in great apes) motor imitation follows a similar developmental course (Dore & Dumas, 1987); the opposite is true in avian species (Moore, 1992). Mitchell's (1994a, 1995a) reviews suggest several evolutionary step-like changes in the influence of perceptual modality on imitative sophistication (Table 6.2).

Imitation in a single perceptual modality, especially kinesthetic–kinesthetic or auditory–auditory matching, occurs in many nonhuman species. Mammals are adept at kinesthetic–kinesthetic matching in that they readily reproduce their own previous actions contingent on predictable circumstances. Primates are especially adept at voluntarily reproducing their own previous actions outside normal circumstances so as to induce their predictable consequences, or self-simulation. For instance, primates feign limping to induce sympathy (Byrne & Whiten, 1988; Mitchell & Thompson, 1986; so do some dogs—Mitchell, 1994a). Auditory–auditory matching is common in birds and nonhuman primates (e.g., vervets, chimpanzees), again as self-simulation; common examples are false alarm calls. In all of this self-simulation, actors engage in what could be interpreted as self-pretense and deception: They act as though doing one thing while actually doing some-

TABLE 6.2
The Evolution of Simulation

Evolutionary Steps	Evidence	Organisms
1a self-simulation to influence others (kinesthetic–kinesthetic matching)	deceptive self-pretense	birds, mammals
b self-simulation to influence others (auditory–auditory matching)	false alarm calls	birds, vervets chimpanzees
c recognition of simulation of others' actions or of objects (visual–visual matching)	skepticism	birds, mammals
	use of mirrors to locate objects	monkeys, great apes, humans
2a simulation of others' activities (kinesthetic–visual matching)	imitation of others	monkeys (?) great apes humans
	pretend play	great apes humans
b use of internal or external props for oneself (kinesthetic–visual matching)	imitative play	monkeys (?) great apes humans
	planning	great apes humans
	insightful tool use	great apes humans
c recognition of self (kinesthetic–visual matching)	mirror self-recognition	great apes humans
	recognition of others' imitation of self	great apes humans
d use of props for others (kinesthetic–visual matching)	teaching with objects	great apes humans

thing else, to deceive others for personal gain. This amounts to a constrained use of pretense for deception in nonhuman species; it contrasts with the unconstrained use of pretense in human activities. It suggests that pretense evolved initially for deceptive social manipulation and it became independent of this narrow function in the great apes and then more extensively in humans, perhaps with the prolongation of ontogeny.

Imitation within the visual modality, or visual–visual matching, occurs when individuals recognize others' actions as simulations. As such, visual–visual matching probably represents a later evolutionary step. Probably many nonhuman primates can recognize others' simulations, although little attention has been given to this issue. Existing evidence shows that great apes, like humans, recognize when a partner could be self-simulating and respond with distrust, counterdeception, or inhibition of their own responses (e.g., Menzel, 1973). The sign-language trained orangutan, Chantek, recognized when his caregivers used self-simulation to deceive him and attempted to verify their actions. Some dogs also show this capacity; they can inhibit chasing a ball until their owners actually throw it, if their owners previously faked throwing. Some primates can recognize some artifactual simulations in that they can use mirror or video images of items to locate the real items. Great apes show this capacity at sophisticated levels: Chimpanzees were almost as good at finding a caregiver who disappeared in a familiar area from video records of the disappearance as they were from direct observation. Their capacities do not, however, achieve the sophistication found in humans. Chimpanzees have difficulty with three dimensional models and only some recognize objects in photographs whereas children 2½ years old can recognize spatial models as representations of something else on the basis of similarities between the model and what it represents (although difficulties can intrude on their recognition) (see Mitchell, 1994a, for details).

Imitation between modalities, especially matching between the visual and the kinesthetic (matching what was observed with motor behavior), appears to have evolved rarely. Species adept at simulating their own actions, including nonhuman primates, are not necessarily good at simulating what they see others do—they may not be able to match their visual with their kinesthetic experience. Mitchell and Anderson (1993) tried to train a long-tailed macaque to imitate a human model's scratching by rewarding him when he scratched at the same time and place as the model did; the macaque never succeeded. Reports of kinesthetic–visual matching in conspecific-reared monkeys are likewise rare. One possible example is that of the female rhesus monkey who carried a coconut shell the same way she saw a mother carry her baby (Breuggeman, 1973). Kinesthetic–visual matching is more common in great apes. Juvenile captive chimpanzees, for example, imitated the crooked gait of a misshapen female and the limping gait of an injured male (de Waal, 1982); and a wild adolescent male imitated, three times in succession, a favorite older male's display of "vigorous leaping and jumping from branch to branch ... [after which he] jumped down to the ground and slapstamped down-slope." (Plooij, 1978, pp. 128–129). It is still less common than in humans.

Where kinesthetic–visual matching has evolved, it appears to have important consequences for psychosocial and cognitive development. It suggests a complex intersensory form of integration (Abravanel, 1981) that co-occurs with and may be a prerequisite to all the high level imitative abilities (Mitchell, 1995a). Motor imitative learning requires the ability for kinesthetic–visual matching because it involves the learner's generating motor patterns on the basis of visual information alone. The imitator must have mechanisms for translating visual input into kinesthetic patterns and the reverse in order to establish matches—that is, to know what its own actions look like. Pretense and planning likewise imply the ability to translate back and forth between the visual-like image of oneself and the kinesthetically based movements of one's own bodily actions needed to enact the plan. Although many of the mechanisms involved may be cognitive, these patterns suggest that some may well be noncognitive.

Evolutionary Mechanisms: Selection and Function

Lefebvre's work underscores the importance of an ecological approach to reconstructing the evolution of true imitation. The ecological approach is particularly valuable in guiding comparative research because its theoretical framework is solidly based in evolutionary biology and behavioral ecology (Bednekoff, Balda, Kamil, & Hile, 1997; Kamil, 1988; Shettleworth, 1993; Yoerg, 1991). It is certainly preferable to either the haphazard choice of species or a narrowly anthropocentric framework haunted by the ghost of the 19th century *scala naturae* approach to comparative cognition. Given that true imitation may be distributed across species that are not closely related, the ecological approach may offer one of the few avenues to establishing general comparative principles associated with its evolution. Consideration of the selection pressures that could have shaped the evolution of true imitation and the corresponding function(s) it evolved to serve may also clarify the cognitive evolution that would have been involved.

There have been some attempts to incorporate ecological selection pressures into evolutionary reconstructions of true imitation. Evidence suggests three general ecological factors that may have been influential in the evolution of true imitation: Opportunistic-generalist versus conservative-specialist lifestyles (Klopfer, 1961), scramble versus interference competition (Dolman et al., 1996), and foraging pressures that select for complex motor techniques versus simpler ones (e.g., embedded foods vs. leaves or grains).

Such social and physical ecological factors could help explain the distribution of true imitation in species as diverse as great apes and nonmimid avians.

Social Ecology. That behavioral imitation is a social phenomenon has repeatedly been pointed out, only to be repeatedly overlooked. It is well accepted that human imitation should be viewed in the context of social interaction as well as of individual cognition: Social relationships are important motivators for imitation, and imitation often enhances social attunement (e.g., Bandura, 1971; Bruner, 1972; Yando et al., 1978). Meltzoff and Moore (1992), for instance, argued that early infant cross-modal imitation functions only in social communicative settings. The importance of social context should, if anything, increase for true imitation: Children's relationships with models likely increase in importance after about 9 months of age. Some argue that imitation evolved in humans to serve an interpersonal function as well as the better known learning one (Uzgiris, 1981; Yando et al., 1978).

The most commonly cited adaptive advantages of imitative behavior in the nonhuman world are also social, not physical, ones. Many nonhuman primates may hone innately guided signals to standard imitative forms and uses (e.g., Seyfarth, Cheney, & Marler, 1980; Tomasello, George, Kruger, Farrar, & Evans, 1985); wild bottlenose dolphins' signature whistles, which act as social identifiers, may derive from imitation (Sayigh et al., 1993); mimetic birds may use imitation in handling social encounters (Moore, 1992; Pepperberg, 1988); nonmimids may use it in the face of particular kinds of social competition (Lefebvre et al., 1996, 1997); and, as we argued earlier, pretense may have evolved for deceptive social manipulation. Imitation tends to enhance social communication and group harmony because of the value of standardization, but not physical world skills because they must be fine-tuned to physical, not social, conditions—they outdate rapidly, for instance, in changeable environments (e.g., Galef, 1992).

Likewise for true imitation, the advantages seem greatest in the context of sociality (Palameta & Lefebvre, 1985). In species capable of true imitation, social communication is an important adaptive dimension and social conditions are important motivationally (Boesch, 1993a, 1993b; Custance & Bard, 1994; Lefebvre et al., 1997; Moore, 1992; Pepperberg, 1988; Russon & Galdikas, 1995; Sayigh et al., 1993; Tyack, 1986). True imitation helps great apes, and perhaps dolphins and grackles, acquire physical world skills but it also contributes to the repertoire of social gestures and to social competition (Boesch, 1996; Moore, 1992; Sayigh et al., 1993; Tayler & Saayman, 1973); and the Grey parrot's true imitation appeared to concern social display (although it was not used socially) and have nothing to do with the physical environment.

For great apes and Grey parrots, some basis exists for reconstructing the social platform on which true imitation evolved because the imitative abilities of related species are relatively well studied. Social learning that generates imitative behavior, complex social interactions like coalitions and deceptive self-pretense, and elaborate social structures occur in many Old World monkey species (e.g., Byrne & Whiten, 1988; Huffman, 1984; Itani & Nishimura, 1973; Mitchell & Thompson, 1986; Nishida, 1987). Likewise, other avian mimids use mimicry and social learning (Moore, 1992). True imitation may then have evolved in lineages where sociality and social learning, with the attendant value of social communication and of matching others' behavior, were critical precursors.

The centrality of sociality in true imitation is consistent with one influential hypothesis about cognitive evolution, that complex cognition evolved to handle social complexity. The hypothesis follows from arguments that animal communication signals may have been selected for manipulating others to the signaller's advantage rather than for honest information transfer; this would in turn pressure dupes to enhance their abilities to uncover the honest information behind the misleading signals, or to mindread. These arguments apply across animal species and mindreading becomes the ultimate cognitive prize issuing from these spiraling evolutionary pressures (e.g., Krebs & Dawkins, 1984; Whiten, 1996; Whiten & Byrne, 1991). This hypothesis then has potential for explaining primate (and perhaps dolphin) true imitation (e.g., Byrne & Whiten, 1988; Jolly, 1966; Humphrey, 1976; Kummer, 1982; Marino et al., 1994). Mindreading is a constituent of the cognitive ability clusters linked to primate true imitation, and other constituents are also prominently social abilities—self-awareness, pretense, self–other representation, and complementary role-taking (see Mitchell, 1993a, 1994a; Parker, 1996; Whiten, 1996; Whiten & Byrne, 1991).

A strictly social scenario for the evolution of true imitation, at least in primates, is not without difficulties. (1) The social intelligence view ties true imitation to integrating self with other representations (e.g., representing the demonstrator's representation, translated into one's own perspective—Whiten, 1996), but some argue that true imitation operates perfectly well on the basis of reading overt behavior (e.g., Heyes, 1993; Mitchell, 1993a, 1993b). It also emerges too early in ontogeny to enlist such processes. (2) The social view offers little help in explaining the gap in imitative capacity between great apes and other nonhuman primates (e.g., Byrne, 1997) because evolutionary change is ascribed to a sort of runaway social selection geared to outwitting social competitors. True imitation does offer a method *par excellence* for exploiting others' knowledge, but the social pattern associated with primate imitation, whatever cognitive mechanisms govern it, is affiliative or cooperative imitator–demonstrator relationships—preferred demonstrators are mothers, high-ranking group members, then siblings and peer playmates (e.g., Boesch, 1993a, 1993b; Huffman, 1984; Russon & Galdikas, 1995; Yando et al., 1978). There are no evident differences in this pattern between great apes and other nonhuman primates, or between great apes and humans for that matter. Other key social parameters like group size, philopatry, or social structure likewise offer little guidance (e.g., Byrne, 1997; Parker & Russon, 1996). (3) The ability cluster tied to primate true imitation includes enhanced nonsocial abilities like the sophisticated use and manufacture of tools, which are handled by causal and logico-mathematical cognition. A social scenario for the evolution of true imitation has to explain enhancements to these physical world abilities as side-effects of enhanced social cognition; this is hard to reconcile with the view that they underpin great apes' solutions to their mounting technical problems, especially their foraging skills (Byrne, 1997; Byrne & Byrne, 1991, 1993; McGrew, 1992; Parker & Gibson, 1977, 1979).

Physical Ecology. Promising, then, is Parker's (1996) apprenticeship model that associates the evolution of primate true imitation with the physical pressures of a difficult feeding niche, embedded foods. Embedded foods demand complex foraging skills. Prolonging ontogeny improves the conditions for acquiring them. Prolonged ontogeny is one of several life history parameters (e.g., life span, body and brain size, age at weaning/puberty/first reproduction) that do differentiate great apes and humans from other nonhuman primates. Prolonging ontogeny in primates also, however, intensifies parental dependency; some suggest the hominoid prolongation of ontogeny was punishing to mothers, interfering with further reproduction (Gibson, 1986; Parker & Gibson, 1977, 1979). Orangutans, the extreme example, remain semidependent until they are strapping juveniles 7 or 8 years old and interbirth intervals exceed 7 years (Galdikas & Wood, 1990). The apprenticeship complex, which includes true imitation, may have evolved to relieve maternal burdens by boosting offsprings' acquisition of the tool-assisted extractive foraging techniques they need to achieve independence in this feeding niche. Notably, demonstration teaching entails mindreading but more in the spirit of cooperative and truthful communication than of competition and deceit; and great apes attain true imitation at the onset of juvenility as the most complex facets of foraging skills are likely being acquired.

THE COGNITIVE EVOLUTION OF TRUE IMITATION REVISITED: THE EVOLUTION OF GREAT APE COGNITION

In light of these potential contributors to the evolution of true imitation, we revisit its cognitive evolution in primates. To recap, our review dates its emergence in the great ape–human (hominoid) ancestor. Evolutionary selection pressures probably include a combination of social and ecological pressures, the latter likely associated with the hominoid feeding niche. Lively debates surround the particulars and balance of these pressures but tend to hold to the premise that greater behavioral flexibility by way of enhanced cognition was the focus of evolutionary change, not just a fortuitous side effect (e.g., Byrne, 1997; Byrne & Whiten, 1988; Gibson, 1993c; Parker, 1996; Povinelli & Cant, 1992). By the most recent common hominoid ancestor, cognitive mechanisms differentiating them from other nonhuman primates were generalized or at least broad reaching, affording a package of interrelated abilities with true imitation as a pivotal constituent. In this case, unraveling the cognitive evolution of true imitation entails understanding the cognitive evolution of the whole package—by no means a settled issue. With no intent to resolve this issue in a few short paragraphs, we sketch some current views.

If great ape cognitive abilities constitute a package, the search logically turns to general purpose cognitive mechanisms that could generate the lot. This premise is implicitly already in place: Evolutionary reconstructions of primate true imitation (social intelligence, apprenticeship) are modifications of hypotheses originally designed to explain, respectively, the evolution of primate and of human cognitive systems. Suggestions for such general purpose cognitive mechanisms stem mainly from constructionist views that model human cognitive abilities, up to rudimentary symbolic levels, as developmental products of a suite of relatively generalized cognitive processes (e.g., Case, 1985; Langer, 1980, 1986; Piaget, 1954). Two have been identified as likely foci of evolutionary change, hierarchical mental construction and structural integration (e.g., Gibson, 1993c; Langer, 1994, 1996). Hierarchical mental construction involves keeping several cognitive units in mind concurrently, combining them into new, higher-order units, then embedding new units as subunits in further cognitive compositions. Integration is an organizational term covering the notion that cognitive achievements are made through interplay among different types of cognitions—that is, relatively independent sets of special purpose cognitive structures, like language, causal cognition, and logical cognition.

Hierarchical mental construction entails combinatorial and recursive mechanisms. Combinatorial mechanisms handle multiple mental items at a time, combining and recombining several together into ensembles (e.g., Gibson, 1993d). Recursion involves taking the products of cognition and piping them back as input—that is, applying cognition to existing cognitions, not just to direct sensorimotor experience (e.g., Langer, 1993). It generates hierarchization, in which more complex cognitions take the form of higher level ones built on the basis of compositions of lower ones. These two mechanisms could be central to great ape cognition because they support complex sequencing of behavior (e.g., Calvin, 1993; Gibson & Ingold, 1993). Long sequences requiring unitary processing strain combinatorial capacity, so increasing the latter boosts cognitive capacity. Hierarchization offers a way of reducing combinatorial load: By generating fewer high-level mental items in place of many original ones, it reduces the number of items to be processed concurrently. This fits great apes. They use long, complex sequences of behavior in food processing techniques and social strategies (e.g., Boesch & Boesch, 1984; Byrne & Byrne, 1991, 1993; de Waal, 1982; Menzel, 1973; Russon & Galdikas, 1994) and their complex abilities seem to be built on the basis of simpler ones (e.g., Gibson, 1993c; Jolly, 1972; Langer, 1993; Mitchell, 1987; Parker & Gibson, 1979, 1990; Whiten & Byrne, 1991).

Comparative evidence is consonant with the hypothesis that these two mechanisms could have been foci of the evolutionary changes resulting in the cognition found in great apes (e.g., Antinucci, 1989; Case, 1985; Langer, 1980, 1986; Spinozzi, 1993). Combinatorial abilities are found in monkeys, great apes, and humans and likely underlie their developing rather similar basic cognitive abilities (Langer, 1996). Monkeys' combinatorial capacities appear very limited in comparison with humans', and great apes' appear to lie between the two—more extensive than monkeys' but less so than humans' and developing at an intermediate rate.

The hierarchization central to human cognitive development is not hailed as a feature of monkey cognition—hailed, if anything, is its absence (e.g., Anderson, 1996; Byrne, 1997; Langer, 1993; Visalberghi & Limongelli, 1996). Increasing numbers of scholars are arguing for its centrality in the great ape cognitive package. Whiten and Byrne (1991; Whiten, 1996) argued that all the constituent abilities rest on secondary representation, the mental representation of other mental representations. Russon (1995) argued that great ape imitative learning may commonly operate at the level of secondary rather than primary representation, and Byrne (1994; Byrne & Byrne, 1991, 1993), that great ape true imitation is hierarchically organized. Langer (1996) argued for hierarchization in great apes' causal and logico-mathematical cognition, both of which are linked to true imitation (Russon, 1995, 1996; Visalberghi, 1993).

The integration characterizing human cognition may likewise owe to two mechanisms, hierarchization plus developmental synchronization. Developmental synchronization constitutes yoking developmental progress across different types of cognition (e.g., logical and causal—Langer, 1993). Humans' increased cognitive capacity has been linked to its integration. Many problems are best solved, or only solvable, by the interaction of different types of cognitive ability rather than one type alone; and distinct abilities can advance if they can exploit other abilities (e.g., the logical ability of classification can be extended by classifying by causal utility—Langer, 1993). Great apes evidence some cognitive integration: They can substitute tools or create logically ordered tool sets, for example (e.g., McGrew, 1992; Russon, 1996). Hierarchization is essential to integration because the latter involves combining cognitions themselves. Synchronization may play a more subtle role.

Synchronization is one of several possible patterns of evolutionary change to developmental timing collectively called heterochrony (Gould, 1977; McKinney & McNamara, 1991). Heterochrony constitutes altering onset and termination of developmental events; according to their pattern, this can change developmental rates (retardation or acceleration) or organization (the timing of developmental events or of structural developments relative to one another). A well known example is neotony, the slowing of developmental rates, which results in preservation of juvenile features. Langer (1996) considered that organizational heterochronies are major mechanisms of cognitive evolution. They disrupt established relations among a number of generalized processes that orchestrate development, like growth, differentiation, centralization, and hierarchic integration; the new relations established likely induce cascading changes to ontogeny and its resulting cognitive products. Synchronization provides the best of the timing patterns possible for cognitive integration by setting the most favorable conditions for cognitive interaction (Langer, 1993, 1994, 1996). Diverse types of cognition can then develop on a common experiential base; this offers a bridge between normally segregated cognitive structures that promotes interplay between them.

The synchronization hypothesis is founded on recent comparative evidence. Humans show developmental synchrony: They begin building causal and logical cognitive abilities at about the same age in infancy and advance in both at a similar pace (e.g., Langer, 1993). Monkeys show asynchrony: They begin building causal cognition early in infancy, but they achieve their most advanced causal abilities before they even begin building rudimentary logical ones (Antinucci, 1989; Langer, 1993, 1996). Chimpanzees' cognitive development appears more synchronized than monkeys' but less than humans' (Langer, 1996; Poti', 1997; Spinozzi, 1993). They retain a lag in the onset of logical relative to causal cognition but begin building logical abilities while their causal development is still ongoing. This temporal overlap in development supports cognitive integration through the common experiential basis it provides, but the support is weaker than that afforded by synchrony because it comes available only relatively late in development and when the abilities involved are out of phase with one other (Langer, 1996).

These three—combinatorial mechanisms, recursion, synchronization—appear to be distinct, complementary, and plausible. This opens the possibility that great ape cognitive evolution involved a suite of changes. How these changes were orchestrated between the original and the most recent common hominoid ancestor—that is, between hominoid divergence from the haplorhine stem and its differentiation into what became the modern great apes and humans—is as yet virtually unchartable because there are no living descendants stemming from this period. Some clarity can be gained by factoring in the brain and possible interplay among the three.

Evolutionary increases to combinatorial capacity merely entail incrementation because great apes evolved from a line already endowed with combinatorial mechanisms. Even a small increase in the number of items that can be combined in a single composition could substantially increase combinatorial capacity because its effect on the size and range of compositions is multiplicative. Gibson (1993c) considered evolutionary changes to the neocortex that could subserve this incrementation. Combinatorial capacity should increase with the numbers of cortical processing units possessed and capable of firing in parallel; these increase with the absolute size of neocortical association areas, which in turn increases with absolute brain size. Great apes have larger brains and neocortices than other nonhuman primates but smaller ones than humans (e.g., Stephan, Frahm, & Baron, 1981), neatly jibing with their increased but intermediate combinatorial capacity.

At least one reading of current evidence, however, is that great ape cognition is not reasonably explained by evolutionary changes in the absolute size of the brain or the neocortex (Byrne, 1997). Great ape brains are not notably larger than those of lesser apes and monkeys when considered in relation to their body size, nor do they show relatively any greater investment in neocortex tissue compared to the rest of their brain volume (Deacon, 1990; Dunbar, 1992; Gibson, 1996). This weighs against investment in brain size as the main evolutionary mechanism for increasing great apes' mental capacity (Byrne, 1997). The alternative is reorganization of the brain; this is consistent with hierarchization and synchronization insofar as their effects owe to reorganization more than to size.

Hierarchization ushers in symbolic thought, one of the most venerable of our sacred cognitive cows. That it may have appeared in hominoids rather than in hominids does not detract from its importance as a landmark in cognitive evolution. It is also, currently, the most often singled out as the key mechanism underpinning great apes' cognitive capacities. An evolutionary move to hierarchization in concert with a boost to combinatorial capacity might account for many of the cognitive abilities newly apparent in great apes—if, as some propose, a level of hierarchical integration generates a major stage-like increase in capacity and compositions of the new, higher level cognitions generate further substage-like increments (e.g., Case, 1985). Great apes' higher abilities, including imitative ones, all represent cognition in the secondary range, beyond threshold but not to advanced levels (e.g., Byrne, 1995; Gibson & Ingold, 1993; Langer, 1993; Premack, 1988; Russon et al., 1996).

Comparative evidence for sychronization as an evolutionary mechanism shaping great ape cognition is as yet very limited (Langer, 1996). It reflects few primate species, few nonhuman primate subjects, and nonhuman primates reared in atypical conditions; among them, the great apes are the least well studied. The findings show developmental overlap between great apes' causal and logical cognition only due to displaced offset—causal development continues after logical development starts. This could result from extending causal development via hierarchization. Evidence for synchronization as a separate mechanism would require an explicit shift in causal-logical developmental timing—that is, displaced onset of logical relative to causal cognition. This can be seen between monkeys and humans but it is not yet clear between monkeys and great apes. Further, synchronization fosters cognitive progress only at hierarchical levels: It promotes interaction between cognitions, an impossibility at sensorimotor levels, and monkeys master sensorimotor cognition without it. Finally, hierarchization appears possible without synchronization: It can proceed within the bounds of a single type of cognition (e.g., Langer, 1993, 1996); and great apes achieve hierarchization under conditions of imperfect synchrony and without evidence of explicit synchronization. Developmental synchronization as an evolutionary mechanism may then have arisen after hierarchization, perhaps after hominid divergence. Hierarchization may have occasioned the initial temporal overlap, perhaps as a side effect, that later evolutionary changes capitalized on.

Beyond these three evolutionary mechanisms, it is likely that others also came into play. Pre-cognitive perceptual changes to a common hominoid ancestor, like visual–kinesthetic matching, may have altered the whole of cognitive development. The case is also growing for organizational heterochronies other than synchronization that could affect great ape cognition, in the form of ontogenetic displacements in the sensorimotor period. One example is the timing of voluntary motor control relative to sensorimotor development (e.g., independent locomotion, prehension—Antinucci, 1989; Poti' & Spinozzi, 1994); this is an important gateway to cognitive progress because of the increased range of manipulation it affords. Displacements also occur in the timing of cognitive achievements relative to one other and to major life periods. Great apes and humans progress through lower sensorimotor levels more slowly than monkeys but through higher ones more rapidly; humans in turn progress more slowly, then more rapidly, than great apes (e.g., Chevalier-Skolnikoff, 1983; Doré & Dumas, 1987; Mathieu & Bergeron, 1981; Russon, 1990). Age at attaining highest cognitive capacity is also displaced: upper sensorimotor level, from juvenility in monkeys to infancy in great apes, and upper secondary level, from late juvenility in great apes to early juvenility in humans (e.g., Parker & Poti', 1990; Schiller, 1952; Visalberghi & Limongelli, 1996). These changes affect the experiential basis of development as well as the mental mechanisms available to tap it, and so its cognitive products.

This evidence has implications for the form of evolutionary change that engendered great ape cognition, including true imitation. Early models proposed terminal addition because great apes' cognitive capacity surpasses levels previously attained. The material reviewed here suggests that these models may be simplistic. Terminal addition may describe the most evident cognitive products of these evolutionary changes but it does not span the range of mental changes induced nor of the mental mechanisms that likely generated them. A possible exception is hierarchization: Although it represents a central constructive mechanism rather than a cognitive product, it resembles terminal addition because it appears to add a mechanism at the end of cognitive development to take cognition beyond the sensorimotor ceiling. Evidence weighs more strongly toward the view that great apes' enhanced cognition owes to evolutionary changes to mechanisms operative earlier in ontogeny that provide the foundations to sustain extended cognitive construction and channel its progress (e.g., Gibson, 1993d).

CONCLUSION

This review leaves an image of imitation as a heterogeneous rather than a homogeneous phenomenon; even mentally, and in only one of the three evolutionary lines that appear to have generated it, it appears to operate via complex sets of mechanisms that incorporate cognitive, motivational, social, and perceptual processes. True imitation, the focus of most evolutionary reconstructions to date, is itself heterogeneous. It occurs at multiple cognitive levels and it likely derives from diverse processes, given the range of species that exhibit it. In its various manifestations, it seems to serve an ensemble of purposes, sometimes ecological but more commonly social. This makes it likely that true imitative abilities commonly evolved from a platform of complex sociality, in response to diverse clusters of ecological pressures. The associated evolutionary changes to the brain probably affected imitation via several of its component processes, among them perceptual and cognitive ones. Several distinct evolutionary changes may have been involved, for instance, perceptual and social ones that preceded cognitive ones, and perhaps several cognitive ones. It is likely that these changes occurred in different patterns and clusters in the diverse species lines that share apparently similar capacities for high level imitation. It seems unlikely that any single explanation can account for the evolution of high level imitation.

It must be kept in mind that extant methods, evidence, and models still offer only glimmerings of the evolution of imitation. Methodologically, we need procedures to remove confounding variables from interspecific tests— among others, controls for the effects of species differences in neophobia and general learning, tasks that test predictable imitative and confounding differences between species, and interpretations based on species-by-task interactions rather than simple species effects (Lefebvre & Giraldeau, 1996). Theoretically, we need a conceptual framework that more clearly delimits forms of imitation of potential evolutionary significance and we need to incorporate ecological, social, and non-cognitive frameworks in addition to cognitive ones in making predictions about qualitative and quantitative differences in imitation between species. Appropriate methods and models are obvious prerequisites to building a valid and representative corpus of evidence; all are still sorely lacking. Even in the primates, a key order, few species of monkeys have been systematically studied concerning imitation, little is known of the lesser apes, and data on great apes are far from comprehensive. Revitalized interest in the comparative evolutionary study of imitation, increased recognition of the complexities involved, and increased attention to social learning, the set of processes encompassing true imitation and its neglected simpler forms, all offer hope that we will yet make further inroads in teasing out a coherent picture (e.g., Box, 1984; Heyes & Galef, 1996; Zentall & Galef, 1988).

In looking for the cognitive roots of true imitation, at least in the primates, it seems to make more sense to frame the search not in terms of a distinct ability but in terms of the much broader realm of species' levels and ways of understanding. True imitation constitutes creating resemblances, where resemblances derive from observers' representations of behavioral phenomena constructed without direct experience. This depends on the sorts of mental representations observers can create and their abilities to reuse them in other cognitions—a function of the broader cognitive system, not of imitation alone. True imitation may still be best construed as simply imitation, the creating of resemblances; it may differ mainly in having access to more powerful and more generalized systems of cognition.

REFERENCES

Abravanel, E. (1981). Integrating the information from eyes and hands: A developmental account. In R. D. Walk & H. L. Pick (Eds.), *Intersensory perception and sensory integration* (pp. 71–105). New York: Plenum.

Abravanel, E. (1991). Does immediate imitation influence long-term memory for observed actions? *Journal of Experimental Child Psychology, 51*, 235–244.

Abravanel, E., Ferguson, S., & Vourlekis, D. (1993). Observing and imitating the formation of object classes during the second year of life. *Canadian Journal of Experimental Psychology, 47*, 477–492.

Abravanel, E., & Gingold, H. (1985). Learning via observation during the second year of life. *Developmental Psychology, 21*, 614–623.

Abravanel, E., Levan-Goldschmidt, E., & Stevenson, M. B. (1976). Action imitation: The early phase of infancy. *Child Development, 47*, 1032–1044.

Abravanel, E., & Sigafoos, A. D. (1984). Exploring the presence of imitation during early infancy. *Child Development, 5*, 381–392.

Anderson, J. R. (1996). Chimpanzees and capuchin monkeys: Comparative cognition. In A. E. Russon, K. A. Bard, & S. T. Parker (Eds.), *Reaching into thought: The minds of the great apes* (pp. 23–56). Cambridge, England: Cambridge University Press.

Anisfeld, M. (1991). Neonatal imitation. *Developmental Review, 11*, 60–97.

Antinucci, F. (Ed.). (1989). *Cognitive structure and development in nonhuman primates.* Hillsdale, NJ: Lawrence Erlbaum Associates.

Aronfreed, J. (1969). The problem of imitation. In L. P. Lipsitt & H. W. Reese (Eds.), *Advances in child development and behavior* (Vol. 4, pp. 210–306). New York: Academic Press.

Baldwin, J. M. (1894). *Mental development in the child and the race.* New York: Macmillan.

Bandura, A. (1971). Analysis of social modeling processes. In A. Bandura (Ed.), *Psychological modeling* (pp. 1–62). Chicago: Aldine-Atherton.

Bard, K. A. (1998). Social-experiential contributions to imitation and emotion in chimpanzees. In S. Brates (Ed.), *Intersubjective communication and emotion in ontogeny.*

Beck, B. B. (1980). *Animal tool behavior: The use and manufacture of tools by animals.* New York: Garland STPM Press.

Bednekoff, D. A., Balda, R. P., Kamil, A. C., & Hile, A. G. (1997). Long-term spatial memory in 4 seed-catching corvid species. *Animal Behaviour, 53*, 335–341.

Boesch, C. (1991). Teaching among wild chimpanzees. *Animal Behaviour, 41*, 530–532.

Boesch, C. (1993a). Towards a new image of culture in wild chimpanzees? *Behavioral and Brain Sciences, 16*, 514–515.

Boesch, C. (1993b). Aspects of transmission of tool-use in wild chimpanzees. In K. R. Gibson & T. Ingold (Eds.), *Tools, language, and cognition in human evolution* (pp. 171–183). Cambridge, England: Cambridge University Press.

Boesch, C. (1996). Three approaches for assessing chimpanzee culture. In A. E. Russon, K. A. Bard, & S. T. Parker (Eds.), *Reaching into thought: The minds of the great apes* (pp. 404–429). Cambridge, England: Cambridge University Press.

Boesch, C., & Boesch, H. (1984). Mental maps in wild chimpanzees: An analysis of hammer transports for nut cracking. *Primates, 25*, 160–170.

Box, H. D. (1984). *Primate behavior and social ecology.* London: Chapman & Hall.

Breuggeman, J. A. (1973). Parental care in a group of free-ranging rhesus monkeys (*Macaca mulatta*). *Folia Primatologica, 20*, 178–210.

Bruner, J. (1972). Nature and uses of immaturity. *American Psychologist, 19*, 1–15.

Byrne, R. W. (1994). The evolution of intelligence. In P. J. B. Slater & T. R. Halliday (Eds.), *Behaviour and evolution* (pp. 223–265). Cambridge, England: Cambridge University Press.

Byrne, R. W. (1995). *The thinking ape: Evolutionary origins of intelligence.* Oxford, England: Oxford University Press.

Byrne, R. W. (1997). The technical intelligence hypothesis: An alternative evolutionary stimulus to intelligence? In R. W. Byrne & A. Whiten (Eds.), *Machiavellian intelligence II: Extensions and evaluations* (pp. 289–311). Cambridge, England: Cambridge University Press.

Byrne, R. W., & Byrne, J. M. E. (1991). Hand preferences in the skilled gathering tasks of mountain gorillas (*Gorilla gorilla berengei*). *Cortex, 27*, 521–546.

Byrne, R. W., & Byrne, J. M. E. (1993). Complex leaf-gathering skills of mountain gorillas (*Gorilla g. berengei*): Variability and standardization. *American Journal of Primatology, 31*, 241–261.

Byrne, R. W., & Tomasello, M. (1995). Do rats ape? *Animal Behaviour, 50*, 1417–1420.

Byrne, R. W., & Whiten, A. (Eds.). (1988). *Machiavellian intelligence.* Oxford, England: Oxford University Press.

Call, J., & Tomasello, M. (1994). The social learning of tool use by orangutans (*Pongo pygmaeus*). *Human Evolution, 9*, 297–313.

Calvin, W. H. (1993). The unitary hypothesis: A common neural circuitry for novel manipulations, language, plan-ahead, and throwing? In K. R. Gibson & T. Ingold (Eds.), *Tools, language and cognition in human evolution* (pp. 230–250). Cambridge, England: Cambridge University Press.

Case, R. (1985). *Intellectual development: Birth to adulthood.* New York: Academic Press.

Chevalier-Skolnikoff, S. (1983). Sensorimotor development in orangutan and other primates. *Journal of Human Evolution, 12*, 545–561.

Custance, D., & Bard, K. A. (1994). The comparative and developmental study of self-recognition and imitation: The importance of social factors. In S. T. Parker, R. W. Mitchell, & M. L. Boccia (Eds.), *Self-awareness in animals and humans: Developmental perspectives* (pp. 207–226). Cambridge, England: Cambridge University Press.

Custance, D. M., Whiten, A., & Bard, K. A. (1994). The development of gestural imitation and self-recognition in chimpanzees. In J. J. Roeder, B. Thierry, J. R. Anderson, & N. Herrenschmidt (Eds.), *Current primatology: Selected proceedings of the XIVth Congress of the International Primatological Society, Strasbourg, Vol. 2: Social development, learning and behaviour* (pp. 381–387). Strasbourg: Université Louis Pasteur.

Custance, D., Whiten, A., & Bard, K. A. (1995). Can young chimpanzees imitate arbitrary actions? Hayes and Hayes (1952) revisited. *Behaviour, 132,* 839–858.

Darwin, C. (1871). *The descent of man and selection in relation to sex.* London: Murray.

Dawson, B. V., & Foss, B. M. (1965). Observational learning in budgerigars. *Animal Behaviour, 13,* 470–474.

de Waal, F. B. M. (1982). *Chimpanzee politics.* London: Jonathan Cape.

Deacon, T. W. (1990). Fallacies of progression in theories of brain-size evolution. *International Journal of Primatology, 11,* 193–236.

Dolman, C., Templeton, J., & Lefebvre, L. (1996). Mode of foraging competition is related to tutor preference in *Zenaida aurita. Journal of Comparative Psychology, 110,* 45–54.

Doré, F. Y., & Dumas, C. (1987). Psychology of animal cognition: Piagetian studies. *Psychological Bulletin, 102,* 219–233.

Dunbar, R. I. M. (1992). Neocortex size as a constraint on group size in primates. *Journal of Human Evolution, 20,* 469–493.

French, R. (1994). *Ancient natural history.* London: Routledge.

Galdikas, B., & Wood, J. W. (1990). Birth spacing in humans and apes. *Primates, 83,* 185–191.

Galef, B. G., Jr. (1988). Imitation in animals: History, definition, and interpretation of data from the psychological laboratory. In T. R. Zentall & B. G. Galef, Jr. (Eds.), *Social learning: Psychological and biological perspectives* (pp. 3–28). Hillsdale, NJ: Lawrence Erlbaum Associates.

Galef, B. G., Jr. (1992). The question of animal culture. *Human Nature, 3,* 157–178.

Gallup, G. G. (1977). Self-recognition in primates. *American Psychologist, 32,* 329–338.

Gallup, G. G. (1982). Self-awareness and the emergence of mind in primates. *American Journal of Primatology, 2,* 237–248.

Gibson, K. R. (1986). Cognition, brain size and extraction of embedded foods. In J. C. Else & P. C. Lee (Eds.), *Primate ontogeny and social behaviour* (pp. 93–105). New York: Cambridge University Press.

Gibson, K. R. (1993a). Animal minds, human minds. In K. R. Gibson & T. Ingold (Eds.), *Tools, language and cognition in human evolution* (pp. 3–19). Cambridge, England: Cambridge University Press.

Gibson, K. R. (1993b). Generative interplay between technical capacities, social relations, imitation and cognition. In K. R. Gibson & T. Ingold (Eds.), *Tools, language and cognition in human evolution* (pp. 131–137). Cambridge, England: Cambridge University Press.

Gibson, K. R. (1993c). Tool use, language and social behavior in relationship to information processing capacities. In K. R. Gibson & T. Ingold (Eds.), *Tools, language and cognition in human evolution* (pp. 251–269). Cambridge, England: Cambridge University Press.

Gibson, K. R. (1993d). Beyond neoteny and recapitulation: New approaches to the evolution of cognitive development. In K. R. Gibson, & T. Ingold (Eds.), *Tools, language and cognition in human evolution* (pp. 273–278). Cambridge, England: Cambridge University Press.

Gibson, K. R. (1996, August). *Monkey versus ape and human cognition: Implications of absolute brain size.* Symposium contribution to Ape mind, monkey mind (A. Whiten, organizer), XVIth Congress of the International Primatological Society, Madison.

Gibson, K. R., & Ingold, T. (Eds.). (1993). *Tools, language and cognition in human evolution.* Cambridge, England: Cambridge University Press.

Goodall, J. (1986). *The chimpanzees of Gombe: Patterns of behavior.* Cambridge, MA: Harvard University Press.

Gopnik, A. (1982). Words and plans: Early language and the development of intelligent action. *Journal of Child Language, 9,* 303–318.

Gopnik, A., & Meltzoff, A. N. (1994). Minds, bodies and persons: Young children's understanding of the self and others as reflected in imitation and theory of mind research. In S. T. Parker, R. W. Mitchell, & M. Boccia (Eds.), *Self-awareness in animals and humans: Developmental perspectives* (pp. 166–186). New York: Cambridge University Press.

Gould, S. J. (1977). *Ontogeny and phylogeny.* Cambridge, MA: Harvard University Press.

Green, S. (1975). Dialects in Japanese monkeys: Vocal learning and cultural transmission in locale-specific behaviour? *Zeitschrift fur Tierpsychologie, 38,* 304–314.

Greenberg, R. (1984). Differences in feeding neophobia in the tropical migrant warblers, *Dendroica castanea* and *D. pennsylvanica. Journal of Comparative Psychology, 98,* 131–136.

Greenberg, R. (1989). Neophobia, aversion to open space and ecological plasticity in Song and Swamp sparrows. *Canadian Journal of Zoology, 67,* 1194–1199.

Greenfield, P. M. (1991). Language, tools and the brain: The ontogeny and phylogeny of hierarchically organized sequential behavior. *Behavioral and Brain Sciences, 14,* 531–595.

Guillaume, P. (1926/1971). *Imitation in children* (2nd ed.). Chicago: University of Chicago Press.

Hart, D., & Fegley, S. (1994). Social imitation and the emergence of a mental model of the self. In S. T. Parker, R. W. Mitchell, & M. Boccia (Eds.), *Self-awareness in animals and humans: Developmental perspectives* (pp. 149–165). New York: Cambridge University Press.

Hauser, M. D. (1988). Invention and social transmission: New data from wild vervet monkeys. In R. W. Byrne & A. Whiten (Eds.), *Machiavellian intelligence* (pp. 327–343). Oxford, England: Clarendon.

Hayes, C. (1951). *The ape in our house.* New York: Harper & Brothers.

Hayes, K. J., & Hayes, C. (1952). Imitation in a home-reared chimpanzee. *Journal of Comparative Physiological Psychology, 45,* 450–459.

Herman, L. M. (Ed.). (1980). *Cetacean behavior, mechanisms and functions.* New York: Wiley.

Heyes, C. M. (1993). Imitation without perspective-taking. *Behavioral and Brain Sciences, 16,* 524–525.

Heyes, C. M., & Dawson, G. R. (1990). A demonstration of observational learning in rats using a bidirectional control. *Quarterly Journal of Experimental Psychology, 42B,* 59–71.

Heyes, C. M., & Dawson, G. R., & Nokes, T. (1992). Imitation in rats: Initial responding and transfer evidence. *Quarterly Journal of Experimental Psychology, 45B,* 229–240.

Heyes, C. M., & Galef, B. G., Jr. (Eds.). (1996). *Social learning in animals: The roots of culture.* New York: Academic Press.

Heyes, C. M., Jaldow, E., Nokes, T., & Dawson, G. R. (1994). Imitation in rats (*Rattus norvegicus*): The role of demonstrator action. *Behavioral Processes, 32,* 173–182.

Hilton, S. C., & Krebs, J. R. (1990). Spatial memory of four species of Parus: performance on an open field analogue of a radial maze. *Quarterly Journal of Experimental Psychology, 42B,* 345–368.

Huffman, M. A. (1984). Stone-play of *Macaca fuscata* in Arashiyama B troop: Transmission of a non-adaptive behavior. *Journal of Human Evolution, 13,* 725–735.

Humphrey, N. K. (1976). The social function of intellect. In P. P. G. Bateson & R. A. Hinde (Eds.), *Growing points in ethology* (pp. 303–317). Cambridge, England: Cambridge University Press.

Itani, J., & Nishimura, A. (1973). The study of infrahuman culture in Japan. In E. W. Menzel (Ed.), *Symposia of the Fourth International Congress of Primatology, Vol. 1: Precultural primate behavior* (pp. 26–50). Basel: S. Karger.

Jolly, A. (1966). Lemur social behaviour and primate intelligence. *Science, 153,* 501–506.

Jolly, A. (1972). *The evolution of primate behavior.* New York: Macmillan.

Kaitz, M., Meschulach-Sarfaty, O., Auerbach, J., & Eidelman, A. (1988). A re-examination of newborns' ability to imitate facial expressions. *Developmental Psychology, 24,* 3–7.

Kamil, A. C. (1988). A synthetic approach to the study of animal intelligence. In D. W. Leger (Ed.), *Comparative perpectives in modern psychology. Nebraska symposium on motivation* (Vol. 35, pp. 257–308). Lincoln: University of Nebraska Press.

Klopfer, P. H. (1961). Observational learning in birds: The establishment of behavioural modes. *Behaviour, 17,* 71–80.

Kohler, W. (1927). *The mentality of apes.* (E. Winter, trans., from 2nd rev. ed.). New York: Humanities Press.

Krebs, J. R., & Dawkins, R. (1984). Animal signals: Mind reading and manipulation. In J. R. Krebs & N. B. Davies (Eds.), *Behavioral ecology: An evolutionary approach* (2nd ed., pp. 340–401). Oxford, England: Blackwell Scientific.

Kummer, H. (1982). Social knowledge in free-ranging primates. In D. R. Griffin (Ed.), *Animal mind—Human mind* (pp. 113–130). New York: Springer-Verlag.

Langer, J. (1980). *The origins of logic: Six to twelve months.* New York: Academic Press.

Langer, J. (1986). *The origins of logic: One to two years.* New York: Academic Press.

Langer, J. (1993). Comparative cognitive development. In K. R. Gibson & T. Ingold (Eds.), *Tools, language and cognition in human evolution* (pp. 300–313). Cambridge, England: Cambridge University Press.

Langer, J. (1994). From acting to understanding: The comparative development of meaning. In W. F. Overton & P. Palermo (Eds.), *The nature and ontogenesis of meaning.* Hillsdale, NJ: Lawrence Erlbaum Associates.

Langer, J. (1996). Heterochrony and the evolution of primate cognitive development. In A. E. Russon, K. A. Bard, & S. T. Parker (Eds.), *Reaching into thought: The minds of the great apes* (pp. 257–277). Cambridge, England: Cambridge University Press.

Lawick-Goodall, J. van (1973). Cultural elements in a chimpanzee community. In E. Menzel (Ed.), *Precultural primate behavior* (pp. 144–184). New York: Karger.

Lefebvre, L. (1996). Ecological correlates of social learning: problems and solutions for the comparative method. *Behavior Processes, 35,* 163–171.

Lefebvre, L., & Giraldeau, L. A. (1996). Is social learning an adaptive specialization? In C. M. Heyes & B. G. Galef, Jr. (Eds.), *Social learning in animals: The roots of culture* (pp. 107–128). New York: Academic Press.

Lefebvre, L., Koelle, M., Brown, K., & Templeton, J. (1997). Carib grackles copy the motor variant used by their conspecific or Zenaida dove tutor. (in press).

Lefebvre, L., Palameta, B., & Hatch, K. K. (1996). Is group-living associated with social learning? A comparative test of a gregarious and a territorial Columbid. *Behaviour, 133,* 241–261.

MacPhail, E. M. (1982). *Brain and intelligence in vertebrates.* Oxford, England: Clarendon Press.

Marino, L., Reiss, D., & Gallup, G. G., Jr. (1994). Mirror self-recognition in bottlenose dolphins: Implications for comparative investigations of highly dissimilar species. In S. T. Parker, R. W. Mitchell, & M. L. Boccia (Eds.), *Self-awareness in animals and humans* (pp. 380–391). New York: Cambridge University Press.

Marten, K., & Psarakos, S. (1994). Evidence of self-awareness in the bottlenose dolphin (*Tursiops truncatus*). In S. T. Parker, R. W. Mitchell, & M. L. Boccia (Eds.), *Self-awareness in animals and humans* (pp. 361–379). New York: Cambridge University Press.

Marten, K., Shariff, K., Psarakos, S., & White, J. (1996). Ring bubbles of dolphins. *Scientific American, 275*(2), 83–87.

Mathieu, M., & Bergeron, G. (1981). Piagetian assessment on cognitive development in chimpanzee (*Pan troglodytes*). In A. B. Chiarelli & R. S. Corruccini (Eds.), *Primate behavior and sociobiology* (pp. 142–147). Berlin: Springer-Verlag.

Matsuzawa, T. (1994). Field experiments on use of stone tools by chimpanzees in the wild. In R. W. Wrangham, W. C. McGrew, F. B. M. de Waal, & P. G. Heltne (Eds.), *Chimpanzee cultures* (pp. 351–370). Cambridge, MA: Harvard University Press.

McGrew, W. C. (1992). *Chimpanzee material culture: Implications for human evolution.* Cambridge, England: Cambridge University Press.

McKinney, M. L., & McNamara, J. K. (1991). *Heterochrony: The evolution of ontogeny.* New York: Plenum.

Meinel, M., & Russon, A. E. (1996, August). Eliciting true imitation of object use in captive orangutans. Presented at XVIth Congress of the International Primatological Society, Madison.

Meltzoff, A. N. (1988a). Imitation, objects, tools, and the rudiments of language in human ontogeny. *Human Evolution, 3,* 45–64.

Meltzoff, A. N. (1988b). The human infant as *Homo imitans.* In T. Zentall & B. G. Galef, Jr. (Eds.), *Social learning: Psychological and biological perspectives* (pp. 319–341). Hillsdale, NJ: Lawrence Erlbaum Associates.

Meltzoff, A. N. (1996). The human infant as imitative generalist: A 20-year progress report on infant imitation with implications for comparative psychology. In B. G. Galef & C. M. Heyes (Eds.), *Social learning in animals: The roots of culture* (pp. 347–370). New York: Academic Press.

Meltzoff, A. N., & Moore, M. K. (1977). Imitation of facial and manual gestures by human neonates. *Science, 198,* 75–78.

Meltzoff, A. N., & Moore, M. K. (1992). Early imitation within a functional framework: The importance of person identity, movement, and development. *Infant Behavior and Development, 15,* 479–505.

Meltzoff, A. N., & Moore, M. K. (1994). Imitation, memory, and the representation of persons. *Infant Behavior and Development, 17,* 83–99.

Menzel, E. W., Jr. (1973). Leadership and communication in young chimpanzees. In E. W. Menzel, Jr. (Ed.), *Precultural primate behavior. Symposia of the Fourth International Congress of Primatology* (Vol. 1, pp. 192–225). Basel, Switzerland: Karger.

Miles, H. L., Mitchell, R. W., & Harper, S. (1996). Imitation, pretense and self-awareness in a signing orangutan. In A. E. Russon, K. A. Bard, & S. T. Parker (Eds.), *Reaching into thought: The minds of the great apes* (pp. 278–299). Cambridge, England: Cambridge University Press.

Mitchell, R. W. (1987). A comparative developmental approach to understanding imitation. In P. P. G. Bateson & P. H. Klopfer (Eds.), *Perspectives in ethology* (Vol. 7, pp. 183–215). New York: Plenum.

Mitchell, R. W. (1990). A theory of play. In M. Bekoff & D. Jamieson (Eds.), *Interpretation and explanation in the study of animal behavior* (Vol. 1, pp. 197–227). Boulder, CO: Westview Press.

Mitchell, R. W. (1991). Kinesthetic-visual matching, perspective taking and reflective self-awareness in cultural learning. *Behavioral and Brain Sciences, 16,* 530–531.

Mitchell, R. W. (1992). Developing concepts in infancy: Animals, self-perception, and two theories of mirror self-recognition. *Psychological Inquiry, 3,* 127–130.

Mitchell, R. W. (1993a). Mental models of mirror-self-recognition: Two theories. *New Ideas in Psychology, 11,* 295–325.

Mitchell, R. W. (1993b). Recognizing one's self in a mirror? A reply to Gallup and Povinelli, Anderson, de Lannoy, and Byrne. *New Ideas in Psychology, 11,* 351–377.

Mitchell, R. W. (1994a). Primate cognition: Simulation, self-knowledge, and knowledge of other minds. In D. Quiatt & J. Itani (Eds.), *Hominid culture in primate perspective* (pp. 177–232). Nivet: University Press of Colorado.

Mitchell, R. W. (1994b). Multiplicities of self. In S. T. Parker, R. W. Mitchell, & M. L. Boccia (Eds.), *Self-awareness in animals and humans* (pp. 81–107). New York: Cambridge University Press.

Mitchell, R. W. (1995a, June). *Imitation as a perceptual process.* Contribution to Imitation in comparative evolutionary perspective, invited symposium (A. Russon, organizer), 25th annual Symposium of the Jean Piaget Society, Berkeley, CA.

Mitchell, R. W. (1995b, May). *Bodily imitation, kinesthetic-visual matching, and animals.* Contribution to the invited symposium on Social learning and tradition in animals, 67th Annual Meeting of the Midwestern Psychological Association, Chicago.

Mitchell, R. W., & Anderson, J. R. (1993). Discrimination learning of scratching, but failure to obtain imitation and self-recognition in a long-tailed macaque. *Primates, 34,* 301–309.

Mitchell, R. W., & Thompson, N. S. (Eds.). (1986). *Deception: Perspectives on human and nonhuman deceit.* Albany: State University of New York Press.

Moerk, E. L. (1989). The fuzzy set called "imitations." In G. E. Speidel & K. E. Nelson (Eds.), *The many faces of imitation in language learning* (pp. 277–303). New York: Springer-Verlag.

Moore, B. R. (1992). Avian movement imitation and a new form of mimicry: Tracing the evolution of a complex form of learning. *Behaviour, 122,* 231–263.

Morgan, C. L. (1894). *An introduction to comparative psychology.* London: Walter Scott.

Morgan, C. L. (1900). *Animal behaviour.* London: Edward Arnold.

Morgane, P. J., Jacobs, M. S., & Galaburda, A. (1986). Evolutionary morphology of the dolphin brain. In R. J. Schusterman, J. A. Thomas, & F. G. Wood (Eds.), *Dolphin cognition and behavior: A comparative approach.* Hillsdale, NJ: Lawrence Erlbaum Associates.

Myoma, M. (1996). Imitation of facial gestures by an infant chimpanzee. *Primates, 37*(2), 207–213.

Nagell, K., Olguin, R. S., & Tomasello, M. (1993). Processes of social learning in the tool use of chimpanzees *(Pan troglodytes)* and human children *(Homo sapiens). Journal of Comparative Psychology, 107,* 174–186.

Nishida, T. (1987). Local traditions and cultural transmission. In S. Smuts, D. L. Cheney, R. M. Seyfarth, R. W. Wrangham, & T. T. Struhsaker (Eds.), *Primate societies* (pp. 462–474). Chicago: University of Chicago Press.

Norris, K. S. (1974). *The porpoise watcher.* New York: Norton.

Palameta, B. (1989). *The importance of socially transmitted information in the acquisition of novel foraging skills by pigeons and canaries.* Unpublished doctoral dissertation, Cambridge University.

Palameta, B., & Lefebvre, L. (1985). The social transmission of a food-finding technique in pigeons: What is learned? *Animal Behaviour, 33,* 892–896.

Paquette, D. (1992). Discovering and learning tool-use for fishing honey by captive chimpanzees. *Human Evolution, 7,* 17–30.

Parker, S. T. (1977). Piaget's sensorimotor series in an infant macaque: A model for comparing unstereotyped behavior and intelligence in human and nonhuman primates. In S. Chevalier–Skolnikoff & F. E. Poirier (Eds.), *Primate biosocial development* (pp. 43–112). New York: Garland Press.

Parker, S. T. (1991). A developmental approach to the origins of self-recognition in great apes. *Human Evolution, 6,* 435–449.

Parker, S. T. (1996). Apprenticeship in tool-mediated extractive foraging: Imitation, teaching and self-awareness in great apes. In A. E. Russon, K. A. Bard, & S. T. Parker (Eds.), *Reaching into thought: The minds of the great apes* (pp. 348–370). Cambridge, England: Cambridge University Press.

Parker, S. T., & Gibson, K. R. (1977). Object manipulation, tool use, and sensorimotor intelligence as feeding adaptation in cebus monkeys and great apes. *Journal of Human Evolution, 6,* 623–641.

Parker, S. T., & Gibson, K. R. (1979). A developmental model for the evolution of language and intelligence in early hominids. *Behavioral and Brain Sciences, 2,* 367–408.

Parker, S. T., & Gibson, K. R. (Eds.). (1990). *"Language" and intelligence in monkeys and apes: Comparative developmental perspectives.* New York: Cambridge University Press.

Parker, S. T., Mitchell, R. W., & Boccia, M. L. (Eds.). (1994). *Self-awareness in animals and humans.* New York: Cambridge University Press.

Parker, S. T., & Poti', P. (1990). The role of innate motor patterns in ontogenetic and experiential development of intelligent use of sticks in cebus monkeys. In S. T. Parker & K. R. Gibson (Eds.), *"Language" and intelligence in monkeys and apes* (pp. 219–246). New York: Cambridge University Press.

Parker, S. T., & Russon, A. E. (1996). On the wild side of culture and cognition in the great apes. In A. E. Russon, K. A. Bard, & S. T. Parker (Eds.), *Reaching into thought: The minds of the great apes* (pp. 430–450). Cambridge, England: Cambridge University Press.

Pepperberg, I. M. (1988). The importance of social interaction and observation in the acquisition of communicative competence: Possible parallels between avian and human learning. In T. R. Zentall & B. G. Galef, Jr. (Eds.), *Social learning: Psychological and biological perspectives* (pp. 279–300). Hillsdale, NJ: Lawrence Erlbaum Associates.

Piaget, J. (1945/1962). *Play, dreams, and imitation in childhood*. New York: Norton.

Piaget, J. (1954). *The construction of reality in the child*. New York: Basic Books.

Plooij, F. X. (1978). Some basic traits of language in wild chimpanzees? In A. Lock (Ed.), *Action, gesture, and symbol: The emergence of language* (pp. 111–131). London: Academic Press.

Poti', P. (1997). Logical structures of young chimpanzees' spontaneous object grouping. *International Journal of Primatology, 18*(1), 33–59.

Poti', P., & Spinozzi, G. (1994). Early sensorimotor development in chimpanzees. *Journal of Comparative Psychology, 108*(1), 93–103.

Povinelli, D. J., & Cant, J. G. H. (1992, August). *Orangutan clambering and the evolutionary origins of self-conception*. Presented at XIVth Congress of the International Primatological Society, Strasbourg.

Premack, D. (1988). "Does the chimpanzee have a theory of mind?" revisited. In R. W. Byrne & A. Whiten (Eds.), *Machiavellian intelligence* (pp. 160–179). Oxford, England: Clarendon.

Pryor, K. (1975). *Lads before the wind*. New York: Harper & Row.

Quine, W. V. (1969). *Ontological relativity and other essays*. New York: Columbia University Press.

Reynolds, P. C. (1982). The primate constructional system: The theory and description of instrumental tool use in humans and chimpanzees. In M. Van Cranach & R. Harré (Eds.), *The analysis of action: Recent theoretical and empirical advances* (pp. 343–385). Cambridge, England: Cambridge University Press.

Russon, A. E. (1990). The development of peer social interaction in infant chimpanzees: Comparative social, Piagetian, and brain perspectives. In S. T. Parker & K. R. Gibson (Eds.), *"Language" and intelligence in monkeys and apes* (pp. 379–419). Cambridge, England: Cambridge University Press.

Russon, A. E. (1995, June). *Aping imitation*. Contribution to Imitation in comparative evolutionary perspective, invited symposium. 25th annual Jean Piaget Society Symposium, Berkeley, CA.

Russon, A. E. (1996). Imitation in everyday use: Matching and rehearsal in the spontaneous imitation of rehabilitant orangutans (*Pongo pygmaeus*). In A. E. Russon, K. A. Bard, & S. T. Parker (Eds.), *Reaching into thought: The minds of the great apes* (pp. 152–176). Cambridge, England: Cambridge University Press.

Russon, A. E., Bard, K. A., & Parker, S. T. (Eds.). (1996). *Reaching into thought: The minds of the great apes*. Cambridge, England: Cambridge University Press.

Russon, A. E., & Galdikas, B. M. F. (1993). Imitation in free-ranging rehabilitant orangutans (*Pongo pygmaeus*). *Journal of Comparative Psychology, 107*, 147–161.

Russon, A. E., & Galdikas, B. M. F. (1994, August). *Hierarchical organization in rehabilitant orangutan object manipulations*. Symposium contribution to "Hierarchical organization in primate intelligence," XVth Congress of the International Primatological Society, Bali.

Russon, A. E., & Galdikas, B. M. F. (1995). Constraints on great apes' imitation: Model and action selectivity in rehabilitant orangutan (*Pongo pygmaeus*) imitation. *Journal of Comparative Psychology, 109*, 5–17.

Sayigh, L. S., Tyack, P. L., & Wells, R. S. (1993, September). *Signature whistle development in bottlenose dolphins is affected by early experience*. 23rd International Ethological Conference, Torremolinos, Spain.

Schiller, P. H. (1952). Innate constituents of complex responses in primates. *Psychological Review, 59*, 177–191.

Seyfarth, R. M., Cheney, D. L., & Marler, P. (1980). Monkey responses to three different alarm calls: Evidence for predator classification and semantic communication. *Science, 210*, 801–803.

Shettleworth, S. J. (1993). Where is the comparison in comparative cognition? Alternative research programs. *Psychological Sciences, 4*, 179–184.

Spinozzi, G. (1993). The development of spontaneous classificatory behavior in chimpanzees (*Pan troglodytes*). *Journal of Comparative Psychology, 107*, 193–200.

Stephan, H., Frahm, H., & Baron, G. (1981). New and revised data on volumes of brain structures in insectivores and primates. *Folia Primatologica, 35*, 1–29.

Stern, W. (1924/1975). *The psychology of early childhood: Up to the sixth year of life.* New York: Arno Press.

Tanner, J. (1985). Koko and Michael, Gorilla gourmets. *Gorilla, 9*, 3.

Tayler, C. K., & Saayman, G. S. (1973). Imitative behaviour by Indian Ocean bottlenose dolphins (*Tursiops aduncus*) in captivity. *Behaviour, 44*, 286–298.

Thorndike, E. L. (1898). Animal Intelligence: An experimental study of the associative processes in animals. *Psychological Review Monographs, 2*, 551–553.

Thorpe, W. H. (1963). *Learning and instinct in animals* (2nd ed.). London: Methuen.

Tomasello, M. (1990). Cultural transmission in the tool use and communicatory signaling of chimpanzees? In S. T. Parker & K. R. Gibson (Eds.), *"Language" and intelligence in monkeys and apes* (pp. 274–311). Cambridge, England: Cambridge University Press.

Tomasello, M., Davis-Dasilva, M., Camak, L., & Bard, K. (1987). Observational learning of tool use by young chimpanzees. *Human Evolution, 2*, 175–183.

Tomasello, M., George, B., Kruger, A., Farrar, J., & Evans, E. (1985). The development of gestural communication in young chimpanzees. *Journal of Human Evolution, 14*, 175–186.

Tomasello, M., Kruger, A., & Ratner, A. (1993). Cultural learning. *Behavioral and Brain Sciences, 16*, 495–592.

Tomasello, M., Savage-Rumbaugh, S. E., & Kruger, A. C. (1993). Imitative learning of actions on objects by children, chimpanzees, and enculturated chimpanzees. *Child Development, 64*, 1688–1705.

Tyack, P. (1986). Population biology, social behavior and communication in whales and dolphins. *Trends in Ecology and Evolution, 1*, 175–188.

Uzgiris, I. (1981). Two functions of imitation during infancy. *International Journal of Behavioural Development, 4*, 1–12.

Visalberghi, E. (1993). Capuchin monkeys: A window into tool use in apes and humans. In K. R. Gibson & T. Ingold (Eds.), *Tools, language and cognition in human evolution* (pp. 138–150). Cambridge, England: Cambridge University Press.

Visalberghi, E., & Fragaszy, D. (1990). Do monkeys ape? In S. T. Parker & K. R. Gibson (Eds.), *"Language" and intelligence in monkeys and apes* (pp. 247–273). Cambridge, England: Cambridge University Press.

Visalberghi, E., & Limongelli, L. (1996). Acting and understanding: Tool use revisited through the minds of capuchin monkeys. In A. E. Russon, K. A. Bard, & S. T. Parker (Eds.), *Reaching into thought: The minds of the great apes* (pp. 57–79). Cambridge, England: Cambridge University Press.

Whiten, A. (1996). Imitation, pretence and mindreading: Secondary representation in comparative primatology and developmental psychology. In A. E. Russon, K. A. Bard, & S. T. Parker (Eds.), *Reaching into thought: The minds of the great apes* (pp. 300–324). Cambridge, England: Cambridge University Press.

Whiten, A., & Byrne, R. W. (1991). The emergence of metarepresentation in human ontogeny and primate phylogeny. In A. Whiten (Ed.), *Natural theories of mind: Evolution, development and simulation of everyday mindreading* (pp. 267–281). Oxford, England: Basil Blackwell.

Whiten, A., Custance, D. M., Gòmez, J. C., Teixidor, P., & Bard, K. A. (1996). Imitative learning of artificial fruit processing in children (*Homo sapiens*) and chimpanzees (*Pan troglodytes*). *Journal of Comparative Psychology, 110*, 3–14.

Whiten, A., & Ham, R. (1992). On the nature and evolution of imitation in the animal kingdom: Reappraisal of a century of research. In P. J. B. Slater, J. S. Rosenblatt, C. Beer, & C. Milinski (Eds.), *Advances in the study of behavior* (Vol. 21, pp. 238–283). New York: Academic Press.

Wood, D. (1989). Social interaction as tutoring. In M. H. Bornstein & J. S. Bruner (Eds.), *Interaction in human development* (pp. 59–80). Hillsdale, NJ: Lawrence Erlbaum Associates.

Yando, R., Seitz, V., & Zigler, E. (1978). *Imitation: A developmental perspective.* Hillsdale, NJ: Lawrence Erlbaum Associates.

Yoerg, S. I. (1991). Ecological frames of mind: The role of cognition in behavioral ecology. *Quarterly Review of Biology, 66,* 287–301.

Zentall, T. R., & Galef, B. G., Jr. (Eds.). (1988). *Social learning: Psychological and biological perspectives.* Hillsdale, NJ: Lawrence Erlbaum Associates.

7

SCIENTIFIC SCHIZOPHRENIA WITH REGARD TO THE LANGUAGE ACT

Sue Savage-Rumbaugh
Georgia State University

IS HIGHER ORDER COGNITION LANGUAGE DEPENDENT?

Humans have traditionally viewed their capacity for language as something special and unique among the creatures of the planet. We typically describe the communication systems of all other animals as *nonverbal*—a term imply-ing the absence of intentionality, symbolic encoding, and internal structure (Feldman & Rime, 1991; Hinde, 1972). The term *nonverbal communication* is also applied to everything humans do while communicating, other than using language, including gestures, facial expressions, body postures, and so forth (von Cranach & Vine, 1973).

Because animals have not been observed to produce sounds that are the obvious equivalent of speech, students of animal behavior have tended to assume that animal communications are primitive and biologically endowed with little room for modification. This has been particularly true following Romanes' (1882) uncritical evaluation of invalidated accounts of animal intelligence. In addition, Morgan's Cannon (1894) was then raised as the criterion by which we must evaluate every behavior emitted by an animal. Even in cases where sounds produced by animals are obviously learned (as in parrots, for example), it is assumed that the modifications reflect style rather than substance; that is, they remain indicative of the animal's imme-diate emotional state and arise as an involuntary manifestation of that state, rather than from a desire or intent to communicate with a conspecific (Chomsky, 1986; Lenneberg, 1967; Lieberman, 1984).

These presuppositions have prevented us from attempting to interpret the communication systems of animals in the same way that we interpret our own communications. By presupposing the absence of symbolic communications and studying only the relationship between a given sound and the actions of conspecifics which ensue shortly thereafter, we necessarily preclude the possibility of finding forms of symbolic communication that function in a language-like manner (Harré, 1984; Taylor, 1994).

IMPLICIT LANGUAGE FUNCTION ASSUMPTIONS

Scientists who wish to study the communication systems of nonhuman primates, or other complex mammals in a way that permits them to find a symbolically based system of communication, should it exist, will have to approach the problem the same way they approach the learning of language in their own species. That is, they will have to make a number of assumptions that have never before characterized the study of animal communication, but which constantly characterize studies of child language. They will have to:

1. assume that communications are purposeful and that the speaker has a specific intent that he or she is attempting to convey to the listener;
2. assume that this intent can be encoded in complex ways that differ from time to time and which depend in large part upon context for their meaning;
3. assume that the effect of the message on the listener may not alter his immediate behavior in any specific manner but that the information he or she has received may cause him or her to make different decisions at some future time than he or she would have made had such information not been available;
4. assume that it will be extremely difficult in most cases to specify any specific point in time that the symbolic communication from a speaker will have any sort of predetermined effect on the listener.

All of these assumptions undergird current assessments of the development of language in children, regardless of the theoretical framework that is employed. This is reflected in the measurements we make of language development such as the first 50 words, mean length of utterance, child word meanings, and so forth. Such measurements are currently absent from all studies of animals (Brunner, 1983; Greenfield & Smith, 1976; Tomasello, 1992; Nelson, 1985; Pinker, 1994). These assumptions are not explicitly stated, rather they undergird all child language in an implicit manner. Many researchers are not even aware that the fundamental assumptions of *aboutness* are applied to the words of children without a moment's hesitation, yet denied most strenuously to the communications of all animals.

When attempting to determine the meanings children assign to words we also have the privilege of *insider's knowledge* of the adult meaning of the word. By combining our implicit assumptions with our *insider's knowledge*, we can construct hypotheses regarding child meaning. We then interpret the development of *meaning* as a reflection of the development of child mind.

CHILDREN'S MEANINGS

This approach leads to findings such as that of Smiley and Huttenlocher (1995) who identified the child meanings for 17 words (three performatives: *hi, bye-bye*, and *night-night*; nine spatial prepositions: *down, up, off, out*; verbs: *open, ride, rock, sit*; two adjectives: *more, my/mine*; one adverb: *there*; one noun: *door*; and two others: *all-gone, uh-oh*). Their methodology entailed the analysis of words that were produced by four or more children and used in contexts of entity movement or change to determine whether children used their words to encode appearance-based categories of simple movement or salient changes of state in entities, or goal-based categories of actions produced by the self or other people (Smiley & Huttenlocher, 1995). Thus when a child used one of the aforementioned words, Smiley and Huttenlocher's coders assumed the child had a referent for the word "in mind" and scored only such things as whether the child's intended referent was present or absent, whether the word expressed a preexisting or current state of movement, change of state, or state of disarray; whether it indicated observed events or functioned as a request for someone to enact a desired event, and so forth. No a priori proof that the child was able to referentially encode any of these things was required for category assignment. All possible categories implicitly assumed the existence of proper referential skills.

In order to determine whether a sound encodes simple movement, change of state, or goal-based action, one must implicitly attribute to the child, the four assumptions previously listed. It also requires a broad interpretation of the context of the utterance on the part of the adult. Given the current state of acceptable methodology in the study of nonhuman primate communication, it would be impermissible to observe a monkey or an ape vocalizing to others and assign categories such as entity of movement, changes of state entity, and so forth, to various vocalizations as they occurred. For to do so, scientists would need to have some external method of determining what the monkey or ape meant by the sound. Although scientists believe that attributions of this sort are perfectly legitimate for the vocalizations of young children, they believe with equal certainty that such attributions to the sounds of apes and monkeys are anthropomorphic at best. Consequently they require an external validation of meaning that is not only absent when they study members of their own species, but one which is essentially unobtainable.

Had Smiley and Huttenlocher (1995) been required to employ the techniques of study commonly used by primatologists interested in the communication systems of nonhuman primates, they would have been limited to recording what the child, or the child's playmate, did immediately after each vocalization. In addition, if the spectrographs of the vocalizations differed between two utterances of the same word, as is typically the case, they would not even have been able to classify different utterances of a word such as "all gone," as the same word.

By using the techniques currently accepted in studies of nonhuman primate communication, Smiley and Huttenlocher (1995) might have found, at best, that children produce a wide array of graded grunt like sounds, as well as graded clicks and click-vowel combinations that appear to somewhat more variable than those of other nonhuman primates and that these vocalizations are under considerable respiratory control. Little, if any, meaning could be assigned to the sounds, since each sound would have occurred in a setting that was unique to that sound. The most likely interpretation would then have been that the sounds reflected the emotional state of the child, with some indicating arousal, others apparent appeasement toward conspecifics, etc.

The assumptions that underlie the differential analysis of human and nonhuman primate communication are so fundamentally different and pervasive, that any evolutionary commonality that might potentially exist between the two systems is precluded *before* data are gathered. Consequently, it is currently impossible to study the evolutionary continuity of natural language systems in nonhuman primates and man. To study continuity, one must apply similar methods of analysis to similar phenomenon that are assumed to vary along a continuum. When the assumption of continuity is precluded at the outset and common techniques of study are essentially disbarred, continuity cannot be found because legitimate questions regarding its nature cannot be raised.

APE LANGUAGE STUDIES— AND INSIDER'S KNOWLEDGE

The ape language studies have come to represent a kind of odd break in this conceptual barricade. Ape language studies have achieved this caveat by virtue of the *insider's knowledge*. The adults who study apes, like those who study children, have a separate understanding of the important components of the communication system. They know what words are, how they function, and generally what these words mean to other adults. Equally important, unlike other investigators interested in primate communication, ape language researchers are not faced with a stack of spectrograms and the task of deciding which sounds are and are not common instances of the same utterance. These two caveats set ape language studies apart from other investigations of primate communication and are made possible by the fact that, for the first time, the system of communication under study in another species is one that is proscribed by the investigators themselves, rather than the animals under study (Gardner & Gardner, 1971; Matsuzawa, 1985; Miles, 1983; Patterson, 1978; Premack, 1976; Rumbaugh, 1977).

Because animal language researchers have an insider's knowledge of the elements of the communication system that is equivalent to those possessed by investigators of child language, ape language researchers can, and have, adopted such techniques as asking questions about ape word meaning that are not unlike those asked by Smiley and Huttenlocher (1995). Although the *insider's knowledge* possessed by the researcher is itself not controversial, the applicability of this knowledge in the same manner to animals and children is controversial. Applying insider's knowledge not only requires a knowledgeable insider, but a set of assumptions regarding the subject as well. The controversies in ape language take many guises but they essentially pivot on the legitimacy of accepting the four assumptions noted earlier as applicable to apes.

Skeptics of ape language studies point out that even though we can apply insider's knowledge to language using apes in a manner that is impossible to do for free-living apes, by what justification do we do so? How, it is asked, is it possible to know that the assumptions traditionally reserved for human language appropriately characterize the utterances of apes and therefore legitimize the application of a completely different modus operandi of investigation?

This has been the little understood and oft maligned central issue in the so-called ape-language debates. The superficial focus on syntax has only served to obscure the more basic issues raised in the earlier four assumptions. At this juncture, it must be noted that we have no independent proof of the validity of the four assumptions in human communication. We know only that human beings behave as if they believed these four assumptions accurately characterize both the nature of their own communications as well as that of other humans and that babies, somewhere between 6 and 9 months of age begin to behave in a similar manner.

A number of researchers including Trevarthan and Hubley (1978), Lock (1980), Bruner (1990) and others have suggested that the reason infants come to behave in a fashion that validates these assumptions is that they are treated in a manner that simultaneously expects, facilitates, and requires the emergence of what we tend to call *intentional symbolic communication*. By *symbolic*, we mean that the gesture or utterance has a meaning that is not inherent in the movement or sound itself and by *intentional*, we mean that there is a preassigned intent or effect that the speaker wishes and/or expects to obtain from the listener at the time the utterance is conceived and produced.

WHAT KINDS OF ASSUMPTIONS CAN WE MAKE ABOUT APES?

Were we to make similar assumptions about animal communication, it would completely change not only the way we study animal communication but the way we view and interpret all animal behavior. How are we to determine whether or not such assumptions are warranted? Before we can answer that question we must first observe that there are no preexisting standards by which investigators of child language determine whether or not it is possible to apply the assumptions to the utterances of human children. It is simply a given that they do.

To attempt to determine whether or not these assumptions should be made for all animal communications entails a treatment of the topic that goes far beyond the scope of this chapter. Here, we attempt only to tackle the more limited question of whether the communications of linguistically competent apes meet the four assumptions and thus are amenable to the same types of analysis as are currently applied to human children.

Lacking an acknowledged standard by which to judge whether or not these implicit assumptions are warranted, the student of ape language must arrive at one *de neauveux*. The issue is further complicated by the fact that although symbolic communicative abilities arise spontaneously in the child, this was not, at least initially, the case with apes (Gardner & Gardner, 1971; Miles, 1983, Rumbaugh, 1977). Unless they were given repeated training with reinforced pairings between an item and a sign or lexigram, apes did not initially use human symbols. The fact that apes, unlike children, had to be taught symbols seemed to validate the prevalent assumption of a fundamental and unbridgeable system of communication between man and ape. Teaching, in the case of apes, was initially synonymous with shaping (Terrace, 1981).

One could get animals to do many things through a method called *successive approximations* in which the animal was rewarded for behaviors that were closer and closer approximations to the desired, or target, action. The difficulty in this approach was that the animal produced the behavior for the reward itself, often having little understanding or concern for the nature of the behavior. Thus an ape tossing a basketball in a hoop was not trying to become a good basketball player, but rather was doing something in order to earn a bit of food. In this case it seemed to make sense to say that the ape knew something about the specific components of basketball, but yet he was not really playing a game of basketball.

Several decades of work by investigators of animal learning had illustrated how behaviors that appear at first glance to be insightful and intuitive can be built up in small increments. In these cases, the ostensive goal of the behavior is not really the controlling stimulus. Such findings made many psychologists leery of ape language claims, because the training techniques that led apes to use symbols consisted of shaping techniques well known to produce behaviors that were routine and proscribed. Moreover, just from the use of a symbol or a group of symbols, one could tell little about the animal's internal intent to communicate or the internal meaning, if any, that it assigned to the symbols it elected to employ at any given time.

Ape symbols were, it was argued, subject to the same ambiguities that plagued the study of nonhuman communication systems when it came to assigning intentionality and inferring meaning. Without some means of independent verification, how could one take an ape at their word? Or more precisely, how was it possible to know that what an ape meant or intended by a word was similar to what a human being meant or intended or even that an ape meant or intended at all? Such was the force behind Terrace's (1981) complaint that apes only requested things that were of interest to them, that they did not produce symbols for the sheer informative value of so doing.

The implicit assumptions that lent meaning, validity, and intepretability to child utterances were denied to the sounds, and/or learned symbols, of apes on the grounds that words used by apes lacked any external verification of intentionality. Apes were *trained*, therefore their utterances were assumed to be conditional responses, lacking communicative intent. Their goal was assumed to be a *reward*, not a communication.

At approximately the same time that language skills were first being claimed to exist in apes, Goodall (1968) began to report discoveries of tool use among wild chimpanzees in the Gombe Reserve. It was found that chimpanzees regularly stripped small twigs of bark and pushed them into termite mounds, causing clumps of termites to attack the stick as though it were an intruder. Prior to this time it had been widely declared that man, and only man, was a tool-maker. Tool-making, like language, was viewed as a hallmark of human intelligence, planning, and intentionality. However, with Goodall's initial report, this definition of man was shattered at once (Gibson & Ingold, 1993).

Unlike the claims for language, tool construction met with much broader acceptance from the scientific community. Scientists generally agreed that ape tool manufacture and use, albeit primitive, was contiguous with that of human tool construction. It is instructive to inquire as to why tool construction was readily accepted as intentional behavior, guided by a mind whose goal was apparent and whose intent appeared self-evident. After all, many arguments against accepting this as "real" tool construction could have been put forth. There was, for example, no independent means of verifying that the chimpanzees intended to make a tool with a specific planned form and structure—as is the case with human tool construction. They did select twigs that fit into the holes, but the precise characteristics of each twig varied greatly and were not altered by the chimpanzee in any systematic manner to make a more perfect tool. The fact that they stripped off the bark could have been the result of their habit of doing this with many other pieces of bark that were partially eaten. Perhaps the flavor of the pith inside the bark simply tasted good to the chimpanzee and so they peeled it off. Perhaps the fact that the stick was made had little to do with how attractive it was to the termites. Would the termites cling to the stick even if it was not stripped of bark?

It was also the case that many different species of twigs were used, hence it is unlikely that any properties of the twig itself were realized as important by the chimpanzee. When humans similarly use twigs they select a special root that is attached to the end of the twig; this particular root has some properties that cause the termites to attack. Similarly, humans make a new hole in the termite mound and blow smoke of particular plants into this hole while uttering specific vocal refrains. The human activity of termiting is clearly highly deliberate and well planned by contrast with the chimpanzee version of termiting. Could it be that chimpanzees accidentally discovered their version of termiting while simply playing with twigs, which they seem predisposed to insert into holes, even when reared in captivity without termite mounds?

If further arguments are needed to show that important discontinuities exist between the termiting activities of chimpanzees and those of man, it could be noted that there is no evidence that chimpanzees intentionally pass this skill along to their offspring through deliberate instruction. Indeed, more recent studies suggest that young chimpanzees learn the skill mostly by trial and error as they play around the termite mounds of their mothers (Tomasello, 1990). Children are repeatedly instructed in tool manufacture and usage, and it is entirely improbable that they would acquire complex skills such as basket weaving or stone knapping if left to their own initiative. The instruction is not always linguistic in nature as the teacher may intentionally show the student or help the student correct mistakes without uttering a word; nonetheless, instruction is an important component of passing the skills of tool construction from one generation to the next among human groups (Gibson & Ingold, 1993).

It might also be argued that chimpanzee tools are different from human ones in that they are used only for a single purpose, whereas a single human tool has many uses. If a chimpanzee tool, such as wadge of leaves placed in the hollow of a tree has only a single purpose, how can it be argued that the maker of the tool draws a conceptual distinction between the tool and its function? That is, does the chimpanzee really conceive of the tool as a tool in the sense that we do so as human beings? Certainly it is possible that chimpanzees found leaves already in the hollow of a tree and as they were scooping water out with their hands, they found that leaves held water. It is also possible that they found sticks that had accidentally landed in an opening in a termite mound and they extracted the twig out of curiosity only to find termites. These chance occurrences could then have led to a repetition of the events much as occurs in nontool feeding situations when a chimpanzee learns for example how to effectively open and eat certain fruits.

A final difference in tool use between ape and man lies in the fact that nearly all chimpanzee tool use is associated with extractive foraging (McGrew, 1992). If chimpanzees did not need to extract a consumable item from a difficult location, it is not likely that they would employ anything resembling tools. Humans, by contrast, use tools for the sheer interest in the skill of object manipulation itself. The tools are made to a certain plan long in advance of their use and are prized for their form and shape. They are kept long after their initial use and will be reused many times in the future in most cases. Each tool often is used for many different purposes, thus indicating that the maker clearly distinguishes between the tool and its many different functions.

The arguments regarding the discontinuity of tool use between man and ape are offered to illustrate how easy it would have been for the scientific community to reject the discoveries of tool use and manufacture by apes as precursors of human tool use. After all, many previous examples of tool use and construction in other animals were widely recognized (bird nests, beaver dams) that were not assumed to be related to hominid tool use. Yet tool manufacture and use by apes was heralded as an important discovery and held to be a significant evolutionary precursor to the emergence of these skills in our own species. This is to say, although it is not often put this way, that apes were widely acknowledged to be making their tools with a goal in mind and that they intended to make them to some predetermined specifications, albeit crude in nature. It has even been argued that the intellectual requirement of tool-making apes are equivalent to those encountered by the hominids who produced Oldawan tools (McGrew, 1992).

Why were scholars prepared to conclude that *tools* were constructed with foresight, intention, and purpose but that *words* were simply successive approximations shaped to look like language but lacking any real substance? And, even more curiously, why was a mind that could intentionally devise, construct, and appropriately employ a tool not able to devise, construct, and appropriately employ a word?

The answer is deceptively simple. When an ape is constructing and using a tool, we can clearly see the goal and all adjustments made in achieving the goal. The behaviors are externalized by the sheer fact that they are directed toward an inanimate object in the environment that does not, itself, behave or reply. Symbolic communicative behaviors are, by their nature, directed toward another willful animate being. Willful animate beings cannot be manipulated and prodded independently of their own reactions until one's goal is reached. Such beings themselves have goals and actions that must constantly be perceived and adjusted to, making it far more difficult to localize intentionality in an ape that is attempting to communicate than in one that is attempting to use a tool. In sum, scientists are willing to attribute intentionality in the domain of tool construction because they feel that they can actually see the intent being made manifest toward a constant tangible goal. They will never be able to *see* the intent of a communication manifest in the same sense that they can see the intent of the tool constructor. If scientists are ever to grasp the evolutionary continuity between the communication systems of man and those of other animals, they must be willing to devise means of granting communicative intentionality to other creatures.

The current bifurcation of intentionality between man and animal that characterizes our way of viewing animal communication presents us with an interesting dilemma. We are prepared to grant that apes can plan ahead sufficiently to construct tools as well as to carry them to sites that are considerably distant from the point of construction. We also know that prior to the onset of language, such deliberate planning behavior is uncharacteristic of children who are able to use language. Yet somehow we are unprepared to assume that apes are capable of similar intentional planning with regard to their use of symbols, both in the wild and in cases where they have acquired human symbols.

APES DO NOT NEED "LANGUAGE TRAINING"

The primary stumbling block to accepting the intentionality of ape communications has been the suspicion that shaping via successive approximations may account for what appears to be language-like behavior in apes. This suspicion has been removed by the discovery that apes raised in a language rich environment do acquire language skills through observation alone, without direct instruction. This finding, initially made with the bonobo Kanzi, and now replicated with three additional apes including one common chimpanzee, rules out the learning by "successive approximations" explanation of ape capacities. If the language skills of apes no longer need not be inculcated by a series of successive approximations and rewards, it becomes legitimate to conclude that apes are not uttering words in mindless manner only for rewards (Savage-Rumbaugh, 1990, 1991; Savage-Rumbaugh, Murphy, Sevcik, Brakke, Williams, & Rumbaugh, 1993).

It is suggested that in cases where apes, like children, have acquired language skills through observing the language usage of competent speakers, it is reasonable to apply the four above assumptions to the analysis of their utterances. The power in this position lies in the fact a child or ape *must employ the same four implicit assumptions* that adults use to interpret child utterances, to the break the linguistic code itself. To determine what is being said by others around them, children or apes must impute intentionally to others. They must somehow *make sense* of communications directed to them in order to interpret what is said and map the words to the intent. Should children (or apes) fail to realize that the communications of others are referential and intentional, it would not be possible to learn language through the process of normal rearing. Washoe did fail to do this, that is why the Gardner's resorted to training (Gardner & Gardner, 1971). Similarly, Lana, Sherman, and Austin failed in this task and that is why we resorted to training (Rumbaugh, 1977; Savage-Rumbaugh, 1986). Kanzi, Panbanisha, and Panzee did not fail in this endeavor. They linked intent to both spoken and printed words and began the process of translation and spontaneous language acquisition (Savage-Rumbaugh & Lewin, 1994). Training was not utilized in their case, because it was not needed.

Although little is currently known about the nature of this *sense-making* process, it is clear that it is highly complex. It depends on the child or ape's ability to interpret the situation from the viewpoint of the speaker, as opposed to their own—at least part of the time—and the ability of the child or ape to infer the speaker's focus of attention as well as the nature of the intent that underlies the speaker's utterance (Tomasello, 1995a). In addition, the child or ape must recognize that the speaker's intent and his own may differ, a concept that implies that the child or ape has formed a self-identity and has recognized that its goals and those of others are not always unimorphic.

The child or ape who is attempting to understand the adult communications directed toward it, must, like the adult attempting to understand children's language, credit the speaker with certain fundamental capacities. Specifically, the child or ape must assume that the speaker's words are purposeful and convey a specific intent. The child or ape must also assume that there may be no relationship between what the speaker says and what he or she does immediately after speaking. The child or ape must recognize that the speaker rarely repeats him or herself in precisely the same manner and that one must understand the speaker's goal if one is understand his utterances. If such assumptions are not made, the child or ape cannot engage in sufficient *sense making* to extract the content of the utterance and when a child or ape cannot determine what the adult means by the words with which they address them, they cannot learn language by observation alone.

The major problem faced by the child or ape is not that of decoding syntax as many linguists would argue, but is that of attempting to determine the speaker's message and intent without really knowing the language. The child or ape must use every available piece of information at hand to make this determination. Having made it, they must then try to determine which bit of language maps to the intention they have discerned and finally they must make some guesses about the syntactic mapping rules.

The child or ape's task is made easier by adults who try to clarify their intent by simplifying their actions in ways that they typically do not do for other adults. Nonetheless, the interpretive burden on the child or ape who learns language by observing others is great and the fact that the feat itself can be accomplished is sufficient to credit that child or ape with the four capacities necessary for a functioning symbolic system *at the moment that begins to produce its own utterances.*

LANGUAGE COMPREHENDING
AND SENSE MAKING

The intellectual scope of the feat of language learning through observation has been severely underestimated. Indeed, it is widely assumed that understanding language is a far less demanding task than producing it. This view was so prevalent that in the early investigations of ape-language no one attempted to test for comprehension. It was assumed an ape that could produce a sign or symbol, could understand any usage of that symbol by others. When we reported that Kanzi acquired language by comprehending, rather than by reward, critics argued that Kanzi's skills were similar to those regularly displayed by dogs trained to serve as seeing eye and/or law enforcement companions.

Indeed, when it is said that an animal understands language, the example that most quickly comes to mind is that of the trained dog. It is generally accepted that dogs can be taught to respond to a large number of verbal commands such as sit, heel, fetch, and so forth. What is not well understood is that this process is very different from what is underway when a child is attempting to decode the meaning of another's utterance. In the case of the dog, the response is achieved either through the route of successive approximations or by physically placing the dog's body in the proper position in response to the command. The dog is not attempting to decode the intent of the speaker. Instead, it is being shown how to respond to a particular set of sounds and gestures. The dog is then expected to respond to this set of sounds and gestures in the same manner on all future occasions. The dog can assume (a) that some action is always expected of him in response to a command, and (b) that the action that is expected will always be related to the sounds and gestures in a reliable manner.

KANZI AND SENSE MAKING

By contrast, a child or ape attempting to understand language cannot assume that the utterances they need to understand will always be directed to them or that these utterances will require a specific action from them. Nor can they assume that whatever actions are appropriately associated with an utterance at time A will be those that are to be associated with the same utterance at time B. This is because for them, unlike the dog, the context of the utterances will need to be taken into account to determine the meaning. All natural language utterances are heavily dependent on joint understanding of the contextual situation for their interpretation. In addition, many of the utterances directed toward the child are not designed to elicit any behavioral response, much less a particular response. They are simply informative and/or descriptive. Often they describe the ensuing action or intent of the speaker.

Tomasello (1995b) demonstrated, for example, that children can learn verbs by hearing the mother make statements about impending actions such as "I will punk X." Whereas children and certain apes appear to be able to decode such statements and to profit from them, no dogs have been reported to acquire word understanding in such a manner. Thus trainers do not teach "sit" to a dog, by saying, "I am going to sit," and then demonstrate this action for the dog. Children and apes do learn words through imitation. Moreover, children, unlike dogs, do not need to be shaped to perform the action or rewarded. Rather, they engage in the process of *sense making* with regard to interpreting the utterances of others (i.e., they understand both meaning of "sit" and the intent of the speaker).

Given their success in this *sense-making* process and the necessity of utilizing the four assumptions to interpret the utterances of others, it is reasonable to assume that all utterances of a child or ape who has acquired symbolic communication skills by observational means will reflect intentionality. Because they had to be able to employ the four assumptions to decode the utterances of adults, it becomes legitimate to utilize these same assumptions in attempting to determine the meanings of their utterances. One cannot make this argument for apes, dogs, or other animals whose communication skills were acquired through a process of shaping and successive approximations. Therefore, a sensitivity to the manner in which communicative skills are acquired, as well as the fact that they exist, is important for determining which procedures can be legitimately utilized in attempts to understand the scope or domain of the communicative competencies in question.

When signs are taught to chimpanzees by shaping techniques, as was the case with Nim in Terrace's project, for example, it is fruitless to raise questions regarding the existence of syntax. Why should we expect syntax to emerge when shaping rather than *sense making* was driving the acquisition of signing behavior? It is not possible for the developing mind to decode the syntax of an utterance if one is not even attempting to make sense of those utterances.

By contrast, the sense-making process did drive the acquisition of language skills in Kanzi, Panbanisha, and Panzee. Let us look at some examples of the sense-making process in operation. In a study designed to determine the relative degree of language comprehension, novel sentences were presented to Kanzi, a 9-year-old bonobo who had acquired language skills through observation alone (Savage-Rumbaugh, Murphy, Sevcik, Brakke, Williams, & Rumbaugh, 1993). When Kanzi heard the sentences he was surrounded by a group of objects as well as locations and people. Because each sentence was novel and different, each required its own interpretation. Having never seen or heard such sentences before, Kanzi had to make some sense of the intent of the speaker based on the objects that were available to him and the utterance that he heard. In many cases, the intent of the speaker was obscure and required second-order reflection (Savage-Rumbaugh, 1990, 1991; Savage-Rumbaugh, Murphy, Sevcik, Brakke, Williams, & Rumbaugh, 1993).

For example, in one case Kanzi was presented with the sentence "Can you feed your ball some tomato." Included in the objects in front of him was a round soft sponge halloween pumpkin with a small soft sponge face sculpted into the body of the pumpkin. The round soft sponge pumpkin resembled a ball, but had not been referred to by Kanzi or by others with him as a ball. Nonetheless, when he heard this sentence, after looking over the other items in the display, Kanzi turned over the pumpkin until its face was facing forward and them pretended to put the tomato in the mouth of the pumpkin. To accomplish this task, he had to understand that the speaker was using the word *ball* to refer to the pumpkin-shaped object and that for some reason, he was being requested to feed this ball—certainly an activity he had never before oriented toward a ball. It this case, the intent of the speaker was for Kanzi to treat real objects as though they represented something else and to pretend to carry out actions that are not logically possible. Kanzi was able to carry out such actions readily, having no difficulty inferring the intent of the speaker from the utterance he heard. He responded to each utterance on the first occasion, without prior demonstration of any such activity.

In another example, he was asked to "Put some water on the carrot." Kanzi inferred that the intent of the speaker was that the carrot be made wet and so he tossed it outdoors in the rain. The speaker had assumed that Kanzi would take some water out of bin and put it on the carrot. However his response indicated that he was able to make his own inference of the intent behind the speaker's utterance. Many other examples confirmed this interpretation. Thus when asked to "Go to the potty and get the sparklers" Kanzi assumed that he was being asked to retrieve the sparklers from the potty, rather then to execute the separate actions of using the potty and then handing the speaker some sparklers. In response to the sentence "Put the milk in the water," Kanzi did not take a can of milk and set it in a bowl of water. (This would have been an acceptable response and was, in fact, the one the speaker anticipated.) Instead, Kanzi inferred that the speaker's intent was to have the milk and the water mixed together. Consequently he proceeded to try as many ways as possible to open the can of milk so that he could pour the milk in the water. In so doing, he was clearly attempting to make sense of the request rather than to carry out what was literally spoken.

In another instance Kanzi was presented with the sentence "Put the shoe in the raisins" and in front of him, among other objects, was a shoe and an open box of raisins. Because the shoe would not fit in the raisins, the intent expressed by the speaker seemed nonsensical to Kanzi. (The speaker had assumed that Kanzi would try to fit the shoe into the box of raisins—not the raisins themselves.) Kanzi took the raisins out of the box and put them in a bowl as though the speaker must have meant to ask for such a logical action. When the sentence was repeated, Kanzi appeared greatly puzzled as though he simply could not comprehend how to put a shoe into a raisin. Finally he picked up one small raisin and put it in the shoe, appearing to think that this had to be the probable intent of the speaker. Kanzi simply did not understand how a shoe could be put in a raisin and, literally speaking, it cannot. Although it could also be argued that Kanzi simply did not process the syntax inherent in the sentence, his ability to both "Put the raisins in the water" and "Put the water in the raisins," on hearing these sentences, belies this view.

CHILDREN AND SENSE MAKING

When language is engaged as a sense-making activity, the context, the previous history of the speaker and the listener; and the facial expressions, body posture, and many other factors in the situation are taken into consideration in attempting to discern the intent of the speaker's utterance. It is these additional factors that make the eventual interpretation of syntax possible. Once syntactical interpretation begins, the task of determining the speaker's intent may become simpler since some information does get encoded at the syntactical level. The listener may not need to attend as closely to the world of the speaker, if he can infer, from the speech alone his or her intent.

In attempting to determine exactly how children go about this sort of sense making Tomasello (1995a) focused on the acquisition of new verbs. He pointed out that unlike nouns, verbs refer to actions that occur across the dimension of time and are thus not "point-at-able." How, he asks, do children know to which action and/or which components of a given action a new verb is to be applied. He referred to this as the packaging problem. While admitting that our current methods of determining how the child (or ape) solves the packaging problem are incomplete at best, Tomasello (1995a) nonetheless offered three suggestions. The first is that adults tend to name the novel or changing elements in a situation rather than the static ones. The second is that children may rely on their knowledge of other words in a sentence to figure out the referent of a new verb (of course this begs the question of how they acquired that knowledge in the first instance and whether the meaning of the other words is the same as it was in previous sentences—because words often do not mean the same things in different combinations). The third alternative is that of the salience of the action. Tomasello (1995a) concluded that whatever information the child is using, it must all be coupled with knowledge of the kinds of things in which adults might be interested in particular social and discourse contexts. In other words, the child must, to some extent put themselves in the place of the adult to engage in sense making with the utterances of adults. Similarly, adults must put themselves in the place of the child to engage in sense making with regard to the utterances of children.

The fact that apes such as Kanzi, Panbanisha, and Panzee have all proved sufficiently adept at *sense making* to be able to acquire words and a primitive grammar not unlike that of human children suggests that the basic cognitive substrates for language are present in apes. Because these skills appeared with exposure to language using humans without training or special encouragement, it is reasonable to conclude that apes in the wild must have such capacities as well. The fact that they have not yet been discerned most likely reflects our inability to decode the relevant aspects of the apes' environment.

Unlike investigators of child language, field researchers do not attempt to understand communications by inferring the intent of individual apes in the field. They do not engage in joint regard or joint perspective-taking with an ape, nor do they generally try to determine what the goals of a given ape may be. Field researchers, for the most part, focus their attention on distal and biological determinants of behavior rather than proximal and psychological determinants. Consequently, it should not prove surprising that language-like communications could exist in the wild without having yet being recognized.

It seems reasonable to conclude that if the four symbolic assumptions can now be legitimately applied to captive apes, it should also be possible to begin to look at the communications of wild apes from this new perspective.

WHAT ARE BONOBOS DOING IN THE WILD
WITH THE LINGUISTIC SENSE-MAKING SKILLS?

In order to determine whether or not apes might be communicating symbolically in the wild, one must begin by asking what kinds of things might
they need to communicate? This approach was taken with a group of wild
bonobos in the Luo Reserve of the Congo at a site maintained by Kano since
the early 1970s. Observations of wild bonobos reveal that these apes, unlike
others, live in very large social groups that do not always travel as a unit,
but which nearly always utilize the same feeding resources and sleeping
resources (Kano, 1992). Therefore, an obvious communicative need arises
from this travel pattern; if they do not travel together, how is it that they
arrive at similar feeding and sleeping resources in a coordinated manner
(Savage-Rumbaugh, Williams, Furuichi, & Kano, 1996)?

Bonobos are both arboreal and terrestrial travelers (Kano, 1992). With
arboreal movement it is possible to follow bonobos by watching the movement of trees. They are large animals and branches bend considerably under
their weight as they move. They often vocalize prior to beginning to travel,
and at rather regular intervals while they travel. These vocalizations enable
listeners (both human and bonobo) to localize the spatial arrangement of
the entire group, even though they are frequently so spread out that group
members cannot see one another. Two hundred yards or more may separate
subparty members of a single group as they travel through the trees.

On the ground, things are quite different. Bonobos vocalize far less often
and rarely use the localizing "Waah" call that permits them to pinpoint the
location of other individuals. Moreover, because foliage is extremely dense
it is often impossible for them to locate each other visually. When moving
as a group on the ground, they typically space themselves into separate
subparties that travel along at distances of 200 yards or more from the
nearest adjacent party. They also tend to move in single file along specific
paths; most are bonobo paths, but unlike human paths, the bonobo paths
vanish at certain points only to pick up later. Sometimes vanishing points
occur in swampy areas, others times they occur in areas where the nature
of the ground cover makes it difficult to discern, and other times they vanish
because the bonobos take to the treetops. All bonobo paths are very feint
compared to human paths, but they are more plentiful and they tend to
crisscross one another more frequently. As the bonobos move from one
feeding and/or resting area to another on these ground paths, males often
engage in branch dragging displays prior to departure.

Given that 100 or more bonobos are traveling through the forest in
subparties that are out of visual contact as long as they are on the forest
floor, bonobos face a specific and unusual problem among primates. Group
members need to stay together but they cannot see each other for the dense

vegetation. While on the ground they also need to avoid giving away their location by vocalizing frequently.

Chimpanzees do not travel together in such large parties nor do all members of the group attempt to nest in close proximity each night (Goodall, 1986). Chimpanzees keep in semicontact with pant-hoot calls, but appear to be far more independent than bonobos. As a result, they do not need to solve the problem of precisely knowing the travel patterns of one another. Gorilla groups travel together, but stay so close as to nearly always be able to see the location of the nearest group members or to hear soft grunting vocalizations. Consequently, they also do not face the problem of coordination of travel that presents itself to the bonobo (Fossy, 1983).

How are bonobo parties able to know the movements of group members when they are moving quietly on the forest floor, and unable to see their companions? And how do they end up at similar locations even though they do not appear to be following their companions? Human trackers are able to follow bonobo parties by looking for signs of passage in the vegetation. Could bonobos be tracking each other by a similar method? Human trackers follow groups through the forest with great ease, only rarely stopping to look closely at the ground. On occasions when they do look closely, it often indicates that the trail is not clear and the group ahead has been lost. How then do they follow so quickly? Fortunately, human trackers can be interviewed; they explain their ability to quickly track bonobos by following bonobo paths and by looking for signs mainly at path junctions or crossings. At such locations, there is generally flattened vegetation which indicates the path bonobos ahead have taken.

Vegetation near path junctions appears to be purposefully and obviously disturbed. At other locations along the trail, it is extremely difficult, though not impossible, to detect that anyone has passed that way. At trail junctures, however, the firm stomping of plants two to three times the size of a bonobo foot and the breaking and placing on the trail of branches 4 to 6 feet in length can be observed. This sort of extensive disturbance is not the result of simply walking through the forest.

To attempt to systematically determine whether the alterations of vegetation seen at path crossings occurred by chance, every instance of vegetation alteration, as well as the type of displacement and the location of the displacement was recorded during two complete daily follows. The recordings were done while following identified groups known to be traveling on the ground. Vegetation that was completely flattened on the trail, with all the flattened leaves or foliage oriented in a specific direction, or any branches that were broken off and placed on the trail, was considered to be an instance of intentionally flattened or broken vegetation and was recorded, no matter where it occurred. A more complete presentation of the results can be found in Savage-Rumbaugh, Williams, Furuichi, and Kano (1996), however several examples will be presented here to give an impression of the kind of path marking system that appears to used by wild bonobos.

The examples that follow are taken from field notes while a group of traveling bonobos was being tracked. A number of subparties, each approximately 20 minutes or more apart in time, were traveling through the forest. The observer was behind the last group, because traveling in between the subgroups was not tolerated by the bonobos.

Field Notes

We continue to follow the bonobo path until again it crosses another bonobo path where we find four smashed plants, two of one species and two of another species, one plant is to the right of the trail and three are to the left of the trail. A small branch has been broken off and laid on the trail pointing to the left. We take a left here and began following another bonobo path.

We continue on this path for another hundred feet, coming across two more smashed plants in the middle of the path, both smashed down in the direction of travel, just a few feet before we cross another bonobo path then again a few feet after we cross that path (Fig. 7.1).

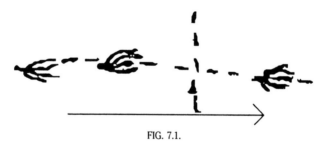

FIG. 7.1.

We cross another bonobo path and a few feet later encounter another smashed plant (Fig. 7.2).

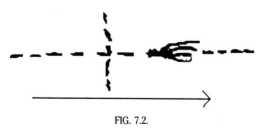

FIG. 7.2.

We cross another bonobo trail and find a broad leaf smashed plant just beyond the crossing point (Fig. 7.3).

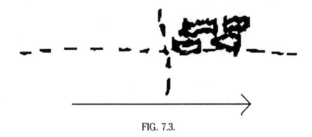

FIG. 7.3.

We continue along the path but it becomes too feint to follow, as it does so however, the soil also becomes rather soft and it is now possible to see bonobo footprints every so often (which was not possible to do earlier). We find we can continue by following footprints alone.

The data from these follows indicated that the altered vegetation was not occurring in a random pattern. Out of a total of 110 cases, it was found that the systematically altered vegetation nearly always occurred when two trails crossed or when the trail split into two directions, or when the trail was unclear. There were 72 instances in which the trail crossing or splits were marked by deliberately altered vegetation and only three instances where this was not the case. In all other instances, the marking *correctly indicated* the direction of travel as was confirmed by actually locating the bonobo group after traveling in the indicated direction. There were *no cases* in which the altered vegetation indicated the incorrect direction of travel.

On two occasions, the trackers elected to take a direction *other than* that indicated by the deliberate flattening of vegetation. On both of these occasions they then quickly lost the bonobo group and had to circle until the trail was recovered. Once it was recovered it could be ascertained that had the trackers proceeded in the direction indicated by the vegetation, they would not have lost the bonobo group. There were only four occasions when deliberately altered vegetation did not indicate either direction of travel, an area for resting, an area for arboreal travel, or an area for digging. In these four cases the altered vegetation served no apparent purpose, however it may have been that the message was not interpretable by the observer.

Systematic data collection thus supported the hypothesis that bonobos are using a symbolic system of communication to indicate, at minimum, direction of travel. Of course, we cannot "interview" the bonobos to ask about the correctness of this interpretation. However, critiques of this view must explain why it is that vegetation is altered only a trail junctions and not haphazardly along the way if it has no intentional communicative value? And how is it that the human trackers are able to use these cues to follow the bonobos rapidly and efficiently if that is not their purpose? And why human trackers loose the bonobos when they elect not to follow these cues?

In our world of civilization, it is not easy to understand how quickly one can get lost in the forest from companions, nor to grasp the danger of calling out in such cases. It is also not easy to understand how difficult it can be to track any creature, human or animal, in extraordinarily dense vegetation. Human groups, using the same forest as bonobos, make use of system of trails and vegetation alteration at trail crossings, to inform followers of the direction to take. It is the most efficient means of communication, when vocalization is precluded. While we cannot directly interview the bonobos as to their intentions, we can say that it is only by interviewing humans that we would come to learn of their system of trail marking. Seeing the markings alone would not prove that they were deliberate.

Such a system, if deliberate, would require that the producer of the signal realize that other bonobos will be traveling the same route but at a later point in time. It also requires that the followers know where to look, as well as how to interpret, such signals. Surely, both skills must require a long learning period. Furthermore, no system could arise in a species that did not have a well developed understanding of the fact that different informational states can exist in different individuals, a feat which is popularly called a *Theory of Mind*. While more data is needed to confirm the hypothesis offered here, it is the case that all current data strongly support the view that bonobos are capable of intentionally altering the vegetation in a specific and deliberate manner *to leave written messages* for those to come.

CONCLUSION

For too long, we have thought of animals as creatures who are incapable of rational thought and goal directed behavior. We have assumed that their behaviors and their communications are, unlike ourselves, stimulus driven responses to the circumstances that surround them. These assumptions have been legitimized by the adoption of two different sets of research methods, one for the study of human communication and behavior and another for the study of animal communication and behavior. As long as we continue to permit ourselves to make inferences regarding our own competencies while declaring equally probable inferences out of bounds when we study animals, we bar ourselves from understanding the evolution of communication and mind.

We may well have to face the simple fact that intentionality is produced, in a communicative context, by the attribution of intention by others and that it is a fundamental characteristic of a great deal of animal communication. Human language emerged as an intentional system that permitted intentions to eventually be encoded on paper in written form and to transcend time and space, but it was built up, not from whole cloth, but from a rich basis of learned, intentional, highly inferential nonverbal communication. How far "down" the phylogentic scale does intentional communication go? Certainly there is strong evidence of its existence in birds and many species of mammals (Barber, 1993; Bekoff, 1995; Evans & Marler, 1995; Griffen, 1976; Moss, 1988; Pepperberg, 1991; Ristau, 1991; Thomas, 1993). It may have developed from the need to track prey animals or the need to locate other groups of apes for purposes of attack.

While the attribution of intentionality to animals is fraught with difficulty, the only other comparative option is to treat ourselves as mindless creatures and apply to our own behavior the standards we currently reserve for animals. The latter does not seem to be a viable option, since by the very act of setting about to understand our own behavior, we assume that we are capable of goals, intents and purposes that can be internalized to a certain degree and that such actions, driven as they are by mind, are comprehensible to the frameworks constructed by the mind.

An institutionalized fear of violating Morgan's Cannon prevents us from making obvious statements about the intentionality of animals. We bow to the critiques of Romanes and are apologetic every time we use language that suggests an animal is behaving with intent and purpose. When we study animals we actively avoid the perspectives of joint attention, joint regard, and joint inference that permit us to understand one another as human beings.

Scientists often seem to fear that if they attempt to understand animals as they attempt to understand others human beings, they will meet only folly. We suggest that this fear is completely unfounded, yet so often repeated that scientists have not dared to ask why they have the fear and whether or not it is reasonable. The greater fear should be that we will learn nothing about animal communication until we adopt a different view point and that what we do learn about human beings will be hopelessly egocentric until we drop our human-centric view of communicative processes.

Would it not be more productive to ascribe intent and mental processes to animals and let the checks and balances of science function to keep erroneous conclusions in check? If the most simplistic explanation possible were given for many human behaviors, they to, would appear trivial. Therefore the greater danger is not in some outlandish claim that can be readily rebutted, but in no claim at all.

It is, in sum, quite easy to conclude that animals are doing nothing. How can anyone attack this position in today's scientific framework? However, to demonstrate that complex mental processes underlie their behavior is not easy and such demonstrations will always remain open to question. Yet they must be attempted, for to leave animals in the limbo of nonthought, nonintentions, nongoals, and nonpurpose is to deny fundamental facts that are now squarely in front of us provided by Kanzi and other bonobos.

Animals can do things that were assumed our prerogative alone. If we do not study the communicative capacities in animals within the same framework we study our own communications, we are cheating both them and ourselves out of the rightful gain to be had from better understanding of one another.

ACKNOWLEDGMENTS

This chapter is truly the product of the efforts of many of the staff and faculty of the Language Research Center, including Michael Baron, Mary Chapelo, Sherry Elrod, Heidi Lynn, Linda McGarra, Liz Pugh, Dan Rice, Sara Root, and Shelly Williams. All have contributed in significant ways to the ideas and content presented here. The author is responsible for this particular exposition of these ideas and findings, but the ideas and findings themselves are the result of a group effort. Gratitude is also extended to the editors of this volume for their effective and helpful critiques and suggestions and for the opportunity to present the ideas in this forum.

This research was funded by the National Institutes of Health Grant NICHD-06016 which supports the Language Research Center of Georgia State University. The college of Arts and Sciences of Georgia State University also supports this research and the Language Research Center.

REFERENCES

Barber, X. (1993). *The human nature of birds: A scientific discovery with startling implications*. New York: St. Martin's Press.

Bekoff, M. (1995). Cognitive ethology and the explanation of nonhuman animal beahvior. In H. Roitblat & J. A. Meyer (Eds.), *Comparative approaches to cognitive science* (pp. 119–150). Cambridge, MA: MIT Press.

Brunner, J. (1983). *Child's talk: Learning to use language*. New York: W. W. Norton.

Bruner, J. (1990). *Acts of meaning*. Cambridge, MA: Harvard University Press.

Chomsky, N. (1986). *Knowledge of language: Its nature, origin, and use*. New York: Praeger.

von Cranach, M., & Vine, I. (1973). *Social communication and movement: Studies of interaction and expression in man and chimpanzee*. London: Academic Press.

Evans, C. S., & Marler, P. (1995). Language and animal communication: Parallels and contrasts. In H. Roitblat & J. A. Meyer (Eds.), *Comparative approaches to cognitive science* (pp. 341–382). Cambridge, MA: MIT Press.

Feldman, R. S., & Rime, B. (1991). *Fundamentals of nonverbal behavior*. Cambridge, England: Cambridge University Press.

Fossy, D. (1983). *Gorillas in the mist*. New York: Houghton Mifflin.

Gardner, B. T., & Gardner, R. A. (1971). Two-way communication with an infant chimpanzee. In A. M. Schrier & F. Stollnitz (Eds.), *Behavior of nonhuman primates* (Vol. 4, pp. 117–183). New York: Academic Press.

Gibson, K. R., & Ingold, T. (1993). *Tools, language and cognition in human evolution*. Cambridge, England: Cambridge University Press.

Goodall, J. (1986). The behavior of free-living chimpanzees in the Gombe Stream Reserve. *Animal Behavior Monographs, 1*, 161–311.

Greenfield, P. M., & Smith, J. H. (1976). *The structure of communication in early language development*. New York: Academic Press.

Griffen, D. (1976). *The question of amimal awareness*. New York: Rockefeller University Press.

Harré, R. (1984). Must monkeys mean? In R. Harre & V. Reynolds (Eds.), *The meaning of primate signals* (pp. 116–137). Cambridge, England: Cambridge University Press.

Hinde, R. (1972). *Non-verbal communication*. Cambridge, England: Cambridge University Press.

Kano, T. (1991). *The last ape: Ecology and behavior of pygmy chimpanzee* (E. O. Vineberg, trans.). Palo Alto, CA: Stanford University Press.

Lenneberg, E. H. (1967). *Biological foundations of language*. New York: Wiley.

Lieberman, P. (1984). *The biology and evolution of language*. Cambridge, MA: Harvard University Press.

Lock, A. (1980). *The guided reinvention of language*. New York: Academic Press.

Matsuzawa, T. (1985). Color naming and classification in a chimpanzee (Pan troglodytes). *Journal of Human Evolution, 14*, 283–291.

McGrew, W. C. (1992). *Chimpanzee material culture: Implications for human evolution*. Cambridge, England: Cambridge University Press.

Miles, L. H. (1983). Apes and language: The search for communictive competence. In J. de Luce & H. T. Wilder (Eds.), *Language in primates: Perspective and implications* (pp. 43–61). New York: Springer.

Morgan, C. L. (1894). *Introduction to comparative psychology*. New York: Scribner's.

Moss, C. (1988). *Elephant memories: Thirteen years in the life of an elephant family*. New York: Fawcett Columbine.

Nelson, K. (1985). Making sense: *The acquisition of shared meaning*. Orlando, FL: Academic Press.

Patterson, F. G. (1978). The gestures of a gorilla: Language acquistion in another pongid. *Brain and Language, 5*, 72–97.

Pepperberg, I. M. (1991). A communicative approach to animal cognition: A study of conceptual abilities of an African grey parrot. In C. A. Ristua (Ed.), *Cognitive ethology: The minds of other animals* (pp. 153–186). Hillsdale, NJ: Lawrence Erlbaum Associates.

Pinker, S. (1994). *The language instinct*. New York: HarperPerennial.

Premack, D. (1976). *Intelligence in ape and man*. Hillsdale, NJ: Lawrence Erlbaum Associates.

Ristau, C. A. (1991). *Cognitive ethology: The minds of other animals*. Hillsdale, NJ: Lawrence Erlbaum Associates.

Romanes, G. (1882). *Animal intelligence*. New York: Appleton.

Rumbaugh, D. (1977). *Language learning by a chimpanzee*. New York: Academic Press.

Savage-Rumbaugh, E. S. (1986). *Ape language: From conditioned response to symbol*. New York: Columbia University Press.

Savage-Rumbaugh, E. S. (1990). Language acquisition in a nonhuman species: Implications for the innateness debate. *Developmental Psychobiology, 23*, 599–620.

Savage-Rumbaugh, E. S. (1991). Language learning in the bonobo: How and why they learn. In N. A. Krasnegor, D. M. Rumbaugh, R. L. Schiefelbusch, & M. Studdert-Kennedy (Eds.), *Biological and behavioral determinants of language development*. Hillsdale, NJ: Lawrence Erlbaum Associates.

Savage-Rumbaugh, E. S., & Lewin, R. (1994). *Kanzi: The ape at the brink of human mind*. New York: Wiley.

Savage-Rumbaugh, E. S., Murphy, J., Sevcik, R. A., Brakke, K. E., Williams, S. L., & Rumbaugh, D. M. (1993). Language comprehension in ape and child. *Monographs of the Society for Research in Child Development*, Vol. 58(3–4), pp. 1–254.

Savage-Rumbaugh, E. S., Williams, S. L., Furuichi, T., & Kano, T. (1996). Language perceived: *Paniscus* branches out. In W. C. McGrew, L. F. Marchant, & T. Nishida (Eds.), *Great ape societies* (pp. 173–184).

Smiley, P., & Huttenlocher, J. (1995). Conceptual development and the child's early words for events, objects, and persons. In M. Tomasello & W. E. Merriman (Eds.), *Beyond names for things* (pp. 21–61). Hillsdale, NJ: Lawrence Erlbaum Associates.

Taylor, T. J. (1994). The anthropomorhpic and the skeptical. *Language & Communication, 14,* 115–127.

Terrace, H. S. (1981). A report to an academy, 1980. *Annals of the New York Academy of Sciences, 364,* 94–114.

Thomas, E. M. (1993). *The hidden life of dogs.* Boston: Houghton Mifflin.

Tomasello, M. (1990). Cultural transmission in the tool use and communicatory signalling of chimpanzees? In S. T. Parker & K. R. Gibson (Eds.), *Language and intelligence in monkeys and apes* (pp. 274–311). Cambridge, England: Cambridge University Press.

Tomasello, M. (1992). *First verbs: A case study of early grammatical development.* New York: Cambridge University Press.

Tomasello, M. (1995a). Pragmatic contexts for early verb learning. In M. Tomasello & W. E. Merriman (Eds.), *Beyond names for things: Young children's acquisition of verbs* (pp. 115–146). Hillsdale, NJ: Lawrence Erlbaum Associates.

Tomasello, M. (1995b). Two-year-olds use pragmatic cues to differentiate reference to objects and actions. *Cognitive Development, 10,* 201–224.

Trevarthen, C., & Hubley, P. (1978). Secondary intersubjectivity: Confidence, confiding, and acts of meaning in the first year. In A. Lock (Ed.), *Action, gesture, and symbol: The emergence of language* (pp. 183–229).

8

THE EVOLUTION AND DEVELOPMENT OF SELF-KNOWLEDGE: ADAPTATIONS FOR ASSESSING THE NATURE OF SELF RELATIVE TO THAT OF CONSPECIFICS

Sue Taylor Parker
Sonoma State University

What is self-knowledge? What forms does it take in great apes and humans? What forms does it take in other species? How does it develop? What cognitive mechanisms underlie its various forms and sequences? What is the evolutionary history of these forms? And, finally, what is their adaptive significance? In this chapter, I address these questions in terms of an integrated research program derived from developmental psychology, comparative psychology, and evolutionary biology.

I begin this effort by suggesting a broad functional definition of self-knowledge that can be used for comparative purposes: Self-knowledge is organisms' knowledge that some aspect of their own being is located in or originates in their bodies. This knowledge arises from their species-specific ability to process and map information about their own chemistry, odors, actions, spatial orientation, appearance, sounds, and/or feedback from responses to these features, onto representations of their own bodies. As this definition reveals, I am using the term *self-knowledge* in a very general sense that embraces a variety of levels and kinds of information processing, perceptual, sensorimotor, and/or cognitive. It is the nature of these levels and kinds that distinguish species.

Even simple organisms manifest a large array of perceptual, sensory, and motoric abilities. Clearly, manifestation of such abilities often occurs without conscious awareness of the actor. In fact, in the absence of specifically designed feedback systems, organisms lack awareness of their own perceptions and actions. This seems to be as true of humans as of other species. Cognitive scientists, for example, argue that most cognitive processes are necessarily unconscious (Varela, Thompson, & Rosch, 1991). Moreover, even in adult humans, they are fleeting phenomena.

As this definition suggests, the self is first and last corporeal. Arguably, the body in the mind—the mapping of the body's spatial organization, its sensory receptors, and its motor programs—is the source of self-knowledge as well as the source of knowledge of the rest of the world (Johnson, 1989). This is true both in a developmental and in an evolutionary sense. We develop our self-knowledge through our corporeal experiences, and we differ from other species in the evolved nature and processing of those corporeal experiences, and hence in the nature of our self-knowledge.

Various forms of self-knowledge have evolved in animals. These include 1) chemical recognition of self by the immune system, 2) self-detection through olfactory matching, 3) self-detection through vestibular and proprioceptive matching of temporal contingencies between actions and experience, 4) kinesthetic–visual matching between actions of the self and those of a model in imitative learning, and 5) evaluation of actions of the self against social standards. See Table 8.1 on forms of self-knowledge in animals.

Please note that each level of self-knowledge in Table 8.1 is subsumed under each succeeding level. Humans, for example, manifest all of the forms present in the other taxa as well as those unique to themselves. Note also that early developmental levels in humans correspond roughly to the various levels in adults of other related species. Before addressing the comparative data and evolutionary issues, I briefly summarize relevant aspects of the emerging picture of development of self-knowledge in human infants and children.

THE ONTOGENY OF SELF-KNOWLEDGE IN HUMANS

Given the comparative thrust of this chapter, I focus on stages of the development of self-knowledge in human children that are crucial to comparisons with great apes. The first is the stage of development of mirror self-recognition, which occurs during the sensorimotor period between 15 and 24 months. It is accompanied by what Lewis and Brooks-Gunn (1979) called the self-conscious emotions (coyness) and by contingency play or exploration of the effects on one's movements on the mirror image. The second is the development of the self-evaluative emotions of shame and pride (Lewis, Sullivan, Stanger, & Weiss, 1989). These emotions develop during the preoperations period at about 36 months of age as children begin

TABLE 8.1

Proposed Levels and Functions of Self-Knowledge in Animals

Taxonomic Group and/ or Developmental Level	Mechanisms for Self-Knowledge	Probable Functions of Self-Knowledge	Arenas for Development of Self-Knowledge
Cells & Tissues in Multicellular Animals	Self-Detection Through Cell Membrane Lock & Key Devices	Assessment of Non-Self for Immunological Self-Defense	Cell Differentiation
Anthropods & Vertebrates	Self-Detection Through Odor Matching & Other Modality Specific Matching	Assessment of Genetic Relatedness for Mate Choice & Nepotism	Olfactory Lobe Development
Mammals	Self-Detection Through Vestibular & Proprioceptive Mapping	Assessment of Fighting Abilities of Self vs. Others	Sensorimotor Abilities: Primary Circular Reactions & Rough & Tumble Play
Juvenile Great Apes & Human Infants	Kinesthetic–Visual Matching, Self-Conscious Emotions, Self-Labeling	Comparative Assessment for Imitative Learning	Sensorimotor Abilities: Tertiary Circular Reactions & Contingency Play
Human Children in Early Childhood	Self-Evaluative Emotions, Incipient Autobiography, Theory of Mind	Comparative Assessment for Imitation of Same Gender Models	Preoperational Abilities, Symbolic Play, & Pretend Teaching
Human Children in Middle Childhood	Self-Concept Regarding Physical & Social Abilities	Comparative Assessment Shapes Physical & Social Strategies	Concrete Operational Abilities, Games With Rules, & Apprenticeship
Human Children in Adolescence	Integrated Psychological Self-Concept	Comparative Assessment Shapes Productive & Reproductive Strategies	Formal Operational Abilities, Cooperative Problem Solving, Mentorship

to internalize social standards. A third stage, role playing, begins at about 2 years of age at the beginning of the preoperations period. It continues until about 13 years of age at the end of the concrete operations period (Watson, 1981, 1984). The early stages of role playing also have implications for comparative studies (Parker & Milbrath, 1994).

Mirror self-recognition (MSR), which begins to emerge between 15 and 21 months of age, seems to develop out of the infant's realization that the mirror image is perfectly tracking its own behaviors. This realization seems to emerge in response to feedback from a variety of self-initiated behaviors that test the contingencies between the actions of the self and the actions of the image. Self-conscious responses to contingent images of the self just precede or co-occur with MSR. Likewise, verbal self-labeling and expressions of verbal possessiveness just follow or co-occur with MSR. MSR is succeeded by recognition of images of the self in photographs (Lewis & Brooks-Gunn, 1979).

At about three years of age, children begin to manifest what Lewis and his colleagues (Lewis et al., 1989) called the self-evaluative emotions of guilt and shame, pride and hubris. The onset of these emotions seems to reflect the nascent internalization of social expectations (Kagan, Garcia Coll, & Reznick, 1984). Indeed, each period of cognitive development entails new constellations of affect about self and others. The intuitive affects of preoperational intelligence allow the child to estimate his superiority or inferiority relative to others (Piaget, 1981).

THE PROXIMATE MECHANISMS UNDERLYING DEVELOPMENT OF SELF-KNOWLEDGE IN HUMANS

Before addressing the evolution and adaptive significance of self-knowledge in hominoids, I would like to address the proximate mechanisms involved in the expression and development of self knowledge. Rather than reviewing various alternative models, I briefly summarize a model for construction of self-knowledge through social play. This model is based on ideas of George Herbert Mead, James Mark Baldwin, and Jean Piaget (Baldwin, 1897; Mead, 1970; Piaget, 1962, 1965).

Baldwin emphasized the role of imitation in the development of self-knowledge (Baldwin, 1897; Hart & Fegley, 1994; Mead, 1970; Piaget, 1962, 1965). Mead (Fein, 1984; Mead, 1970) emphasized the role of play in the development of social knowledge. Piaget (1962, 1965) described stages of development of imitation, symbolic play, and games with rules in the broader context of intellectual development. In this chapter I use a Baldwinian-Piagetian-Meadean model to show that ritualized social play interactions lead to the development of self-knowledge. The easiest way to present this model is to focus on the nature of play interactions in three periods of development: 1) mother-caretaker play in infancy; 2) pretend play in early childhood; and 3) games with rules in later childhood.

Beginning at about 3 months of age, infants in many societies engage with their mothers in face-to-face interactions that Watson (1972) labeled The Game. The game involves what Piaget (1952) called secondary circular re-actions (SCR). These are rounds of contingent facial movements and vocali-zations that seem to be motivated by the baby's pleasure in controlling the contingent behavior of the mother. These face-to-face contingency games play an important role in language acquisition, particularly in the form of conversational turn-taking (Stern, 1977). They are unique to humans (Parker, 1993).

Before 12 months of age, babies engage in social imitation of novel actions of their caretakers. This occurs in body part identification games (Piaget, 1952, 1962) and in rounds of mutual facial, gestural, and vocal imitation (Meltzoff, 1988). The imitation of novel coordinated actions seems to coin-cide with and depend on what Piaget (1952) called tertiary circular reactions (TCR). These elaborated circular reactions entail systematic variation in schemes with the goal of testing the contingent effects of these variations. These games are important in the establishment of joint structures of atten-tion (Bruner, 1983; Trevarthan & Hubley, 1978).

Baldwin (1897) noted that imitation helps infants to develop a sense of self by allowing them to take other's actions into themselves and project them back onto others. Meltzoff (1990) showed that 14-month-old infants understand when they are being imitated and that they prefer models who imitate them to those who perform other contingent actions. He argued that self develops in part through the social mirror provided by parental imita-tion of infants' actions. This social mirror provides a means whereby infants can see their own actions reflected. Meltzoff argued that the great appeal of parental imitation for infants lies in their recognition that it is a reflection of what they have just done. Research by Hart and Fegley (1994) shows a close association between the frequency of social imitation and the onset of MSR. This research suggests that MSR is an artifact of the self-recognition that develops through interactions with social mirrors.

Developmentally, the mutual imitation games of infants and caretakers are precursors of the symbolic games young children play with caretakers and with one another during early childhood (Piaget, 1962). During the period of preoperations from about 2 to 5 years, children are using their newly developed symbolic capacities to construct their grammatical sys-tems and to make pictorial representations of objects. At this time, they are also engaging in increasingly complex and elaborated forms of pretend play (Piaget, 1962). Pretend play is a highly ritualized form of event repre-sentation (Nelson, 1983; Nelson & Gruendel, 1986; Nelson & Seidman, 1984) that recreates and practices various social roles (Watson, 1990). Various investigators have described similar developmental sequences from simple representation of the self's actions in a new context to representing actions of others in passive and then active modes, and so forth (Bretherton, 1984; Watson, 1981).

As Mead (1970) pointed out long ago, symbolic games provide a major arena for the development of self-knowledge. In representing simple everyday events, children project themselves into a variety of stereotyped roles. They also practice complementary roles in response to the play of other children, thereby assuming the identity of another. Then they engage in role reversals that allow them to experience the same event from different perspectives (e.g., Fein, 1984). These games provide a complex series of social mirrors that are crucial for developing knowledge of social roles, social self, and social others. The reciprocal growth of understanding of self and other is consistent with the interpretation that the theory of other minds develops concurrently with the theory of one's own mind (Gopnik & Meltzoff, 1994). Just as pretend play is an elaboration of imitation, theory of mind seems to grow out of pretend play (Leslie, 1988).

Just as pretend games in early childhood grow out of the mutual imitation games of infancy, so games with rules in middle childhood grow out of pretend play. At about 5 to 7 years of age as they move toward concrete operational thinking, children begin to understand the concept of rules (Piaget, 1965). Like pretend games, games with rules provide children with repeated opportunities to play a variety of roles in highly ritualized forms of event representation.

These games differ from pretend games, however, in the complexity and variety of events and roles they represent and in their focus on extra domestic, extra work settings. Many such games involve highly ritualized political contests or battles over resources. In addition to practicing various roles, children practice a variety of strategies and counterstrategies for achieving their goals (Parker, 1984). Games with rules provide the most complex social mirrors found in any form of play. Children also engage in simple rough-and-tumble play fighting games similar to those found in other young mammals (e.g., Aldis, 1975; Fagen, 1981). The roles and role reversals in these games are much simpler, however, than those seen in the forms of play previously outlined.

I should note that this model of self-construction through social play is based primarily on studies of children in Western urban societies. Data on child development in non-Western societies suggest some significant differences in the nature and frequency of face-to-face interaction among infants and caretakers (LeVine, 1990). These and other cross-cultural data suggest cultural differences not only in the nature of self-knowledge, but its acquisition.

COMPARATIVE DATA ON SELF-KNOWLEDGE IN MONKEYS AND APES

Recently, primatologists have been using frameworks from developmental psychology to study monkey and ape cognition. There are several advantages to such studies. First, because they are based on human behavior, they are unlikely to underestimate the complexity of the behavior of other species. Second, insofar as they describe epigenetic sequences of behavioral development, they provide a natural scale for judging the relative cognitive complexity of the behavior of other species. Third, because they are multidimensional, they provide a variety of developmental scales for identifying species differences in achievements across domains (decalages or displacements in Piaget's model). Fourth, because they are developmental, they provide a scale for comparing rates of development in human and nonhuman primates (Parker, 1990).

Some might object that comparative use of models from human developmental psychology is anthropomorphic. I would say that anthropomorphism is the null hypothesis in comparative developmental studies. Indeed, comparative developmental studies can provide a finer scale for identifying species differences among anthropoid primates than can other approaches. As more developmental stages are studied in more domains, this will be increasingly true (Parker, 1996a).

Which models from developmental psychology have been used in comparative studies of self-knowledge? Ironically, Gallup's (1970) landmark study of mirror self-recognition in primates was not inspired by human developmental psychology. To the contrary, Gallup's methodology stimulated new studies of MSR in human infants (Amsterdam, 1972; Lewis & Brooks-Gunn, 1979). In his original paper, Gallup reported that chimpanzees passed the mark test, whereas rhesus monkeys did not. Gallup's mark test entails comparing an individual's behaviors in front of a mirror before and after marking his face. A part of the face the individual is unable to see without a mirror is marked with an odorless dye while he is anesthetized. Visually directed touching of the marked spot is taken as evidence for MSR. Gallup developed the mark test to verify his suspicion that chimpanzees who were using the mirror to examine parts of their bodies had MSR. Gallup's MSR methodology dominated comparative studies of self-awareness from 1970 through 1990.

A series of MSR studies published during that period showed that orangutans and chimpanzees display MSR, but gorillas and monkeys do not (Anderson, 1984; Gallup, 1977; Ledbetter & Basen, 1982). Patterson and Cohn (1994), however, have provided evidence for MSR in two signing gorillas. Meanwhile, work by Swartz and Evans (1991) has revealed that MSR is variable among both gorillas and chimpanzees even when they are socially reared. Reasons for this intraspecific variation in frequencies of MSR in gorillas as compared to chimpanzees remain to be explored (Patterson & Cohn, 1994; Povinelli, 1994). Patterson and Cohn (1994) suggested that gorillas show lower frequencies of MSR than chimpanzees do because they are shier and more self-conscious. Observations of gorillas suggest that they experience self-conscious and even self-evaluative emotions. Various anecdotes in the literature suggest that they do (Hart & Kamel, 1996).

Most of the early work on self-knowledge in monkeys and apes involved replication of Gallup's test on adult animals. Since then, however, a few primatologists have begun to publish studies of the development of MSR in immature apes. Bard and her colleagues at Yerkes Laboratory, for example, have studied the development of MSR in young chimpanzees. They assessed MSR by the occurrence of contingency testing behaviors, self-addressed behaviors, and mark-directed behaviors described in human infants (Custance & Bard, 1994; Linn, Bard, & Anderson, 1992). They found increasing percentages of these behaviors in chimpanzees 2½ through 5 years of age with 4- and 5-year-olds showing relatively high frequencies.

Likewise, Boysen, Bryan, and Shreyer (1994) found that two chimpanzees 4- and 4½-years old displayed evidence of MSR in the form of contingency testing behaviors and self-directed movements. Povinelli, Rulf, and Bierschwale (Povinelli, Rulf, Landau, & Bierschwale, 1993) found that most chimpanzees younger than 4½ years failed to show MSR. Like Bard, Miles (1994) also saw the first evidence for MSR in Chantek, the signing orangutan, when he was 2 years of age. Miles noted that Chantek's MSR was inconsistent, as it is in young human children, until he was 3½ years old.

Miles (1994) broadened the inquiry by distinguishing the following 3 stages of development of self-awareness in Chantek: 1) the instrumental association stage, from 9 to 24 months, culminating in fifth-stage sensorimotor understandings and a beginning interest in mirrors and in signing his own name; 2) the subjective representation stage, from 2 to 4½ years, during which he displayed MSR, the use of the pronoun *me*, and began engaging in pretend play; 3) the objective representation stage, from 4½ to 8 years, during which he began spontaneously labeling his mirror image and using the mirror in more elaborate ways to groom and adorn himself. He also showed the ability to take his caretaker's perspective by waiting for eye contact before initiating signing.

Although the few studies of the development of MSR in captive great apes report somewhat different developmental ages, they all indicate that MSR develops considerably later in great apes than in human infants. Please note that MSR is merely a convenient means for diagnosing a certain level of self-knowledge present in human infants and juvenile great apes. Clearly,

MSR is an index of kinds of self-knowledge that are manifested in contexts that predate the invention of mirrors. For this reason, it is important to find other indices of self-knowledge that can be used to study monkeys and apes living in social groups in captivity and in the wild. Some alternative indices of self-knowledge include social imitation, role playing, empathy, deception, and self-consciousness and/or shame.

If we want to understand self-knowledge in natural settings, we need to know the cognitive correlates of MSR and other landmarks in the development of self-knowledge. Two Piagetian models have been proposed. First, Bertanthal and Fischer (1978) argued that object permanence correlates with MSR. More recently, Gergely (1994) elaborated this argument on the grounds that sixth-stage object permanence entails mental representation. Lewis and Brooks-Gunn (1979) argued that object permanence was necessary but not sufficient for MSR.

Second, Parker (1991) and Mitchell (1993) independently argued that imitation or kinesthetic–visual matching is necessary for MSR. On the basis of their studies of imitation and MSR in chimpanzees, Custance and Bard (1994) doubted this correlation, arguing that mental representation is the key. It is likely that object permanence, fourth- or fifth-stage imitation, and fifth- or sixth-stage objectified causality (Piaget, 1954) are all necessary for MSR. The question is which set of abilities is necessary but insufficient, and which is necessary and sufficient. Resolution of this matter awaits further developmental research. Questions regarding the extent and limits of imitative abilities in great apes are also at issue in this controversy (Russon, 1996; Russon & Galdikas, 1993, 1995; Tomasello, Gust, & Frost, 1989; Tomasello, Kruger, & Ratner, 1993) also see Savage-Rumbaugh (this volume) and Tomasello (this volume).[1]

We can see from this review that primatologists are beginning to do developmental studies of self-awareness. Moreover, these studies are expanding their perview to incorporate criteria used in studies of human infants and children (see especially Miles, 1994). Comparative research is limited, however, by the lack of understanding of the kinds of cognitive abilities that underlie specific forms of self-knowledge that emerge early in human development. As such a model emerges, it will surely reverberate in comparative studies.

---

[1]The question regarding the imitative abilities of great apes is a complex one. Part of the issue revolves around differing concepts of imitation. If imitation is defined as perfect replication of all aspects of a novel scheme after one observation of a model, then great apes rarely imitate. On the other hand, most human children also fail to imitate by this standard. Continuing research on imitation in human children suggests that it is a complex phenomena involving interrupted, partial, and repeated replications of various elements of a model's behavior (see Russon, 1996, for discussion).

THE PHYLOGENY OF SELF-KNOWLEDGE
IN ANTHROPOID PRIMATES

The cladistic method of analysis allows us to reconstruct the evolution of various levels of self-knowledge that have been distinguished in monkeys, apes, and humans. Specifically, Hennig's cladistic methodology allows us to infer the evolutionary origins of shared derived characters that have been inherited from a common ancestor (Hennig, 1979; Wiley, 1981). Such characters as elongated digits with tactile pads and nails, for example, are shared derived characteristics inherited from the common ancestor of all primates.

We can identify shared derived characters by comparing the characters of a group of related species (the in-group) with those of more distantly related species (the out-group). If, for example, the apes were selected as a putatively related in-group and the Old World monkeys are selected as the out-group, we would compare the characteristics of the apes and the monkeys. Such comparisons yield the information that the climbing by grasping complex is present in both groups although the brachiation complex is present only among the among apes. This analysis tells us that the brachiation complex is a shared, derived character that was inherited from the common ancestor of all the great apes.

The cladistic method then involves reconstructing the common ancestry of particular structures and behaviors, climbing by grasping and brachiation in the previous examples. We can use this method to reconstruct the evolutionary history of behaviors using phylogenies constructed from other characters (Brooks & McLennan, 1991). (It is against the rules in cladistics to use the same characters to construct your phylogeny and to reconstruct the evolution of behaviors.)

Because the phylogeny of anthropoid primates is well known from molecular data, we can use this phylogeny to map the characters whose evolutionary history we are interested in reconstructing. In this case, we can use this method to map the distribution of MSR and other sensorimotor and symbolic abilities in these species. See Fig. 8.1 for a mapping of MSR and various sensorimotor and symbolic abilities onto a cladogram of anthropoid primates.[2]

Cladistic mapping suggests that the capacity for MSR, imitation, tool use, and rudimentary symbol use first arose in the common ancestor of great apes approximately 14 million years ago. If so, these capacities must have been present in the earliest hominid species that diverged from the common ancestor with chimpanzees approximately 5 million years ago (Parker, 1991).

---

[2]The general picture of primate phylogeny is well agreed. There is, however, at least one major bone of contention. Controversy rages over the branching of the African apes and hominids: Some argue that chimpanzees and hominids diverged later than chimpanzees and gorillas, others argue that gorillas, chimpanzees, and hominids diverged at the same time. There is a growing consensus that chimpanzees and humans diverged last (Ruvolo, 1994).

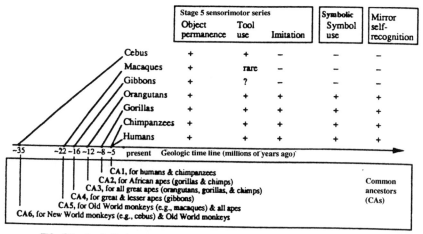

	Stage 5 sensorimotor series			Symbolic Symbol use	Mirror self-recognition
	Object permanence	Tool use	Imitation		
Cebus	+	+	–	–	–
Macaques	+	rare	–	–	–
Gibbons	+	?	–	–	–
Orangutans	+	+	+	+	+
Gorillas	+	+	+	+	+
Chimpanzees	+	+	+	+	+
Humans	+	+	+	+	+

-35   -22 -16 -12 -8 -5   present   Geologic time line (millions of years ago)

CA1, for humans & chimpanzees
CA2, for African apes (gorillas & chimps)
CA3, for all great apes (orangutans, gorillas, & chimps)
CA4, for great & lesser apes (gibbons)
CA5, for Old World monkeys (e.g., macaques) & all apes
CA6, for New World monkeys (e.g., cebus) & Old World monkeys

Common ancestors (CAs)

FIG. 8.1. A cladistic mapping of sensorimotor and symbolic abilities in monkeys, apes, and human children (Parker & Mitchell, 1994).

Also note that tool use, which also arose independently in cebus monkeys from Central and South America, is not necessarily associated with imitation and MSR. Likewise, fifth-stage object permanence, which apparently occurs in all monkeys and apes, is not necessarily associated with MSR. This pattern suggests that abilities other than object permanence and understanding of causality are necessary for MSR. Evidence cited previously suggests that imitation is the requisite other ability.

THE ADAPTIVE SIGNIFICANCE OF SELF-KNOWLEDGE IN GREAT APES

Procedures for discovering the adaptive significance of characters are less straightforward than are those for reconstructing their common ancestry (e.g., Clutton-Brock & Harvey, 1984). The first step is identification of shared derived character states (Coddington, 1988). A second step is identification of functional analogies among distantly related species that have evolved convergent specializations. If we use MSR as an index of self-knowledge, we find only one distantly related group with convergent abilities, that is, dolphins (Martens & Psarakos, 1994). This single convergence is informative, however. In addition to displaying MSR, dolphins display tool use, imitation, and some symbolic capacities. This is the same complex of abilities that we find in the great apes. Unfortunately, the functional significance of this complex in dolphins is unclear.[3]

---

[3]Convergent specializations for similar activities (analogous characters) have evolved independently in distantly related species whose common ancestor lacked such specializations. Echo location, for example, has evolved independently not only in distantly related mammals, two groups of bats and dolphins, but also in two distantly related birds, Cave swifts and oil

Another methodological strategy for reconstructing adaptive significance is to examine contextual expressions of correlated behaviors that are unique in the taxonomic in-group in question (Clutton-Brock & Harvey, 1984). Great apes are unique among primates in displaying a correlated complex of cognitive abilities including true imitation, intelligent tool use, demonstration teaching, symbolic capacities, and MSR. Contextual expression of these abilities suggests that they functioned as a means for imitative learning of subsistence and social skills in the common ancestor of great apes (Parker, 1991, 1996b). This scenario is based on recent reports revealing that juvenile chimpanzees in the wild imitate their mothers' tool-using procedures and that mothers sometimes demonstrate these procedures for their offspring (Boesch, 1991).

Imitation involves kinesthetic–visual matching of actions of the self with those of the model (Mitchell, 1993). Teaching by demonstration involves accommodating demonstrated actions to the capacities of the pupil. This involves selecting, isolating, slowing down, and repeating key elements of the demonstrated action as well as tracking changes in the pupil's ongoing imitative performance (Wood, 1989; Wood, Bruner, & Ross, 1976). This suggests that the kinesthetic visual matching/imitative skills associated with MSR may have arisen as adaptations for imitative learning and teaching of tool use (Parker, 1996b). The primary context of tool use in great apes suggests that it was favored as an adaptation for feeding on a variety of high energy embedded foods. These foods can only be exploited if they are extracted from their matrix with the aid of tools (Parker & Gibson, 1977, 1979). Self-knowledge in hominoids also facilitates assessment of the abilities of the self as compared to those of potential rivals in reproductive competition. Among great apes, this function seems to be motivated by an element of identification with and imitation of successful models and potential allies. All of these functions are apparently practiced in imitative play (Goodall, 1986).

The various forms of self-knowledge sequentially manifested during human development provide ever more powerful cognitive means for assessing and monitoring changing abilities relative to those of competitors for scarce resources. Such assessment is a prerequisite for choice of and training for particular reproductive and subsistence strategies and roles. These roles vary according to individual abilities and to local conditions across populations, habitats, and cultural traditions.

Modern humans display two forms of play that facilitate the development of culturally variable forms of self-knowledge and assessment: 1) Contingency games during infancy facilitate the development of linguistic commu-

---

birds (Dawkins, 1986). If the adaptive significance of such a specialization is unclear in one species, then comparisons with convergent specializations in distantly related species may provide clues as to functions. In the case of echo location, the common function seems to be identification of moving prey in a medium in which vision is occluded.

nication that underpins the autobiographical self and social manipulation through language (Parker, 1985; Stern, 1977; Watson, 1972), and 2) games with rules during middle childhood facilitate the development of cognitively mediated competitive strategies such as formation of political alliances and strategic deployment of force (Parker, 1984; Piaget, 1965).

The foregoing model addresses the adaptive significance of self-knowledge in anthropoid apes and humans but leaves unexplored the adaptive significance of self-knowledge in monkeys and other mammals. In the following section, I explore a more comprehensive model that sheds light back on my taxonomically restricted model. This comprehensive model is implicit in the broader definition of self-knowledge proposed above: Self-knowledge is the knowledge organisms have that some aspect of their own being emanates from their bodies. This knowledge results from their species-specific ability to process and map information about their features onto representations of their own bodies.

Self-knowledge provides the standard for assessing the nature of the self relative to that of others. The specific aspects of self that are assessed and the mechanisms for assessing these aspects vary from species to species. Modern evolutionary formulations suggest that the general function of assessment is to guide choices among available alternative strategies for growth and development, defense, maintenance, and/or reproduction. A short digression into the rudiments of what biologists call life-history strategy (LHS) theory provides necessary background for understanding this interpretation.

LIFE-HISTORY STRATEGY THEORY AND SELF-KNOWLEDGE AS A STANDARD FOR ASSESSMENT

According to LHS theory, organisms compete with other organisms of the same species (conspecifics) for limited resources. Individuals in social species often cooperate with close kin in competing with conspecifics. Competitors are scored in terms of their relative lifetime reproductive success. This mechanism of differential reproductive success has produced organisms capable of making strategic choices among limited alternatives. Animals' life cycles represent the most successful lifetime distribution of limited energy budgets among the basic functions of growth and development, maintenance, defense, and reproduction under ancestral conditions of their lineage (Horn & Rubenstein, 1984).

Two contrasting life history patterns may clarify this concept. *K* strategists are large bodied, slow developing, long lived species with low reproductive rates and high parental investment in their young. In contrast, *r* strategists are small bodied, rapidly developing species with high reproductive rates (MacArthur & Wilson, 1967). This typology is best used to describe closely related species in an order or family. In primates, for example, mouse lemurs are r strategists as compared to gorillas, who are K strategists. As large mammals, gorillas and other anthropoid apes allocate a considerable portion of their life energy to growth and development (Harvey, Martin, & Clutton-Brock, 1987). Mouse lemurs weigh 80 grams, whereas gorillas weigh 93 kilograms. Mouse lemurs have their first offspring at 11.5 months, whereas gorillas have theirs at about 120 months. Mouse lemurs have two offspring a year, whereas gorillas have one offspring every 4 years. Owing to the more rapid generation time and the exponential nature of reproduction, a mouse lemur could leave 10 million descendants by the time a gorilla had one (Harvey, 1990).

Evolved life history patterns entail patterns of allocation of energy among the four basic life functions in any given circumstance, as well as their allocation across the life span. Among mammals, for example, the following features are involved: gestation length, timing of locomotor development, deciduous teeth, weaning, onset of puberty, first reproductive effort, number of offspring per reproductive effort, frequency of reproductive effort, relative balance of mating and parental investment, and total life span. In other words, evolutionary biologists view not only bodily structures and behaviors, but life histories as products of past selection operating in various developmental and phylogenetic constraints. Selection favors classes of individuals whose investment patterns result in the greatest lifetime reproductive success or inclusive fitness in a species. (It is important to note, however, that, as a consequence of random reshuffling of genes in reproduction as well as mutations, populations always include unsuccessful variants.)

Life histories also can be described in terms of differential investments in conspecifics. Conspecifics generally fall into one of the following classes: 1) potential carriers of the actor's genes, 2) potential mates, 3) potential allies, and 4) potential competitors. Close relatives share genes and are more likely than other conspecifics to benefit from cooperating with one another. Therefore, kin recognition is vital to allocation of cooperation. Although kin recognition can occur through a variety of mechanisms, it often relies on phenotypic matching. This, in turn, relies on olfactory or other self-knowledge. Adaptive mate choice depends on an optimal degree of genetic distance between mates. Self-knowledge and phenotype matching in this context are mechanisms for avoiding extreme inbreeding or outbreeding (Slater, 1994). Finally, assessment of the qualities of the self relative to others becomes important whenever animals may benefit or suffer from competing with a given rival. Assessment becomes an important issue when rivals are apparently closely matched in their strength and abilities.

In other words, assessment of the net benefits of investing in a given course of action relative to a given conspecific is prerequisite for strategic choices. Assessment implies a means for assessing the nature of the self relative to that of conspecifics: Self-knowledge is the standard for such assessment. Assessment of the qualities of potential interactants relative to the self becomes important whenever animals may benefit from investing energy in interactions with one individual as opposed to another. When a female chooses of one mate versus another mate, when a parent invests more in one offspring than another, when someone aids one relative as opposed to another, or competes with one potential rival instead of another, these choices have consequences for their reproductive success. A few examples should help clarify this idea.

Assessment is important in male competition. Among male red deer, for example, assessing their own strength relative to that of rivals is crucial for deciding whether it is cost-effective to engage in combat with a given rival. Roaring contests are one means for such assessment. These contests effectively gauge the relative size and strength of two rivals because the loudness of roaring depends on body size. It is therefore a relatively honest signal for assessment in contrast to antler size, which may not be such a good index (Clutton-Brock & Albon, 1979).

Likewise, assessment of the relative reproductive value of their offspring allows parents to discriminate accordingly in their parental investment in a manner that increases their own reproductive success (Alexander, 1974). One reason for this is that high-ranking mothers may receive a greater reproductive payoff from investing more in male than female offspring in polygynous species (Trivers & Williard, 1973). Likewise, parents benefit from assessing the degrees of dependency of their offspring in deciding when to reduce their investment (for example, by weaning) in that offspring preparatory to investing in another offspring (Trivers, 1974).

The ability to assess qualities of conspecifics relative to self (and relative to one another) and to make choices based on their assessment is widespread among animal species. Although this may surprise nonbiologists, reflection on the nature of natural selection reveals the reason. Given any variation in such abilities, selection would weed out those individuals who made poorer choices and hence those who were poorer at assessment. Even nonsocial species are constantly engaging in assessments of potential prey choices or potential predators as well as potential mates. Indeed, the nervous systems of animals seem to have evolved largely for such assessments.

CONDITIONS FAVORING THE EVOLUTION OF ASSESSMENT AND SELF-KNOWLEDGE

Ethologists classify signals that can be probed by the receiver to test the qualities of the signaler as assessable signals. They note that assessable signals involve costs (as well as benefits) not only to the sender but also to the receiver (Dawkins & Guilford, 1991). Producing such signals is costly to the sender because they depend on high cost organ systems and involve considerable energy expenditure. Eliciting such signals is costly to the receiver because in most cases he must emit similar signals to elicit continuing production by the sender (Dawkins & Guilford, 1991). Therefore, assessable signals tend to be rarer than lower cost, nonassessable conventionalized signals that can be easily faked. Conventionalized signals such as hair and plumage provide less information about the quality of their bearers, but they are cheap to produce. They demand no assessment energy by the receiver.

Assessment is important among social species with long memories, individual recognition, and stable social groups. In such species, assessment is more important under some conditions than under others. Under stable conditions, conventionalized signaling is a desirably low-cost option. This is true, for example, in the case of a stable dominance hierarchy. Assessment becomes important under conditions of change when new information is vital to reduce uncertainty. This occurs, for example, when strength changes rapidly during the breeding season (Dawkins & Guilford, 1991). It probably also occurs under the following conditions: 1) when young males in a group mature and older males decline to the degree that a takeover of the alpha position in the dominance hierarchy becomes feasible, 2) when group composition changes owing to immigration and/or emigration of sexually mature adults, 3) when different individuals are present with or without their respective allies, 4) when significant ecological changes occur (food and other resources open up, or conversely decline), and 5) when new skills are invented or imported.

When there are several stage-like transitions in the life cycle, when there are complex social groups, when the environmental niche is complex and unstable, when adaptation depends on learned technology and social traditions, then assessable signals become adaptive. In other words, it seems likely that assessable signals should be more prevalent among species with so-called K LHS than among species with so-called r LHS.

Given these stipulations, It also seems likely that assessable signals would be especially advantageous during developmental transitions. In particular, they should be prominent in parent–infant interactions, in peer play interactions, and in apprenticeship or teaching interactions. Therefore, I argue that play and apprenticeship are important contexts for mutual assessment in anthropoid primates. Parent–infant play, peer play, and apprenticeship are all characterized by reciprocal, highly contingent interactions that involve mutual assessments. Participants are more or less constantly monitoring and/or receiving feedback from one another.

Comparative data suggest that vestibular and proprioceptive feedback in play fighting in monkeys and some other social mammals allows these organisms to assess their fighting abilities relative to those of future competitors. Furthermore, kin interventions in play allow monkeys to assess the relative size and rank of their playmate's kin groups (Aldis, 1975; Fagen, 1981; Symons, 1978). This in turn may aid them in devising appropriate social strategies and roles, particularly strategies in mate competition (Symons, 1978). Other more primitive forms of assessment occur in other vertebrate species. See Table 8.1 for a summary of proposed assessment functions for various kinds and levels of self-knowledge in various taxa.

The assessment model of self-knowledge presented is a more general formulation than the preceding apprenticeship model of self-knowledge in great apes and humans. How does apprenticeship fit the broader model? Apprenticeship involves assessment by the pupil of his own actions relative to the teacher, and reciprocally, assessment by the teacher of his own actions relative to the abilities of the pupil. In other words, apprenticeship also entails assessment of the self's abilities relative to those of conspecifics. More advanced forms of self-awareness such as self-evaluative emotions (Lewis et al., 1989) and the narrative or autobiographical self (e.g., Snow, 1990) in humans involve more elaborate forms of self-assessment.

SUMMARY AND CONCLUSIONS

In Baldwin's tradition, I have suggested an integrated comparative approach to understanding the evolution and development of self-knowledge in animals. This approach is based on several steps. The first step was to use models from human development to identify levels of self-knowledge and their developmental patterns in anthropoid primate species. The second was to use Mead's model for the development of self through social play as a frame for analyzing mechanisms of self-knowledge. The third was to use cladistic methodology to map the distribution of these abilities onto primate phylogenies in order to identify the common ancestry of particular kinds of abilities. The fourth was to use comparative data on the distribution of various kinds of self-knowledge among various species to generate functional hypotheses concerning the adaptive significance of self-knowledge.

LHS theory suggests that self-knowledge in animals has the general function of allowing them to assess their own nature relative to that of conspecifics. This allows them to identify conspecifics as kin, potential mates, or potential competitors, and to assess their abilities relative to those of potential competitors. Such assessment is prerequisite to making strategic choices among available alternative investments in mating effort, parental effort, nepotism, and competition.

Application of LHS theory in relation to monkeys and other social mammals suggests that these species use vestibular and proprioceptive cues during rough-and-tumble play to assess their fighting abilities and kin network relative to those of competitors. Comparative analysis suggests that self-awareness in great apes and human infants is central to assessment in imitation and teaching in apprenticeship in tool use in ancestral great apes (Parker, 1996b). It also suggests that great apes selectively imitate successful models to develop their competitive strategies. Finally, this analysis suggests that humans have added new cognitive dimensions of self-knowledge and self-assessment through the evolution of linguistic and cultural means that are practiced in new forms of play.

ACKNOWLEDGMENTS

I would like to thank the editors of this volume, Melanie Killen and Jonas Langer, for inviting me to speak at the Jean Piaget Society Meetings in Berkeley in 1995 and for their comments on the first draft of this chapter. I also want to thank the following colleagues for helpful suggestions on earlier drafts of this paper: Constance Milbrath, Sulamith Hines Potter, Pamela Plumb Dhindsa, and Andrew Wilson.

REFERENCES

Aldis, O. (1975). *Play fighting*. New York: Academic Press.
Alexander, R. (1974). The evolution of social behaviour. *Annual Review of Ecology and Systematics, 5*, 325–383.
Amsterdam, B. K. (1972). Mirror self-image reactions before two years of age. *Developmental Psychobiology, 5*, 297–305.
Anderson, J. R. (1984). The development of self-recognition: A review. *Developmental Psychobiology, 17*(1), 35–49.
Baldwin, J. M. (1897). *Social and ethical interpretations of mental development*. New York: Macmillan.
Bertanthal, B. L., & Fischer, K. W. (1978). Development of self-recognition in the infant. *Developmental Psychology, 14*, 44–50.
Boesch, C. (1991). Teaching among wild chimpanzees. *Animal Behaviour, 41*, 530–532.
Boysen, S. T., Bryan, K. M., & Shreyer, T. A. (1994). Shadows and mirrors: Alternative avenues to the development of self-recognition in chimpanzees. In S. T. Parker, R. W. Mitchell, & M. L. Boccia (Eds.), *Self-awareness in animals and humans* (pp. 227–240). New York: Cambridge University Press.
Bretherton, I. (1984). Representing the social world in symbolic play: Reality and fantasy. In I. Bretherton (Ed.), *Symbolic play: The development of social understanding* (pp. 32–41). New York: Academic Press.
Brooks, D., & McLennan, D. (1991). *Phylogeny, ecology, and behavior*. Chicago: University of Chicago Press.
Bruner, J. (1983). *Child's talk*. New York: Norton.
Clutton-Brock, T., & Albon, S. D. (1979). The roaring of red deer and the evolution of honest advertisement. *Animal Behaviour, 69*, 145–170.

Clutton-Brock, T., & Harvey, P. (1984). Comparative approaches to investigating adaptation. In J. R. Krebs & N. B. Davies (Eds.), *Behavioural ecology* (2nd ed., pp. 7–29). London: Blackwell.

Coddington, J. A. (1988). Cladistic tests of adaptational hypotheses. *Cladistics, 4,* 3–22.

Custance, D., & Bard, K. (1994). The comparative and developmental study of self-recognition and imitation: The importance of social factors. In S. T. Parker, R. W. Mitchell, & M. L. Boccia (Eds.), *Self-awareness in animals and humans* (pp. 207–226). New York: Cambridge University Press.

Dawkins, M. S. (1986). *Unravelling animal behaviour.* Essex, England: Longman.

Dawkins, M. S., & Guilford, T. (1991). The corruption of honest signaling. *Animal Behaviour, 41,* 865–873.

Fagen, R. (1981). *Animal play behavior.* New York: Oxford University Press.

Fein, G. G. (1984). The self-building potential of pretend play, or "I got a fish all by myself." In T. D. Yawkey & A. D. Pelligrini (Eds.), *Child's play: Developmental and applied* (pp. 125–141). Hillsdale, NJ: Lawrence Erlbaum Associates.

Gallup, G. G., Jr. (1970). Chimpanzees: Self-recognition. *Science, 167,* 86–87.

Gallup, G. G., Jr. (1977). Self-recognition in primates. *American Psychologist, 32,* 329–338.

Gergely, G. (1994). From self-recognition to theory of mind. In S. T. Parker, R. W. Mitchell, & M. L. Boccia (Eds.), *Self-awareness in animals and humans* (pp. 51–60). New York: Cambridge University Press.

Goodall, J. (1986). *Chimpanzees of the Gombe.* Cambridge, MA: Harvard University Press.

Gopnik, A., & Meltzoff, A. (1994). Minds, bodies and persons: Young children's understanding of the self and others as reflected in imitation and theory of mind research. In S. T. Parker, R. W. Mitchell, & M. L. Boccia (Eds.), *Self-awareness in animals and humans* (pp. 166–185). New York: Cambridge University Press.

Hart, D., & Fegley, S. (1994). Social imitation and the emergence of a mental model of self. In S. T. Parker, R. W. Mitchell, & M. L. Boccia (Eds.), *Self-awareness in animals and humans* (pp. 149–165). New York: Cambridge University Press.

Hart, D., & Kamel, M. P. (1996). Self-awareness and self-knowledge in humans, apes, and monkeys. In A. E. Russon, K. A. Bard, & S. T. Parker (Eds.), *Reaching into thought: The minds of the great apes* (pp. 325–357). Cambridge, England: Cambridge University Press.

Harvey, P., Martin, R. D., & Clutton-Brock, T. (1987). Life histories in comparative perspective. In B. Smuts, D. Cheney, R. Seyfarth, R. Wrangham, & T. Struhsaker (Eds.), *Primate societies* (pp. 181–196). Chicago: University of Chicago Press.

Harvey, P. H. (1990). Life-history variation: Size and mortality patterns. In C. J. D. Rousseau (Ed.), *Primate life history and evolution* (pp. 81–88). New York: Wiley.

Hennig, W. (1979). *Phylogenetic systematics.* Urbana: University of Illinois Press.

Horn, H., & Rubenstein, D. (1984). Behavioural adaptations and life history. In J. R. Krebs & N. B. Davies (Eds.), *Behavioural ecology: An evolutionary approach* (2nd ed., pp. 279–298). London: Blackwell.

Johnson, M. (1989). *The body in the mind.* Chicago: University of Chicago Press.

Kagan, J., Garcia Coll, C., & Reznick, J. (1984). Behavioral inhibition in young children. *Child Development, 55,* 1005–1009.

Ledbetter, D. H., & Basen, J. A. (1982). Failure to demonstrate self-recognition in gorillas. *American Journal of Primatology, 2,* 307–310.

Leslie, A. M. (1988). Some implications of pretense for mechanisms underlying the child's theory of mind. In J. Astington, P. Harris, & D. Olsen (Eds.), *Developing theories of mind* (pp. 19–46). Cambridge, England: Cambridge University Press.

LeVine, R. (1990). Enculturation: A biocultural perspective on the development of self. In D. Cicchetti & M. Beeghly (Eds.), *The self in transition: Infancy to childhood* (pp. 99–128). Chicago: University of Chicago Press.

Lewis, M., & Brooks-Gunn, J. (1979). *Social cognition and the acquisition of self.* New York: Plenum.

Lewis, M., Sullivan, M. W., Stanger, C., & Weiss, M. (1989). Self-development and self-conscious emotions. *Child Development, 60,* 146–156.

Linn, A., Bard, K., & Anderson, J. R. (1992). Development of self-recognition in chimpanzees. *Journal of Comparative Psychology, 106,* 120–127.

MacArthur, R. H., & Wilson, E. O. (1967). *Theory of island biogeography.* Princeton, NJ: Princeton University Press.

Martens, K., & Psarakos, S. (1994). Evidence of self-awareness in the bottlenose dolphin (*Tursiops truncattus*). In S. T. Parker, R. W. Mitchell, & M. L. Boccia (Eds.), *Self-awareness in animals and humans* (pp. 380–391). New York: Cambridge University Press.

Mead, G. H. (1970). *Mind, self and society.* Chicago: University of Chicago Press.

Meltzoff, A. (1988). Imitation, objects, tools and the rudiments of language in human ontogeny. *Human Evolution, 3,* 45–64.

Meltzoff, A. (1990). Foundations for developing a concept of self: The role of imitation in relating self to other and the value of social mirroring, social modeling, and self practice in infancy. In D. Cicchetti & M. Beeghly (Eds.), *The self in transition: Infancy to childhood.* Chicago: University of Chicago Press.

Miles, H. L. (1994). Me Chantek: The development of self-awareness in a signing gorilla. In S. T. Parker, R. W. Mitchell, & M. L. Boccia (Eds.), *Self-awareness in animals and humans* (pp. 254–272). New York: Cambridge University Press.

Mitchell, R. W. (1993). Mental models of mirror-self-recognition: Two theories. *New Ideas in Psychology, 11,* 295–325.

Nelson, K. (1983). The derivation of concepts and categories from event representations. In E. Scholnick (Ed.), *New trends in conceptual representation: Challenges to Piagetian theory* (pp. 129–149). Hillsdale, NJ: Lawrence Erlbaum Associates.

Nelson, K., & Gruendel, J. (1986). Children's scripts. In K. Nelson (Ed.), *Event knowledge* (pp. 21–45). Hillsdale, NJ: Lawrence Erlbaum Associates.

Nelson, K., & Seidman, S. (1984). Playing with scripts. In I. Bretherton (Ed.), *Symbolic play* (pp. 45–72). New York: Academic Press.

Parker, S. T. (1984). Playing for keeps: An evolutionary perspective on human games. In P. K. Smith (Ed.), *Play in animals and humans* (pp. 271–293). London: Blackwell.

Parker, S. T. (1985). A social technological model for the evolution of language. *Current Anthropology, 26*(5), 617–639.

Parker, S. T. (1990). The origins of comparative developmental evolutionary studies of primate mental abilities. In S. T. Parker & K. R. Gibson (Eds.), *"Language" and intelligence in monkeys and apes* (pp. 3–64). New York: Cambridge University Press.

Parker, S. T. (1991). A developmental approach to the origins of self-recognition in great apes and human infants. *Human Evolution, 6,* 435–449.

Parker, S. T. (1993). Imitation and circular reactions as evolved mechanisms for cognitive construction. *Human Development, 36,* 309–323.

Parker, S. T. (1996a). Anthropomorphism is the null hypothesis and recapitulation is the Bogey man in comparative developmental evolutionary studies. In R. Mitchell, N. Thompson, & H. L. Miles (Eds.), *Anthropomorphism, anecdotes and animals* (pp. 348–362). Albany: State University of New York Press.

Parker, S. T. (1996b). Apprenticeship in tool-mediated extractive foraging. In A. Russon, K. Bard, & S. T. Parker (Eds.), *Reaching into thought: The minds of the great apes* (pp. 348–370). Cambridge, England: Cambridge University Press.

Parker, S. T., & Gibson, K. R. (1977). Object manipulation, tool use, and sensorimotor intelligence as feeding adaptations in cebus monkeys and great apes. *Journal of Human Evolution, 6,* 623–641.

Parker, S. T., & Gibson, K. R. (1979). A developmental model for the evolution of language and intelligence in early hominids. *Behavioral and Brain Sciences, 2,* 367–408.

Parker, S. T., & Milbrath, C. (1994). Contributions of imitation and role-playing games to the construction of self in primates. In S. T. Parker, R. W. Mitchell, & M. L. Boccia (Eds.), *Self-awareness in animals and humans* (pp. 108–128). New York: Cambridge University Press.

Parker, S. T., & Mitchell, R. W. (1994). Evolving self-awareness. In S. T. Parker, R. W. Mitchell, & M. L. Boccia (Eds.), *Self-awareness in animals and humans* (pp. 413–428). New York: Cambridge University Press.

Patterson, F., & Cohn, R. (1994). Self-recognition and self-awareness in lowland gorillas. In S. T. Parker, R. W. Mitchell, & M. L. Boccia (Eds.), *Self-awareness in animals and humans* (pp. 273–290). New York: Cambridge University Press.

Piaget, J. (1952). *The origins of intelligence in children.* New York: International Universities Press.

Piaget, J. (1954). *The construction of reality in the child.* New York: Basic Books.

Piaget, J. (1962). *Play, dreams, and imitation.* New York: Norton.

Piaget, J. (1965). *The moral judgment of the child.* New York: The Free Press.

Piaget, J. (1981). *Intelligence and affectivity: Their relationship during child development* (T. A. Brown, C. E. Kaegi, Trans.). Palo Alto, CA: Annual Reviews.

Povinelli, D. (1994). How to create a self-recognizing gorillas (but don't try it on macaques). In S. T. Parker, R. W. Mitchell, & M. L. Boccia (Eds.), *Self-awareness in animals and humans* (pp. 291–300). New York: Cambridge University Press.

Povinelli, D., Rulf, A., Landau, K., & Bierschwale, D. (1993). Self-recognition in chimpanzees (*Pan troglodytes*): Distribution, ontogeny, and patterns of emergence. *Journal of Comparative Psychology, 107*(4), 347–372.

Russon, A. (1996). Imitation in everyday use: Matching and rehearsal in the spontaneous imitation of rehabilitant orangutans (*Pongo pygmaeus*). In A. Russon, K. Bard, & S. T. Parker (Eds.), *Reaching into thought: The minds of the great apes* (pp. 152–176). Cambridge, England: Cambridge University Press.

Russon, A., & Galdikas, B. (1993). Imitation in free-ranging rehabilitant orangutans (*Pongo pygmaeus*). *Journal of Comparative Psychology, 107*(2), 147–161.

Russon, A., & Galdikas, B. (1995). Constraints on great ape imitation: Model and action selectivity in rehabilitant orangutan (*Pongo pygmaeus*) imitation. *Journal of Comparative Psychology, 109,* 5–17.

Ruvolo, M. (1994). Molecular evolutionary processes and conflicting gene trees: The hominoid case. *American Journal of Physical Anthropology, 94,* 89–113.

Slater, P. J. B. (1994). Kinship and altruism. In P. J. B. Slater & T. R. Halliday (Eds.), *Behaviour and evolution* (pp. 193–222). Cambridge, England: Cambridge University Press.

Snow, C. E. (1990). Building memories: The ontogeny of autobiography. In D. Cicchetti & M. Beeghly (Eds.), *The self in transition: Infancy to childhood* (pp. 213–242). Chicago: University of Chicago Press.

Stern, D. (1977). *The first relationship.* Cambridge, MA: Harvard University Press.

Swartz, K., & Evans, S. (1991). Not all chimpanzees (*Pan troglodytes*) show self-recognition. *Primates, 32,* 483–496.

Symons, D. (1978). *Play and aggression: A study of rhesus monkeys.* New York: Columbia University Press.

Tomasello, M., Gust, D., & Frost, T. (1989). A longitudinal investigation of gestural communication in young chimpanzees. *Primates, 30*(1), 35–50.

Tomasello, M., Kruger, A. C., & Ratner, H. H. (1993). Cultural learning. *Behavioral and Brain Sciences, 16,* 495–552.

Trevarthan, C., & Hubley, P. (1978). Secondary intersubjectivity: Confidence, confiding and acts of meaning in the first year. In A. Lock (Ed.), *Action, gesture and symbol* (pp. 183–229). New York: Academic Press.

Trivers, R. (1974). Parent–offspring conflict. *American Zoologist, 14,* 249–264.

Trivers, R., & Williard, D. E. (1973). Natural selection of parental ability to vary the sex ratio of offspring. *Science, 191,* 249–263.

Varela, F. J., Thompson, E., & Rosch, E. (1991). *The embodied mind*. Boston: MIT Press.

Watson, J. S. (1972). Smiling, cooing, and "the game." *Merrill Palmer Quarterly, 18*, 323–339.

Watson, M. (1990). Aspects of self development as reflected in children's role playing. In D. Cicchetti & M. Beeghly (Eds.), *The self in transition* (pp. 265–280). Chicago: University of Chicago Press.

Watson, M. W. (1981). The development of social roles: A sequence of social-cognitive development. In K. W. Fischer (Ed.), *New directions for child development* (Vol. 12, pp. 33–41). New York: Jossey–Bass.

Watson, M. W. (1984). Development of social role understanding. *Developmental Review, 4*, 192–213.

Wiley, E. O. (1981). *Phylogenetics: The theory and practice of phylogenetic systematics*. New York: Wiley.

Wood, D. (1989). Social interaction as tutoring. In M. H. Bornstein & J. S. Bruner (Eds.), *Interaction in human development* (pp. 59–82). Hillsdale, NJ: Lawrence Erlbaum Associates.

Wood, D., Bruner, J., & Ross, G. (1976). The role of tutoring in problem solving. *Journal of Child Psychology and Psychiatry, 17*, 89–100.

9

CONFLICT RESOLUTION IN HUMAN AND NONHUMAN PRIMATES

Marina Cords
Columbia University

Melanie Killen
University of Maryland, College Park

In a Tanzanian forest, an adult male chimpanzee named Goliath attacked a younger male named Figan. Shortly afterward, Figan approached his former adversary, screaming submissively. Goliath moved toward Figan, reaching out his arm to pat the younger male gently, after which Figan stopped screaming and visibly relaxed (Goodall, 1986).

At the foot of their sleeping cliff in the Ethiopian desert, the adult male members of a clan of hamadryas baboons decide on the direction of their daily march. Individual males appear to make proposals by taking a few steps in one direction, sometimes inviting another male to follow by presenting the conspicuous red hindquarters. Proposals may be followed by counterproposals or by refusals, in which a male lowers his head abruptly, averting his gaze from the proposal being made. Eventually, the males reach a consensus on a direction and the band sets off on a half-day's journey to a distant water hole, whose direction from the sleeping cliff is exactly that on which they agreed (Kummer, 1995).

In a Japanese preschool, two children, Hana and Aya, are putting away some cards that they were playing with during free time. Aya gives the card box to Hana. Hana puts her cards in the box and gives it back to Aya. Aya begins looking through Hana's cards.

Hana: Don't touch my cards!

Aya: I'm only looking through them.

Hana: No, you don't have to! (she puts her hands over the cards)

Aya: Okay, I won't look at them if you help me clean up the rest of the cards.

Hana: Alright. (she puts away the rest of the cards)

Aya: (closes the box and refrains from looking at Hana's cards). (Killen & Sueyoshi, 1995).

In a preschool in the United States, three children are at a table playing with 10 to 12 small toys. Luke takes the cookie monster truck.

Martha: Hey, no fair, I want that one (to Luke). You have all the good toys.

Rebecca: Yeah, and I got none!

Luke: Well, I didn't have any yesterday.

Martha: I know . . . Luke, if you give that one to Rebecca and I give this one (red car) to you then you can give me the cookie monster. Then, we'll each have one!

Luke: Okay, here Rebecca (gives her the blue car and then gives Martha the cookie monster truck and takes the red car from Martha).

Rebecca: (takes blue car) Does it go like this? Vrrooommm! (Killen & Naigles, 1995).

These are typical examples of conflict resolution in children and in non-human primates. Individuals begin in a state of conflict, in which their behavioral acts or beliefs are incompatible, and end up with their conflict resolved. Conflicts may be aggressive or not, and resolution may take many forms, including negotiation and making up. Recent studies have shown not only that resolution of conflicts occurs widely across the primate order, even in very young individuals, but also that such resolution allows individuals to maintain important social relationships. In the case of human children, engaging in conflict resolution also encourages the development of social and moral reasoning.

The comparative evidence for these general findings now appears strong, and our chapter reviews this evidence. We also note that these conclusions are fairly new and result from recent changes in the foci of research on interindividual conflict in both human children and nonhuman primates. Early studies focused on aggressive conflict (children: Shantz & Hartup, 1992; nonhuman primates, Mason, 1993), which was seen as potentially or actually maladaptive. More recently, the research theme has broadened in two important ways. First, the notions of conflict and aggression have been at least partially dissociated so that nonaggressive conflict has also become a subject of study. Second, there has been a greater focus on resolution of conflict. As a result of both of these developments, conflict and its aftermaths have come to be recognized as potentially constructive and positive events in individuals' lives (e.g., Killen, 1995; Lyons, 1993; Ross & Conant, 1992; Shantz, 1987).

In this chapter, we highlight some of the specific similarities and differences that have emerged from studies of conflict resolution in human children and nonhuman primates. In so doing, we wish to call attention to aspects of this behavior that appear to show evolutionary continuity in the primate order, as well as those that seem to differentiate members of this order. In addition, we propose that much complexity in how human and nonhuman primates resolve conflicts has been overlooked because of an overemphasis on aggressive, rather than nonaggressive, conflicts. Recent research findings, from studies both of human children and nonhuman primates, have begun to alter the course of scientific explorations in this area.

THE STUDY OF INTERPERSONAL
CONFLICT RESOLUTION: TWO HISTORIES,
TWO PERSPECTIVES

Our task is complicated by differences in the perspectives that guide the study of conflict resolution in nonhuman primates and in human children. Ethological studies of nonhuman animals have emerged from a zoological tradition that emphasized evolutionary perspectives on behavior, both in its focus on cross-species comparisons, and in its analysis of the costs and benefits (measured ultimately in the currency of lifetime reproductive success) of particular behavioral programs. In the 1960s, Lorenz (1966) and Ardrey (1966) portrayed aggression as the product of an innate drive, reflecting primarily an individual's internal state and ubiquitously present among animals. With the advent of sociobiological thinking in the 1970s, there was greater emphasis on how aggression is a flexible and adaptive response, elicited by and ultimately terminating conflicts of interest between competitors. Game theoretical models of animal conflicts (e.g., Maynard Smith & Price, 1973), formulated to enrich understanding of the evolution of various agonistic strategies, focused attention on the balance of benefits and costs of a greater variety of conflict types; however, the costs included in these models (e.g., lost time, risk of injury, loss of a resource) were not social costs. More recently, the social costs of conflict have been considered more carefully, largely as a result of studies of nonhuman primates whose conflicts usually occur in the context of enduring social relationships. Some forms of conflict have the potential for disturbing these relationships, which are viewed as adaptive responses to ecological challenges set by the environment in which these animals live. The discovery of apparent mechanisms of conflict resolution in chimpanzees (namely postconflict reconciliation; de Waal & van Roosmalen, 1979) stimulated researchers to look for similar behavior in other taxa: Such behavioral mechanisms, it was thought, should be widespread in animals who depend on social relationships for survival and reproduction because conflict resolution should be important in managing these vital relationships. Alongside a growing number of studies that demonstrated apparent postconflict reconciliation behavior in various non-human primate species, research has concentrated on demonstrating the efficacy of such behavior in promoting (correlates of) survival and reproduction and the factors that determine how and to what degree such conflict resolution occurs in particular situations, dyads, and species. In addition, a small but significant literature has been growing that addresses a wider variety of conflict types (e.g., noncompetitive, nonaggressive conflicts) and forms of conflict resolution other than postaggression peacemaking (de Waal, 1996a; Mason & Mendoza, 1993). A few studies have addressed the development of strategies of conflict resolution in juveniles (Cords & Aureli, 1993; de Waal & Johanowicz, 1993).

Developmental psychologists have placed more emphasis on the ways in which the experience of social conflict influences the acquisition of social skills and concepts such as negotiation (Hay & Ross, 1982), perspective-taking (Selman, 1980), reciprocity (Piaget, 1932), morality (Dunn, Slomkowski, Donelan, & Herrera, 1995; Killen, 1995; Piaget, 1932; Youniss, 1980) and a sense of self (Damon & Hart, 1988). This emphasis stems partly from developmental theory that postulates that conflict facilitates change in development. Specifically, individuals strive to maintain a sense of cognitive equilibrium; when the individual experiences cognitive disequilibrium (e.g., something occurs that she/he doesn't understand), attempts are made to figure out the nature of the problem (Piaget, 1971, 1985/1975; see Shantz, 1987). This is true for the infant striving to understand object permanence and for the child struggling to understand fairness. Piaget theorized that adult–child interactions, which are asymmetrical and characterized by constraint, inhibit the child's ability to construct fairness and reciprocity. In contrast, peer interactions, which are symmetrical and characterized by cooperation, promote the child's understanding. In particular, peer conflict forces children to take another's perspective and, by a process of reciprocity and abstraction, develop a sense of justice. Piaget's findings led him to postulate that peer conflict may provide a special form of interaction for children, one that leads them to develop moral judgment (Piaget, 1932). Thus, historically, the focus was on conflict and conflict resolution among peers. Recent studies have included parent–child, teacher–child, and sibling interactions as well, however, as researchers have moved away from Piaget's (1932) view that social reciprocity and morality are an outcome solely of peer interactions (because adult–child interactions are not always characterized by constraint, nor are peer interactions always characterized by cooperation). By examining a broader range of social relationships and interactions in which young children engage, including various kinds of conflict as well as various kinds of opponents, contemporary researchers aim to understand more thoroughly how social behavior contributes to the development of social knowledge. Thus, their purpose in chronicling ontogenetic change is not only to document social coping skills and the factors that influence their expression (as with nonhuman primates), but also to determine the consequences of those emerging skills for sociocognitive development.

Despite somewhat different aims, both evolutionary biologists and developmental psychologists view conflict resolution as generally adaptive in that it maintains group harmony. The way in which researchers in these two disciplines conceive of adaptation is somewhat different, but, we feel, not incompatible. In biology, adaptation is related to the notion of evolutionary change. Traits viewed as adaptations become prevalent in populations through the evolutionary process of natural selection because individuals possessing those traits have an advantage in terms of lifetime reproductive success over individuals lacking those traits. This view assumes that at least originally, some variation in the expression of a trait was related to variation in the genetic make up of individual organisms. Developmental psychologists describe those traits that contribute to the development of fully functional adult humans as adaptive. Their view does not necessarily imply anything about evolutionary processes or genetic underpinnings to variations in behavior. Researchers in both fields would measure adaptiveness in terms of the effects that particular behavioral traits have on the individuals who express them. Although the biologist is ultimately interested in the trait's effect on lifetime reproductive success, this effect may be difficult to measure, especially in long-lived organisms. Instead, one usually assesses the trait's effect on a variable (such as food intake, immune function, or the successful performance of some behavioral strategy) believed to be correlated with lifetime reproductive success (Hinde, 1982). The kind of adaptiveness considered by psychologists could exemplify such a correlated effect: Behavioral traits that contribute to the development of social (and, for humans, moral) abilities that underpin primate society should also be biologically adaptive, insofar as all primates are committed in an evolutionary sense to life in complex societies whose workings depend on those skills. When we consider conflict resolution as adaptive, we thus consider the ways in which it contributes to the development of social and moral skills and knowledge (in children) and to the maintenance of social relationships in which conflict occurs (in children and in nonhuman primates). These are the proximate mechanisms through which conflict resolution may ultimately influence reproductive output. In this chapter, we review the evidence that supports the existence of these proximate mechanisms and conclude that conflict management and resolution may have significant impacts on the lives of all primates.

SOME DEFINITIONS

It is important to consider at the outset what exactly is meant by the term *conflict*, as this term has been used in various ways by developmental psychologists and primatologists alike. We limit ourselves here to interindividual conflict (henceforth simply *conflict*), acknowledging that the term has also been applied to conflicts in individuals and between groups of individuals. Conflict arises when individuals express incompatible goals, interests, or actions (Hand, 1986; Hay, 1984; Hay & Ross, 1982; Shantz, 1987). It seems that human psychologists first called attention to the fact that conflict and aggression are separate concepts (see review by Shantz, 1987), with aggression being defined as behavior aimed at harming or injuring another individual (Hinde, 1974; Parke & Slaby, 1983; Shantz, 1987). Aggression need not arise from conflict (for example, frustration or pain can elicit aggression). Aggression is nevertheless likely to create conflict, insofar as the victim of aggression tries to avoid being harmed or injured. Conflict need not be aggressive at all, however (for example, when two interacting individuals disagree about what they will do next). Thus, although aggression may reliably indicate conflict, conflict also can (and often does) occur in the absence of aggression.

Evolutionary biologists studying animal behavior have generally not used the term *conflict* when referring to actual behavior (see Hand, 1986, for an exception), although it has been applied to theoretical situations in which the evolutionary interests of different individuals are incompatible (e.g., parent–offspring conflict, Trivers, 1974). Conflict in its behavioral sense is implied, however, in sociobiological definitions of aggression as a mechanism of competition (e.g., Barash, 1982). In the animal literature generally, and in studies of nonhuman primates in particular, an association of conflict (namely competition) with aggression is widespread. Only recently has the independence of these two concepts been explicitly reiterated for primatologists (Mason, 1993; Mason & Mendoza, 1993), and it is probably no coincidence that two animal *psychologists* were responsible. Such a reiteration was timely because most recent empirical work on conflict resolution in nonhuman primates has been limited to the sequelae and resolution of aggressive conflicts. Several chapters in Mason and Mendoza's (1993) book provide interesting exceptions (e.g., Mason, Long, & Mendoza, 1993; Menzel, 1993).

Whereas students of child development and nonhuman primates might agree on a conceptual definition of conflict, there are differences in the operational definitions they use to recognize such conflict, especially in studies of conflict resolution. Developmental psychologists typically focus on the expression of opposition as a hallmark of conflict. Conflict is recognized when at least one opponent protests, resists, or disagrees with the actions or utterances of another (Shantz, 1987), and "conflicts begin when opposition becomes apparent" (Ross & Conant, 1992, p. 155). Most studies of nonhuman primates have focused on aggressive conflicts, and thus recognize conflict in acts of aggression. Typically, however, observers limit their study to cases in which the recipient of aggression shows some behavioral reaction to the aggressor, most often protective responses like flight, but occasionally counteraggression. Although they have not been explicitly identified as such in the nonhuman literature, even protective responses are expressions of opposition, inasmuch as the victim of aggression thereby attempts to interfere with the aggressor's immediate goal of inflicting harm. However, such flight responses make up the vast majority of oppositional responses in the aggressive conflicts studied among nonhuman primates, whereas opposition takes more various forms in the conflicts studied among human children. This is not surprising, given that studies of children's conflict include many nonaggressive conflicts to which protective responses are unnecessary.

These differences in the defining features of conflict probably reflect practical convenience more than any fundamental difference in animal and human conflict. A focus on opposition as defining human conflict is made possible by the fact that opposition is often expressed verbally, and hence easily recognized. A focus on opposition is called for if nonaggressive conflicts are to be included, as the intentions of an instigator in such a conflict are hard to discern behaviorally. A protest from a recipient reveals that the instigator's act was perturbing. An act might look perturbing to an observer (e.g., one child taking a toy from another) but could be interpreted as unoffensive by the recipient (e.g., turn-taking exchanges may have begun before an observer was present). Because they lack language, nonhuman primates generally show opposition in less easily detectable forms (e.g., Kummer, 1995; Menzel, 1993). The one exception is a protective response to received aggression. Because aggression itself, and protective responses to it, are easily recognized, studies of these animals often focus on aggressive conflicts. For the purposes of the present discussion, we simply note that these differences exist. These differences are important insofar as the population of conflicts sampled by developmental psychologists and primatologists differ, and this difference in samples could lead to apparently diverse conclusions.

THE CONTEXT OF CONFLICT AMONG PRIMATES

Much interindividual conflict among primates, both human and nonhuman, occurs in the context of social relationships. Social relationships are, in fact, one of the hallmarks of primate societies, and many aspects of social behavior, including conflict, are likely to influence these relationships. What exactly do we mean by the term *social relationship*?

Psychologists and biologists have defined social relationships in terms of the behavior exhibited by social partners. Hinde (1979), for example, used this term to refer in a descriptive way to the content, patterning, and quality of interactions between two individuals. These parameters are important characterizations of the dyad because of the specific ways in which each individual responds, and has responded previously, to the other. From such descriptive characterizations, it is possible to abstract emergent qualities of the relationship, such as reciprocity, and to infer underlying affective systems. Ross and colleagues (e.g., Ross, Conant, Cheyne, & Alevizos, 1992) have emphasized, perhaps even more than Hinde, the ways in which each partner's response to the other is unique. Relationships are inferred to exist "when individuals act toward one another in ways that cannot be predicted from their interactions in other social contexts" (Ross, Conant, Cheyne, & Alevizos, 1992, p. 2). The relationship is thus expressed as a statistical interaction effect between the behavioral propensities of two individuals.

Social relationships like these do not occur among all animals, even all social animals. Their existence depends on (1) repeated or long-term associations, in which (2) animals recognize and respond to one another as individuals, (3) in such a way that earlier interactions influence later ones. Insect societies and schools of fish are characterized by long-term associations of certain animals, but interactions are not individualized. These animals respond to one another only as members of groups, which are defined in terms of morphological structure, chemical signature, or perhaps, in the case of schooling fish, relative spatial position. Thus societies and social groups can and do exist in the absence of individualized social relationships.

If they are not prerequisites for social life generally, then what are such relationships for? There are, of course, multiple answers to this question, depending on one's perspective and level of analysis. An evolutionary answer was given by Kummer (1978), an ethologist/zoologist, who viewed relationships as investments that benefit the individuals involved. Benefit is measured in the evolutionary currency of lifetime reproductive success. In this context, interactions are viewed as ways of shaping the relationship to maximize the value of the social partner, as well as expressions of the relationship's adaptive benefit for one or both partners. A social partner is valuable insofar as interactions with that partner increase one's lifetime reproductive success. How valuable she is will depend on her intrinsic qualities (like sex, strength, social connectedness), her behavioral tendencies (how likely she is to behave in particular ways in particular circumstances), and her availability as an interaction partner (e.g., is she accessible when needed or desired?). Even if a social partner's value is negative, so that she decreases ego's chances of survival and reproduction, a relationship with her that influences her qualities, behavioral tendencies or availability will be advantageous if it makes her value less negative.

Among primates, social relationships probably have several particular adaptive functions (Cords, 1997). When members of the dyad have common reproductive interests (e.g., parent and offspring, mates), the adaptive function is obvious. But relationships are not limited to dyads whose members have common interests of this sort. Considering nonhuman primates, researchers have distinguished between the benefits of having relationships generally, and those associated with a subclass of relationships termed friendships. Among gregarious species, all group-mates typically have relationships with one another that are different when compared to their relations with other members of their population. Members of the same group are relatively tolerant of one another in feeding and social contexts, provide protection against predators through alarm calling or active defense, and may support each other in contests with other groups over feeding areas or territorial boundaries. Special friends, whose relationships are characterized by extraordinary levels of affiliation, may show even higher degrees of tolerance, may support one another in aggressive interactions with third parties, or may make food or social resources available to one another in several ways (Cords, 1997).

A social–developmental answer to the question of what relationships are for would differ from an evolutionary one because it would focus on the acquisition of social skills and social concepts as an outcome of conflict resolution, rather than on competitive ability or safety from predators. Decades of research have shown that close relationships provide an important context that enables children to develop social, emotional, and cognitive abilities. These relationships include parent–child attachments (Bowlby, 1971), as well as close and intimate friendships (Bukowski, Newcomb, & Hartup, 1996; Hartup, 1992). Space limitations do not permit an in-depth review here.

In general, the capacity to engage in social relationships, and the tendency to do so, is so broadly characteristic of the primate order, including humans, that it is likely an evolutionarily old trait. The precise fitness benefits that modern humans get from forming such relationships may differ from those documented more extensively for our nonhuman relatives. Yet, the same sorts of broad categories, namely cooperative defense against external threats, improving access to various resources, alliance formation to increase individuals' power, and development of social abilities may apply to all primates. For the purposes of this chapter, the exact way in which such relationships are adaptive in extant humans is less important than the more general proposition that they are adaptive, a proposition supported by investigations of many nonhuman primate species.

THE COSTS OF CONFLICT

Although social relationships are valuable, social partners will sometimes find themselves in a state of conflict. This state is both unavoidable and potentially beneficial, insofar as it leads each individual to accomodate the behavior, goals, or beliefs of a regular social partner in an ongoing series of interactions (de Waal, 1996a). At the same time, however, a state of conflict may impose costs on one or both partners if it undermines their social relationship. Over the short term, conflict may lead social partners to avoid each other so that beneficial interactions between them cease. In nonhuman primates, aggressive conflicts frequently result in the immediate spatial separation of opponents, and experimental tests have demonstrated that mutual tolerance in a dyad is decreased in the minutes after aggression (Cords, 1992). Among children and adolescents, conflict with certain partners may similarly lead to the immediate disruption of their social interactions (Hartup, Laursen, Stewart, & Eastenson, 1988; Laursen, 1996; Sackin & Thelen, 1984), or to disruption in the larger group of children to which they belong (Berndt, 1996).

It is also possible, at least in principle, that unresolved conflict would damage a relationship in a more enduring, long-term way, either because particular types of conflict are severe enough to lead to prolonged avoidance or because an accumulation of short-term damage gradually undermines stable, predictable interaction patterns. Nonhuman primates whose time together is characterized (over periods of months) by frequent aggression show a correspondingly low rate of affiliative interactions (e.g., Bernstein, Judge, & Ruehlmann, 1993; Watts, 1994). In children, the formation and maintenance of important positive social relationships seems to be closely related to the frequency with which conflicts are constructively resolved (Bukowski & Sippola, 1996; Dodge, Coie, Petit, & Price, 1990; Hartup et al., 1988; Newcomb & Bagwell, 1996; Vespo & Caplan, 1993).

Conflict may entail other costs beside those relevant to social relationships. Individuals who are in conflict may be unable to achieve their immediate goals, whether they require cooperative activities, such as sharing or jointly acquiring a resource, or independent activities, such as moving from one place to another, which cannot be carried out. Some forms of conflict (especially aggressive conflict) are also physically and psychologically stressful for the individuals engaged in them. For example, studies of male baboons have shown that during periods of reorganization of dominance relationships in the troop, high-ranking individuals participate frequently in aggression with unpredictable outcomes and show physiological profiles associated with stress that predispose them to ill health; when the dominance hierarchy is stable, however, these males do not show high rates of aggression and lack the physiological indicators of stress (Sapolsky, 1993).

In childhood, group settings characterized by unresolved conflicts are not conducive for learning and development. Children's motivation for academic achievement is highly related to a positive social environment in the classroom (Deci & Ryan, 1985; Wentzel, 1993).

MANAGING CONFLICT AND CONFLICT RESOLUTION

Insofar as conflict is inevitable in social animals, and yet has potentially harmful effects on social relationships and on individuals, one might expect that organisms would be under selective pressure to evolve mechanisms of avoiding these effects. In fact, there is evidence that such behavioral mechanisms exist among primates.

First, some primates (as well as other animals) use conventions to settle potential conflicts before they have escalated to the level of aggression, or even the level of protest. In a sense, conventions obviate conflict. Ritualized dominance relationships (LaFreniere & Charlesworth, 1983; Mendoza, 1993), respect for possession (Kummer & Cords, 1991; Ross & Conant, 1992) and the development of routines (Menzel, 1993), are examples of such conventions (Hand, 1986). Among children, the use of peer group entry rituals has been shown to reduce conflict (Corsaro, 1985; Putallaz & Sheppard, 1992).

Second, some primates appear to anticipate periods of potential conflict (Koyama & Dunbar, 1996), and engage in marked displays of preconflict reassurance, appeasement, or (in the case of humans) pacifying discourse. For example, captive chimpanzees who see a bundle of coveted food conspicuously embrace, kiss, and touch one another even before the food is made accessible to them. These celebrations reduce the frequency of aggressive conflict when the food is finally delivered (de Waal, 1989). Similar, although less dramatic, behavior has also been reported for captive stumptailed macaques, which increased their grooming of high-ranking, powerful group members before food was presented. Although the effects of this affiliative behavior were not documented, the authors interpreted it as a tension-reduction mechanism (Mayagoitia, Santillan-Doherty, Lopez-Vergara, & Mondragon-Ceballos, 1993). Children's anticipation of conflict is marked by their use of pragmatic suggestions for relieving impending conflict. For example, children use verbal counterpropositions, reasons, bargaining suggestions, and affirmations as ways to prevent conflict (Eisenberg & Garvey, 1981; Killen & Naigles, 1995). Quite strikingly, conflict diminishes even when very young children (3½ years of age) use reasons and justifications.

Third, should conflict nevertheless occur, it may be relatively mild in form or short in duration. Theoretical models of the escalation of aggressive conflict in animal societies predict that mild forms of conflict (threat dis-

204 CORDS AND KILLEN

plays) should predominate over more escalated forms (combat) precisely because of the risks involved in the latter (Maynard Smith & Price, 1973). Empirical studies of monkeys have shown that even in aggressive conflicts, only a small fraction of interactions involves the sort of contact aggression (namely biting) that is likely to cause physical injury; threats and spatial displacements are far more common (Bernstein & Ehardt, 1985). Similarly, among young children, physical aggression characterizes only a small fraction of conflicts (Killen & Turiel, 1991; Ross & Conant, 1992). There is also evidence that primates possess behavioral strategies to end escalated conflicts quickly. Nonhuman primate victims will sometimes redirect aggression they are receiving onto a new target, with the result that the aggressor's focus is distracted from its original victim (e.g., Aureli & van Schaik, 1991). Also, interference by powerful third parties often brings a quick end to ongoing aggression in nonhuman primates (Boehm, 1992; Petit & Thierry, 1994), as well as in human children (e.g., Bayer, Whaley, & May, 1995; Killen & Turiel, 1991; Ross, Tesla, Kenyon, & Lollis, 1990).

A fourth strategy involves a different sort of involvement by third parties, who may help relieve the deleterious effects of conflict by consoling or reassuring one or both of the opponents. Such consolation may not end the state of conflict per se, but it may relieve the stress associated with such a state. Consolation and responding to another's distress is well known in humans (Hoffman, 1983; Zahn-Waxler, Radke-Yarrow, & King, 1979). Apparent consolation, as evidenced by an increased likelihood of friendly contact with third parties after escalated conflict has ceased, has also been reported for chimpanzees, although it has not been found among macaques (de Waal & Aureli, 1996).

A fifth strategy that may be used to lessen the deleterious consequences of conflict is resolution. When a conflict has been resolved, the attitudes or goals of the former opponents are no longer incompatible, but rather in alignment, as a result of communication between the opponents. In developmental terms, the interaction has been restored to a state of equilibrium.

Opponents who simply drop the conflict have not resolved it. Many forms of conflict resolution involve changes in the behavior or attitudes of both opponents. Examples include compromise, sharing, and reconciliation. In principle, however, resolution might occur when only one individual willingly adjusts its attitude to match its opponent's. This would include cases of acquiescence or formally giving up a resource, priority, or point of view. In practice, it may be difficult to distinguish such acquiescent resolution from mere submission, in which one opponent gives up its position reluctantly to avoid further escalation of the conflict. Such a distinction requires observers to know the motivation of the opponent who is giving up, and this would seem to be particularly difficult in conflicts that do not include language. It is a critical distinction, however, because resolution is not mere submission. Finally, two opponents might agree to disagree. In this case, the differences that originally caused a state of conflict still persist, but opponents have aligned their attitudes about the significance of those differences and in this sense have resolved their conflict. Agreeing to disagree is not the same as dropping a conflict: The former involves communication between the agreeing parties, whereas the latter involves no communication about a conflict's ending.

We have so far argued that resolution, among other forms of conflict management, is adaptive because it allows valuable social relationships to persevere. This idea stems mainly from studies of nonhuman primates by evolutionary biologists. Developmental psychologists have contributed another perspective to the adaptive nature of conflict resolution, at least for humans, by focusing on its role in promoting the development of social skills and social cognition. From participation in conflict resolution, children develop an understanding of reciprocity, mutuality, and negotiation, all essential concepts for interacting with others in the social world. Such knowledge contributes not only to children's social competence but also to their social competence as adults.

EVIDENCE FOR CONFLICT RESOLUTION IN NONHUMAN PRIMATES

As we mentioned previously, most studies of conflict in nonhuman primates have focused on aggressive conflict. Perhaps because most of these conflicts (at least among species whose conflicts have been well studied) end with a clearly submissive loser, studies of conflict resolution in nonhuman primates have focused on the events occurring after behavioral indicators of conflict (i.e., aggression) have ceased. The term *reconciliation* was first applied to nonhuman primates by de Waal and van Roosmalen (1979), who observed that captive chimpanzees that had recently interacted aggressively frequently came together after hostilities had ended and engaged in apparently reassuring and friendly body contact. Because the forms of contact were special to this social situation, and contact was sought selectively with former opponents, it seemed that these friendly reunions might have the function of repairing their social relationship. Subsequent work on about 20 species of nonhuman primates used more rigorous methods to demonstrate that aggressive conflict elevates the rate of friendly interaction between former opponents over baseline rates and that these postconflict reunions are directed selectively to former opponents (reviews in de Waal, 1993; Kappeler & van Schaik, 1992).

Other experimental and observational studies have corroborated the interpretation of such friendly reunions as reconciliations. Opponents who have just fought are less tolerant of one another than normal, and the victim is likely to receive further aggression from the original aggressor and others at an elevated rate. Friendly reunions with the opponent restore characteristic tolerance levels (Cords, 1992) and reduce the rate of further aggression received by the victim. They also reduce the victim's tension, which is presumably related to the risk of further attack (Aureli & van Schaik, 1991).

The actual forms that these friendly postconflict reunions take is variable across species (reviewed in de Waal, 1993). For example, chimpanzees include mouth-to-mouth kissing and embracing, whereas stumptail macaques clutch each other's hips. In these species, the particular forms of affiliation are special to the postconflict context but gorillas and other monkey species show affiliative reunions whose form is indistinguishable from that shown in other contexts. One study of long-tailed macaques showed that the particular form of affiliation characterizing postconflict reunions did not influence how effectively baseline levels of social tolerance were restored (Cords, 1993), and as far as we know, the differences between species in the form of reunion do not translate into differences in the effectiveness of this behavior. Similarly, it appears that the forms of reunion shown by juvenile animals differ little from those shown by adults of the same species, although play may be somewhat more common in younger animals (Cords, 1988; Cords & Aureli, 1993; de Waal & Johanowicz, 1993). Although further research would help to explain species differences in the form of postconflict reunions, so far it appears that in nonhuman primates, it matters more *that* former opponents interact in a friendly way after aggression than what particular form such interaction takes.

The ontogeny of postconflict reconciliation has not been well studied in nonhuman primates. De Waal (1996b) suggested that the roots of postconflict reunions may lie in mother–infant weaning conflicts, in which conflict over access to the nipple is interspersed with suckling. There is some evidence that the social experience of juveniles can influence their tendency to reconcile (de Waal & Johanowicz, 1993). However reconciliatory behavior develops, macaque juveniles in their second year of life (macaques typically become sexually mature at about 3 to 4 years if females, 4 to 6 years if males) are already reconciling aggressive conflicts, and in at least one of the three species studied, they reconcile equal proportions of their conflicts as adults (Cords & Aureli, 1993; de Waal & Johanowicz, 1993). An evolutionary view of the early development of this behavior would hold that these social skills are already adaptive early in the lifespan, and that they therefore develop when animals are young (Cords & Aureli, 1993).

How postconflict reconciliation is adaptive is suggested by analyses of the patterning of this behavior. In nonhuman primates, not all aggressive conflicts are reconciled (values of 7–56% have been reported, Cords & Thurnheer, 1993). An area of continuing research concerns factors that influence whether particular conflicts are reconciled or not. A number of studies have shown that the social relationship of the opponents is an important factor: Generally, reconciliation is more likely if the opponents have valuable relationships with one another. For example, among macaques, matrilineal family members cooperate closely in competing with other matrilines in their groups, and most studies have shown that reconciliation occurs more often between matrilineally related opponents than among nonrelatives (Aureli, Das, & Veenema, 1993; Aureli, van Schaik, & van Hooff, 1989; DeMaria & Thierry, 1992). Among chimpanzees, females have weak relationships with each other and correspondingly low reconciliation rates, especially relative to males who form strategic alliances with one another (de Waal, 1986). Among gorillas, which typically live in groups with a single adult silverback male, females also have weak relations and low reconciliation rates, but reconciliation rates are high after aggression between the male and his females: Females depend on protection from males, and are valuable to those males as mates (Watts, 1995). One experimental study has backed up the general conclusion of correlative studies such as these. When macaque partners depended on one another to get food in a cooperative task, they reconciled three times more often than when cooperation was not required of them (Cords & Thurnheer, 1993). The study dyads were used as their own controls, so these results also show that the likelihood of reconciling conflicts can be adjusted as the value of the partner changes. In other words, these monkeys appear to use reconciliation in an adaptively strategic way.

Although the value of the partner may be an important, and perhaps the most critical, aspect of a relationship that influences the likelihood of postconflict reconciliation, other aspects may also have an effect. Cords and Aureli (1993) proposed that relationships that are less secure might also be more likely to be reconciled, as they might need more explicit nurturance. At a more immediate level, the compatibility or accessibility of partners might also influence how easy it is for them to achieve a friendly postconflict reunion. The roles of these two factors, and the way they might interact with each other and with partner value, have not yet been studied systematically.

Although aggressive conflict and subsequent reconciliation have received much attention and have been documented in many nonhuman primate species, other forms of conflict and conflict resolution also occur. Mason (1993) described the ubiquity of conflict in the social lives of primates. A similar review of the various forms of conflict resolution has not been written, but we mention two of them here.

First, at least some nonhuman primates begin resolving conflicts by engaging immediately in conspicuous appeasement behavior rather than waiting for signs of conflict to cease. For example, bonobos, both in captivity and in the wild, increase their performance of sociosexual behavior when provisioned with food (de Waal, 1987, 1993). The food is coveted by the animals, and its mode of distribution (a rich clump) makes it possible for certain individuals to monopolize it: This is why provisioning leads to conflict. The kinds of behavior shown by bonobos in the presence of provisioned food are identical to those used in postconflict reconciliations, and the performance of such behavior leads to more assertive behavior on the part of subordinate animals, suggesting that the behavior mitigates conflict (de Waal, 1987).

Second, some nonhuman primates appear to engage in interindividual negotiations to resolve conflicts. Among hamadryas baboons, greeting behavior between males, which occurs often in the context of rivalry over females, has been interpreted as a way in which individuals both assess and influence the behavior of rivals, and thus avoid dangerous escalated aggression (Colmenares, 1991). Other examples of negotiation come from situations in which group members disagree, but must come to a consensus, about a common direction of travel. Among hamadryas baboons and South American titi monkeys, individuals appear to propose a direction of travel by making tentative forays in a particular direction. If other group members do not follow, the initial proposal is not followed through, and a new proposal (perhaps by another animal) is made (Kummer, 1995; Menzel, 1993). Through a series of such proposals, counterproposals and passive refusals, group members come to an agreement on a common travel route. De Waal (1996a) described several additional scenarios involving social negotiation in chimpanzees.

EVIDENCE FOR CONFLICT RESOLUTION IN HUMAN CHILDREN

Studies of conflict involving children have focused more explicitly than those involving nonhuman primates on how the source of conflict and the type of opponent influence the conflict's outcome, both over the short term (for example, is the conflict resolved and how?) and over the long term (what do children gain from their experience?). Social–cognitive theories have provided useful categories for interpreting and understanding the nature of social conflicts (see Smetana, 1995; Turiel, 1983). Issues that instigate conflicts have been categorized as stemming from moral, social–conventional, and psychological considerations (Dunn, 1988; Killen, 1991; Killen & Nucci, 1995; Ross & Conant, 1992; Shantz, 1987). For example, moral conflicts would be those that involve a victim such as the infliction of physical harm on another (e.g., aggression), psychological harm (e.g., teasing), a lack of a fair distribution of resources (e.g., not sharing toys) and a lack of concern for rights (e.g., use of space). Social–conventional conflicts are those that disrupt the smooth functioning of social order such as the violation of a school rule or disagreements about how to structure an activity or play a game (e.g., "let's build the bridge here," "No! Let's build it over there"). Recently, Nucci (1996) indentified a third arena of children's psychological development referred to as the personal domain, in which conflicts frequently involve issues of autonomy, personal choice, and friendship. Typically, moral conflicts among peers pertain to such issues as the distribution of resources, whereas social–conventional conflicts among peers pertain to the structuring of activities. Conflicts in the personal domain seldom occur among peers, but do characterize interactions between adults and children. It is important to identify the source of conflict because different sources lead to different outcomes and these outcomes serve as the bases for the construction of different categories of social knowledge.

A child's social relationships with his or her opponent influences not only the type of conflict in which they typically engage, but also the outcome of these conflicts (Dunn & Slomkowski, 1992). Analyses of conflict and conflict resolution in different kinds of relationships have included adult–child and peer relationships (Youniss, 1980; Youniss & Smollar, 1985), familial and nonfamilial relationships (Cummings & Davies, 1994; Dunn, 1988; Pitrowski, 1995; Ross, Filyer, Loolis, Perlman, & Martin, 1994), and friends and non-friends (Dunn & Slomkowski, 1992; Slomkowski & Killen, 1992; Vespo & Caplan, 1993). Adult–child and peer conflict and resolution methods provide very different experiential sources for children's social development. Adults typically respond to children's protests by using commands, rule statements, rationales, and sanctions. The goal of most adult responses to children's protests is pedagogical, namely to teach children social skills and social understanding. Peer conflict, however, appears to serve a different function. Through peer conflict, children develop an awareness about the other in terms of others' needs, desires, and expectations of social interaction. Children's identification with peers (rather than with adults) enables them to abstract norms of reciprocity ("do unto others as you would have them do unto you") and mutuality. Research has shown that young children pay close attention to the affect displayed by instigators and recipients in conflict episodes (Arsenio & Killen, 1995; Lennon & Eisenberg, 1987) as well as the use of specific sociolinguistic markers and utterances (Eisenberg & Garvey, 1981; Killen & Naigles, 1995).

Clearly, how children abstract information depends on the cognitive developmental level of the individual as well as the nature of the conflict and its outcome. Conflicts that are aggressive probably do not play a positive role in promoting reciprocity because of the more irreversible nature of the harm inflicted. In contrast, conflicts regarding the sharing of toys or turn-taking seem to play a positive role because of the reversible nature of the act (e.g., a toy can be returned, a turn can be relinquished).

The research literature on adult intervention in peer conflicts is fairly minimal. Adults frequently intervene in children's conflicts (e.g., Killen, 1989) but they do so in inconsistent and ineffective ways. Ross and Conant (1992) demonstrated how adults use inconsistent goals such as ignoring ownership rights of some children and acknowledging such claims by other children. Research by Bayer et al. (1995) showed that when adults suggest how children might interact with one another, even toddlers resolve conflicts using negotiation. Bayer also found that, unfortunately, adults use this strategy only 10% of the time. In general, intervening adults use commands (e.g., "Stop. Don't do that") that do not promote peer resolution techniques but are designed only to stop the conflict. Adults appear to underestimate children's abilities to resolve conflicts, both when the child is one of the opponents and when it intervenes in the conflicts of other children. Even children as young as 33 months intervene in familial disputes as third-party participants (Pitrowski, 1995); in particular, older siblings often instruct younger siblings about conflict-resolution techniques (Dunn, 1988).

One of the goals of research with nonhuman primates has been to document the ways in which friendship, or other mutually beneficial social relationships, influence the form and frequency of conflict resolution. Studies of humans have also revealed that friendship relationships play an important role in the development of constructive methods of conflict resolution. Children use more constructive kinds of conflict resolution with friends more often than with nonfriends and make conceptual distinctions between acts that instigate conflicts with friends and those that instigate conflicts with nonfriends (Bukowski, Newcomb, & Hartup, 1996; Dunn & Slomkowski, 1992; Shantz & Hartup, 1992; Slomkowski & Killen, 1992; Vespo & Caplan, 1993). These results provide further evidence for the argument that social relationships influence conflict strategies and outcomes.

Although studies of nonhuman primates have focused on postconflict reconciliation, there are no published studies of this method of conflict resolution in children. Recently, however, a few primatologists have changed their study subjects and have documented postconflict reconciliation in human children as well, using similar methods (Butovskaya, 1997; Verbeek, 1996, 1997; Westlund, Forsberg, & Ljungberg, 1997). One reason why these postconflict interactions may have been overlooked in prior studies relates to the high rate of nonaggressive, low-affect conflicts that are immediately resolved during the course of normal interaction among children. For example, in object disputes (a frequent source of conflict), the back-and-forth exchange about who has what toy is often long and involved. Immediate resolution terminates the conflict so there is little reason for postconflict reconciliation. Future studies should examine the factors that influence these alternative strategies of conflict resolution among children (see Verbeek, 1996).

Consequences of successful conflict resolution by children have been studied both in the short and long terms. Preschoolers who resolve their conflicts in a conciliatory way are much more likely to interact subsequently in a friendly manner than those whose conflicts end with submission/subordination (Sackin & Thelen, 1984; Vespo & Caplan, 1993). Studies using sociometric analyses (peer popularity status) have shown that aggressive children are often rejected by their peers and are at risk for academic achievement (Dodge, Cole, Petit, & Price, 1990), whereas children who are socially skillful and who use negotiation and compromise with one another are well liked and generally socially competent (Putallaz & Sheppard, 1992). Although friends and nonfriends may experience conflict at similar rates when the amount of time they are together is taken into account, friends resolve conflicts more often than nonfriends. This pattern has been interpreted as reflecting the commitment that friends have to their relationship, implying that constructive conflict resolution is an important tool for preserving childhood friendships (Newcomb & Bagwell, 1996).

A COMPARISON OF CONFLICT RESOLUTION IN CHILDREN AND IN NONHUMAN PRIMATES

The apparent ubiquity of conciliatory behavioral mechanisms of conflict resolution among primate species is a strong argument that such mechanisms have a long evolutionary history in these social mammals. A consideration of the context of conflict in social relationships, and the adaptive significance of such relationships in the lives of these fundamentally social animals, makes it clear why mechanisms of conflict resolution would be adaptive. Although there is insufficient comparative information on the ontogeny of conflict-resolving behavior to specify the details of its biological basis, we would agree with de Waal (1992) that our own species shares with its closest relatives an evolved predisposition to manage social conflict, partly through conflict resolution. This predisposition is already apparent in very young animals. Such a comparative perspective supports the Piagetian view that human children are not inherently self-centered or asocial, but that they (too) are predisposed to attend to social experience with a variety of partners, and to develop the social skills related to conflict management that characterize the order of mammals to which they belong.

Further support for the notion that behavioral mechanisms of conflict resolution are important comes from the concordant evidence, from children and nonhuman primates, that conflicts occurring in certain types of social relationships are more likely to be resolved than those occurring in other relationships. Developmental psychologists have not used the evolutionary term *value* (as in Kummer, 1978), but instead have compared friends to nonfriends when considering peer relations. Because friends are desirable social partners, and because there is much evidence that relationships with friends are important to children's development (Bukowski et al., 1996; Hartup, 1992; Hartup et al., 1988), it seems reasonable to take friendship as an indicator of value measured in the currency of lifetime reproductive success. Thus, whereas nonhuman primates are more likely to resolve conflicts with valuable social partners, human children resolve more conflicts, or reach more equitable and mature resolutions of conflicts, with friends than with nonfriends (Hartup, 1992; Nelson & Aboud, 1985; Newcomb & Bagwell, 1996; Verbeek, 1997). From a developmental perspective, we propose that friendship plays an important role in the acquisition of social–cognitive abilities, and that this, in turn, enables the child to function in his or her social world.

We think that these parallel avenues of research have the potential to inform each other about new research directions. Studies of nonhuman primates suggest that a closer examination of postconflict reconciliation, and perhaps also mediation and consolation, in children would be valuable. Do instigators offer ways of making amends with those protesting their actions? How are third parties involved in postconflict strategies of resolution? Do children develop different kinds of social knowledge from these delayed resolutions of conflict? The work with children indicates that nonaggressive conflicts, and their sequelae, take different forms from aggressive ones and may play different roles in the facilitation of social development. To understand more fully the evolutionary context of conflict management strategies, primatologists could profit by adopting a broader view of conflict and including in their investigations a consequently greater variety of conflict resolution strategies.

Although there are noteworthy similarities in the conflict resolution behavior of children and nonhuman primates, there are also several differences. The most obvious are the linguistic and social–cognitive differences. By 3½ years of age, children have developed the capacity to use reasons, justifications, and rationales with one another. The use of such statements during disputes serves to resolve conflict and harmonize group relationships. Further, research indicates that a critical experiential source for the acquisition of social–cognitive concepts such as friendship, morality, and justice is conflict and conflict resolution. Among nonhuman primates, there is some evidence that opponents may negotiate with each other, but at present we cannot reject the view that such negotiations occur only at the level of assessing and trying to influence others' motivation, not their beliefs. The complex ways in which even young children resolve their conflicts, and the relations between these kinds of resolution and their social–cognitive development, suggest that studies of conflict resolution in nonhuman primates might help to assess their capacities for social and proto-moral cognition as well (e.g., Cords, 1997; de Waal, 1996b). In a parallel manner, research on a theory of mind in young children provided the impetus for investigating deception abilities in nonhuman primates (see Whiten, this volume).

Cross-species comparison of conflict resolution provides a directional guide for research with nonhuman primates (can the social and proto-moral orientations of nonhuman primates be inferred from their conflict resolution behavior?) and an evolutionary foundation for research with children. Recently, educators have turned to conflict resolution as a pedagogical tool for classroom management (see DeVries & Zan, 1994). In prior decades, conflict resolution techniques were not part of general classroom management or the curriculum training of teachers. Instead, discipline in the classroom was maintained through rewards and punishments, even though developmental researchers such as Kohlberg (1969, 1984), proposed that the Socratic method of learning was most effective for promoting development. Current educators and psychologists have acknowledged that assisting chidren with the acquitistion of conflict resolution skills is a powerful way both to facilitate academic achievement and to establish group identity and social order in the classroom (DeVries & Zan, 1994; Watson, Solomon, Battisstich, Schaps, & Solomon, 1989). Demonstrating that there is an evolutionary basis for conflict resolution provides further evidence of the significance of this aspect of social interaction among humans as well as among nonhuman primates.

ACKNOWLEDGMENTS

We thank Frans de Waal, Peter Kahn, Jonas Langer, and Hildy Ross for helpful comments on the manuscript.

REFERENCES

Ardrey, R. (1966). *The territorial imperative*. New York: Atheneum.

Arsenio, W., & Killen, M. (1996). Conflict-related emotions during peer disputes. *Early Education and Development, 7*, 43–57.

Aureli, F., Das, M., & Veenema, H. C. (1993). Interspecific differences in the effect of kinship on reconiliation frequency in macaques. *Abstract Book of the 30th Annual Meeting of the Animal Behavior Society, 5*.

Aureli, F., & van Schaik, C. P. (1991). Post-conflict behaviour in long-tailed macaques (*Macaca fascicularis*), II. Coping with the uncertainty. *Ethology, 89*, 101–114.

Aureli, F., van Schaik, C. P., & van Hooff, J. A. R. A. M. (1989). Functional aspects of reconciliation among captive long-tailed macaques (*Macaca fascicularis*). *American Journal of Primatology, 19*, 39–51.

Barash, D. P. (1982). *Sociobiology and behavior*. New York: Elsevier.

Bayer, C. L., Whaley, K. L., & May, S. E. (1995). Strategic assistance in toddler disputes, II. Sequences and patterns of teachers' message strategies. *Early Education and Development, 6,* 405–432.

Berndt, T. J. (1996). Exploring the effects of friendship quality on social development. In W. M. Bukowski, A. F. Newcomb, & W. W. Hartup (Eds.), *The company they keep: Friendship in childhood and adolescence* (pp. 346–365). Cambridge, England: Cambridge University Press.

Bernstein, I. S., & Ehardt, C. L. (1985). Intragroup agonistic behavior in rhesus monkeys (*Macaca mulatta*). *International Journal of Primatology, 6,* 209–226.

Bernstein, I. S., Judge, P. G., & Ruehlmann, T. E. (1993). Kinship, association and social relationships in rhesus monkeys (*Macaca mulatta*). *American Journal of Primatology, 31,* 41–53.

Boehm, C. (1992). Segmentary 'warfare' and the management of conflicts: Comparison of East African chimpanzees and patrilineal-patrilocal humans. In A. H. Harcourt & F. B. M. de Waal (Eds.), *Coalitions and alliances in humans and other animals* (pp. 137–173). Oxford, England: Oxford University Press.

Bowlby, J. (1971). *Attachment and loss.* London: Pelican Press.

Bukowski, W. M., Newcomb, A. F., & Hartup, W. W. (1996). *The company they keep: Friendship in childhood and adolescence.* Cambridge, England: Cambridge University Press.

Bukowski, W. M., & Sippola, L. K. (1996). Friendship and morality: (How) are they related? In W. M. Bukowski, A. F. Newcomb, & W. W. Hartup (Eds.), *The company they keep: Friendship in childhood and adolescence* (pp. 185–210). Cambridge, England: Cambridge University Press.

Butovskaya, M. (1997). Aggression and reconciliation in primary school children. *Advances in Ethology, 32,* 154.

Colmenares, F. (1991). Greeting behavior between male baboons, oestrous females, rivalry and negotiation. *Animal Behaviour, 41,* 49–60.

Cords, M. (1988). Resolution of aggressive conflicts by immature long-tailed macaques, *Macaca fascicularis. Animal Behaviour, 36,* 1124–1135.

Cords, M. (1992). Post-conflict reunions and reconciliation in long-tailed macaques. *Animal Behaviour, 44,* 57–61.

Cords, M. (1993). On operationally defining reconciliation. *American Journal of Primatology, 29,* 255–267.

Cords, M. (1997). Friendships, alliances, reciprocity and repair. In A. Whiten & R. W. Byrne (Eds.), *Machiavellian intelligence II* (pp. 29–49). Cambridge, England: Cambridge University Press.

Cords, M., & Aureli, F. (1993). Patterns of reconciliation among juvenile long-tailed macaques. In M. E. Pereira & L. A. Fairbanks (Eds.), *Juvenile primates: Life history, development and behavior* (pp. 271–284). New York: Oxford University Press.

Cords, M., & Thurnheer, S. (1993). Reconciliation with valuable partners by long-tailed macaques. *Ethology, 93,* 315–325.

Corsaro, W. (1985). *Friendship and peer culture in the early years.* Norwood, NJ: Ablex.

Cummings, E. M., & Davies, P. (1994). *Children and marital conflict: The impact of family dispute and resolution.* New York: Guilford.

Damon, W., & Hart, D. (1988). *Self understanding from childhood to adolescence.* Cambridge, England: Cambridge University Press.

Deci, E. L., & Ryan, R. M. (1985). *Intrinsic motivation and self determination in human behavior.* New York: Plenum.

DeMaria, C., & Thierry, B. (1992). The ability to reconcile in Tonkean and rhesus macaques. *Abstract Book of the 14th Congress of the International Primatological Society,* 101.

DeVries, R., & Zan, B. (1994). *Moral classrooms, moral children.* New York: Teachers College Press.

de Waal, F. B. M. (1986). Integration of dominance and social bonding in primates. *Quarterly Review of Biology, 61,* 459–479.

de Waal, F. B. M. (1987). Tension regulation and nonreproductive functions of sex among captive bonobos (Pan paniscus). *National Geographic Research, 3,* 318–335.

de Waal, F. B. M. (1989). Food sharing and reciprocal obligations among chimpanzees. *Journal of Human Evolution, 18*, 433–459.

de Waal, F. B. M. (1992). *Peacemaking among primates*. Cambridge, MA: Harvard University Press.

de Waal, F. B. M. (1993). Reconciliation among primates: A review of empirical evidence and unresolved issues. In W. A. Mason & S. P. Mendoza (Eds.), *Primate social conflict* (pp. 111–144). Albany: State University of New York Press.

de Waal, F. B. M. (1996a). Conflict as negotiation. In W. C. McGrew, L. F. Marchant, & T. Nishida (Eds.), *Great ape societies* (pp. 159–172). Cambridge, England: Cambridge University Press.

de Waal, F. B. M. (1996b). *Good natured: The origins of right and wrong in humans and other animals*. Cambridge, MA: Harvard University Press.

de Waal, F. B. M., & Aureli, F. (1996). Consolation, reconciliation and a possible cognitive difference between macaques and chimpanzees. In A. E. Russon, K. A. Bard, & S. T. Parker (Eds.), *Reaching into thought: The mind of the great apes* (pp. 80–110). Cambridge, England: Cambridge University Press.

de Waal, F. B. M., & Johanowicz, D. L. (1993). Modification of reconciliation behavior through social experience: An experiment with two macaques species. *Child Development, 64*, 897–908.

de Waal, F. B. M., & van Roosmalen, A. (1979). Reconciliation and consolation among chimpanzees. *Behavioural Ecology and Sociobiology, 5*, 55–66.

Dodge, K., Coie, J., Petit, G. S., & Price, J. M. (1990). Peer status and aggression in boys' groups: Developmental and contextual analyses. *Child Development, 61*, 1289–1309.

Dunn, J. (1988). *The beginnings of social understanding*. Cambridge, MA: Harvard University Press.

Dunn, J., & Slomkowski, C. (1992). Conflict and the development of social understanding. In C. U. Shantz & W. W. Hartup (Eds.), *Conflict in child and adolescent development* (pp. 70–92). Cambridge, England: Cambridge University Press.

Dunn, J., Slomkowski, C., Donelan, N., & Herrera, C. (1995). Conflict, understanding and relationships: Developments and differences in the preschool years. *Early Education and Development, 6*, 303–316.

Eisenberg, A. R., & Garvey, C. (1981). Children's use of verbal strategies in resolving conflicts. *Discourse Processes, 4*, 149–170.

Goodall, J. (1986). *The chimpanzees of Gombe*. Cambridge, MA: Harvard University Press.

Hand, J. L. (1986). Resolution of social conflicts: dominance, egalitarianism, spheres of dominance, and game theory. *Quarterly Review of Biology*, 61, 201–220.

Hartup, W. W. (1992). Conflict and friendship relations. In C. U. Shantz & W. W. Hartup (Eds), *Conflict in child and adolescent development* (pp. 186–215). Cambridge, England: Cambridge University Press.

Hartup, W. W., Laursen, B., Stewart, M. I., & Eastenson, A. (1988). Conflict and the friendship relations of young children. *Child Development, 59*, 1590–1600.

Hay, D. F. (1984). Social conflict in early childhood. In G. Whitehurst (Ed.), *Annals of child development* (Vol. 1, pp. 1–44). Greenwich, CT: JAI.

Hay, D. F., & Ross, H. (1982). The social nature of early conflict. *Child Development, 53*, 105–113.

Hinde, R. A. (1974). *Biological bases of human social behaviour*. New York: McGraw-Hill.

Hinde, R. A. (1979). *Towards understanding relationships*. London: Academic Press.

Hinde, R. A. (1982). *Ethology: Its nature and relations with other sciences*. New York: Oxford University Press.

Hoffman, M. L. (1983). Empathy, guilt and social cognition. In W. Overton (Ed.), *The relationship between social and cognitive development*. Hillsdale, NJ: Lawrence Erlbaum Associates.

Kappeler, P. M., & van Schaik, E. P. (1992). Methodological and evolutionary aspects of reconciliation among primates. *Ethology, 92*, 51–69.

Killen, M. (1989). Context, conflict and coordination in social development. In L. Winegar (Ed.), *Social interaction and the development of children's understanding* (pp. 119–146). Norwood, NJ: Ablex.

Killen, M. (1991). Social and moral development in early childhood. In W. M. Kurtines & J. L. Gewirtz (Eds.), *Handbook of moral behavior and development, Vol. 2* (pp. 115–138). Hillsdale, NJ: Lawrence Erlbaum Associates.

Killen, M. (1995). Conflict resolution in social development: Sociality, morality, and individuality. *Early Education and Development, 6,* 1–5.

Killen, M., & Naigles, L. (1995). Preschool children pay attention to their addressees: The effects of gender composition on peer disputes. *Discourse Processes, 19,* 329–346.

Killen, M., & Nucci, L. (1995). Morality, autonomy, and social conflict. In M. Killen & D. Hart (Eds.), *Morality in everyday life: Developmental perspectives* (pp. 52–86). Cambridge, England: Cambridge University Press.

Killen, M., & Sueyoshi, L. (1995). Conflict resolution in Japanese social interactions. *Early Education and Development, 6,* 313–330.

Killen, M., & Turiel, E. (1991). Conflict resolution in preschool social interactions. *Early Education and Development, 2,* 240–255.

Kohlberg, L. (1969). Stage and sequence: The cognitive-developmental approach to socialization. In D. A. Goslin (Ed.), *Handbook of socialization theory and research* (pp. 347–480). Chicago: Rand-McNally.

Kohlberg, L. (1984). *Essays in moral development: Vol. II: The psychology of moral development: Moral stages, their nature and validity.* San Francisco: Harper & Row.

Koyama, N. F., & Dunbar, R. I. M. (1996). Anticipation of conflict by chimpanzees. *Primates, 37,* 79–86.

Kummer, H. (1978). On the value of social relationships to nonhuman primates: A heuristic scheme. *Social Science Information, 17,* 687–705.

Kummer, H. (1995). *In quest of the sacred baboon.* Princeton, NJ: Princeton University Press.

Kummer, H., & Cords, M. (1991). Cues of ownership in *Macaca fascicularis. Animal Behaviour, 42,* 529–549.

LaFreniere, P., & Charlesworth, W. R. (1983). Dominance, attention and affiliation in a peer group: A nine-month longitudinal study. *Ethology and Sociobiology, 4,* 55–67.

Laursen, B. (1996). Closeness and conflict in adolescent peer relationships, interdependence with friends and romantic partners. In W. M. Bukowski, A. F. Newcomb, & W. W. Hartup (Eds.), *The company they keep: Friendship in childhood and adolescence* (pp. 185–210). Cambridge, England: Cambridge University Press.

Lennon, R., & Eisenberg, N. (1987). Emotional displays associated with preschoolers' prosocial behavior. *Child Development, 58,* 992–1000.

Lorenz, K. (1966). *On aggression.* New York: Harcourt, Brace.

Lyons, D. (1993). Conflict as a constructive force in social life. In W. A. Mason & S. P. Mendoza (Eds.), *Primate social conflict* (pp. 387–408). Albany: State University of New York Press.

Mason, W. A. (1993). The nature of social conflict. In W. A. Mason & S. P. Mendoza (Eds.), *Primate social conflict* (pp. 13–47). Albany: State University of New York Press.

Mason, W. A., Long, D. D., & Mendoza, S. P. (1993). Temperament and mother-infant conflict in macaques: A transactional analysis. In W. A. Mason & S. P. Mendoza (Eds.), *Primate social conflict* (pp. 205–227). Albany: State University of New York Press.

Mason, W. A., & Mendoza, S. P. (1993). Primate social conflict: An overview of sources, forms and consequences. In W. A. Mason & S. P. Mendoza (Eds.), *Primate social conflict* (pp. 1–11). Albany: State University of New York Press.

Maynard Smith, J., & Price, G. R. (1973). The logic of animal conflict. *Nature, 246,* 15–18.

Mayagoitia, L., Santillan-Doherty, A. M., Lopez-Vergara, L., & Mondragon-Ceballos, R. (1993). Affiliation tactics prior to a period of competition in captive groups of stumptail macaques. *Ethology, Ecology and Evolution, 5,* 435–446.

Mendoza, S. P. (1993). Social conflict on first encounters. In W. A. Mason & S. P. Mendoza (Eds.), *Primate social conflict* (pp. 85–110). Albany: State University of New York Press.

Menzel, C. R. (1993). Coordination and conflict in Callicebus social groups. In W. A. Mason & S. P. Mendoza (Eds.), *Primate social conflict* (pp. 253-290). Albany: State University of New York Press.

Nelson, J., & Aboud, F. E. (1985). The resolution of social conflict between friends. *Child Development, 56,* 1009-1017.

Newcomb, A. F., & Bagwell, C. L. (1996). The developmental significance of children's friendship relations. In W. M. Bukowski, A. F. Newcomb, & W. W. Hartup (Eds.), *The company they keep: Friendship in childhood and adolescence* (pp. 289-321). Cambridge, England: Cambridge University Press.

Nucci, L. P. (1996). Morality and the personal sphere of actions. In E. Reed, E. Turiel, & T. Brown (Eds.), *Values and knowledge.* Mahwah, NJ: Lawrence Erlbaum Associates.

Parke, R. D., & Slaby, R. G. (1983). The development of aggression. In E. M. Hetherington (Ed.), *Handbook of child psychology: Vol. R. Socialization, personality, and social development, 4th ed.* (pp. 547-641). New York: Wiley.

Petit, O., & Thierry, B. (1994). Aggressive and peaceful interventions in conflicts in Tonkean macaques. *Animal Behavior, 48,* 1427-1436.

Piaget, J. (1932). *The moral judgment of the child.* New York: Free Press.

Piaget, J. (1971). *Biology and knowledge.* Chicago: University of Chicago Press. (Originally published 1967)

Piaget, J. (1985/1975). *The equilibration of cognitive structures* (T. Brown & K. Thampy, trans.). Chicago: University of Chicago Press.

Pitrowski, C. (1995). Children's interventions into family conflict: Links with the quality of siblings relationships. *Early Education and Development, 6,* 377-404.

Putallaz, M., & Sheppard, B. (1992). Conflict management and social competence. In C. U. Shantz & W. W. Hartup (Eds.), *Conflict in child and adolescent development* (pp. 330-355). Cambridge, England: Cambridge University Press.

Ross, H. S., & Conant, C. L. (1992). The social structure of early conflict, interaction, relationships and alliances. In C. U. Shantz & W. W. Hartup (Eds.), *Conflict in child and adolescent development* (pp. 153-185). Cambridge, England: Cambridge University Press.

Ross, H. S., Conant, C. L., Cheyne, J. A., & Alevizos, E. (1992). Relationships and alliances in the social interaction of kibbutz toddlers. *Social Development, 1,* 1-17.

Ross, H. S., Filyer, R., Loolis, S, Perlman, M., & Martin, J. (1994). Administering justice in the family. *Journal of Family Psychology, 8,* 254-273.

Ross, H. S., Tesla, C., Kenyon, B., & Lollis, S. (1990). Maternal intervention in toddler peer conflict: The socialization of principles of justice. *Developmental Psychology, 26,* 994-1003.

Sackin, S., & Thelen, E. (1984). An ethological study of peaceful associative outcomes to conflict in preschool children. *Child Development, 55,* 1098-1102.

Sapolsky, R. M. (1993). The physiology of dominance. In W. A. Mason & S. P. Mendoza (Eds.), *Primate social conflict* (pp. 171-204). Albany: State University of New York Press.

Selman, R. (1980). *The growth of interpersonal understanding.* New York: Academic Press.

Shantz, C. U. (1987). Conflicts between children. *Child Development, 58,* 283-305.

Shantz, C. U., & Hartup, W. W. (1992). *Conflict in child and adolescent development.* Cambridge, England: Cambridge University Press.

Slomkowski, C., & Killen, M. (1992). Young children's conceptions of transgressions with friends and nonfriends. *International Journal of Behavioral Development, 15,* 247-258.

Smetana, J. G. (1995). Morality in context: Abstractions, ambiguities, and applications. In R. Vasta (Ed.), *Annals of Child Development, 10,* 83-130.

Trivers, R. L. (1974). Parent offspring conflict. *American Zoologist, 14,* 249-264.

Turiel, E. (1983). *The development of social knowledge: Morality and convention.* Cambridge, England: Cambridge University Press.

Veerbeek, P. (1996). *Peacemaking of young children.* Unpublished doctoral dissertation, Emory University, Atlanta, GA.

Veerbeek, P. (1997, August). How do young children make up after a fight with a peer? Paper presented at a symposium entitled "Conflict Resolution in Primates and Non-primates" at the 25th International Ethological Conference, Vienna, Austria.

Vespo, J. E., & Caplan, M. (1993). Preschoolers' differential conflict behavior with friends and acquaintances. Early Education and Development, 4, 45–53.

Watson, M., Solomon, D., Battisstich, V., Schaps, E., & Solomon, J. (1989). The Child Development Project: Combining traditional and developmental approaches to education. In L. P. Nucci (Ed.), Moral development and character education (pp. 51–92). Berkeley, CA: McCutchan Publishing.

Watts, D. P. (1994). Social relationships of immigrant and resident female mountain gorillas, II. Relatedness, residence and relationships between females. American Journal of Primatology, 32, 13–30.

Watts, D. P. (1995). Post-conflict social events in wild mountain gorillas (Mammalia, Hominoidea). I. Social interactions between opponents. Ethology, 100, 139–157.

Wentzel, K. (1993). Does being good make the grade? Social behavior and academic competence in middle school. Journal of Educational Psychology, 85, 357–364.

Westlund, K., Forsberg, A. J. L., & Ljungberg, T. (1997). Reconciliatory behaviours in pre-school children. Advances in Ethology, 32, 158.

Youniss, J. (1980). Parents and peers in social development. Chicago: University of Chicago Press.

Youniss, J., & Smollar, J. (1985). Adolescent relations with mothers, fathers, and friends. Chicago: University of Chicago Press.

Zahn-Waxler, C., Radke-Yarrow, M., & King, R. (1979). Child rearing and children's initiations towards victims of distress. Child Development, 50, 319–330.

PART

III

CULTURAL DEVELOPMENT

10

SOCIAL COGNITION AND THE
EVOLUTION OF CULTURE

Michael Tomasello
Emory University

Taking a comparative perspective on human cognition presents an immediate puzzle. Human beings shared an ancestor with their nearest primate relative, the chimpanzee, a mere 6 to 8 million years ago—a very brief time evolutionarily. But the cognitive skills of the two species seem very different. Just to highlight the obvious, human beings have whatever cognitive skills are necessary to create products such as languages, complex cumulative technologies, and social institutions—whereas, to our knowledge, chimpanzees do not. The problem is that there simply has not been enough evolutionary time for very large differences of cognitive processes to have evolved. The general solution to this puzzle must be some small difference of cognitive process that makes a big difference in the cognitive products that may be created.

In my view there is only one plausible candidate for this small difference that makes a big difference. Human beings have become ultrasocial, and this has changed their cognition from an individual enterprise to a social–collective enterprise. This cultural view of human cognition is the fundamental premise of the newly emerging paradigm of Cultural Psychology which, following Vygotsky (1978), posits that human cognition is the way that it is because human children grow up in a particular kind of social world (e.g., Bruner, 1990; Cole, 1996; Rogoff, 1990; Saxe, 1994; Stigler, Shweder, & Herdt, 1990). It is not just that children benefit from the information gathered by others, which they do, but it is also that their cognition is shaped in very basic ways by the social–cultural context in which it develops. Thus, from a very early age, children are exposed to a variety of artifacts, including both material tools such as spoons and hoes and symbolic tools such as language and Arabic numerals. The structure of these artifacts is social–cultural because each one embodies the collective wisdom of the many different persons who contributed to its creation over historical time. As children learn to use an artifact for understanding and dealing with a situation, they participate in this wisdom—and this includes learning to use linguistic symbols, through which children learn something of how members of their culture perceive and categorize the world.

In addition, and just as important as artifacts, from a very early age, human children participate in a variety of social practices that antedate their arrival in the culture—including games, scripts, rituals, instructional formats, and other forms of prepackaged communal activities (often involving artifacts). These social practices serve to motivate children toward certain goals, to instruct them in the pursuit of those goals, and, in general, to potentiate cognitive skills that would not develop in social isolation (Candland, 1993; Gauvain, 1995). Together, the artifacts and structured social practices that human children inherit from their forebears—along with their ability to tune in to those artifacts and practices, of course—makes human cognition social and cultural, indeed collective, in a very fundamental way (Tomasello, Kruger, & Ratner, 1993).

It is in this context that I have become interested in the claims of some behavioral biologists that other animal species also live in cultures and that their cognitive ontogenies also benefit from the social contexts in which they develop (e.g., Boesch, 1993, in press; McGrew, 1993). Many of these scientists claim that while there are clearly quantitative differences in the amount of information transmitted by different species, the basic processes of cultural transmission are similar in all cases. If true, this would be astounding because it would mean that the kind of collective cognition that characterizes the human species is not unique, as most anthropologists and psychologists assume, but rather that human culture has much deeper evolutionary roots. These claims have been made most energetically for chimpanzees, and they clearly have much merit: Chimpanzee societies do resemble human cultures in some very important ways. However, it is also true—for me at least—that human cultures differ from the societies of other animal species in some fundamental respects, and that human cognitive development is unique in the extent to which and the ways in which it is socially constituted.

In this chapter I argue for the uniqueness of human culture—and the uniqueness of human cognition as a result—by comparing it with the culture of our nearest primate relatives. My procedure is as follows. I begin by describing very briefly the social cognition and cultural learning that takes place during human children's initial entry into culture. I then ask and attempt to answer three main questions: (1) Do chimpanzees and other apes engage in cultural learning? (2) Do chimpanzees and other apes understand the actions of others in terms of the underlying intentions and beliefs involved (an important question because some scientists, including myself, have argued that such an understanding is necessary for truly cultural learning)? and (3) In what ways do apes respond to attempts at human enculturation? Note that in asking this third question as a separate question, I place many of our most famous ape individuals—Viki, Washoe, and Kanzi, to name three—in a special category. This is because I am interested primarily in whether apes have created something like human cultures on their own. The study of apes raised in human-like cultural environments is relevant to this question, but in a special way.

THE ENCULTURATION OF HUMAN CHILDREN

Whenever there is a discussion of culture, definitional problems immediately arise. Tomasello, Kruger, and Ratner (1993) sought to avoid some of these by looking at culture not as a product but as a process. We argued that social influences on individual learning take many forms, ranging from the fact that mammalian young stay close to their mothers and so are exposed to things they might otherwise not be exposed to, to the fact that the young of some bird species learn their species-typical song by mimicking precisely that of their parents. In this context, we argued that some species, human beings in particular, engage in an especially powerful form of social learning called cultural learning. Cultural learning takes place not when a learner simply has its attention drawn to things by the behavior of others, but when a learner makes active attempts to discern what others are doing and why they are doing it—to take their perspective, in fact. We tried to capture this distinction by saying that in this case the learner is not learning **from** the other, but rather **through** the other. We hypothesized that what allows organisms to engage in cultural learning is a particular form of social cognition in which the behavior of others is understood as intentional. We proposed three levels of this social understanding in human ontogeny: the understanding of intentional agents at one year of age, the understanding of mental agents at 3 to 4 years of age, and the understanding of reflective agents at 6 to 7 years of age. For current purposes, the most important of these is the ontogenetically first.

Human infants are social creatures from birth, but around their first birthdays, they undergo a kind of social–cognitive revolution in which for the first time they begin to understand others in terms of their intentional relations to the world. This understanding manifests itself as infants both tune into adults and invite adults to tune into them. Infants at this age begin to tune into the intentional relations of adults by looking at objects adults are looking at (gaze following), adopting toward those objects attitudes adults are adopting toward them (social referencing), and doing with those objects what adults are doing with them (imitative learning). Infants get adults to tune into their intentional relations by actively directing their attention to outside objects with ritualized gestures and vocalizations, for both imperative and declarative purposes (i.e., as requests and comments). All of these skills emerge together in early development quite simply because they are all manifestations of the same thing: They are all manifestations of the infant's emerging ability to understand other persons as intentional agents whose attention and behavior to objects may be actively followed into, directed, and shared (Tomasello, 1995).

This social–cognitive revolution sets the stage for the infants' second year of life in which they begin to imitatively learn the use of all kinds of tools, artifacts, and symbols. For example, in a study by Meltzoff (1988) 14-month-old children observed an adult bend at the waist and touch its head to a panel, thus turning on a light. They followed suit. Infants engaged in this somewhat unusual and awkward behavior, even though it would have been easier and more natural for them simply to push the panel with their hand. One interpretation of this behavior is that infants understood that (a) the adult had the goal of illuminating the light and then chose one means for doing so, from among other possible means; and (b) if they had the same goal, they could choose the same means. Cultural learning of this type thus relies fundamentally on infants' tendency to identify with adults and on their ability to distinguish in the actions of others the underlying goal and the different means that might be used to achieve it. This interpretation is supported by the more recent finding of Meltzoff (1995) that 18-month-old children also imitatively learn actions that adults intend to perform, even if they are unsuccessful in doing so.

Another excellent example is word learning. In a recent experimental study, Tomasello, Strosberg, and Akhtar (1996) had an adult announce to 18-month-old children, "Let's go find the modi." Using no language after this, she then proceeded to a row of buckets and extracted several objects with a scowl on her face, and then an object that brought her obvious glee. Almost all the children knew immediately that the first objects extracted were not the modi—she had scowled at them—and that the last object extracted was the modi—she had smiled on it. They knew this because they understood that the adult had an intention to find this thing called a modi and that all of her subsequent actions were means directed at that end. The frowns thus meant not that she did not like those objects, or that she had a sudden fit of depression, but simply that they were not the modi. The smile meant fulfillment of the intention and thus that the modi had been found. Although it is not widely appreciated, it is a fact that all word learning relies on intention reading of this type. It should also be noted that it is at around this same age—18 months—that infants for the first time begin to predicate multiple things about objects to which they and the adult are jointly attending, for example, by saying that this ball is wet or big or mine (Reed, 1995; Tomasello, 1988, 1995). Predication demonstrates young children's understanding that others have attentional states over which they have voluntary control, independent of eye gaze direction.

The overall picture is thus as follows. Human infants are born into a world of preexisting artifacts, tools, and symbols. As they begin to understand the intentional relations that others have to these outside entities, they become able to adopt their attitudes, goals, and behaviors toward them, that is, to engage in cultural learning. This allows them to appropriate (to use Rogoff's, 1990, felicitous term) these cultural materials for their own use, which has ramifications for all aspects of human cognitive development, including many not touched on in this brief account. The question of central interest here is the extent to which our nearest primate relatives also fit with this basic description.

QUESTION 1:
DO APES ENGAGE IN CULTURAL LEARNING?

Tool Use. The observation that has done most to promote the idea of culture in a nonhuman species is depicted in Fig. 10.1. In their natural habitats in central Africa, different populations of chimpanzees (*Pan troglodytes*) learn to use tools differently and these differences seem to persist across generations—a seemingly clear-cut case of cultural variation and transmission. The problem in the current context is that some population differences of behavior involve things that are not socially transmitted. For example, chimpanzees living in different parts of Africa construct their nightly nests in different ways. But in the analysis of McGrew (1993), these differences are fairly straightforward reflections of the differing local ecologies of the different groups, that is, the different nest-building materials available in the different environments, the different trees in which nests may be built in the different environments, the relative risk of predators, and other relevant ecological differences.

Similarly in the case of tool use, some chimpanzees in Eastern Africa carefully fish for termites by inserting leaves and twigs down the tunnels of their mounds, whereas other chimpanzees in West-Central Africa simply destroy termite mounds with large sticks and scoop up the inhabitants by the handful (McGrew, 1993). The reason for this difference is that because of the small amount of rainfall in Eastern Africa, the termite mounds there are too cement-like to be destroyed with a stick whereas in Western Africa,

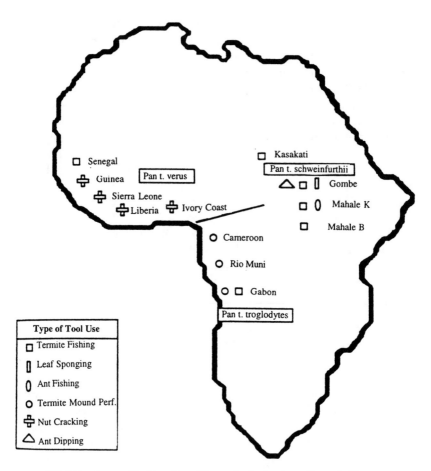

FIG. 10.1. Geographical location of the major tool use practices of chimpanzees (taken from Tomasello, 1990). For a few updates, see McGrew (1993).

they are much softer. The point is that in at least some cases, population
differences of behavior may be produced not by social or cultural learning
but by the individuals of different groups adapting individually to their own
local ecologies (Tomasello, 1990, 1994, 1996). Behavioral traditions of this
type clearly indicate cognitive flexibility and skills of individual learning, but
if the behavior is not learned from others, it is cultural only in an extended
use of that term. The main problem in the current context is that types of
learning processes involved in naturally occurring behavioral traditions can
never be determined from naturalistic observations alone; even when detailed ecological analyses are performed (e.g., Boesch, Marchesi, Marchesi,
Fruth, & Joulian, 1994), it is always possible that some unobserved ecological
differences are at work. What is needed are experimental studies in which

different subjects are systematically exposed to different types of tool-use activities.

There exist basically four experimental studies of chimpanzees or other apes learning to use tools under different observational conditions. First, Tomasello, Davis-Dasilva, Camak, and Bard (1987) trained an adult chimpanzee demonstrator to rake food items into her cage with a metal T-bar. She then went on to develop two very distinctive two-step strategies when the food was located in difficult places along the side or against the back of the platform's raised edges. When chimpanzee youngsters were then given the opportunity to observe this demonstrator, many learned to use the tool, but they employed a wide variety of different raking-in procedures, and none of them learned either of the two-step strategies. This suggested to us the possibility that what they had learned from their observations was not a behavioral strategy of the demonstrator's, but rather something about the changes of state in the environment that the demonstrator's use of the tool had brought about. They then used one of their own, already-known behavioral strategies to attempt to re-create that change of state. Because it served to reproduce the effect, not the means, of the demonstrator's behavior, we called this emulation learning.

In a second experimental study, Nagell, Olguin, and Tomasello (1993) attempted to investigate the emulation hypothesis more directly (see also Call & Tomasello, 1994). We presented juvenile and adult chimpanzees and 2-year-old human children with a rake-like tool and a desirable but out-of-reach object. The tool was such that it could be used in either of two ways, leading to the same end result—the logic being that if all subjects were attending to was the end result, they would not be affected by the method they saw demonstrated. For each species, one group of subjects observed a human demonstrator employ one method of tool use (a less efficient method, rake-side down, so that the food slipped through the prongs) and another group of subjects observed another method of tool use (a more efficient method in which the rake was conspicuously flipped to the edge-side down orientation). What we found was that whereas human children in general copied the behavioral method of the demonstrator in each of the two observation conditions, chimpanzees used the same methods no matter which demonstration they observed: They flipped or failed to flip equally in the two conditions. From this pattern of results we concluded, once again, that chimpanzees were paying attention to the changes of state in the environment the demonstrator brought about but they were not attending to the behavioral strategies employed; they were engaged in emulation learning.

In a relatively direct test of the emulation hypothesis, Call and Tomasello (1995) designed a task whose goal it was to effectively prevent emulation and other forms of individual learning—the logic in this case being that if these forms of learning were prevented, and all there was to observe was behavior, apes should be basically lost in the task. Subjects were juvenile and adult orangutans. What they saw was a human demonstrator manipulate a stick protruding from an opaque box in one of four particular ways and then receive a reward from a protruding tube. They could not see how the manipulations led to the result, and so could not employ their own individual intelligence to decide what to do. When subjects were then given the opportunity to solve the problem themselves, they performed the four possible actions indiscrimantly, no matter which demonstration they saw, and thus enjoyed only a chance rate of success. On the other hand, a majority of human 3- and 4-year-old children did learn to imitate the requisite actions of the demonstrator. This study, then, provides further evidence for the emulation hypothesis: Preventing emulation learning by apes leads to basically random performance.

Finally, Whiten, Custance, Gòmez, Teixidor, and Bard (1996) have recently conducted an experiment in which chimpanzees were shown different ways to open an artificially constructed fruit. There were two mechanisms, each with two techniques of operation: a bolt that could be either pushed or pulled free of a doorway and a latch that had two modes of operation. Each subject was shown one of the two techniques for each mechanism. For the latch mechanism, subjects behaved in the same way no matter which demonstration they saw. For the bolt mechanism, there was a difference. Subjects behaved differently when they saw a human demonstrator push a bolt through a lock versus a condition in which she reached around and pulled that bolt through the lock with a twisting motion. Because the demonstration drew subjects' attention to different ends of the bolt, however, it is very likely that subjects were not imitating the demonstrator's behavioral strategy as much as they were having their attention drawn to the end of the bolt the demonstrator touched. It is also noteworthy that 3-year-old human children in this study imitatively learned the demonstrator's technique much more often and more faithfully than did the chimpanzees for both mechanisms.

Overall, what these studies suggest, I believe, is that apes are very intelligent and creative in using tools and understanding changes in the environment brought about by the tool use of others. But they do not understand the actual behavioral strategies of others in the same ways as do humans. For humans, the goal or intention of the demonstrator is a central part of what they perceive, and indeed the goal is understood as something separate from the behavioral means. This understanding thus highlights the demonstrator's method or strategy of tool use—the way she is attempting to accomplish the goal, given the possibility of other means of accomplishing it. Humans also understand that when they have the same goal as another, they can use the same strategy (presumably based on some kind of identification with the other, perhaps as hypothesized by Meltzoff & Gopnik, 1993, or by Barresi & Moore, 1996). For apes, on the other hand, what is salient in the demonstration is the tool, the food, and their spatial–temporal–causal relations; the intentional states of the demonstrator, and thus her strategies as distinct behavioral entities, are simply not perceived or understood.

Let us return to the wild with the emulation hypothesis in hand. One possibility is this: Perhaps one chimpanzee in Western Africa invented nut cracking. Her behavior would have then left a stone hammer, some unopened nuts, and some opened nuts all in one place near a suitable substrate—very propitious learning conditions that might facilitate the individual learning of others. Moreover, her behavior would also have been quite noisy and would have attracted the attention of groupmates and, if observed, would illustrate certain causal relations among stones and the opening of nuts. There is thus clearly social transmission going on here—young chimpanzees would not have learned how to use the tool if they had not observed the original inventor. But it is different from the cultural transmission that takes place with human children who actually copy the behavioral strategies of others. If this distinction seems like a subtle one, let me just point out that it has important implications for the nature of the resulting behavioral traditions (Tomasello, 1994). Most importantly, chimpanzee behavioral traditions do not seem to be characterized by the so-called ratchet effect. That is, human artifacts and social practices accumulate modifications over time as one generation adapts to a situation in a new way and then subsequent generations adopt that new way via some form of cultural learning—and so on over time so that they can look at the history (the ratcheting up) of such things as hammers and languages. No behavioral traditions of apes seems to have this accumulative, historical character (but cf. Boesch, 1993)—in my view because there is no way that reproducing environmental effects in idiosyncratic ways can be as stable over generations of tool users as can the direct appropriation of specific behavioral strategies.

Gestural Communication. The other well-known case of relevance to the current discussion is the gestural communication of chimpanzees, for which there also seem to be some population-specific behaviors in the wild—although these have never been systematically studied (see Tomasello, 1990, for a review). The most detailed studies come from a captive colony of chimpanzees. At regular intervals since 1983, my collaborators and I have been observing the gestural signaling of a group of chimpanzees living at the Yerkes Primate Center Field Station. In our first study, we observed the infants and juveniles of the group (1 to 4 years old), with special emphasis on how they used their signals (Tomasello, George, Kruger, Farrar, & Evans,

1985). Looking only at learned, intentional signals accompanied by gaze alternation or response waiting (both indicating the expectation of a response), we found a number of striking developmental patterns. For example, we found that juveniles used many gestures not used by adults, that adults used some gestures not used by juveniles, and that some juvenile gestures for particular functions were replaced by more adult-like forms at later developmental periods. None of these patterns was consistent with the idea that infant and juvenile chimpanzees acquire their gestural signals by imitating adults.

In a longitudinal follow-up to these observations, Tomasello, Gust, and Frost (1989) observed the same juvenile chimpanzees in the same group setting 4 years later (at 5 to 9 years old). We were mainly interested in whether the youngsters acquire their gestures by means of imitative learning or ontogenetic ritualization. In ontogenetic ritualization, a communicative signal is created by two organisms shaping each others' behavior in repeated instances of a social interaction (see Fig. 10.2). For example, an infant may initiate nursing by going directly for the mother's nipple, perhaps grabbing and moving her arm in the process. In some future encounter, the mother might anticipate the infant's behavior at the first touch of her arm, and so become receptive at that point. Noting this anticipation then leads the infant to abbreviate its behavior to a touch on the arm in order to initiate nursing. A good analogy from the human domain is infants learning to hold their arms above their heads to be picked up. No one teaches them this and they do not learn it by imitating other infants; they ritualize it with adults individually. The important point for current purposes is that in ritualization neither individual is seeking to reproduce the behavior of the other; they are just interacting and anticipating and a signal results. The main observation in this study that suggested ritualization, not imitation, as a learning process was the existence of a number of idiosyncratic gestures used by single individuals—that obviously could not have been learned by imitation (Goodall, 1986, also reports this for the wild group she observes).

We have recently completed a third set of longitudinal observations of the gestures of this group (Tomasello, Call, Nagell, Olguin, & Carpenter, 1994).

ENCOUNTER 1: A does x (to B)

ENCOUNTER 2: B reacts to x (perhaps anticipating it) by doing y

ENCOUNTER 3: A notices that B does y when s/he does x

ENCOUNTER 4: A produces x **in order to** get B's reaction y

FIG. 10.2. The process of ontogenetic ritualization by means of which chimpanzees learn most, if not all, of their gestures. (Human infants learn some of their gestures in this way as well.)

In this study, a completely new generation of youngers was the object of the study, that is, 1- to 4-year-olds who were not even born at the time of the last observations. In order to investigate the question of potential learning processes, we made systematic comparisons of the concordance rates of all individuals with all other individuals across the three longitudinal time points; that is, each youngster's gestures were compared with those of each other youngster. The analysis revealed, by both qualitative and quantitative comparisons, that there was much individuality in the use of gestures, with much individual variability both within and across generations. It was not even the case that offspring resembled their mothers more than they resembled other adults. All of this individual variability would not seem compatible with a hypothesis of imitative learning. It is also important that many of the gestures that were widespread in the group were gestures that are also used quite frequently by captive youngsters raised in peer groups with no opportunity to observe older conspecifics—again suggesting ontogenetic ritualization.

Let me mention finally, and very tentatively, that we have also recently completed a small pilot study in which we removed an individual from this same group and taught her two different arbitrary signals by means of which she obtained desired food from a human. When she was then returned to the group and used these same gestures in full view of other group members, there was not one instance of another individual imitating. This pilot study has several limitations (e.g., this is a situation in which most chimpanzees had already used other gestures successfully in the past), and so it should not be relied on heavily until further studies are conducted. However, given its agreement with the naturalistic observations, it is at least worthy of a brief mention.

This overall pattern of results suggests that chimpanzee youngsters acquire the majority, if not the totality, of their gestures by individually ritualizing them with one another. The explanation for this is analogous to the explanation for emulation learning in the case of tool use. Like emulation learning, ontogenetic ritualization does not require individuals to understand the intentions of others in the same way as does imitative learning. Ritualizing a touch-side as a request for nursing requires only an anticipation of the future behavior of a conspecific and the ability to translate this anticipation into an instrumental action of one's own. Imitatively learning a touch-side from another infant, on the other hand, requires that a learner understand that: (a) that infant wishes to nurse; (b) that infant is using the touch-side gesture, as opposed to other possible methods, to accomplish that goal; and (c) when she, the learner, has the same goal, she can use the same gesture. Chimpanzees do not engage in this kind of learning sequence because they do not identify their own behavior with that of others and so differentiate in the behavior of others their goals and the means they use to accomplish those goals.

Teaching. Let me conclude this consideration of the first question with a brief comment on teaching—the other, top-down side of culture and cultural learning. A number of fieldworkers have reported observations that they interpret as an ape mother teaching her offspring, for example, a chimpanzee mother may take a poisonous plant away from her child (Goodall, 1986). But the mother's motive in such cases is unclear. Certainly she intends to prevent her child from eating the poisonous plant, but there is no evidence that she intends to teach her child about plants—she does not persist until her child acquires the avoidance behavior on its own, for example. It is also worth noting that in many years of observing chimpanzees crack nuts, Boesch (1991) reported only two instances of what he considered to be intentional instruction in this context, and both of these have other nonpedagogical interpretations. In any case, by no one's account is intentional instruction a pervasive aspect of ape social life, and indeed apes in the wild have not even been observed to simply point to things or to show them to others—perhaps the simplest form of instruction. In contrast, Kruger and Tomasello (1996) recently reviewed a wealth of anthropological data and found that in all human cultures, intentional instruction, in which adults actively instruct youngsters in ways that clearly reveal their intention that the child learn something, is pervasive. This behavioral difference is presumably due to some difference of social cognition as well, perhaps in the understanding of others as mental agents who have the possibility of being either knowledgeable or ignorant.

QUESTION 2: DO APES UNDERSTAND OTHERS INTENTIONALLY?

Because of the emphasis I have placed on the intentional understanding of others as a determining factor in cultural learning, it is also important to assess ape social–cognitive skills in general, outside of learning contexts. In particular, it is important to investigate their understanding of others in terms of their intentions and beliefs. In human children the understanding of intentions first occurs during the social–cognitive revolution at 1 year of age, and the understanding of beliefs occurs as they engage in such things as deception and the comprehension of false beliefs at 3 to 4 years of age. Although it is widely believed that apes have considerable skills in this domain, the fact is that the experimental foundation on which this conclusion rests is very weak, resting almost totally on three experimental studies.

Intentions. The first study to assess experimentally the social cognition of apes was Premack and Woodruff's (1978) famous investigation that asked whether chimpanzees have a theory of mind. The language-trained chimpanzee Sarah was shown videotapes of human actors coming on obstacles in problem-solving situations. For example, Sarah saw a human trying to exit through a locked cage door, or a human trying to operate a hose that was unattached to a faucet. The videotape was then stopped and Sarah was presented with a pair of photographs, one of which represented, from the human point of view, a solution to the problem: such things as a key to open the door, or hose attached to a faucet. In general, Sarah performed quite well on these tasks. Premack and Woodruff thus concluded that Sarah's choices constituted evidence that she "recognized the videotape as representing a problem, understood the actor's purpose, and chose alternatives compatible with that purpose" (p. 515).

The difficulty is that there are clear alternative interpretations of this famous study involving simple associations between items in the videotaped problems and items in the response choices. In a commentary on the paper that is very little cited, Savage-Rumbaugh, Rumbaugh, and Boysen (1978) examined each item with which Sarah was presented and found that, in general, the items for which associative strategies were most straightforward given Sarah's past experience were the ones Sarah did best on (e.g., the key with lock, hose with faucet—both common associations in her everyday life); those that were more difficult associatively were items Sarah did more poorly on. To explore this possibility further, Savage-Rumbaugh et al. presented two of their own language-trained chimpanzees, Austin and Sherman, with a match-to-sample procedure in which they were shown, for example, a picture of a foot and asked to choose between pictures of a shoe and a key. What happened was that both subjects chose the closely associated objects on almost all trials, suggesting that Sarah may have done something similar. Savage-Rumbaugh et al. (1978) also have a very telling critique of the two control studies that Premack and Woodruff performed that were meant to rule out such associative strategies.

The upshot is that this experiment has some very plausible interpretations in terms of Sarah's experimental strategies that do not involve her seeing the videotaped sequences as problems, defined intentionally from the human actor's point of view. It thus begs for replication or confirmation using a different methodology. In one attempt to do this, Premack (1986) reported very briefly on his attempt to train Sarah to discriminate between videotaped sequences that depicted intentional actions versus those that depicted nonintentional actions. Although no details of the procedure are given, he reported that Sarah never learned the discrimination (1986, p. 85). Some ongoing work by Povinelli is also finding negative results. In his procedure, juvenile chimpanzees witness a mean actor pour their juice onto the floor intentionally and a clumsy actor spill their juice onto the floor accidentally; they then get to choose which actor will bring them their juice on the next trial. The findings to date provide no support for chimpanzees' ability to distinguish intentional from accidental human actions.

Beliefs. The second and third experimental studies of ape social cognition concern knowledge or beliefs. The second was conducted by Povinelli, Nelson, and Boysen (1990), based on a previous attempt reported briefly by Premack (1988). They had four chimpanzees witness a human bait one of four cups behind an occluder (so that the chimpanzees could not tell which cup contained the food). Another human remained outside the room and consequently could not see which cup was being baited. After this ignorant human entered the room, subjects could choose either the ignorant human or the knowledgeable human to inform them of the whereabouts of the food. If they chose the knowledgeable human, they invariably got the food; if they chose the ignorant human, they invariably did not. Results indicated that three of the four chimpanzees learned to choose the knowledgeable human significantly more often than the ignorant human, two after 100 to 150 trials and the third after 250 to 300 trials. The interesting twist in this experiment was that there now came a transfer phase consisting of 30 trials in which a neutral experimenter baited the cups. The difference was that this time, instead of remaining outside the room during the baiting process, the ignorant human now stayed inside the room but with a bag over his head; a knowledgeable human watched the baiting process. All three subjects maintained their successful performance during this transfer phase, suggesting that what they learned during the first phase was something more general than a simple discrimination based on the physical presence of a human—something more like who had witnessed the baiting process visually.

There are two problems with this interpretation, however. The first is that in a subsequent reanalysis of the data for the transfer (bag-on head) trials, Povinelli (1994) reported that in the first five transfer trials, subjects did not discriminate the knowledgeable and ignorant humans; only after these initial trials did they learn to choose consistently the human who had witnessed the hiding. This raises the possibility that in the transfer phase, as in the original phase, subjects were simply learning a discrimination—although in the transfer phase they did so more quickly due to a process of learning set formation, that is, learning to learn. The second problem is that when this study was replicated with 4-year-old nursery-raised chimpanzees, all six subjects failed to differentiate between the knowledgeable and ignorant experimenters. Although Povinelli, Rulf, and Bierschwale (1994) attributed their failure to replicate the previous findings to the age of the subjects, these data—in concert with the reanalysis of the transfer data of the original experiment—raise the possibility that apes simply do not understand the knowledge states of others, although they may in some circumstances learn cues for deciding who can get them food and who cannot.

Ape skills of so-called deception are also relevant here—because deception is also thought to depend on an understanding of the beliefs of others. First of all, there are many reported anecdotes of ape deception solicited and collected by Whiten and Byrne (1988). For example, de Waal (1986) reported that a chimpanzee who was angry at another held out her hand in an appeasement gesture and when the other approached, attacked him; this happened repeatedly so it is unlikely to have been a chance confluence of events. The central question in such instances is whether the perpetrator is attempting to create a false belief in the other or whether she is simply attempting to influence the other's behavior. Thus, if an individual has noticed that others approach when she holds out her hand and she wishes one to approach now (for whatever reason), she can hold out her hand to get him to do so. This is clearly an intelligent and insightful social strategy, but it requires no talk of beliefs or false beliefs.

This interpretation would seem to be supported by the third experimental study of ape social cognition. Woodruff and Premack (1979) taught four juvenile chimpanzees to indicate to a naive human trainer which of two opaque buckets contained food, at which point they got it. After learning to do this, two different types of human trainers were introduced. First, a cooperative trainer acted as before, locating the hidden food and then giving it to the subject. A competitive trainer also attempted to locate the food, but when he found it, he kept it and ate it himself. The question was whether the subjects would learn to provide accurate information for the cooperative trainer but not for the competitive trainer. In the first phase of the experiment, three of four subjects pointed in a similar manner for both the cooperative and competitive trainers, with no attempts to withhold information or actively deceive either; the other subject began to differentiate between the trainers in the second block of 24 trials. In the second phase of the experiment, which took place 6 months later and included some methodological changes (and lasted 14 months), all of the subjects began to withhold information from the competitive trainer, and two of the subjects actually induced the competitive trainer to choose the wrong bucket by orienting to it (after several hundred trials in each case).

The investigators interpreted these findings as evidence for chimpanzee skills of intentional deception. But it should be noted that the chimpanzees' skills emerged only gradually over many trials. This suggests the possibility that, as in the case of the anecdotes from the wild, what the chimpanzees in this study were doing was learning to use creative, intelligent social strategies to get what they wanted, that is, they learned over many trials to induce the competitive trainer to go to the bucket without food and the cooperative trainer to go to the bucket with food. They were manipulating the behavior, not the belief states of the trainers.

Visual Perception. Finally, let me say a brief word about ape understanding of visual perception. Apes seem to know some things about whether others are looking at them, and, in some cases, where others are looking—

especially those who have had extensive contact with humans. But there are also some curious gaps in their understanding, for example, the inability to discriminate cases in which a human's eyes are covered from cases in which they are not (Povinelli & Eddy, 1996). In any case, following the gaze of others does not automatically indicate an understanding of their attention, if what we mean by attention is something that can be voluntarily or intentionally focused on different aspects of experience even in the same visual orientation. And I would contend that an understanding of the intentional dimension of perception—namely, attention—is necessary for truly cultural learning (Tomasello, 1995).

Summary. Overall, then, I do not find strong evidence that apes understand the behavior of others in terms of intentions or beliefs. This conclusion seems implausible to some primatologists because they see much complexity in the social interactions of apes, and this complexity would seem to require human-like forms of social cognition. But this complexity may be generated by other means. That is, it is clear that apes understand that others are directed to things in the environment which sometimes allows them to predict their behavior (see Fig. 10.3a). Thus, for example, from past experience in similar contexts an individual may predict that when food appears, others are likely to go for it and eat it. Certain cues in the behavior of others may also be used for prediction; for instance, the fact that others are excited or fearful predicts what they are likely to do next. It may even be that the direction of travel and/or eye gaze may be used as cues to predict the behavior of others, as in Menzel's (1971) famous experiments.

This reading of contextual and behavioral cues becomes even more sophisticated as it combines with apes' understanding of the complex social field in which they operate. This consists of a recognition of individual groupmates, a knowledge of their own relationship to these groupmates based on past interactions with them, and an understanding of the relationships that other individuals have with one another based on their past

FIG. 10.3a. Depiction of how nonhuman primates understand the behavior of others: directed toward an object or change of state in the environment (A → B).

interactions. (Indeed, it is precisely in this understanding of third-party social relationships that primate social cognition distinguishes itself from the social cognition of other mammalian species; Tomasello & Call, 1994). The combination of cue detection with this kind of social knowledge allows apes to predict the behavior of others in many creative ways, for example: Who can attempt to mate with whom in the presence of whom; who is headed for food; who can attempt to take food from whom in the presence of whom; who is about to leave the area; who will retaliate if a juvenile is attacked; who is likely to be a strong ally in a fight; where a frightening object or predator might be located; and who is likely to form an alliance against whom in the future. Social strategies of this nature make for what de Waal (1982) called primate politics in which individuals seek to gain advantage over their rivals. But it does not make for a theory of mind or intentions, as all of these strategies may be formulated on the basis of a knowledge of the behavior of others.

What apes do not do, in my opinion, is understand intentional behavior as an integrated process containing as separable components goals, behavioral means, and perceptual monitoring (Fig. 10.3b). That is to say, understanding behavior intentionally means understanding, first, that an organism may have different behavioral means to achieve the same goal in different contexts—that is, has choices to make—and, second, that an organism's attention is also under voluntary control—again, there are choices to be made—as it monitors its progress toward that goal. The goal thus serves as a kind of invariant in social cognition, providing coherence to different behavioral and perceptual activities. Human infants simply see their mothers trying to open a cabinet, not moving her arms around randomly, and thus they know that her attention and behavior are organized around that goal. This basically control-system view of behavior is what allows human

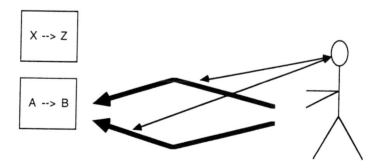

FIG. 10.3b. Depiction of how humans understand the behavior of others: directed at one of several possible changes of state, using one of several possible behavioral means, and monitoring the behavioral means via voluntary attention.

infants to understand, from 1 year of age, that means are separate from ends, that attention is separate from bodily orientation or eye gaze direction, and, in general, that the intentional is separate from the behavioral.

QUESTION 3: IN WHAT WAYS DO APES RESPOND TO HUMAN ENCULTURATION?

It is well-known that apes raised by humans acquire some human-like skills that they otherwise would not acquire. In a comprehensive review of the effects of humans on the cognitive development of apes, Call and Tomasello (1996) found that in the domain of physical knowledge, this effect was limited to exposure: Apes who are exposed to human objects learn to manipulate them in various interesting ways through their own explorations and emulation of humans. In the social domain, on the other hand, there is some evidence that human intervention may lead to some more profound changes in cognitive development. In the current context, the most important behavioral domain is imitation. The relevant findings follow:

First, Hayes and Hayes (1952) trained their human-raised chimpanzee Viki to mimic various of their movements and gestures, for example, blinking the eyes or clapping the hands. They trained her throughout her daily life in their home for a period of more than 17 months before systematic testing began. The training consisted of a human performing a behavior and then using various shaping and molding techniques, with rewards, to get Viki to "Do this." After she had become skillful, some novel behaviors were systematically introduced to Viki. She reproduced many of them faithfully and quickly; she had clearly gotten the idea of the mimicking game. Recently, Custance, Whiten, and Bard (1995) demonstrated in a more rigorous fashion similar abilities in two nursery-reared chimpanzees after they were trained for a period of several months in a manner similar to Viki. The main issue in these two studies, of course, is what the animals are learning over their several months of training. Parrots mimic human speech with no understanding of its communicative significance. If this is all the apes in these studies are doing, then their performance is interesting only from the point of view of the ability to make sensorimotor correspondences between one's own body and that of another—not from the point of view of understanding the intentions of others in a way that allows for the reproduction of instrumental actions or strategies of the type necessary for participating in culture.

Second, Tomasello, Savage-Rumbaugh, and Kruger (1993)—in a study comparing captive apes, human-raised apes, and 2-year-old human children—demonstrated to subjects two different actions on each of 24 different objects. Children were told in the experiment to "Do this," and the apes were pretrained to reproduce modeled actions. The major result was that the mother-reared apes very rarely produced both the end and means of the novel actions (i.e., imitatively learned them), and there was not one instance of a mother-reared ape performing both demonstrated actions on one object. In contrast, the human-raised apes and the human children imitatively learned the novel actions much more frequently, and they did not differ from one another in this learning. Again the interpretive problem, however, is that the subjects were not solving any problems here; their goal was only to reproduce the human actions in order to please their human caregiver, not to produce an instrumentally effective action. That this may be a problem is demonstrated by Call and Tomasello (1995) who found that a human-raised, sign-language-using orangutan, who played the mimicking game quite well with arbitrary actions (even on objects), did very poorly when confronted with an instrumental problem, shown its solution, and told to "Do this" as in the mimicking game.

Also relevant is a recent study by Russon and Galdikas (1993). The subjects of their study were rehabilitant orangutans who had been raised in various ways by humans and then introduced to a human camp on the edge of a forest. What Russon and Galdikas observed in the behavior of a few individuals (one in particular) was a number of actions that were so unlike the typical actions of orangutans, and so unlikely to have been learned by individuals on their own, that imitative learning was inferred. These behaviors almost all involved the manipulation of human artifacts in human-like ways—such things as brushing the teeth, applying insect repellent, using a knife, and so forth. Although we do not know precisely what the orangutans observed of these actions, or what they were attempting to accomplish with the objects as they manipulated them, or what they could have learned from exploring the objects by themselves, or what kinds of experiences with humans they had early in life, clearly something very interesting is going on here. Whether it is apes tuning into humans relating to objects—or whether it is something more akin to mimicking or emulation learning—awaits future studies in which some of these unknowns are experimentally controlled.

Clearly human-raised apes are learning to tune into human behavior in some interesting ways. At this point, the precise nature of this tuning in is open to interpretation, however, as there simply are not enough data. There are two extreme possibilities. On the one hand, it is possible that human beings can, through various processes of enculturation or training over a relatively extended period of time in early ontogeny, lead apes down a developmental path that includes various human-like skills of social cognition and cultural learning. Fundamental to this process would be experiences in which young apes are encouraged to attend to what a human is attending to, with the human trying to make this happen and rewarding the ape when it does; exposed to human artifacts and intentionally instructed in their operation, with social praise and other rewards when the subject reproduces the human's actions; and exposed to forms of gestural and symbolic communication that presuppose a reciprocity of understanding. These kinds of interactions are integral to the process that Vygotsky (1978) called the socialization of attention and they prepare the way for cultural learning in organisms who possess certain kinds of social–cognitive skills, including humans. And it is the case, by the way, that having these experiences early in ontogeny seems important, as apes treated in these ways only later in development seem to be much less responsive (Rumbaugh et al., 1991).

The more conservative interpretation focuses on some of the things that human-raised apes do not do. Whereas human-raised apes often do learn to point for humans (as their conspecifics in the wild do not), this pointing is almost always of the imperative form—asking for an object or to be transported to a location. It is extremely rare that an ape will point to or show an object to others simply to share attention to it, or to make a comment with communicative symbols when the only goal is the sharing of attention (Carpenter, Tomasello, & Savage-Rumbaugh, 1995). And there is still very little, if any, behavior of human-raised apes that one would want to call intentional teaching. It is thus possible that the motivation to share attention with others, and to teach one another, stems from a uniquely human social motivation that no amount of experience or training can ever instill in apes. This might imply that the imitative learning skills of human-raised apes are based on social–cognitive processes different from those of humans, that is, something other than a state of shared intentions and attention. It almost certainly implies that no apes, including human-raised apes, have the motivation to create a cultural environment of material and symbolic artifacts and intentional instruction as an ontogenetic niche for their progeny. Without this top-down part of the process, cultural learning, and thus a human-like culture, cannot evolve.

THE EVOLUTION OF CULTURE

What does all this mean for the evolution of culture? If we could leave human-raised apes out of the picture, the story would be straightforward. Apes, particularly chimpanzees, have some population-specific behavioral traditions, but these do not show the ratchet effect or any other indication of building up complexities over historical time. The reason that their behavioral traditions do not show this historical development is that apes engage in socially influenced individual learning such as emulation and ritualization, but not cultural learning of the human kind. The reason they do not engage in cultural learning is that they do not understand the behavior of others intentionally.

The major implication for human evolution is that human and chimpanzee behavioral traditions are only analogous and not homologous. Although the vast majority of human behavior and cognition is directly inherited from the common ancestor we shared with chimpanzees some 7 million years ago—and this may even include some of the precursors of intentional understanding such as gaze following—the cultural traditions of the two species evolved from separate phylogenetic roots, and thus they rely on different proximate mechanisms. Chimpanzee behavioral traditions rely on an understanding of the directedness of others—leading to such forms of learning as emulation and ritualization—whereas human cultural traditions rely on an understanding of the intentionality of others—leading to various forms of cultural learning such as imitative and collaborative learning. Indeed, in some recent accounts of human evolution, attention has been drawn to the relative lack of cultural variability or historical change in the stone tools of all manifestations of the genus *Homo* prior to the emergence of *Homo sapiens* less than 100,000 to 200,000 years ago. This is several million years after the split from other ape species and implies a very recent origin for human culture as we know it today (Klein, 1989; Noble & Davidson, in press).

The behavior of human-raised apes presents a difficulty for this scenario, however. Not so much because they are better at cultural learning than their conspecifics, but rather because their development implies that to acquire certain skills of social cognition and cultural learning, it is useful, perhaps necessary, that organisms grow up with other organisms showing them how to do things. If this is a correct inference, it means that some form of instruction must have evolved before cultural learning. From a cognitive-developmental point of view this is curious because imitative learning is present at 1 year of age, whereas clearly recognizable attempts at teaching do not seem to be present in an obvious way until perhaps 3 to 4 years of age. This is presumably because imitative learning depends on more basic social–cognitive skills than does intentional instruction. So how could instruction have evolved first?

The solution may be this: Although full-blown intentional instruction involves one organism making sure that another organism acquires some information or skill, it has its ontogenetic roots in something simpler. The ontogenetic roots, in my view, are the protodeclarative behaviors of pointing and showing that we see in young children at the same age they begin to imitatively learn, that is, at the 1-year social–cognitive revolution. Showing a parent a novel object just discovered is, in effect, inviting them to experience something new that they are not now experiencing; it is an act of informing just as an attempt to instruct is an act of informing. Instruction may therefore have an initial manifestation in acts of informing that emerge

in late infancy—depending on an understanding of the intentions and attention of others—whereas other forms of instruction may emerge later and
depend on an understanding of the knowledge and beliefs of others. Perhaps
this initial form of informing is sufficient to encourage cultural learning. If
this were so, it would suggest that in human evolution, skills of cultural
learning and informing may have evolved together: Humans learned to show
things to others and to respond to the attempts of others to show them
things all in one package—perhaps in the last 100,000 years.

In Piaget's genetic epistemology, phylogenetic analyses are an important
complement to ontogenetic analyses. In the current case, when the two
types of analyses are combined, we find that it is the social–cognitive revolution at 1 year of age that is the key ontogenetic event signaling the
uniquely human adaptation for culture. This is clear from all of the things
that 1- to 2-year-old children do—from declarative pointing to the acquisition
of language—that other animals do not do in the natural course of events.
The full-blown theory of mind characteristic of 4-year-old children, which
many researchers have identified as a key human adaptation is, therefore
simply icing on the social–cognitive cake. It is in the understanding of
intentions and attention—phylogenetically and ontogenetically prior to the
understanding of knowledge and beliefs—that humans display their species-
typical and species-unique form of social cognition that, in my view, paved
the way for the evolution of human culture.

ACKNOWLEDGMENTS

Thanks to Nameera Akhtar and Josep Call for helpful comments on an earlier
version of the manuscript.

REFERENCES

Barresi, J., & Moore, C. (1996). Intentional relations and social understanding. *Behavioral and Brain Sciences, 19,* 107–154.
Boesch, C. (1991). Teaching among wild chimpanzees. *Animal Behavior, 41,* 530–532.
Boesch, C. (1993). Toward a new image of culture in wild chimpanzees. *Behavioral and Brain Sciences, 15,* 149–150.
Boesch, C. (in press). The emergence of cultures among wild chimpanzees. In J. Maynard Smith (Ed.), *Evolution of social behavior patterns in primates and man.* London: The British Academy.
Boesch, C., Marchesi, P., Marchesi, N., Fruth, B., & Joulian, F. (1994). Is nut cracking in wild chimpanzees a cultural behavior? *Journal of Human Evolution, 26,* 325–338.
Bruner, J. (1990). *Acts of meaning.* Cambridge, MA: Harvard University Press.
Call, J., & Tomasello, M. (1994). Social learning of tool use by orangutans. *Human Evolution, 4,* 297–313.

Call, J., & Tomasello, M. (1995). The use of social information in the problem-solving of orangutans and human children. *Journal of Comparative Psychology, 109*, 308–320.

Call, J., & Tomasello, M. (1996). The role of humans in the cognitive development of apes. In A. Russon (Ed.), *Reaching into thought: The minds of the great apes* (pp. 371–403). New York: Cambridge University Press.

Candland, D. (1993). *Feral children and clever animals: Reflections on human nature.* New York: Oxford University Press.

Carpenter, M., Tomasello, M., & Savage-Rumbaugh, S. (1995). Joint attention and imitative learning in children, chimpanzees, and enculturated chimpanzees. *Social Development, 4*, 217–237.

Cole, M. (1996). *Cultural psychology: A once and future discipline.* Cambridge, MA: Harvard University Press.

Custance, D., Whiten, A., & Bard, K. (1995). Can young chimpanzees imitate arbitrary actions? Hayes and Hayes (1952) revisited. *Behaviour.*

de Waal, F. (1982). *Chimpanzee politics.* New York: Harper & Row.

de Waal, F. (1986). Deception in the natural communication of chimpanzees. In R. Mitchell & N. Thompson (Eds.), *Deception: Perspectives on human and nonhuman deceit* (pp. 221–244). New York: State University of New York Press.

Gauvain, M. (1995). Thinking in niches: Sociocultural influences on cognitive development. *Human Development, 38*, 25–45.

Goodall, J. (1986). *The chimpanzees of Gombe.* Cambridge, MA: Harvard University Press.

Hayes, K., & Hayes, C. (1952). Imitation in a home-raised chimpanzee. *Journal of comparative and physiological psychology, 45*, 450–459.

Klein, R. (1989). *The human career.* Chicago: University of Chicago Press.

Kruger, A., & Tomasello, M. (1996). Cultural learning and learning culture. In D. Olson (Ed.), *Handbook of education and human development: New models of teaching, learning, and schooling.* London: Blackwell.

McGrew, W. (1993). *Chimpanzee material culture.* New York: Cambridge University Press.

Meltzoff, A. (1988). Infant imitation after a one week delay: Long term memory for novel acts and multiple stimuli. *Developmental Psychology, 24*, 470–476.

Meltzoff, A. (1995). Understanding the intentions of others: Re-enactment of intended acts by 18-month-old children. *Developmental Psychology, 31*, 838–850.

Meltzoff, A., & Gopnik, A. (1993). The role of imitation in understanding persons and developing a theory of mind. In S. Baron-Cohen, H. Tager-Flusberg, & D. Cohen (Eds.), *Understanding other minds: Perspectives from autism* (pp. 335–366). New York: Oxford University Press.

Menzel, E. (1971). Communication about the environment in a group of young chimpanzees. *Folia Primatologica, 15*, 220–232.

Nagell, K., Olguin, K., & Tomasello, M. (1993). Processes of social learning in the tool use of chimpanzees and human children. *Journal of Comparative Psychology, 107*, 174–186.

Noble, W., & Davidson, I. (in press). *Human evolution, language, and mind: A psychological and archeological inquiry.* New York: Cambridge University Press.

Povinelli, D. (1994). What chimpanzees (might) know about the mind. In R. Wrangham, W. McGrew, F. de Waal, & P. Heltne (Eds.), *Chimpanzee cultures* (pp. 285–300). Cambridge, MA: Harvard University Press.

Povinelli, D., & Eddy, T. (1996). What chimpanzees know about seeing. *Society for Research in Child Development Monographs*, No. 247.

Povinelli, D., Nelson, K., & Boysen, S. (1990). Inferences about guessing and knowing by chimpanzees. *Journal of Comparative Psychology, 104*, 203–210.

Povinelli, D., Rulf, A., & Bierschwale, D. (1994). Absence of knowledge attribution and self-recognition in young chimpanzees. *Journal of Comparative Psychology, 108*, 74–80.

Premack, D. (1986). *Gavagai!* Cambridge, MA: MIT Press.

Premack, D. (1988). 'Does the chimpanzee have a theory of mind?' revisited. In R. Byrne & A. Whiten (Eds.), *Machiavellian intelligence: Social expertise and the evolution of intellect in monkeys, apes, and humans* (pp. 160–179). New York: Oxford University Press.

Premack, D., & Woodruff, G. (1978). Does the chimpanzee have a theory of mind? *Behavioral and Brain Sciences, 4*, 515–526.

Reed, E. (1995). The ecological approach to language development. *Language and Communication, 15*, 1–29.

Rogoff, B. (1990). *Apprenticeship in thinking*. New York: Oxford University Press.

Rumbaugh, D., Hopkins, W., Washburn, D., & Savage-Rumbaugh, S. (1991). Comparative perspectives of brain, cognition, and language. In N. Krasnegor, D. Rumbaugh, R. Schieffelbusch, & M. Studdert-Kennedy (Eds.), *Biological and behavioral determinants of language development* (pp. 145–164). Hillsdale, NJ: Lawrence Erlbaum Associates.

Russon, A., & Galdikas, B. (1993). Imitation in ex-captive orangutans. *Journal of Comparative Psychology, 107*, 147–161.

Savage-Rumbaugh, S., Rumbaugh, D., & Boysen, S. (1978). Commentary on Premack and Woodruff (1978). *Behavioral and Brain Sciences, 4*, 527–529.

Saxe, G. (1994). *Culture and cognitive development: Studies in mathematical understanding*. Hillsdale, NJ: Lawrence Erlbaum Associates.

Stigler, J., Shweder, R., & Herdt, G. (1990). *Cultural psychology*. New York: Cambridge University Press.

Tomasello, M. (1988). The role of joint attention in early language development. *Language Sciences, 10*, 69–88.

Tomasello, M. (1990). Cultural transmission in the tool use and communicatory signaling of chimpanzees? In S. Parker & K. Gibson (Eds.), *"Language" and intelligence in primates: Developmental perspectives* (pp. 274–311). New York: Cambridge University Press.

Tomasello, M. (1994). The question of chimpanzee culture. In R. Wrangham, W. McGrew, F. de Waal, & P. Heltne (Eds.), *Chimpanzee cultures* (pp. 301–318). Cambridge, MA: Harvard University Press.

Tomasello, M. (1995). Joint attention as social cognition. In C. Moore & P. Dunham (Eds.), *Joint attention: Its origins and role in development* (pp. 103–130). Hillsdale, NJ: Lawrence Erlbaum Associates.

Tomasello, M. (1996). Do apes ape? In J. Galef & C. Heyes (Eds.), *Social learning in animals: The roots of culture* (pp. 319–346). New York: Academic Press.

Tomasello, M., & Call, J. (1994). The social cognition of monkeys and apes. *Yearbook of Physical Anthropology, 37*, 273–305.

Tomasello, M., Call, J., Nagell, K., Olguin, K., & Carpenter, M. (1994). The learning and use of gestural signals by young chimpanzees? A trans-generational study. *Primates, 35*, 137–154.

Tomasello, M., Davis-Dasilva, M., Camak, L., & Bard, K. (1987). Observational learning of tool-use by young chimpanzees. *Human Evolution, 2*, 175–183.

Tomasello, M., George, B., Kruger, A., Farrar, J., & Evans, E. (1985). The development of gestural communication in young chimpanzees. *Journal of Human Evolution, 14*, 175–186.

Tomasello, M., Gust, D., & Frost, T. (1989). A longitudinal investigation of gestural communication in young chimpanzees. *Primates, 30*, 35–50.

Tomasello, M., Kruger, A., & Ratner, A. (1993). Cultural learning. *Behavioral and Brain Sciences, 16*, 495–511.

Tomasello, M., Savage-Rumbaugh, S., & Kruger, A. (1993). Imitative learning of actions on objects by chimpanzees, enculturated chimpanzees, and human children. *Child Development, 64*, 1688–1705.

Tomasello, M., Strosberg, R., & Akhtar, N. (1996). Eighteen-month-old children learn words in non-ostensive contexts. *Journal of Child Language, 22*, 1–20.

Vygotsky, L. (1978). *Mind in society: The development of higher psychological processes*. Cambridge, MA: Harvard University Press.

Whiten, A., & Byrne, R. (1988). Tactical deception in primates. *Behavioral and Brain Sciences, 11*, 233–244.

Whiten, A., Custance, D., Gomez, J., Teixidor, P., & Bard, K. (1996). Imitative learning of artificial fruit processing in children and chimpanzees. *Journal of Comparative Psychology, 110*, 3–14.

Woodruff, G., & Premack, D. (1979). Intentional communication in the chimpanzee: The development of deception. *Cognition, 7*, 333–362.

11

PREHISTORY AND COGNITIVE DEVELOPMENT

Peter Damerow
Max Planck Institute for the History of Science, Berlin

THE PERSPECTIVE OF GENETIC EPISTEMOLOGY

This chapter deals with cognitive development in prehistory from the perspective of Piaget's genetic epistemology, applying concepts such as the concept of sensorimotor intelligence, preoperational thought, and operational thought to the early development of human intelligence.

Following some introductory remarks on the application of genetic epistemology in cross-cultural and historic comparisons, the origin of man and the Neolithic and the Urban Revolution is briefly examined. The chapter concludes with a discussion of findings about the transition from prehistory to history.

The view of cognitive growth in prehistory presented here is widely based on an analysis of sources documenting the transition process to the historical era. The results of the analysis answer the question of what has been the ultimate level of cognition achieved in prehistory, thus providing a landmark for any correlation of ontogenetic stages with prehistoric cognition.

To show how stages of the development of human intelligence established by cognitive psychology can be correlated with the emergence of human culture in prehistory is, in fact, the predominant aim of this chapter. It is argued that cognitive development in the long Paleolithic Period can be interpreted as transition from sensorimotor intelligence to preoperative thinking. Furthermore, I argue that a specific form of operative thinking emerged together with the transition from prehistory to history. This form of operative thinking was strictly context-dependent, and its emergence should therefore be interpreted as transition from preoperational to concrete operational thinking. It is, however, also shown that thinking in this period lacked certain structures of operational thinking that are usually considered to be universal.

Introductory Remarks

Piaget (see, for instance, Piaget, 1970) developed his conception of genetic epistemology and the categories for describing genetic stages when he became aware of fundamental changes in the thought processes of the developing child. He identified invariant psychological functions such as assimilation, accommodation, equilibration, and reflective abstraction, which generate a discontinuous universal sequence of subsequent stages of cognition, each of which gives rise to specific cognitive achievements.

Sensorimotor intelligence is the level of a practical intelligence based on a close relationship between action and cognition. At this level of cognition, sensory data are assimilated to generalized schemes of coordinated, repeatable actions that can operate at a level below mental representation and conscious thought. These schemes of action or practical concepts are generalized, differentiated, and integrated in the course of sensorimotor activities by accommodation to the growing amount of sensorimotor experience. The cognitive outcome of this development is the mental construction of invariants of replacements and of (irreversible) transformations. The invariants constitute structures that differentiate already between contents and forms, thus establishing a semilogic of internalized actions and mental imagery based on identities and functions (Piaget & Inhelder, 1963; Piaget, Grize, Szeminska, & Bang, 1977; Piaget, Henriques, & Ascher, 1992).

In addition to the development of such cognitive structures of sensorimotor intelligence, preoperational thought is supplemented by the symbolic function; that is, the ability to represent something by symbols and eventually to distinguish objects from their meanings. This ability is a precondition for language acquisition and for symbolic activities such as drawing, painting, and modeling.

The developmental stage of operational thought emerges when internalized actions turn into reversible mental operations and abstract entities such as quantity, time, and space are constructed by reflective abstraction from such systems of mental operations. They constitute the structures of logical and mathematical thinking that are usually assumed to be human cognitive universals.

The extent to which we can reasonably apply psychological categories that describe stages in ontogenesis to phenomena in prehistory is not discussed here in detail. Piaget himself, at least, believed (see e.g., Piaget,

1950a; Piaget & Garcia, 1983) that the basic concepts of his genetic episte-mology not only represented psychological phenomena but also that they were epistemological categories covering cultural and historical aspects of cognitive processes.

One specific theoretical problem in applying these categories to prehis-toric and historic observations, however, must be briefly discussed. Piaget's theory (Piaget, 1950a, 1970) suggests that essential characteristics of the ontogenetic stages of cognitive development are universal. Differences in the environment should have no effect on the sequence in which these stages occur. Furthermore, environmental conditions should not be able to alter the universal, logico-mathematical structures of thinking that are the final cognitive outcome of ontogenesis. Accordingly, diverging develop-ments of thinking that lead to atypical structures should emerge only tem-porarily as sidetracking of a universal adaptive process. Apart from such exceptional developments, there are only two possibilities for the alleged universal cognitive structures not to show up in certain cultures. They may either nevertheless exist as a cognitive potential that is not being used, or they may, in fact, actually be missing. In the first case, certain ecological conditions would be responsible for the cognitive potential to be exercised; in the second case, such conditions would be responsible for the rate of progress through the ontogenetic stages.

These are, indeed, the alternatives according to which genetic epistemol-ogy has commonly been applied to cultural differences. It is generally ac-cepted that ontogenesis reaches or completes the final stage of formal operational thinking only if the environment meets certain requirements. Hence, cultural differences in the development of the structures of thinking are usually attributed to cultural constraints on ontogenesis.

Unfortunately, experts disagree about the degree to which the final level of cognition may vary between cultures. Jahoda (1980), for instance, wrote in a review article on the Piagetian approach to cross-cultural psychology, "It can be stated quite categorically that no society could function at the preoperational stage, and to suggest that a majority of any people are at that level is nonsense almost by definition" (p. 116).

But this is precisely what Piaget originally assumed (others followed him as, for instance, recently Hallpike, 1979). Influenced by the discussions in the 1920s about the interpretation of ethnological findings as evidence for culturally specific modes of thinking and, in particular, by Lévy-Bruhl's (1923) early work on primitive mentality (Lévy-Bruhl later abandoned this idea), he introduced the theory that among primitive people ontogenetic development reaches only the level of preoperative thinking. Piaget (1950a) elaborated his originally strong claim that culture and cognition are closely connected in this way primarily in his monumental *Introduction à l'épistémologie génétique*—which has unfortunately never been translated into English. He argued that there may well exist a seemingly great discrepancy between, on the one hand, the practical intelligence of such people based on mental imagery, intuitive thinking, and symbolic representation, and, on the other hand, their ability to build higher-level concepts by reflective abstractions and deductive thinking.

Later on, Piaget (1966) weakened his assumption. He then left the question open as to which extent cultural differences influence the ontogenetic development of cognition. Taking into account results of empirical studies in Aden, Hong Kong, and South Africa, he argued:

> The question is to know whether a change will be observed for the stages of logical-mathematical operations or whether these operations will be found everywhere with their identical common background; . . . the kind of psychology we develop in our social environments remains conjectural as long as comparative extensive and systematical research is not available. (p. 4)

In a similar way as Piaget (1970) applied categories of genetic epistemology to cross-cultural research, he also envisaged the application of these categories to the study of the development of cognition in prehistory. In his Woodbridge Lectures on genetic epistemology, he argued:

> The fundamental hypothesis of genetic epistemology is that there is a parallelism between the progress made in the logical and rational organization of knowledge and the corresponding formative psychological processes. Well, now, if that is our hypothesis, what will be our field of study? Of course the most fruitful, most obvious field of study would be reconstituting human history—the history of human thinking in prehistoric man. Unfortunately, we are not very well informed about the psychology of Neanderthal man (. . .). Since this field of biogenesis is not available to us, we shall do as biologists do and turn to ontogenesis. (p. 13)

Methodological Difficulties

Our information about the psychology of humans in prehistory is, in fact, extremely limited. The common psychological methods of data collection are irrelevant in archaeological research. Psychologists usually interact with their subjects of investigation by means of interrogations, experiments, and tests and they scrutinize their observations in order to reconstruct the mental processes involved in the observed activities. In the case of prehistoric humans, however, only some extremely durable material remains are transmitted to the modern scientist that can lead to some conclusions concerning the activities that might have been necessary to produce or to use the transmitted artifacts.

In spite of this seemingly hopeless situation, there are ongoing discussions among anthropologists about what can be concluded from the palaeoanthropological findings on topics that are intimately linked to the development of cognition, topics such as the origins of symbolism (Bednarik, 1995; Byers, 1994), imagery (Davis, 1986), and language (Burling, 1993; Chazan, 1995; Corballis, 1992; Dunbar, 1993; Greenfield, 1991; Parker & Gibson, 1979). These discussions, however, rarely refer to concepts and results of genetic epistemology. This may partly be a consequence of severe methodological criticism of the stage concept that has been widely discussed among anthropologists (see the open peer commentary on Brainerd, 1978/1979). There is, however, also an inherent obstacle in genetic epistemology that makes it difficult to identify stages of cognitive growth based on the scare evidence provided by archeology.

According to genetic epistemology, the basic structures of cognition reflect the coordination of actions, not the actions themselves. It is, therefore, not possible to directly infer from an observed behavior the level of cognition involved. The same action—say, walking from one location to the other—may indicate completely different levels of cognition. Such an action may be the immediate outcome of sensorimotor activities. It may result from following a verbal description of those landmarks marking the way, it may have been planned in advance by reading a map, or it may be part of the systematic exploration of an unknown area by a highly competent individual. If there is no possibility to communicate with the subject investigated in order to find out more about the context of the observed behavior, the only way to infer the level of cognition is to observe how the total actions of this individual are coordinated and how they are related to other activities in his social environment.

It is obviously impossible to identify levels of cognition in prehistory according to such strong criteria. In this methodologically hopeless situation, it is tempting to abandon any rigidity by taking identified structures of behavior immediately as indications of corresponding cognitive structures. Wynn (1985, 1989), in particular, inferred in this way, from geometrical shapes of stone tools, levels of cognition. He interpreted, for instance, the production of spherical shapes as an indication of the achievement of a concept of radius, and the production of symmetrical shapes as attestation of a general spacial framework equivalent to a space of euclidean coordinates. Such an application of concepts of genetic epistemology fails to distinguish sufficiently between different levels of cognition that may be represented by a specific behavior, thus leading to unreasonably early datings of cognitive achievements. Hence, Wynn claimed that hominids must have used operational intelligence as early as 300,000 B.C., although Piaget (Piaget & Inhelder, 1963) showed convincingly that the reproduction of geometrical forms and symmetries is already a preoperative achievement of children between 2 and 7 years of age, presupposing only the transition from purely sensorimotor perception to imagery.

The following account of cognition in prehistory is also examining information provided by palaeoanthropology and archaeology about the development of forms and functions of human artifacts and human behavior in order to relate this development to what we know from developmental and cross-cultural psychology about the psychogenesis of fundamental structures of cognition. The method, however, is different from that of Wynn (1989). In view of the gap between what we know about human activities in prehistory and what we need to know in order to reconstruct the correlation of cognitive stages with prehistoric periods, the achievement of a specific level of cognition is assumed only if several converging criteria indicate the emergence of a behavior that would be impossible on the previous level. The overall picture of the development of cognition in prehistory resulting from such a cautious evaluation of available sources may possibly underestimate prehistoric cognitive achievements. It turns out, however, to be in general quite consistent with the results of a number of studies about cognitive growth in prehistory that were carried out in conceptual frameworks different from genetic epistemology (see, for instance, the open peer commentary to Donald, 1993, and the review article of Mellars, 1989).

In addition to studying archaeological findings, three different approaches can be applied in order to achieve at least indirect evidence of the development of cognition in prehistory and to determine the level of cognition that was ultimately achieved in the prehistoric era.

First, animal and human cognition can be compared in order to infer minimal cognitive achievements connected with the origin of mankind.

Second, studies about cognition in extant indigenous people living without contact to modern civilization under conditions comparable to those of prehistoric times can be consulted and can be related to corresponding prehistoric periods.

Third, the earliest written documents of mankind can be studied in order to determine the level of cognition at the end of the prehistoric period that made the transition to literacy possible.

The outcome of an investigation following these lines is presented next.

ORIGIN OF HUMAN COGNITION

The Paleolithic Period

Leaving aside the development of our proto-human ancestors, human development in prehistory covers roughly the timespan from the first appearance of man about 1 million years ago up to the occurrence of the first writing systems around 3000 B.C. Most of this vast period belongs to the so-called Paleolithic, ending about 8000 B.C.

It becomes apparent in this discussion that there is no clear-cut distinction between proto-human primates and early hominids. In the Paleolithic Age, a slowly but continuously growing material culture emerged that became the essential characteristic of human in contrast to animal communities. This material culture finally comprised a variety of tools accompanied by language as a developed means of communication.

Throughout the Paleolithic, man was a hunter and food gatherer producing tools of which only those made of stone, bone, and antler have survived. In general, these tools developed gradually from a few all-purpose tools at the beginning of the Paleolithic Age to a great variety of highly specialized and sophisticated instruments for specific purposes at the end. In the Upper Paleolithic Period, which covers approximately the last 100,000 years of the Paleolithic, regional stone tool industries appeared and basic techniques of drawing, modeling, sculpture, and painting were developed.

Comparison With Animal Intelligence

Given this overall picture of the Paleolithic, some obvious conclusions can be drawn concerning the level of cognition associated with the emergence and development of the human species.

Humans in the Paleolithic were surely equipped with at least those cognitive prerequisites based on sensorimotor skills that make up the intelligence of primates. This should warn us against a careless application of human psychology. The success of Paleolithic man to survive even under extremely harsh living conditions and his superiority to the animals he was hunting is not necessarily an indication of specific human cognitive abilities.

Let us take spatial orientation as an example (Pick & Acredolo, 1983). Certain cognitive structures relative to spatial relationships and their representation in gesture, language, and other external tools of orientation are such fundamental components of human cognition that they seem to be a necessary prerequisite of those activities attested for the Paleolithic humans. It is known, however, that animals may also exhibit an extremely sophisticated performance in spatial orientation (Ellen & Thinus-Blanc, 1987). The behavioral mechanisms available to them in their spatial orientation are not only based on simple adaptation to cues and stimuli. On a higher level of cognitive organization, animals also exhibit rule-governed behavior. They adapt to problems using alternative strategies such as change-after-success or stay-after-success, depending on how the food supply varies at different locations. Many animals show intelligent spatial problem solving based on some kind of cognitive map representing spatial relations. Such mental representations of spatial relations depending on past experience make animals capable of rearranging the patterns of their orientation behavior, taking short cuts in complex spacial arrangements, choosing between alternative routes for reaching a certain goal, and so forth. Primates seem even to be able to decode spatial relationships from spoken human language and to communicate such relationships by gestures, deliberately produced trails, learned symbols, and so forth (Savage-Rumbaugh et al., 1993; see also chapter 7, this volume). In order to decide whether certain activities of Paleolithic humans show any characteristics of typical human cognition, they have to give evidence of cognitive preconditions that according to our knowledge, are qualitatively different from what we know about such intelligent behavior of animals.

Indications of Human Intelligence

Cognitive prerequisites of human activities that exceed the capabilities of animal cognition can indeed be inferred even from the scarce information we have. Neither the ability to communicate information by some kind of language precursor (Savage-Rumbaugh et al., 1993) nor the skill necessary for the use or even the production of tools (McGrew, 1992; McGrew & Marchant, 1992; Westergard & Suomi, 1994) are beyond the cognitive capabilities of animals. Rather, the continuous transmission of knowledge from one generation to the other is the necessary prerequisite of the development of a human language with socially transmitted meanings and of the enduring improvement of the stone implements over the millennia of the Paleolithic era.

Such a transmission constitutes human cultural development. At least in its developed form, it presupposes a powerful means of communication such as human language that is assumed to have emerged in the Paleolithic together with the development of tools (Byers, 1994; Dunbar, 1993; Parker & Gibson, 1979; Wallace, 1989) and has reached its developed form probably during the Middle-to-Upper Paleolithic transition in connection with the appearance of the anatomically modern populations of homo sapiens (see the review in Mellars, 1989). Although the development of such means of communication as language and its presumable precursors in facial expressions, body language, and vocalizations such as screams and cries can only be indirectly inferred from Paleolithic remains (Armstrong, Stokoe, & Wilcox, 1994; Bateman et al., 1990; Davidson & Noble, 1989), so-called Paleolithic art provides evidence of various kinds of pictography and symbolism in the Upper Paleolithic Period. Paleolithic art is expressed in artifacts such as decoration, pictography, personal adornment, graves, sacrificial goods, modeled figurines, and cave paintings. These indications of the representation of mental constructs lead to the conclusion that the development of tools was indeed accompanied by an evolving ability to make use of symbolic representations.

Emergence of Preoperative Thinking

Now, this is exactly what one would expect from the perspective of genetic epistemology if restrictive criteria are applied as they are proposed here. It is precisely the development of the symbolic function at the preoperational stage of the growing child at about the age of 2 years that indicates the ontogenetic bifurcation into independent developmental paths of animal and human cognition. According to Piaget (1950b), at about this age human children—contrary to young primates—achieve the ability not only to react to the signals of sensorimotor intelligence that represent, for the subject, simply a partial aspect of the object indicated, but also to decode the symbols and signs and distinguish them from the objects themselves. The symbolic function supports the preoperative thinking that leads to preconcepts that are the notions attached to the symbols and signs.

The development beginning with animal reactions to signals emitted by their environment and concluding with the creation of complex symbolism in the Middle-to-Upper Paleolithic transition resembles this emergence of preoperative thinking. Whereas animal cognition is essentially based on individual experience Paleolithic art seems to indicate that at least after the Middle-to-Upper Paleolithic, transition symbols and signs were deliberately used to transfer socially transmitted meanings. The difference due to reflection is recognizable when—as in the case of cave paintings—the symbols and signs cannot have been produced without a conscious discrimination of the symbols and their meaning.

Cognitive development in the long Paleolithic Period can, therefore, be characterized as the transition from sensorimotor intelligence to preoperative thinking based on the development of mental imagery and of a semilogic of internalized actions.

Operative Thinking at Stone-Age Level?

Paleolithic art, however, also contains certain elements that are suggestive of arithmetical and geometrical cognition and have sometimes been interpreted as indications of a higher developmental level of cognition than the level of preoperative thinking.

The paintings in the cave of Lascaux, for instance, which have been dated by carbon-14 analysis to about 14,000 B.C., depict primarily animals hunted at that time but also contain some simple drawings composed of straight lines and sequences of dots that may be interpreted as abstract geometrical figures and early numerical representations. However, if, as has been proposed, the drawings depict traps, then the regular shapes are not the result of any geometrical construction or conceptualizing but simply depict artifacts that as a result of material constraints, result in rectangular shapes. And if, as one might conjecture, the series of dots represent the number of animals hunted in a one-to-one correspondence, these dots are still only representations of animals and not representations of numbers. This interpretation of the dots as symbols for objects and not as a representation of numbers is strongly supported by the fact that the dots lack the regular structuring characteristic of all counting sequences.

Another archaeological find believed to constitute an example of early arithmetical activity is a notched bone tool handle excavated at the Mesolithic site of Ishango. The implement is dated to about 7000 B.C. It shows three sequences of grouped notches. The groups of the first of these sequences contain 3, 6, 4, 8, 10, 5, 5, and 7 notches; the groups of the second contain 11, 13, 17 and 19 notches; and the groups of the third contain 11, 21, 19 and 9 notches. There is no obvious, simple regularity in these numbers. The excavator, Jean de Heinzelin, admitted that the grouping might be fortuitous (de Heinzelin, 1962). Nevertheless, he offered the interpretation that the notches were deliberately planned and may represent an arithmetical game. He further argued that if so, the tool provides evidence of the use of a decimal system and of the knowledge of duplication and of prime numbers. Marshack (1972) also assumed that the notches were consciously prepared notations, but offered an alternative interpretation. According to his opinion, based on an analysis of how the notches were carved, the groups can further be subdivided and thus turn out to be astronomical records representing the lunar cycle.

The evidence is weak for both interpretations because the sequences of notches offer no evidence of even the minimal requirements of signs representing arithmetical notations; they do not exhibit the typical regular structure of counting series.

Missing evidence of typical structures of counting sequences does not, of course, prove that such cognitive constructions did not exist in early prehistory. Counting techniques are usually based on language or gestures that do not leave traces in the archaeological records. However, as we know from extant preliterate cultures, even the existence of counting techniques does not necessarily indicate an operatory concept of number. Only an analysis of the use of such techniques allows us to draw conclusions with regard to the level of cognition involved.

We must conclude that with this evidence there is no sufficient justification for the alleged arithmetical activities of man in the Paleolithic Period. Neither the implements that survived from the Paleolithic nor Paleolithic art provide evidence to support the assumption that a level of cognition higher than the level of preoperative thinking was achieved at that time.

THE NEOLITHIC REVOLUTION

In the following time period up to the end of prehistory there were at least two major changes in human social organization: the so-called Neolithic Revolution around 8000 B.C. and the Urban Revolution beginning about 4000 B.C.

The Neolithic Revolution was brought about by the transition from food gathering to life in stable settlements. This revolution probably resulted in a dramatic population increase, and it was accompanied by several innovations that must have had a cognitive impact: techniques for building dwellings; the cultivation of land; animal domestication; the invention of tools like the hoe and later the plow; the development of food preparation techniques such as baking and brewing; the development of weaving techniques, as well as the use of clay and the production of pottery, developing into a striking variety of regionalized and successive styles of painted pottery. There are, furthermore, indications of early forms of trade, in particular the dispersion of luxury objects like shells into areas far away from their places of origins and the distribution of tools such as stone axes manufactured at the source of the stone. At the end of the Neolithic Period, flint and other stone tools were gradually replaced by copper and, eventually, bronze implements.

This brief survey of Neolithic innovations makes evident that it is this period that shows the closest resemblance with what we know from extant indigenous cultures at a stone age level. If, therefore, Piaget's original assumption (Piaget, 1950a) was correct that cognition in such cultures does not exceed the preoperational level, then the Neolithic Revolution in spite of the material progress did not fundamentally change the level of cognition achieved at the end of the Paleolithic Period.

THE URBAN REVOLUTION AND THE EMERGENCE OF COGNITIVE TOOLS

The second change, the so-called Urban Revolution, is indicated by the emergence of large settlements; that is, the early cities, the differentiation of the population into specialized occupational groups, the stratification of the society into social classes with different access to resources, and the emergence of monumental architecture. This process of urbanization was a long-term consequence of the achievements of farming. Intensive agriculture produced a surplus that made possible the proliferation of administrators and specialists, freed from primary subsistence activities. Urbanization emerged in the Near East in the 4th millennium B.C. and approximately at the same time in Egypt, in the Indus valley in the 3rd millennium B.C., in

China probably in the 2nd millennium B.C., and in the New World in the first millennium B.C. From these centers, urbanization spread into the surrounding regions, in particular into Europe and across Asia.

This Urban Revolution as a process of transition from a Neolithic village farming society to the first centralized settlement patterns of the late Neolithic and early Bronze Age was quite different from the earlier Neolithic Revolution. The Neolithic Revolution was an advance in man's control of his environment and the Urban Revolution primarily changed human relations by a transition to a vastly greater complexity of patterns of social organization. These social patterns no longer resemble social structures known from extant preliterate cultures. Thus, we can only refer to archaeological data in order to understand the transition from the Neolithic period to early civilizations.

The extensive excavations in Mesopotamia and in Iran are of particular importance for the study of this urbanization process. They show that urbanization began in prehistory a considerable time before the invention of writing (Algaze, 1989; Nissen, 1988). In the Late Uruk Period in the 4th millennium B.C., the culture of Mesopotamia and the surrounding areas already differed fundamentally from that of Neolithic villages. Urban centers with a highly developed division of labor and social stratification emerged. Remnants of representative buildings in the city centers attest to the existence of temples and palaces that were the administrative centers of a redistributive barter economy. A sophisticated apparatus of officials organized the deployment of labor and supervised the distribution of the products of labor collected in central storehouses.

The Development of Cognitive Tools

The administrative tasks associated with this type of economy could not be accomplished without administrative aids for the qualitative and quantitative control of the economic resources. Contrary to earlier developments in prehistory, the process of urbanization was, therefore, closely associated with the development of genuine cognitive tools that have at least partially survived (Nissen, 1988; Nissen, Damerow, & Englund, 1993). Standardized containers, stamp seals that were pressed into clay surfaces and later cylinder seals that were rolled over the surface of clay objects before they were dried or baked, containers supplied with sealed stoppers or with sealed bullae, signs with numerical meanings, but most importantly a special kind of clay symbols with simple geometric shapes (sphere, cone, pellet, tetrahedron, cylinder, etc.) that were apparently used, among other things, as counters to record quantitative data, served the registration and symbolic representation of economic goods and the designation of those who controlled them (Schmandt-Besserat, 1992; Damerow & Meinzer, 1995). These tools offer evidence of a development of cognition that has no parallel in extant preliterate cultures.

The clay symbols had probably the greatest cognitive impact. Their function is attested to by the fact that combinations of such clay symbols were sometimes kept in closed and sealed clay spheres—apparently for the purpose of preventing the manipulation of the encoded information. Some of these clay spheres exhibit impressions on their surfaces. These impressions generally correspond in type and number to the clay symbols inside the spheres. They can easily be identified as precursors of the numerical signs of the later writing systems. Furthermore, numerous clay tablets—the so-called preliterate numerical tablets—that bear such impressions together with seal impressions can also be dated to the period shortly before the invention of writing (Englund, 1994; Schmandt-Besserat, 1981).

The Invention of Writing

Around the last century of the 4th millennium, a system of pictographs was added to these symbolic means of representation. The introduction of such pictograms is generally considered to be the actual invention of writing. This is, however, merely a matter of definition. It seems that, at least in the beginning, these pictograms did not serve to write down spoken language but exclusively served the purpose of bookkeeping (Nissen et al., 1993). Two different systems of this kind of archaic writing systems emerged in the Near East in quick succession: the so-called proto-cuneiform and the proto-Elamite archaic writing systems. Soon afterwards if not simultaneously, a third system of writing, the Egyptian system, was developed—unfortunately, however, the evidence from the early period of this system is sparse so that it is difficult to draw conclusions with regard to the cognitive processes involved.

The origin of the other two systems, however, can fairly well be studied based on the extant sources. Each system contained more than 1,000 different signs with widely standardized notations and conventionally defined meanings.

The more important system is the proto-cuneiform system of southern Mesopotamia, from which cuneiform writing evolved. To date, approximately 5,600 clay tablets and fragments with this type of writing have been excavated. The oldest are texts from the IVa layer of the ancient city of Uruk, the most important archaeological site yielding proto-cuneiform tablets (Englund, 1994).

The other system, proto-Elamite writing, which is documented by some 1,500 texts—most of them from Susa, the urban center of a region to the southeast of Mesopotamia—was created somewhat later. It adopted the idea and took over, slightly modified, the proto-cuneiform numerical signs (Damerow & Englund, 1989). The system was used for only a short time.

The oldest tablets displaying a developed system of cuneiform writing date back to around the middle of the 3rd millennium B.C. Cuneiform writing was the first genuine writing system, terminating the long prehistoric period (Nissen et al., 1993).

THE ULTIMATE LEVEL
OF PREHISTORIC COGNITION

After this brief outline of the transition from the Neolithic Period to early civilizations, let me now turn to its cognitive implications in order to answer the question of what level of cognition was ultimately achieved in prehistory.

It has been pointed out already that in the course of urbanization, the use of symbolic representations increased dramatically. This development must have been accompanied by a sweeping expansion of the content and form of knowledge. After the invention of writing, we find stratified societies with a highly complex social organization. The cognitive capabilities of leaders and administrators in these societies must have been strikingly higher than those of man in early prehistoric times. These people not only invented the technique of writing but also used developed techniques of measurement and numerical calculation and even early forms of mathematics. Such techniques are usually considered proof of sophisticated operative thinking.

There is obviously a discrepancy between human intelligence at the end of the Paleolithic and in the late Neolithic Period indicating a rapid acceleration of cognitive development in this comparably short timespan. At the end of the Paleolithic Period, man had achieved the ability of intuitive thinking based on mental imagery and a semilogic of internalized actions. As far as cognition is concerned, this ability was a major achievement of the transition from animal to human intelligence. Nevertheless, the simple use of this ability at the end of the Paleolithic, documented by Paleolithic art and symbolism, is not comparable to the sophisticated cognitive techniques that were used after the rise of civilization when writing was invented.

This striking difference between late Paleolithic and late Neolithic symbolism raises three questions:

1. What precisely were the new contents and forms of knowledge that are indicated by the new symbolic representations?
2. To what extent do they indicate a level of cognitive development beyond the level of preoperative thinking?
3. Did this higher level of cognition exist earlier or was it a genuine result of the Urban Revolution?

In order to answer these questions, we have to study the new symbolic representations in somewhat greater detail.

Prehistoric Tokens and Numerical Notations

For the incipient phase of the Urban Revolution, our knowledge about the cognitive tools used by the urban administration is rather limited. Tokens or pebbles believed to be tokens have been found in archaeological layers that date back well into the Neolithic Period, in some cases as early as the 8th millennium B.C. However, there is no archaeological evidence for relating them from the very beginning to administrative activities. Only finds dating to the 4th millennium provide clear evidence of such usage. Not only did the number and variety of tokens increase considerably but they were now sometimes kept in those sealed clay envelopes that have provided us with the key to understanding their arithmetical function. Furthermore, numerical tablets—the precursors of proto-cuneiform writing—now occur for the first time. In view of prevailing speculations attributing arithmetical meaning to repetitive Paleolithic and Neolithic patterns, it is worth noticing that the preliterate combinations of tokens and impressions on clay surfaces from the 4th millennium provide the first reliable evidence of the construction of one-to-one correspondences that eventually resulted in the operatory concept of number.

We get some further clarification of the function of these denotations of quantities in the latest period of prehistory if we compare them with the numerical notations of the later proto-cuneiform and proto-Elamite writing systems. This comparison reveals that the different impressions or tokens already represented measuring and counting units of different kinds and orders found in the later writing systems. However, it also provides indications of a fundamental change of the semiotic function of the signs in the transition from preliterate to proto-cuneiform and proto-Elamite numerical notations.

Contrary to the numerical signs of the later archaic writing systems, the impressions on envelopes of tokens and the impressions on those numerical tablets that can be dated beyond doubt into the preliterate period lack the standardization of later numerical notations. Accordingly, all attempts to identify the measuring and counting units represented by the preliterate tokens and impressions have failed so far (regarding the alleged identifications of Schmandt-Besserat, see the critic of Michalowski, 1993). Furthermore, the comparison shows that contrary to later numerical notations, the repeated units have not necessarily been converted into higher units. On a tablet from Jebel Aruda dating to the middle of the 4th millennium B.C., one of the signs of the notation is even repeated 22 times (van Driel, 1982).

The lower degree of standardization and of strict adherence to semiotic rules strongly suggests that the signs before the invention of the archaic writing systems did not yet represent abstract measuring and counting units but still represented the real objects or containers that made up the quantities to be represented. They indicate, at least, that the prehistoric token and sign combinations were in a transitional stage between the representation of real objects by one-to-one correspondences to tokens and signs and the representation of quantities by semiotically structured numerical notations.

Proto-literate Numerical Notations

Let us now turn to the situation immediately after the invention of writing. The hypothesis of a fundamental change in the symbolic representation of quantities at the end of prehistory receives further support by the results of an analysis of the numerical notations in the proto-cuneiform texts (Damerow & Englund, 1987). These results strongly contradict common expectations. In view of the close resemblance of many of these notations to numerical notations in the later tradition of developed cuneiform writing, it has always been assumed that the numerical signs represented numbers (Falkenstein, 1936, 1937; Langdon, 1928). Inconsistencies of the interpretation of numerical operations resulting from this assumption were explained by errors of the ancient scribes or by the clumsiness of an insufficiently elaborated notation system.

However, as a result of recent analysis it turned out that the numerical notations in the proto-cuneiform texts follow strictly applied semiotic rules and that the alleged errors of the scribes in fact resulted from the mistaken assumption of modern scholars that they represent numbers and accordingly must have definite numerical values. Contrary to all expectations, the proto-cuneiform numerical signs proved to have changed their numerical value depending on the objects they were applied to, and the same turned out to be true for the numerical signs of the proto-Elamite writing system (Damerow & Englund, 1989).

This startling conclusion needs to be explained in some detail. The analysis of proto-cuneiform and proto-Elamite numerical notations showed that the numerical signs represented units of counting and measuring systems with entirely standardized numerical relations between the units. The ranges of these systems from the lowest to the highest units as a rule covered tens of thousands of units and sometimes even more. The precision of many of the numerical notations exceeds what we might consider reasonable limits that might be explained as the result of an exaggerated bureaucracy. At first sight, the oldest written documents of mankind seemed to prove that at the time of the invention of writing, a fully developed number concept and elaborated techniques for numerical calculations existed.

Closer inspection, however, provided puzzling details. Whereas the same signs were often used to designate units of different metrological systems, the numerical relations between the units varied considerably from one metrological system to the other. Moreover, the meaning of the signs, that is, the conventions by which certain units were represented by certain signs, was determined in one system without taking into account how the meaning was determined in other systems. Thus, the numerical values of the signs were entirely dependent on the system for which they were actually used, that is, on the particular context of their application.

A certain sign (N34; see Damerow & Englund, 1987), for instance, represented a unit that is 60 times smaller than another unit represented by another sign (N45) when they were used in a system for counts of certain discrete objects as, for instance, animals. But the same sign was used for a unit 3 times larger than the other one when they represented certain grain measures (Damerow & Englund, 1987).

The details of the different numerical sign systems of the archaic texts cannot be discussed here. Despite the ambiguity of the numerical signs, 14 proto-cuneiform and 8 proto-Elamite numerical sign systems could be identified and their fields of application determined. These areas of application turned out to have been mutually exclusive, but their definitions followed no obvious rules and seem to have been determined simply by tradition. It is remarkable that not even all discrete objects that can be counted were recorded in one and the same system. In the proto-cuneiform texts five systems with two different arithmetical structures and in the proto-Elamite texts four systems with three different arithmetical structures were used to denote different types of discrete objects.

The numerical ambiguity of the numerical signs is not the only indication that the meaning of the signs was dependent on the context in which they were used. Without further explanation, some additional evidence is given next.

The numerical signs inherited from their prehistoric precursors—that is, the tokens and impressions—the function to represent objects and not numbers. In contrast to these precursors, repeated signs were converted as far as possible into higher units; however, the arrangements of the signs were still not consolidated in standardized representations of numbers or quantities. Frequently, there are additive and multiplicative relations between different entries of a text that do not represent abstract operations, however, but correspond always to some material action or transformation. Even the seemingly clear distinction between the numerical signs originating in tokens and the nonnumerical pictographs appearing with the invention of writing appears to be much less clear on closer inspection. Numerical signs could denote objects by some inherent measure as, for instance, the denotation of barley products by the amount of barley necessary for the production of one unit. Conversely, nonnumerical signs such as signs for rations or for special types of beer could also stand for related quantities such as the standard size of a ration or the strength of the beer measured by the amount of grain necessary for the production of the amount held by one jar. Furthermore, numerous composite signs that are graphical combinations of numerical and nonnumerical signs were used in order to express quantitative and qualitative information by means of a single sign.

The overwhelming evidence pointing to a meaning of the numerical signs of proto-writing dependent on their context of application suggests that the arithmetical techniques of archaic bookkeeping were in fact techniques without an integrating number construct. Both the meaning of these signs as well as the way they were used do not correspond to what could be expected if they would have represented numbers or generalized numerically structured concepts such as the abstract concepts of space, time, weight, volume, area, and so on.

What else can the numerical signs and the techniques of handling them have represented if not numbers and numerical operations? We get a convincing answer to this question if we assume that the numerical signs and the way they were used in principle had the same function as the nonnumerical signs and their use (Damerow, 1995). Accordingly, their function must have been to represent the objects and actions of the archaic bookkeeping system. The objects and actions were encoded in categories directly related to each specific context and quantified by mental metrological constructs consisting of relations that were set up by context-specific conventional standardizations and measurement procedures.

A Puzzling Conclusion

This result of an analysis of the proto-literate sign systems answers the first question posed earlier concerning the ultimate level of prehistoric cognition. I asked about the cognitive contents and forms of knowledge represented by the new symbolic representations that were created by officials of early Mesopotamian cities at the dawn of history. It turned out that they represented mental models of their administrative activities. These models were developed and represented by systems of symbols as a means for coordinating collective human actions in a complex social setting.

This answer to the first question, however, makes it even more difficult to answer the second concerning the cognitive level beyond the level of Neolithic preoperative thinking indicated by the new symbolic representations, and the third question concerning the historical origins of such a higher level of cognition. Insofar as these questions are concerned, the results of the analysis of proto-literate sign systems apparently leads to a paradox.

On the one hand, the gap between Neolithic preoperative thinking and the sophisticated cognitive techniques used in early civilization seems to be bridged. The development of the precursors of proto-cuneiform writing demonstrates that first the administrative problems associated with the process of urbanization were solved by exhausting the potentials of proto-arithmetical tools well-known from extant preliterate cultures. At the end of this preliterate period, the officials who were in charge of these tasks had created, by elaborating these potentials, a complex symbolic system representing their activities. This is seemingly a paradigmatic case of reflective abstraction that, according to genetic epistemology, brings about the fundamental structures of logico-mathematical cognition that consists of reversible operations constituting the cognitive level of concrete operational thinking.

The puzzling structure of the numerical notations used in the archaic writing systems shows, on the other hand, that certain cognitive constructions such as the concept of number (see Piaget, 1952) were lacking, which, according to genetic epistemology, should have been developed already because they are essential components of concrete operational thinking. In spite of the complexity of the archaic system of bookkeeping, the analysis of these notations provides strong evidence against the existence of a number construct integrating the context-dependent rules according to which the signs were manipulated.

Is it conceivable that the officials running the administration of a complex redistributive society using highly developed symbol systems in order to control the flow of materials and products were not able to use reversible mental operations, that they still, like members of Neolithic rural communities, solved their problems on a preoperative level of cognition using proto-arithmetical aids?

The discrepancy in the final period of prehistory of the emergence of highly complex symbol systems and the lack of integration of the context-dependent systems by generalized operations, indicating the emergence of mathematical and logical thinking, suggests that neither different rates of progress nor cognitive potentials that are not being used can sufficiently account for fundamental historical differences in levels of cognition. There are no indications in the bookkeeping activities of the scribes for any stagnation on a preoperative level or any reasons why they should not use their full cognitive potential for solving their complex tasks, and yet they solved them without using the alleged universal concept of number for integrating their evidently numerical operations.

According to genetic epistemology, the fundamental structures of logical and mathematical thinking are universal, and this universality is assumed to be based on universal structures of the coordination of human actions. It is true that certain human activities are so deeply rooted in biological preconditions of human action that their coordination gives rise to structures of human cognition that are probably universal. Considering the cross-cultural and historical evidence, structures such as identities and similarities based on the coordination of substitutions as well as ordinal structures based on the transitivity of elementary actions are prominent candidates of such universals. These are, at least, clearly recognizable in the usage of symbols in the early bookkeeping systems. However, the difficulty to identify in the activities of the scribes who invented and used these systems and also such complex structures of operative thinking as the concept of number casts doubts on the culture-independent universality of the entire set of structures constituting logical and mathematical thinking. The basic human activities underlying the cognitive universals do not necessarily determine the development of cognition to such an extent that the outcome of ontogenesis is always the same, universal structure of logical and mathematical thinking, independent of any specific social and cultural environments.

There are, of course, explanations possible for the puzzling use of symbols by the early bookkeepers in genetic epistemology. The domain specific numerical systems may be transitional, representing a level of concrete operational thinking that is still bound to a high degree to specific contexts. Or they may be interpreted as an example of a horizontal décalage due to the towering influence of certain objects of the bookkeeping system.

The puzzling example is, however, not unique. Genetic epistemology as conceived by Piaget (1970) always meets serious difficulties when substantial historical differences in the fundamental structures of thinking have to be explained. Piaget and Garcia (1989), in their famous study on the psychogenesis of basic concepts of scientific thinking, for instance, were compelled to place the psychogenesis of the alleged universal basic concepts of classical mechanics into the time of Newton, and consequently into a completely different historical period than that of the psychogenesis of basic concepts of arithmetic and geometry, which are supposed to have their roots in prehistory and were fully developed in the Greek classical period. But if the structure of such concepts would be entirely independent of any specific social and cultural environments, determined only by fundamental coordination of action, why then should they emerge historically in so different periods?

Such paradoxes inherent in Piaget's genetic epistemology vanish if we assume that operatory cognitive structures may evolve in different forms depending on the nature of the activities and their coordination, from which they are constructed by reflective abstraction. Such an understanding of genetic epistemology would be in agreement with Piaget's theory insofar as neither the universality of basic cognitive functions such as the construction of the structures of logico-mathematical cognition by reflective abstraction, nor the universality of cognitive structures originating in the coordination of universal human actions are questioned. After all, the structures of logico-mathematical cognition would be substantially modified by the cultural setting in which they emerge as soon as culture-specific cognitive tools modify the activities from which these structures are constructed by reflective abstraction. The ultimate cognitive outcome of prehistory can be conceived then as the emergence of a specific form of operative thinking, its structure being determined by its specific origin in the manipulation of the symbols of the archaic bookkeeping system.

Such an understanding of the cognitive outcome of prehistory not only explains the peculiar context-dependent use of archaic symbols. It can, moreover, pave the way for an understanding of the further cognitive development in early civilizations from the perspective of psychogenesis.

It is, for instance, characteristic of early civilizations that a variety of independent and often incompatible symbol systems emerged. This phenomenon is easily understandable as a result of a culture-specific expansion of the universal core structures of logical and mathematical thinking by reflective abstractions from highly specific cognitive tools developed for the narrowly restricted but complex tasks of the administration of early states and centralized economies.

Advancing from such an explanation of the origins of culturally specific mathematical thinking, the general concepts of modern logical and mathematical thinking have to be conceived of as an outcome of the integration of context-dependent cognitive structures under historically specific constraints and not as predetermined in their structure by their origins in the coordination of human action. This provides us with a convincing explanation for the fact that the earliest examples of explicit mathematics did not start with simple concepts and procedures but rather with weird constructions. At the beginning, mathematics did not deal with abstract numbers and Aristotelian logic. We find instead such odd logico-mathematical structures as those of Babylonian mathematics, Egyptian calculations with unit fractions, Chinese proofs by analogical reasoning, and the sophisticated ritual calendar of the Mayas.

REFERENCES

Algaze, G. (1989). The Uruk expansion. *Current Anthropology, 30*, 571–608.

Armstrong, D. F., Stokoe, W. C., & Wilcox, S. E. (1994). Signs of the origin of syntax. *Current Anthropology, 35*, 349–368.

Bateman, R., Goddard, I., O'Grady, R., Funk, V. A., Mooi, R., Kress, W. J., & Cannell, P. (1990). Speaking of forked tongues: The feasibility of reconciling human phylogeny and the history of language. *Current Anthropology, 31*, 1–24.

Bednarik, R. G. (1995). Concept-mediated marking in the lower Palaeolithic. *Current Anthropology, 36*, 605–634.

Brainerd, C. J. (1978/1979). The stage question in cognitive-developmental theory. *The Behavioral and Brain Sciences, 2*, 173–213. With continuing commentary 137–154.

Burling, R. (1993). Primate calls, human language, and nonverbal communication. *Current Anthropology, 34*, 25–53.

Byers, A. M. (1994). Symboling and the middle-upper Palaeolithic transition. *Current Anthropology, 35*, 369–399.

Chazan, M. (1995). The language hypothesis for the middle-to-upper Paleolithic transition. *Current Anthropology, 36*, 749–768.

Corballis, M. C. (1992). On the evolution of language and generativity. *Cognition, 44*, 197–226.

Damerow, P. (1995). *Abstraction and representation: Essays on the cultural evolution of thinking.* Boston Studies in the Philosophy of Science, Vol. 175. Dordrecht, The Netherlands: Kluwer.

Damerow, P., & Englund, R. K. (1987). Die Zahlzeichensysteme der Archaischen Texte aus Uruk. In M. W. Green & H. J. Nissen (Eds.), *Zeichenliste der Archaischen Texte aus Uruk* (pp. 117–166). Berlin: Mann.

Damerow, P., & Englund, R. K. (1989). *The proto-elamite texts from Tepe Yahya.* Cambridge, MA: Harvard University Press.

Damerow, P., & Meinzer, H.-P. (1995). Computertomografische Untersuchung ungeöffneter archaischer Tonkugeln aus Uruk. *Baghdader Mitteilungen, 26*, 7–33 and Tf. 1–4.

Davidson, I., & Noble, W. (1989). The archaeology of perception: Traces of depiction and language. *Current Anthropology, 30*, 125–155, 330–342.

Davis, W. (1986). The origins of image making. *Current Anthropology, 27*, 193–215.

de Heinzelin, J. (1962, June). Ishango. *Scientific American, 206*, 105–116.

Donald, M. (1993). Précis of origins of the modern mind: Three stages in the evolution of culture and cognition. *The Behavioral and Brain Sciences, 16*, 737–791.

Dunbar, R. I. M. (1993). Coevolution of neocortical size, group size and language in humans. *The Behavioral and Brain Sciences, 16*, 681–735.

Ellen, P., & Thinus-Blanc, C. (Ed.). (1987). *Cognitive processes and spatial orientation in animal and man.* NATO ASI Series, No. 36, Vols. 1–2. Dordrecht, The Netherlands: Nijhoff.

Englund, R. K. (1994). *Archaic administrative texts from Uruk: The early campaigns.* Berlin: Mann.

Falkenstein, A. (1936). *Archaische Texte aus Uruk.* Berlin: Harrassowitz.

Falkenstein, A. (1937). Archaische Texte des Iraq-Museums in Bagdad. *Orientalische Literaturzeitung, 40*, 401–410.

Greenfield, P. M. (1991). Language, tools and brain: The ontogeny and phylogeny of hierarchically organized sequential behavior. *The Behavioral and Brain Sciences, 14*, 531–595.

Hallpike, C. R. (1979). *The foundations of primitive thought.* Oxford, England: Clarendon.

Jahoda, G. (1980). Theoretical and systematic approaches in cross-cultural psychology. In H. C. Triandis & A. Heron (Eds.), *Handbook of cross-cultural psychology* (Vol. 1, pp. 69–141). Boston: Allyn & Bacon.

Langdon, S. (1928). *Pictographic inscriptions from Jemdet Nasr.* London: Oxford University Press.

Lévy-Bruhl, L. (1923). *Primitive mentality.* New York: MacMillan.

Marshack, A. (1972). *The roots of civilization: The cognitive beginnings of man's first art, symbol and notation.* London: Weidenfeld & Nicolson.

McGrew, W. C. (1992). *Chimpanzee material culture: Implications for human evolution.* Cambridge, England: Cambridge University Press.

McGrew, W. C., & Marchant, L. F. (1992). Chimpanzees, tools, and termites: Hand preference or handedness. *Current Anthropology, 33*, 114–119.

Mellars, P. (1989). Major issues in the emergence of modern humans. *Current Anthropology, 30*, 349–385.

Michalowski, P. (1993). Tokenism. *American Anthropologist, 95*, 996–999.

Nissen, H. J. (1988). *The early history of ancient Near East, 9000–2000 B.C.* Chicago: Chicago University Press.

Nissen, H. J., Damerow, P., & Englund, R. K. (1993). *Archaic bookkeeping: Early writing and techniques of economic administration in the ancient Near East.* Chicago: Chicago University Press.

Parker, S., & Gibson, K. (1979). A developmental model for the evolution of language and intelligence in early hominids. *The Behavioral and Brain Sciences, 2*, 367–408.

Piaget, J. (1950a). *Introduction à l'épistémologie génétique*, Vol. 1–3. Paris: Presses Universitaires de France.

Piaget, J. (1950b). *The psychology of intelligence*. London: Routledge & Paul.

Piaget, J. (1952). *The child's conception of number*. London: Routledge & Paul.

Piaget, J. (1966). Nécessité et signification des recherches comparatives en psychologie génétique. *International Journal of Psychology, 1*, 3–13.

Piaget, J. (1970). *Genetic epistemology*. New York: Columbia University Press.

Piaget, J., Grize, J. B., Szeminska, A., & Bang, V. (1977). *Epistemology and psychology of functions*. Dordrecht, The Netherlands: Reidel.

Piaget, J., & Garcia, R. (1989). *Psychogenesis and the history of science*. New York: Columbia University Press.

Piaget, J., Henriques, G., & Ascher, E. (1992). *Morphisms and categories: Comparing and transforming*. Hillsdale, NJ: Lawrence Erlbaum Associates.

Piaget, J., & Inhelder, B. (1963). *The child's conception of space*. London: Routledge & Paul.

Pick, H. L., Jr., & Acredolo, L. P. (Eds.). (1983). *Spatial orientation: Theory, research, and application*. New York: Plenum.

Savage-Rumbaugh, E. S., Murphy, J., Sevcik, R. A., Brakke, K. E., Williams, S. L., & Rumbaugh, D. M. (1993). Language comprehension in ape and child. *Monographs of the Society for Research in Child Development, 58*, 1–252.

Schmandt-Besserat, D. (1981). From tokens to tablets: A re-evaluation of the so-called "numerical tablets." *Visible Language, 15*, 321–344.

Schmandt-Besserat, D. (1992). *Before writing*. Austin: University of Texas Press.

van Driel, G. (1982). Tablets from Jebel Aruda. In G. v. Driel (Ed.), *Zikir Shumin* (pp. 12–25). Leiden, The Netherlands: Brill.

Wallace, R. (1989). Cognitive mapping and the origin of language and mind. *Current Anthropology, 30*, 518–526.

Westergard, G. C., & Suomi, S. J. (1994). Stone-tool bone-surface modifications by monkeys. *Current Anthropology, 35*, 468–470.

Wynn, T. (1985). Piaget, stone tools, and the evolution of human intelligence. *World Archaeology, 17*, 32–43.

Wynn, T. (1989). *The evolution of spacial competence*. Urbana: University of Illinois Press.

12

NOTES FROM THE UNDERGROUND: CULTURE, CONFLICT, AND SUBVERSION

Elliot Turiel
University of California, Berkeley

A pervasive theme in writings during the latter part of the 1980s and into the 1990s about America is that the society is in moral crisis and undergoing serious decay. Several causes have been attributed to the supposed moral decay. Among the most frequently stated are: changes in the structure of the family (Bloom, 1987; Etzioni, 1993; Whitehead, 1993; Wilson, 1993); the effects of the culture of the 1960s with its emphasis on freedom, sex, and drugs (Bloom, 1987; Kirkpatrick, 1992); a failure to attend to traditions (Bennett, 1992; Kirkpatrick, 1992; Ryan, 1989; Wynne, 1979, 1986); a questioning of traditions (Etzioni, 1993); the ways youth have been morally educated in the schools (Bennett & Delattre, 1978; Kirkpatrick, 1992; Sommers, 1984); the failure of universities to provide adequate education (Bloom, 1987; Sommers, 1984); too much of an emphasis on rights (Etzioni, 1993); the onset of radical individualism (Bellah, Madsen, Sullivan, Swidler, & Tipton, 1985; Hogan, 1975; Sampson, 1977); the influences of feminism (Bloom, 1987; Kirkpatrick, 1992); and the teachings of elites (intellectuals, scholars) who create theories hostile to the ideas of virtue, character, and the language of morality (Bennett, 1992; Bloom, 1987; Himmelfarb, 1994; Wilson, 1993).

Among those who perceive moral crisis there is an explicit or implicit conception of changes that have occurred and that need to occur in the make up of culture. Some explicitly take the position that there are necessary moral virtues reflected in the fabric of culture and its traditions, and that the culture has lost its way by losing sight of those traditions. For the most part, in these views it is maintained that the moral development of individuals entails a process of acquiring general traits of character and habits of action consistent with cultural traditions (e.g., Bennett, 1992; Bennett & Delattre, 1978; Kirkpatrick, 1992; Ryan, 1989; Wynne, 1979, 1986). It is further asserted that in contemporary times cultural traditions have been displaced, to the detriment of the moral order, by concerns with individual needs and the priority given to personal gratification over community interests.

Others squarely place morality in cultural contexts, draw contrasts in the orientations of different cultures, and claim that the moral crisis in America is due to a cultural ethos of self-contained individualism and extreme independence (Hogan, 1975; Sampson, 1977). The independence and isolation of individualism is contrasted with other (especially non-Western) better adjusted cultures that cohere around interdependence. Similar assessments of the moral decay of American culture are made by those who contrast the contemporary condition with a more balanced and adjusted state that characterized the culture in the past (e.g., Bellah et al., 1985; Etzioni, 1993). For instance, Etzioni claimed that because of a waning of traditional values, without the affirmation of new values, "we live in a state of everlasting moral confusion and social anarchy" (p. 12). The effects of radical individualism, representing a departure from the past's balance of autonomy and commitment to a moral order, are according to Bellah et al. (1985) that "we seem to be hovering on the brink of disaster" (p. 284). They believe that American "individualism may have grown cancerous" (p. vii), and inquire "how can we reverse the slide toward the abyss?" (p. 284).

These propositions regarding moral crisis and cultural disintegration highlight some of the problems in long-standing conceptions of culture, morality, and the role of individual social development. These analyses generally presume that cultures form coherent and consistent patterns of thought and action (Benedict, 1934), and that different cultures have distinct patterns and modes of thought (Shweder & Sullivan, 1993). The emphasis of such cultural analyses has been on harmony, coherence, stability, and continuity over time. Comparative analyses are conducted primarily to demonstrate that cultures have distinctive psychologies. As a consequence, insufficient attention has been given to aspects of culture entailing conflicts, disagreements, internal critiques of social practices and norms, or changes stemming from the make up of cultures. The perceptions of crisis and disintegration may very well reflect disagreements about the course of social practices in American society, embodying critiques and counter-critiques of cultural practices and the ways society is organized.

This chapter addresses the main theme of this volume by considering the evolution of mental development through the interplay of cultural practices, individual moral and social development, and the possible varying perspectives of groups and persons in cultural systems. From that perspective, cultural analyses entail not only comparisons of different cultures to identify distinctive orientations between them, but just as importantly, comparative analyses in cultures so as to identify sources of heterogeneity, conflicts, and inconsistencies. In turn, heterogeneity, conflicts, and inconsistencies are considered as potential sources of tension and change in cultures.

CULTURAL CRITIQUE AND CULTURAL COHERENCE

Consider again the claims that society is undergoing moral crisis and decay. Those perceiving moral crisis appear to include the ideas of cultural conflict and transformations, in the context of the presumption that cultures are harmonious and continuous, by calling for changes (i.e., moral improvements) in the fabric of the culture. One way in which these two sets of propositions could be consistent with each other is insofar as it is proposed that cultures are indeed coherent and consistent and that moral crisis is a consequence or a failure to maintain coherence (e.g., as in Bennett, 1992; Kirkpatrick, 1992; Wynne, 1979). In other words, normal and adaptive cultures are coherent but there can be breakdowns in the system. It is thought that characteristic of contemporary America—in contrast with the past—is a breakdown of the social fabric.

A little in the way of comparative historical analysis is informative with regard to these propositions. Whereas the strength and urgency of the claims of crisis suggest a serious deterioration of the moral state in late 20th century America relative to other cultures and previous times, it is striking that in other places, and at other times in the United States, similar language was invoked to describe society. For instance, in *fin-de-siècle* France (late 19th century) there was similar concern with moral degeneration in the society (Norris, 1996). Many decried what they perceived to be a national decline and called for national renewal. A particular focus, as is the case currently in the United States, was on the deterioration of the morality of youth. Such deterioration was said to be evident in a great propensity for dishonesty on the part of children and in increasing juvenile crime rates.

A decline in the morality of youth was also a major theme in American social commentaries during the 1920s—a time that those who now bemoan that there is societal decay point to positively as one in which American traditions and values prevailed. As detailed by Fass (1977), many during that period were convinced that, especially because of the attitudes and behaviors of youth, there was serious social disorder and cultural disintegration. As a consequence of changes in the family, schools, and church, entailing a loosening of authority and their replacement with undisciplined individualism, personal liberties and rights, self-gratification, traditional values, and a sense of community were being undermined. Referring to those who viewed society in the 1920s as undergoing moral crisis, Fass (1977) stated that:

> The young represented the fruit of social disorder, cultural disintegration, and a personal loss of coherence. They viewed the present from the perspective of what they believed was a formerly stable society which had been shattered, and they taunted themselves with the loss that came with change. (p. 15)

Again, it was perceived that there were alarming increases in juvenile crime rates, which were attributed to the erosion of the family unit (Fass, 1977).

In the 1920s, the view that the culture was in disintegration due to the ways of youth was not the only perspective. At the time, some welcomed the changes in attitudes, behaviors, and in the structure of the family, schools, and church. They believed that there was a progressive moral reorganization of society, through which the old order was being transformed into a more just system with legitimate individual freedoms and more healthy social relationships (Fass, 1977). Disagreements of this sort also exist in contemporary times. Several of the causes attributed to a moral decline by those who see cultural disintegration are events that others view as furthering moral and societal ends. For example, events in the 1960s, seen by some as having a negative effect, are regarded by others as representing movements toward effecting moral change (specifically, the end of the unjust war in Vietnam, achieving greater civil rights for Blacks, and reducing poverty). Similarly, whereas some regard feminism and the assertion of too many rights to have negative effects, others see moral progress in achieving greater justice for women (Okin, 1989) and rights for groups faced with discrimination.

What does the repeated history of intense concern with moral crisis mean? Does it merely show that in many epochs there are disgruntled people who go public with their complaints? Perhaps! But it can be argued that the phenomena of continual critiques and counter-critiques of one's culture reflect neglected but salient aspects of culture: That in a society, there are deep disagreements about cultural practices and about the perceived nature and course of the culture; that such disagreements, in part, stem from a multiplicity of social orientations and goals held by members of a culture; that members of a culture, along with accepting its practices, can find serious moral failings in it; that along with cultural harmony there is a fair amount of conflict in a culture due to varying views and, especially, due to people's varying perspectives in roles, status, privileges, and burdens in the organization of the society; and that cultures are usually undergoing, in part, internally regulated changes—changes that result in negative and positive evaluations. Those claims of moral crisis and degeneration reflect disagreements and conflicts—an historical dialectic among those who critique cultural practices and countercritique the critiques. One example of this process is evident in discussions around feminism as a source of moral crisis (Bloom, 1987; Kirkpatrick, 1992). Feminism entails moral critiques of cultural practices denying women equality, rights, and opportunities in the workplace. It entails moral critique of the role of women and their unequal burdens in the organization of the culture. Those who claim that feminism has contributed to moral decline, in turn, critique it for making what they perceive to be unjustified moral claims and for disrupting family and social order.

Disagreements, varying social orientations, varying perspectives, conflicts, internal subversion, and changes stemming from the very make up of cultures are often neglected because the emphasis of cultural analyses traditionally has been, and continues to be, on coherence, public ideologies, and symbols promulgated by those in positions of dominance and their continuation through reproduction in the socialization of children (for further discussion see Spiro, 1993, and Strauss, 1992). In large measure, the idea of cultural coherence was in reaction to late 19th and early 20th century anthropological orderings of different cultures along dimensions of relative progress (see Hatch, 1983, for details). For the most part, such hierarchical orderings of cultures placed the anthropologist's own Western culture at the apex, with the presumption that other, "more primitive" cultures were not as civilized, morally developed, or conceptually advanced. Cultural anthropologists, seeing bias and a lack of criteria for such orderings, argued that those types of analyses failed to recognize that cultures form different patterns and perspectives that do not allow for comparisons of relative adequacy or progress. Cultural anthropologists did engage in comparative analyses, however. Their comparisons were aimed not at demonstrating progress or advance along a continuum or hierarchy but at demonstrating differences between cultural contexts—differences that could not be evaluated against each other. In the process, the focus was on coherence and integration in cultures as well as on stability in cultures over time.

The emphasis on cultural coherence and comparative analyses seeking divergence in cultural patterns has influenced contemporary analyses, especially in what has been proclaimed as a new discipline of cultural psychology (Shweder, 1990; Shweder & Sullivan, 1993). As put by Shweder and Sullivan:

> cultural psychology has grown up in an intellectual climate suspicious of a one-sided emphasis on fixed essences, intrinsic features, and universally necessary truths—an intellectual climate disposed to revalue processes of constraints that are local, variable, context-dependent, and in some sense made up. (p. 500)

In these frameworks, the local, variable, and context-dependent is located at the fairly general level of cultures. The valued processes of constraints are at the level of the culture as local and as context, with the most significant variations occurring between cultures.

The comparative analyses are, therefore, between coherent and different cultures, which are seen to have distinctive psychologies evident in their respective "emotional and somatic (health) functioning, self organization, moral evaluation, social cognition, and human development" (Shweder & Sullivan, 1993, p. 497). Indeed, many of those currently claiming that American society is undergoing moral crisis and disintegration also presume that cultures form divergently coherent and consistent systems (e.g., Bellah et al., 1985; Hogan, 1975; Sampson, 1977). Although they characterize the coherence of the culture to be based on individualism, they also claim that the dire state of the culture is due to individualism. However, in highlighting differences through coherence in culture, some treat cultural patterns as types of fixed essences by which, in cultures, short shrift is given to divergences, disagreements, conflicts, heterogeneity of social orientations, and change (as discussed in Abu-Lughod, 1991; Spiro, 1993; Strauss, 1992; Turiel, 1998).

SOCIAL CONFLICT AND SOCIAL CHANGE

Concerns with variability, context-dependence, and the local sources of knowledge and development provide an in-road into analyses of differences, conflict, and change in cultures. Variations in contexts occur at levels less broad than culture (Turiel & Wainryb, 1994). Moreover, variations in thought and action occur at levels more local than the general culture. In fact, embedded in the positions of some who espouse cultural psychology are propositions suggesting the need for a reconceptualization of coherence and integration in cultures. One example can be seen in Tomasello's argument (in this volume) that large cognitive differences between humans and chimpanzees (humans' nearest primate relative) are due to social causes. In keeping with his conception of "the newly emerging paradigm of Cultural Psychology" (p. 221), Tomasello maintained that human cognition differs from other species primarily because it is a social-collective rather than an individual enterprise. Human cognition is fundamentally based on artifacts and social practices embodying a collective wisdom accruing over historical time that antedates children's participation in culture. Children inherit from their forebears prepackaged communal activities (including games, scripts, rituals, instructional formats) that makes human cognition cultural in fundamental ways (Tomasello, this volume).

Yet, drawing on other lines of psychological research, Tomasello also maintained that a characteristic of human cognition is an understanding of the behavior of others as intentional. This involves "active attempts to discern what others are doing and why they are doing it—to take their perspectives, in fact" (Tomasello, this volume, p. 223). Because the process is reciprocal, the centrality accorded to understandings of intentionality and the coordination of perspectives implies that there are various levels of individual, social-interactional, and cultural knowledge. Unless it were posited that intentions, goals, beliefs, and perspectives are all culturally based in artifacts and prepackaged communal activities, human cognition includes a good deal of knowledge and thought based on efforts to discern the reasons for people's behaviors and the coordination of the perspectives of others and self.

A more elaborated example of a cultural analysis pointing to the need for re-conceptualization of cultural coherence and the inclusion of multiple types of cognition and social relationships lies in propositions put forth by Bruner (1996). First consider Bruner's central thesis that "culture shapes mind, that it provides us with the toolkit by which we construct not only our worlds but our very conceptions of our selves and our powers" (Bruner, 1996, p. x). Bruner referred to this approach as *culturalism*, based on:

> the evolutionary fact that mind could not exist save for culture. For the evolution of the hominid mind is linked to the development of a way of life where "reality" is represented by a symbolism shared by members of a cultural community in which a technical-social way of life is both organized and construed in terms of that symbolism. This symbolic mode is not only shared by a community, but conserved, elaborated and passed on to succeeding generations who, by virtue of this transmission, continue to maintain the culture's identity and way of life. (p. 3)

Bruner here appears to emphasize a reality that is shared by virtue of culture and a cultural identity that is maintained through transmission from one generation to the next. What seems to be missing in this formulation are the ideas of multiple realities, multiple identifications, that which is not shared, and the transformations in a culture's identities and ways of life occurring from generation to generation. The types of ubiquitous concerns with moral crisis and cultural disintegration considered above have a great deal to do with perceptions of changes in cultural identity and way of life—changes regarded by some as negative and others as positive.[1] More-

---

[1]It is often difficult not to recognize that conflicts exist within a society over significant moral issues (examples in the contemporary scene in America are conflicts over abortion, affirmative action, feminism, and homosexual rights). A common way to preserve the idea that cultures are harmonious and coherent in the context of such conflicts is to portray the conflicts as reflecting cultural wars; that is, the conflicts are said to be between people of different cultures. However, this serves to obscure the substantive issues over which there are disagreements. It also ignores the likelihood that individuals may affiliate with different groups over different issues. In place of analyses and explanations of how individuals in a culture may find themselves in disputes and conflicts, the idea of cultural wars simply treats any difference as a cultural difference.

over, the concerns with moral crises often reflect generational conflicts and, thereby illustrate, as cultural anthropologist Strauss (1992) noted, that cultural values and practices are not simply transmitted from generation to generation:

> This is not a simple problem of "noise" in the fax line from the public social order to individuals' psyches causing imperfect copies. Transmission is more complicated than this because the social order is more complicated than this. If our cultural-ideological milieux were unchanging, unambiguous, and internally consistent, there would be no need to study how social messages are appropriated by individual minds ... yet, as we now recognize, conflicting messages, ambiguity, and change are found in all societies, even "traditional" ones. (p. 8)

Bruner went on, however, to present a position much closer to the one articulated by Strauss through a series of tenets entailing a conception of greater interrelationships between culture and mind and greater differentiations and perspectives in culture and individual thought (see Bruner, 1996). Included among those tenets are the ideas of perspectives that can result in multiple interpretations of reality, cultural multivocality, and the possible divergence between institutional interests and construals of individuals. Bruner also proposed that the forms of meaning in any culture are constrained by the nature of human functioning and that the formation of knowledge is interactional, entailing reciprocity in communications and people learning from each other. Moreover, individuals' identifications with a variety of social institutions can produce conflicting allegiances and the need for the resolution of conflicting interests and goals. Emerging from these tenets is a view of culture that appears substantially different from the seemingly monolithic view in the proposition that there is a reality represented by a shared symbolism passed on from one generation to the next. Bruner explicitly acknowledged conflicts and contradictions in cultures in his contention that educational aims are complex, entailing a set of antinomies. These antinomies bring to center stage the multiple orientations of individual and group, the internal and external aspects of thought, and the local or more general criteria for judging ideas and meanings. One antinomy revolves around the functions of education, on the one hand, to enable individuals to attain their fullest potential (individual realization) and, on the other, to reproduce culture by furthering its economic, political, and other ends. A second set of contradictions revolve around learning that is inside the head or intrapsychic and learning that is situated in and enhanced by the culture. The third antinomy pertains to whether ways of thinking are judged by local knowledge, standards, and functions or by more general, universalistic standards of knowledge and morality.

Unlike some adherents to cultural psychology, Bruner (1996) did not discount individual goals or development in favor of social, cultural, or community goals. He did not discount the intrapsychic quality of thought in favor of collective learning and representations. And he did not discount universalistic standards or ways of thinking in favor of local knowledge and truths. Rather, recognizing the multiplicity of types of functioning, goals and ways of thinking and judging, Bruner saw those as constituting legitimate aims of education posing baffling and complex conflicts. He cautioned against being monopolistically cultural, calling instead for analyses of "the interaction of biological, evolutionary, individual psychological, and cultural insights in helping us grasp the nature of human mental functioning" (p. 161). Combining the biological, individual, social, and cultural in meaningful ways would require accounting for the complex relationships of individuals and culture.

Elements of such an approach were evident in Piaget's (1950/1995) efforts to include cognition and development in sociological explanations. Piaget distinguished between diachronic and synchronic aspects of social interaction. The diachronic refers to analyses of historical influences on society and the dependence of one state on previous ones (traditions and continuity). The synchronic refers to analyses of interactions at a given moment in time, which may be integrated into new functions and can serve to alter historically based meanings. Piaget argued in favor of analyses of the diachronic and synchronic (e.g., as in Marx), rather than those emphasizing one or the other (as in Durkheim's emphasis on the diachronic and Pareto's on the synchronic).[2]

Recent theoretical and empirical works of several anthropologists and psychologists also seriously treat differentiations and heterogeneity in social orientations and attempt to account for tensions, conflicts, and transformations stimulated from within cultures (Abu-Lughod, 1991, 1993; Ap-

---

[2]It is sometimes thought that in his formulation of children's moral development Piaget (1932) regarded judgments based on individuality and independence to constitute a developmentally advanced state. Although Piaget labeled his proposed developmental progression as a shift from heteronomy to autonomy, he meant by autonomy that moral judgments entailing mutual respect, cooperation, and justice are elaborated with the participation of the individual (Piaget, 1960/1995). Furthermore, Piaget proposed that the levels of the development of moral judgments entailed a shift from egocentrism (confusing one's point of view with that of others) to sociocentrism (decentration of self and cooperation among people). With regard to sociological analyses, however, Piaget (1950/1995) put forth a different conception of sociocentricism. He proposed that sociocentricism is linked to ideologies, which entail a centering on the group or collectivity. Parallel with the need in individual development for a shift from egocentrism to a differentiated state, there is need, in societies, for a shift from sociocentricism to a decentered state: "if the development of rational operations presupposes cooperation among individuals, which liberates them from their initial intellectual egocentrism, the sociocentric collective representations are the social equivalent of individual egocentric representations" (Piaget, 1950/1995, p. 74).

padurai, 1988; Edelstein, 1995; Greenfield, 1995; Saxe, 1995; Spiro, 1993; Strauss, 1992). In anthropology, a recognition that the concept of culture can serve as a construct imposing order and uniformity where it does not exist has led some to seek new definitions. Strauss (1992) noted that anthropologists are "beginning to stress conflict, contradiction, and change in cultural under-standings" (p. 1). This is consistent with Abu-Lughod's (1991) view:

> By focusing closely on particular individuals and their changing relationships, one would necessarily subvert the most problematic connotations of culture: homogeneity, coherence, and timelessness. Individuals are confronted with choices, struggle with others, make conflicting statements, argue about points of view on the same events, undergo ups and downs in various relationships and changes in their circumstances and desires, face new pressures, and fail to predict what will happen to them or those around them. (p. 154)

SOURCES OF VARIATION

In one sense, at least, most would acknowledge that a society can include heterogeneity in perspectives and social conflicts. Insofar as different cul-tural groups (or sometimes referred to as subcultures) have contact with each other or inhabit the same social spheres (this is especially true in industrial, modern, Western societies), there may be differences in their personal, social, and moral orientations. From the perspective of culture as shared collective representations, there are a variety of ways that such differences would be said to be played out (e.g., one group dominating and assimilating the other; conflicts eventually resolved through mutual accom-modations and the emergence of new representations; more or less peaceful coexistence in the context of differences). However, this is not the only or main type of heterogeneity in social orientations and perspectives proposed here. Rather, it is that varieties of orientations and perspectives exist in social relationships and collectivities that do not necessarily stem from distinctly different cultural groups in contact with each other. Furthermore, the task is not simply to distinguish between the individual and the social or the private and public spheres. Although such distinctions are important, more to the point for the present purposes is that there are, in cultures, a variety of public spheres, social perspectives, and social realities. One salient reason for the multiplicity of perspectives is that in most societies, different people and groups of people have greater or lesser power, influence, and entitlements. Insofar as there are relationships of inequality, especially ones of dominance and subordination, people do not always share the same perspective.

As a means of illustrating the ways multiple perspectives may exist in cultures, consider examples of two areas of investigation based on propositions of fundamental cultural differences in personal, social, and moral orientations. In the first case, it has been proposed that there are gender differences in concepts of self and morality (e.g., in Gilligan's, 1982, distinction between moralities of care and justice), with the implicit or explicit (e.g., Haste & Baddeley, 1991; Tannen, 1990) claim that the world views of women and men constitute different cultures. In that context, it has been maintained that one consequence of that cultural divide is great difficulty in communications between women and men (Tannen, 1990). It is informative, however, that in another set of proposed cultural distinctions concepts of self and morality in non-Western cultures are described in terms closely resembling descriptions of the orientations of females, whereas Western cultural orientations are described in terms closely resembling the orientations of males (e.g., Markus & Kitayama, 1991; Miller & Bersoff, 1995; Shweder & Bourne, 1982; Triandis, 1990). Briefly, it has been proposed that in non-Western cultures there is an unbounded or sociocentric concept of self and others based on the salience of interpersonal connections and moral understandings of interdependence and duties (this description is similar to the description by Gilligan and others of a morality of care supposedly aligned with females). By contrast, in Western cultures there is a bounded or egocentric concept of self and others based on the salience of the independence of self-contained individuals and moral understandings of personal freedoms and rights (this is similar to the description of a morality of justice aligned with males).

These two sets of propositions cannot be readily integrated with each other. The ways the orientations of Western cultures are described by some are discrepant with the ways others describe the orientations of females in those very same cultures. In turn, the descriptions of orientations in non-Western cultures are discrepant with descriptions of the orientations of males (presumably also in non-Western cultures). This problem has been recognized by Miller and Bersoff (1995), who themselves drew contrasts between Western (e.g., the United States) and non-Western (e.g., India) cultures along the dimensions of cultural meanings of independence or individualism and interdependence or interpersonal obligations. Miller and Bersoff found the proposed gender difference implausible because it would lead to the conclusion that concepts of self and morality of individuals of the same gender from different cultures are more alike than those of males and females from the same culture. They put the matter as follows: Can it be that the concepts of self and morality of a secular American woman are more or less like those of a traditional Hindu Indian woman, whereas the concepts of the Hindu Indian woman differ from those of a traditional Hindu Indian man?

From the perspective of general orientations (e.g., individualism versus collectivism), it makes sense to question the types of gender distinctions that have been proposed because they fail to account for the influence of the different cultural meanings. Hindu Indian women and men would act and judge in similar ways, and differently from American women and men. There is reason, however, to question the dichotomy between the two types of orientations—whether they are applied to gender or cultures—because of the multiple roles and perspectives of women and men in social systems. In most cultures, women and men do not hold equal status nor necessarily engage in the same activities. In Western cultures men generally have greater power and influence than women, women have fewer opportunities for paid work; and in the family, the interests of men are often given priority over those of women (Blood & Wolfe, 1960; Blumstein & Schwartz, 1983; Hochschild, 1989; Okin, 1989, 1996; Turiel, 1996). In many hierarchically organized non-Western cultures, there are clearly delineated distinctions between the genders in power, influence, and status so that women are in subordinate positions and men in positions of dominance (Bumiller, 1990; Goodwin, 1994; Turiel & Wainryb, 1994; Wainryb & Turiel, 1994). As a consequence of social hierarchy, in a given society women's perspectives would differ from those of men. Men have entitlements, prerogatives, areas of power and influence, and spheres of activities that are not shared by women. The perspective of a person in a subordinate position relative to those in dominant positions and to the dominant culture differs from that of a person in a dominant position. Accordingly, there is a sense in which women from different cultures (the American secular woman and the Hindu Indian woman) may share perspectives based on their roles in the hierarchy, status held, and restrictions on freedoms and activities. Similarly, men from different cultures may share perspectives in roles, entitlements, and responsibilities based on the extent to which they are in dominant positions relative to women.

This is not the whole story, however. For at least two reasons, it cannot simply be said that females differ from males in their personal, social, and moral concepts (i.e., that males and females constitute distinct cultures). One reason is that females and males do share a great deal, and there are cultural or societal differences impacting on both genders. Indeed, it cannot be entirely accurate to say that the worlds of women and men constitute different cultures because they share so many experiences and are often in intimate relationships. A second reason is that status of females and males relative to each other intersects with status on the dimension of social class or caste. Whereas in a patriarchal society females may clearly be in a subordinate position relative to men in their family or social class, they may also hold higher status relative to men of lower social classes or social castes. The same would hold for Western cultures that may not be appropriately classified as patriarchal. As an example, an upper-middle-class American woman may hold a perspective of more or less subordination, in the terms just discussed, to upper-middle class men. In significant respects, the American upper-middle-class woman may be in a dominant position (e.g., with greater status, power, and influence) relative to a working class man.

Charting out these intersecting positions does not, in itself, demonstrate that people do form multiple judgments and perspectives—although it is certainly suggestive. It may be that there are cultural or collective meanings, which actually are shared among people in different roles, of different status and of varying entitlements. This would mean that cultural representations are sufficiently powerful and/or that humans are sufficiently predisposed to be part of the collectivity that they do not attend to differences (only to commonalities) nor to their interests or social and economic consequences to self and others. These presumptions are at least implicit in the culturalism of those who draw general contrasts between cultures and who believe those general contrasts produce cultural variations in social practices and taboos. The presumption has been that little variation exists in society, except insofar as it may be comprised of different cultural groups. A commonality in these positions is that wholism (integrated cultural patterns, as manifested in differences like individualism and collectivism) is linked to accepted standards and taboos. As a consequence, little attention has been given to differences in roles, status, and entitlements (Appadurai, 1988).

Alternatively, the intersection of positions and perspectives in a culture can include a complex set of similarities and differences based on place in the hierarchy, the nature of social relationships, and concepts or meanings shared differentially at a broader cultural level and at local levels (which can result in contradictions and inconsistencies). In a society, therefore, people are at once part of the public or dominant culture and apart from it. People are identified with a particular conception of the culture, but at the same time identify with counter-elements of that conception of the culture (including engagement in activities aimed at subverting certain cultural practices). If this were so, it would mean that individuals' development is not solely influenced by collective representations, and that understandings of reality are not only based on sharing a worldview. In addition, individuals would form personal spheres, with concepts of individual entitlements and goals; social spheres, with understandings of different systems of social relationships and interactions; moral spheres, with understandings of how social relationships and social systems ought to be; and abilities to reflect on self, others, and groups, with the potential for opposition to existing frameworks.

CULTURAL PRACTICES: MORE THAN WHAT THEY SEEM

There is evidence from anthropological and psychological research for these propositions. One source of evidence comes from researchers who have been careful to distinguish between public cultural conceptions or ideologies and individuals' conceptions and actions. A comprehensive summary of research serving to question the assumption that cultural conceptions of the self or persons are isomorphic with individual conceptions has been provided by Spiro (1993), who reviewed research conducted in Nepal, Japan, India, and Burma. As an example, in the context of a public Japanese ideology of self as unbounded and interconnected with the group, it has been shown that Northern Japanese villagers are very much concerned with and motivated by self-interest and self-oriented goals (e.g., self-esteem, pride, and power). Similarly, studies of Burmese villagers showed that they held strong beliefs in an ego or a soul. This was so in spite of the central doctrine of Anatta in Theravada Buddhism that there is no ego, soul, or transcendental self. According to Spiro, Burmese villagers hold the concepts at odds with Anatta because they experience a subjective sense of self and because of Buddhist beliefs in reincarnation. Because the quality of a person's acts in the present existence determine the nature of future existences, the villagers reason that one need only be concerned with the quality of one's acts if there is a self (an ego or soul) with continuity to future existences (for more examples see Spiro, 1993).

Beyond discrepancies between cultural conceptions or public ideologies and individual conceptions, researchers who have not restricted their investigations to the judgments and perspectives of those in dominant positions have provided evidence that individuals, even in traditional cultures, do take multiple, and sometimes critical, perspectives on cultural practices. Before considering that research, however, it would be useful to convey the spirit of tension and subversion as it is reflected in recollections by the sociologist Mernissi (1994) of her life as young girl in a harem in Fez, Morocco, during the 1940s. In *Dreams of Trespass*, Mernissi recounted the daily activities of children and women in the harem, their ambitions, discontents, fantasies, and transgressions.

Women's discontents were with many of the cultural practices bearing on male and female relationships, including keeping women behind the walls of the harem, polygamy, and wearing of the veil. Women complained that they were kept in harems so they would remain dependent, and that men believed that by restricting their activities women would not improve their intelligence ("to put our brains to sleep is behind the locks and the walls," Mernissi, 1994, p. 187). Polygamy and the use of the veil were also topics of much conversation; those practices were considered unfair and ways of stigmatizing and denying women their rights (see also Goodwin, 1994). Winds of change were anticipated (certainly, hoped for) by the women, with aspirations for different lives for their daughters. Mothers' hopes for their daughters included greater happiness, freedom, independence, and education.

Complaints were also voiced about the unfairness of traditions and rules. Often, traditions were felt as suffocating ("This tradition is choking me,"

Mernissi's [1994, p. 78] mother told her). Many rules were regarded as designed to deny rights, impose inequality, and place greater burdens on women than men. Referring to ubiquitous implicit rules and behavioral codes (qa'ida), one woman lamented that, "unfortunately, most of the time the qa'ida is against women" (p. 62). And women do not simply accept those rules. Mernissi perceived that "women dreamed of trespassing all the time. The world beyond the gate was their obsession" (pp. 1–2). Nor did they dutifully obey the rules imposed on them. One incident recounted by Mernissi, although it is with regard to a relatively inconsequential activity, provides a rich account of the subversive, hidden activities in the women's daily lives, as well as the mixed messages that may be conveyed to children:

> The men were the only ones in the house supposed to have access to a huge cabinet radio which they kept in the right corner of their salon, with the cabinet doors locked when the radio was not in use. . . . Father was sure that he and Uncle had the only two keys to the radio. However, curiously enough, the women managed to listen to Cairo Radio regularly, when the men were out. Chama and Mother often would be dancing away to its tunes, singing along with the Lebanese princess Asmahan "Ahwa" (I am in love), with no men in sight. And I remember quite clearly the first time the grownups used the word Khain (traitors) to describe Samir and myself; when we told father, who had asked us what we had done while he was away, that we had listened to Radio Cairo. Our answer indicated that there was an unlawful key going around. More specifically, it indicated that the women had stolen the key and made a copy of it. "If they made a copy of the radio key, soon they will make one to open the gate," growled Father. A huge dispute ensued, with the women being interviewed in the men's salon one at a time. But after two days of inquiry, it turned out the key must have fallen from the sky. No one knew where it had come from.
>
> Even so, following the inquiry, the women took their revenge on us children. They said that we were traitors, and ought to be excluded from their games. That was a horrifying prospect, so we defended ourselves by explaining that all we had done was tell the truth. Mother retorted by saying that some things were true, indeed, but you still could not say them: you had to keep them secret. And then she added that what you say and what you keep secret has nothing to do with truth and lies. (pp. 7–8)

Mernissi's account illustrates that people who are identified with their culture nevertheless find ways to counteract practices they consider unduly restrictive of their freedoms. Not only did the women engage in social transgressions, but they did not react with remorse when caught in the act. Mernissi's story also illustrates the ways children receive mixed messages about cultural practices, social relationships, and the structure of power. According to Mernissi's account, in addition to their covert activities the women of the harem understood overt symbolism. Mernissi's mother believed that preventing women from chewing gum was part of a crusade to deny women's rights, and instructed her daughter that "a woman who chews gum is in fact making a revolutionary gesture. Not because she chews gum per se, but because gum chewing is not prescribed by the code" (p. 187).

Like Mernissi's account, Abu-Lughod's (1991, 1993) anthropological investigations of the thoughts and actions of Bedouin women in Egypt provided a window into less public thoughts and into conflicts, tensions, struggles, and the interplay of opposing orientations. Referring to one specific example, Abu-Lughod (1991) concluded that "it becomes difficult to think that the term 'Bedouin culture' makes sense when one tries to piece together and convey what life is like for one old Bedouin matriarch" (p. 154). The picture that emerges of life for the Bedouin matriarch, and for the other Bedouin women of varying ages, is a combination of fulfilling role expectations or prescribed duties in line with public expectations and efforts at subverting those expectations and asserting their own will, desires, and judgments that may not be in accord with social expectations or with the judgments of those in dominant positions.

Abu-Lughod (1993) documented that the Bedouin women often resist cultural practices like arranged marriages and polygamy. The Bedouin matriarch, referred to by Abu-Lughod, on three separate occasions had prevented marriages arranged by her father by screaming, crying, refusing to eat for a number of days, and running away to her uncle's house (it was her uncle's wife, and not her uncle, who gave her refuge). Each time, these strategies akin to civil disobedience wore down her father's resolve with regard to the chosen marriage for his daughter. Another strategy used by young women who were in love with someone else but nevertheless were forced into an arranged marriage was to provoke their husbands to divorce them. When later married and widowed, the matriarch objected to a marriage her sons arranged for one of her daughters. She also castigated her sons for taking more than one wife. She put her disapproval of polygamy into action by attempting to discourage the women from marrying her son or by trying to frighten off the parents of the women (sometimes with success, sometimes not). Furthermore, her daughters-in-law often solicited her advice and aid in conflicts with their husbands. She often supported her daughters-in-law, believing that her sons were treating them unfairly.

With regard to polygamy, another young Bedouin woman put it as follows:

> And the business of marrying more than one wife—I wish they'd change their views on this. It is the biggest sin. The Prophet—it is not forbidden but the Prophet said only if you can treat them fairly. But a man can't, it can't be done. Even if he has money, he can't. As a person, in his thoughts and his actions, he can't be fair. He'll like one more than another. (Abu-Lughod, 1993, p. 238)

Moreover, the women complain more generally about men treating women unfairly and acting on their own needs without attending to those of women. The same young woman complained that Bedouin men "make women work hard and don't pay attention to them. Even if the woman is old, the man won't lift a finger to help, not even to pick up a crying baby" (p. 239). However, young and old Bedouin women also expressed their resistance to these practices when they conveyed to the anthropologist the meaning of an old song they were accustomed to singing: "A woman can't be governed—anyone who tries to guard her will just get tired. Whatever a woman wants to she can do. She's smart and she can think" (p. 78).

Abu-Lughod portrayed the Bedouin women as both identified with the culture and its practices and as forming allegiances to subvert that which they disapprove in the ways women are restricted and treated by men. The strategies women develop to obtain their goals are not solely with regard to arranged marriages. The strategies are also directed toward many aspects of daily life such as leisure activities and alleviating the burdens imposed on them. Females also develop strategies to circumvent the restrictions males place on females' education. Some women believe that men now place more restrictions on women than had been the case in the past. As put by one of the women, "Yes, that's how things were, may God have mercy on past generations. They weren't like this new generation . . . the men now are awful" (Abu-Lughod, 1993, p. 77). This type of nostalgia for a past that may or may not have existed is reminiscent of views of the past and present in *fin-de-siècle* France, the United States of the 1920s, and the United States of the 1990s.

LOCATING THE LOCAL AND THE CONTEXTUAL

The types of analyses of traditional cultures provided by Abu-Lughod (1993) and Spiro (1993), as well as Mernissi's (1994) account of life in a harem, shed a different light on cultural practices. They are not the straightforward, consistent, and easily identifiable ways of doing things representative of a people's worldview. It has been customary to distinguish cultures through contrasting cultural practices. Variations in practices are often taken as self-evident and lists are drawn to illustrate cultural differences; these often include differences, writ large by culture, in attitudes toward taking life, sexuality, marriage, divorce, romantic love, abortion, religion, atheism, and much more (for an earlier version, see Benedict, 1934, and for a later version, see Shweder, 1994). Thus, it may be said that cultures differ by attitudes toward, as examples, arranged marriages or polygamy. In one culture arranged marriages may be acceptable, whereas in another they are seen as abhorrent. People in one culture may regard polygamy as fair and right whereas in another culture it is seen as morally unacceptable. It must be asked, however, where is there room in these types of characterizations of cultural practices for the emotions, thoughts, and strategies of the Bedouin woman who works to preserve her interests and goals by breaking down the resolve of her father to arrange that marriage, and who later labors to foil her son's attempts to marry more than one time? Similarly, where is there room for explanation of the conspiracies of the women in the harem in using a purloined key to the radio cabinet, in refusing to admit they had it—no less how they got it, and in insisting that children should know to act as coconspirators, by not revealing truths, for more worthy ends?

Differences between cultures do need to be taken into account. Clearly, there are differences in cultural practices bearing on the lives of Bedouin women in Egypt or the women of the harem in Morocco and middle-class American women. Indeed, in many ways how and what a woman thinks about harem life is not the same as how and what a woman thinks about her life as a practicing lawyer in a large Wall Street firm. Those differences, however, should not serve to obscure the possible commonalities across cultures nor the variation in cultures—variations that can serve as points of contact between cultures. As stressed by Bruner (1996), in addition to respecting local experiences, it is necessary to account for universal standards. Some of the commonalities across cultures may include the judgments of people in dominant or subordinate positions (e.g., between Bedouin and American men, and perhaps in some respects between a Bedouin man and an upper-middle-class American woman), the nature of conflicts among people in those different positions, efforts to transform cultural practices by the new generation (e.g., young women in Morocco, youth of *fin-de-siècle* France and the 20th century United States), and concerns with fairness, rights, and human welfare.

Yet, as shown by the examples of the activities of the Moroccan and Bedouin women, cultural practices also can be nebulous, with many sides and connotations. Embedded in cultural practices are multiple messages (e.g., bearing differently on people in different social positions) that can be interpreted in varying ways (e.g., by people in the different social positions). Cultural practices are also carried out in multiple ways. The multiple interpretations and actions around cultural practices imply that knowledge can be local and contextualized. The ideas of local knowledge and contextualism are among the mainstays of culturalism (Geertz, 1983; Shweder, 1990), where these ideas are taken to mean that knowledge is local to cultures (and not generalized beyond the culture) and that judgments or actions are dependent on the cultural context (e.g., that they will vary by culture). The problem in such formulations is that the local is not local enough and the contextual is not sufficiently contextual. People attend to knowledge that is more local than the general culture, and their thinking is flexible enough so that they adjust and vary their behavior in accord with contexts more narrow than a general cultural context.

Thought and knowledge can be at a more local level than the general cultural context in the sense that individuals or groups act in ways that are contrary to the public practices or taboos or are in conflict with those in positions of dominance. Thought can also be local insofar as individuals reinterpret public ideologies or make judgments at variance with them. As Spiro (1993) documented, for example, the beliefs of Burmese villagers in an ego or soul, based on their direct experiences, are at variance with the public doctrines of Anatta (the denial of self or soul) in Theravada Buddhism (Spiro provided several additional examples of such discrepancies). Whereas the local concepts of individual villagers are at variance with public or official pronouncements, those concepts may very well be points of contact with individuals in other cultures whose direct experiences also lead them to concepts of an ego or transcendental self. Variations in context, at levels different from cultural context, also result in variations in people's judgments or actions. Naturalistic and experimental studies in Western cultures have demonstrated that situational circumstances have large effects on whether individuals obey authority, conform to the group, are influenced socially, and endorse personal freedoms and rights (for reviews see Ross & Nisbett, 1991; Turiel, 1998; Turiel & Wainryb, 1994). Such variations are not in accord with the idea that cultures and individuals would show consistent patterns (Benedict, 1934). The particular variations observed are not in accord with the pattern of individualism expected in Western cultures because people's actions or judgments shift by situation as to whether they defy or obey authority, go against or conform to the group, or endorse or reject personal freedoms and rights.

Locating context at the cultural level is too broad to account for the observed lack of consistency from situation to situation with regard to these types of social judgments and behaviors. An explanation of contextual variations, however, requires more than locating them at a level of analysis (e.g., universal, or cultural, or in cultures). Although judgments and actions do have features that generalize across cultures, vary by culture, and vary in a culture, it is also the case that, if the variety of judgments individuals make are taken into account, embedded in particular events are a variety of contexts. This is to say that the intersection of individuals' heterogeneous judgments and the multiple features of an event or situation can constitute multiple contexts in an event or situation. This type of contextual variation is evident particularly in relationships between people of differing status or position in social hierarchies, where there are differences not only in the perspectives of people in the different positions but also in perspectives of an individual on the situation.

Research into how people in a traditional culture make judgments about social relationships has revealed that various types of judgments are applied to different facets of interactions of people holding differing status. Studies have been conducted among Druze Arab children, adolescents, and adults who live in segregated villages in Northern Israel (Turiel & Wainryb, 1995; Wainryb & Turiel, 1994). The Druze can be classified as a traditional culture, with social practices that restrict the activities of women in many ways. The restrictions apply, among other activities, to dress, bodily ornaments, sexuality, work, education, and leisure activities (e.g., dancing, going to places of entertainment or beaches). In addition, marriages are arranged and divorce, which is discouraged, is mainly in the control of husbands. The community is arranged around a patrilineal and patriarchal family structure that shapes interactions among men, women, and children. Roles are clearly demarcated, with men in dominant positions and women in subordinate positions. The culture is of the kind that has been identified as collectivistic, with a predominance of an interdependent concept of persons (Markus & Kitayama, 1991; Triandis, 1990).

One set of studies (Wainryb & Turiel, 1994) examined how the Druze make judgments about family decision making, in the context of conflicts or disagreements between people in dominant and subordinate positions. The participants in these studies, who were male and female adolescents and adults, were presented with a number of situations describing disagreements between a husband and wife, or father and daughter, or father and son. In one set of situations, the person in a subordinate position, as culturally defined (i.e., wife, daughter, or son), has chosen an activity to which the person in a dominant position (i.e., father or husband) objects. In another set of situations, the person in the dominant position chose an activity objected to by the person in a subordinate position. These situations depicted several types of activity choices relevant to cultural practices including educational and occupational choices, household chores, friendships, and leisure activities.

Several assessments were made about the situations in which one person has objections to what the other wants to do. These included judgments as to who should make the decision, their reasons for how the decisions should be made, and how they conceptualized the relationships. One unsurprising finding for a patriarchical culture was that both males and females thought that men should have decision-making power and discretion. They judged that wives or daughters should not engage in activities to which a husband or father objects, and, nonreciprocally, that a husband or father should do what he wants and not go along with the objections of a wife or daughter. However, the context of the father-daughter relationship (or husband and wife) differs, for them, from the context of the father-son relationship. Greater reciprocity was evident in judgments about the relationship of a father and son because it was generally thought that a son should not acquiesce to his father's objections, and that a father should not acquiesce to a son's objections.

In one sense, the judgments that men should have decision-making power and discretion over women's activities can be seen to reflect straightforward cultural practices revolving around social hierarchy, as well as a cultural ideology regarding duties, social roles, and interdependence in the hierarchy. Those cultural practices are not so straightforward, however, as embedded in them is a more complex set of varying social concepts, multiple agendas and goals, and undercurrents. In particular, the cultural practices include concepts of duties, role obligations, interdependence, along with concepts of personal autonomy, independence, and entitlements. There are different facets to social relationships, constituting varying contexts for the applications of personal, social, and moral judgments. As shown by the findings regarding judgments about decision making between fathers and sons, we cannot solely speak of one way that relationships are conceptualized (i.e., those relationships are judged in ways differing from male-female relationships).

It is also the case that a particular relationship, say between husband and wife, does not constitute a unitary context—at least when the relationship is unequal and nonreciprocal. This is because hierarchical status and perceived positions of power, influence, and competence result in varying conceptions of persons and the nature of the relationship. In a relationship the context of a person in a dominant position attempting to direct the actions of a person in a subordinate position differs from the context of a person in a subordinate position attempting to direct the actions of a person in a dominant position. Those varying contexts produced, among the Druze, different judgments about persons, morality, and pragmatics. Druze males and females reasoned that a wife or daughter should adhere to the husband's or father's wishes on the basis of fulfilling duties and role responsibilities. They reasoned in terms of the need to maintain interdependence in social relationships. By contrast, with regard to the judgment that a wife or daughter should not interfere with the man's decisions, they emphasized personal autonomy, the need for independent decisions, and the entitlements of individuals. Of course, autonomy, independence, and entitlements were all accorded to the persons in dominant positions (this "individualistic" orientation was also evident in judgments about father-son relationships). A difference in contexts also emerged in the means of discourse about the nature of relationships. The relationships between husband and wife or father and daughter were couched in terms of status, roles, and interdependence in one context (a male objecting to the chosen activity of a female), whereas they were couched in terms of independence, individual choice, and autonomy in the other context (female objecting to the activity of the male).

The heterogeneity of judgments does not stop there. In keeping with the women of the Moroccan harem and the Bedouin women, Druze female adolescents and women are attuned to the power of males. They were quite concerned with pragmatics, believing that a wife should acquiesce with her husband's directives also because of the serious consequences that could ensue if she did not. Among the possible consequences mentioned were abandonment and divorce. These types of pragmatic considerations, which were not part of males' judgments about the conflicts, reflect an awareness on the part of females of both the power accorded to men and of their own vulnerability. They perceive that the cultural practices are not designed to always take care of them. In turn, females, it was found in the studies with the Druze, judge as unfair those cultural practices that allow men to dictate the activities of women and that place women in such vulnerable positions.

The vulnerability of females in patriarchical societies is not solely in the perceptions of the female participants in these studies. Journalistic accounts of the perspectives of women in several Islamic countries (Goodwin, 1994) and India (Bumiller, 1990), for instance, have documented that women are subject to many hardships and inequalities. The hardships range from malnutrition (for young girls when scarce food is given to boys instead), to dowry or bride burnings, to the easy availability of divorce to men, and custody laws favoring men. In a way that captures the roles and vulnerabilities of women and the autonomy accorded to men, an Egyptian woman who is the editor of a woman's magazine told Goodwin that:

> Women are really crushed and maltreated in this society. Men realize that religion gives them a license; even my six-year-old son knows that because he is male he is automatically powerful. The man is the one who can desert or divorce the wife at whim; the man is the one who can do as he pleases, not the woman. It is men who can take secret wives without informing the first wife ... Even with my husband I fear polygamy; it puts all women in jeopardy. Generations of mothers have taught their daughters to give their husbands everything he wants, never confront him, even if they know he is fooling around.
>
> The women I talk to or who write to us tell me that married men care only about their needs. The wife must never express her needs. (p. 337)

We see here points of difference and connection between cultures. Most men in Western cultures do not take secret wives (and legally or by practice cannot take more than one wife), and women do not fear polygamy. However, the Egyptian woman's view that men care only about their needs would indicate that concepts of personal autonomy and entitlements are also part of non-Western cultures. Moreover, in Western cultures there are also struggles over the needs and welfare of husbands and wives. More often than not, men are accorded greater benefits, entitlements, and power than women (Cowan & Cowan, 1992; Hochschild, 1989; Okin, 1989, 1996). In these regards, there are commonalities in perspectives among women from different cultures and among men from different cultures. It may well be that in Western cultures, too, young boys come to believe that because they are male they are more powerful and influential than females. Correspondingly, in each type of culture some young boys and girls may come to believe that because they are part of the higher social classes or castes they are more powerful and influential than people of lower social classes or castes.

CONCLUSIONS

Appadurai (1988) argued that anthropologists have put peoples in places and thereby confine them not only geographically but also mentally. He maintained that even groups of people who have had minimal contact with other peoples "have constituted very complex 'internal' mosaics of trade, marriage, conquest, and linguistic exchange, which suggests that no one grouping among them was ever truly incarcerated in a specific place and confined by a specific mode of thought" (p. 39). It is generally acknowledged that when peoples of different cultures are in contact with each other, differences between them in judgments or social orientations can result in the possibility of conflicts between groups and the potential for changes in cultural patterns. Appadurai's observations suggest that the modes of thought of peoples are not restricted to place or unitary, and that conflict and change can stem from internal dynamics. Places, he argued, should not be "encapsulated by single diacritics (or essences) in order for them to be compared with other places, but would permit several configurations of resemblance and contrast" (p. 46).

Internal dynamics apply to cultures and to individuals. The focus of this chapter has been on how social hierarchy (which is not restricted to any one type of culture), with status, roles, and positions of dominance and subordination, produces heterogeneity of thought and social conflicts. Different perspectives and conflicts do occur among people in cultures. However, internal dynamics and conflicts also occur in individuals. Individuals are not confined to one pattern of thought, but rather develop multiple domains of social reasoning through their direct experiences (Spiro, 1993; Turiel, 1998). These domains include, as we have seen, concepts of persons as independent agents with autonomy and entitlements. They also develop judgments of interdependence in social organizations. Judgments about interdependence include moral concerns with welfare and justice. The heterogeneity of the thinking of individuals is in the context of their multiple perspectives and goals in social hierarchies. That is, individuals may be simultaneously in relative positions of dominance and subordination, and may be simultaneously in harmony and conflict with others or with culture. Therefore, individuals' social judgments are not restricted to collective representations. In turn, collective representations are not restricted to one kind or set of culturally identifiable ideologies or symbols; different groups (e.g., the women of the harem or the Bedouin women) form collective representations along with other collective representations.

There are many sources of innovation and social transformation in cultures, given the heterogeneity of thought, collective representations, and social perspectives. It may be these variations that result in complaints about the moral state of society, aspirations for something different for the new generation, and efforts to transform cultural practices. If so, social conflicts and tensions would not be associated solely with modern, Western multicultural societies. Cultures do not divide into those that are harmonious and those that are multifaceted and conflicted. Social harmony and social conflict are part of social life.

REFERENCES

Abu-Lughod, L. (1991). Writing against culture. In R. E. Fox (Ed.), *Recapturing anthropology: Working in the present* (pp. 137–162). Santa Fe, NM: School of American Research Press.

Abu-Lughod, L. (1993). *Writing women's worlds: Bedouin stories*. Berkeley: University of California Press.

Appadurai, A. (1988). Putting hierarchy in its place. *Cultural Anthropology, 3,* 36–49.

Bellah, R. N., Madsen, R., Sullivan, W. M., Swidler, A., & Tipton, S. M. (1985). *Habits of the heart: Individualism and commitment in American life*. New York: Harper & Row.

Benedict, R. (1934). *Patterns of culture*. Boston: Houghton Mifflin.

Bennett, W. J. (1992). *The de-valuing of America: The fight for our culture and our children*. New York: Simon & Schuster.

Bennett, W. J., & Delattre, E. J. (1978). Moral education in the schools. *The Public Interest, 50,* 81–99.

Blood, R. O., & Wolfe, D. M. (1960). *Husbands and wives: The dynamics of married living*. Glencoe, IL: The Free Press.

Bloom, A. (1987). *The closing of the American mind: How higher education has failed democracy and impoverished the soul of today's students*. New York: Simon & Schuster.

Blumstein, P., & Schwartz, P. (1983). *American couples*. New York: Morrow.

Bruner, J. (1996). *The culture of education*. Cambridge, MA: Harvard University Press.

Bumiller, E. (1990). *May you be the mother of a hundred sons: A journey among the women of India*. New York: Fawcett Columbine.

Cowan, C. P., & Cowan, P. A. (1992). *When partners become parents: The big life changes for couples*. New York: Basic Books.

Edelstein, W. (1995, June). *Individual development in cultural context and the role of educational reform in reciprocal accommodation*. Paper presented at the Annual Symposium of the Jean Piaget Society, Berkeley, CA.

Etzioni, A. (1993). *The spirit of community: The reinvention of American society*. New York: Touchstone.

Fass, P. (1977). *The damned and the beautiful: American youth in the 1920s*. New York: Oxford University Press.

Geertz, C. (1983). *Local knowledge: Further essays in interpretive anthropology*. New York: Basic Books.

Gilligan, C. (1982). *In a different voice: Psychological theory and women's development.* Cambridge, MA: Harvard University Press.

Goodwin, J. (1994). *Price of honor: Muslim women lift the veil of silence on the Islamic world.* New York: Plume/Penguin.

Greenfield, P. (1995, June). *Phylogeny, cultural change, and human development.* Paper presented at the Annual Symposium of the Jean Piaget Society, Berkeley, CA.

Haste, H., & Baddeley, J. (1991). Moral theory and culture: The case of gender. In W. M. Kurtines & J. L. Gewirtz (Eds.), *Handbook of moral behavior and development* (pp. 222–249). Hillsdale, NJ: Lawrence Erlbaum Associates.

Hatch, E. (1983). *Culture and morality: The relativity of values in anthropology.* New York: Columbia University Press.

Himmelfarb, G. (1994). *The demoralization of society: From Victorian virtues to modern values.* New York: Vintage Books.

Hochschild, A. (1989). *The second shift.* New York: Avon Books.

Hogan, R. (1975). Theoretical egocentricism and the problem of compliance. *American Psychologist, 30,* 533–539.

Kirkpatrick, W. (1992). *Why Johnny can't tell right from wrong: Moral illiteracy and the case for character education.* New York: Simon & Schuster.

Markus, H. R., & Kitayama, S. (1991). Culture and the self: Implications for cognition, emotion, and motivation. *Psychological Review, 98,* 224–253.

Mernissi, F. (1994). *Dreams of trespass: Tales of a harem childhood.* Reading, MA: Addison-Wesley.

Miller, J. G., & Bersoff, D. M. (1995). Development in the context of everyday family relationships: Culture, interpersonal morality, and adaptation. In M. Killen & D. Hart (Eds.), *Morality in everyday life: Developmental perspectives* (pp. 259–282). Cambridge, England: Cambridge University Press.

Norris, K. (1996, March). *Lying in the age of innocence: The deceitful child in* fin-de-siècle *France.* Paper presented at the Society for French Historical Studies Annual Meeting, Boston.

Okin, S. M. (1989). *Justice, gender, and the family.* New York: Basic Books.

Okin, S. M. (1996). The gendered family and the development of a sense of justice. In E. S. Reed, E. Turiel, & T. B. Brown (Eds.), *Values and knowledge* (pp. 61–74). Hillsdale, NJ: Lawrence Erlbaum Associates.

Piaget, J. (1932). *The moral judgment of the child.* London: Routledge & Kegan Paul.

Piaget, J. (1950/1995). Explanation in sociology. In J. Piaget, *Sociological studies* (pp. 30–96). London: Routledge.

Piaget, J. (1960/1995). Problems of the social psychology of childhood. In J. Piaget, *Sociological studies* (pp. 287–318). London: Routledge.

Ross, L., & Nisbett, R. M. (1991). *The person and the situation: Perspectives on social psychology.* Philadelphia: Temple University Press.

Ryan, K. (1989). In defense of character education. In L. P. Nucci (Ed.), *Moral development and character education: A dialogue* (pp. 3–18). Berkeley, CA: McCutchan Publishing Corporation.

Sampson, E. E. (1977). Psychology and the American ideal. *Journal of Personality and Social Psychology, 35,* 767–782.

Saxe, G. (1995, June). *Toward a cultural psychology of cognitive development.* Paper presented at the Annual Symposium of the Jean Piaget Society, Berkeley, CA.

Shweder, R. A. (1990). Cultural psychology—What is it? In J. W. Stigler, R. A. Shweder, & G. Herdt (Eds.), *Cultural psychology: Essays on comparative human development* (pp. 1–43). Cambridge, England: Cambridge University Press.

Shweder, R. A. (1994). Are moral intuitions self-evident truths? *Criminal Justice Ethics, 13,* 24–31.

Shweder, R. A., & Bourne, E. J. (1982). Does the concept of person vary cross-culturally? In A. J. Marsella & G. M. White (Eds.), *Cultural conceptions of mental health and therapy* (pp. 97–137). Boston: Reidel.

Shweder, R. A., & Sullivan, M. A. (1993). Cultural psychology: Who needs it? *Annual Review of Psychology, 44,* 497–523.

Sommers, C. H. (1984). Ethics without virtue: Moral education in America. *American Scholar, 53,* 381–389.

Spiro, M. (1993). Is the Western conception of the self "peculiar" within the context of the world cultures? *Ethos, 21,* 107–153.

Strauss, C. (1992). Models and motives. In R. G. D'Andrade & C. Strauss (Eds.), *Human motives and cultural models* (pp. 1–20). Cambridge, England: Cambridge University Press.

Tannen, D. (1990). *You just don't understand: Women and men in conversation.* New York: Morrow.

Triandis, H. C. (1990). Cross-cultural studies of individualism and collectivism. In J. J. Berman (Ed.), *Nebraska Symposium on Motivation: 1989, Vol. 37, Cross-cultural perspectives* (pp. 41–133). Lincoln: University of Nebraska Press.

Turiel, E. (1996). Equality and hierarchy: Conflict in values. In E. S. Reed, E. Turiel, & T. Brown (Eds.), *Values and knowledge* (pp. 71–102). Hillsdale, NJ: Lawrence Erlbum Associates.

Turiel, E. (1998). The development of morality. In W. Damon (Ed.), *Handbook of child psychology, 5th Ed., Vol. 3: N. Eisenberg (Ed.), Social, emotional, and personality development* (pp. 863–932). New York: Wiley.

Turiel, E., & Wainryb, C. (1994). Social reasoning and the varieties of social experience in cultural contexts. In H. W. Reese (Ed.), *Advances in child development and behavior, Vol. 25* (pp. 289–326). New York: Academic Press.

Wainryb, C., & Turiel, E. (1994). Dominance, subordination, and concepts of personal entitlements in cultural contexts. *Child Development, 65,* 1701–1722.

Whitehead, B. D. (1993, April). Dan Quayle was right. *The Atlantic Monthly,* 47–84.

Wilson, J. Q. (1993). *The moral sense.* New York: Free Press.

Wynne, E. A. (1979). The declining character of American youth. *American Educator, 3,* 29–32.

Wynne, E. A. (1986). The great tradition in education: Transmitting moral values. *Educational Leadership, 43,* 4–9.

AUTHOR INDEX

SUBJECT INDEX

A

Accommodation, 10
Adaptation, 171, 174, 181, 182
  feeding tools for, 181, 182
Aggression, 194, 195
  see Conflict resolution
Amnesia
  function without recall, 68, 69
Animal communication, 145-167
  assumptions about, 150
  external validation, 148, 151
  see Ape language studies
Animal intentionality, 151-167
  see Intentionality
Ape language studies, 145-167
  behavior-reward, 150, 151, 156
  Bonobos, 158, 161-167
  conflict resolution, 207, 208
  branch dragging displays, 161-164
  comprehension, 156
  debates on, 149
  decoding syntax, 155, 157-159
  evolutionary continuity, 154
  field research, 160
  implicit assumptions, 151
  inference, 151,152, 159
  insider's knowledge, 148, 149
  intentional symbolic communi-
    cation, 150
  intentionality, 151-156, 158, 159,
    164, 165
  joint understanding, 157, 166
  language-like behavior, 154, 155,
    160
  path marking, 163

self-identity, 155
sense-making process, 155-160
shaping techniques, 157, 158
signing, 158
skeptics of, 149
successive approximations, 150,
  154
symbolic communication, 154,
  157, 161-167
theory of mind, 165
tool use, 151-154
verbal commands, 156
see Tool use
Apes
  adaptation to humans, 240-242
  avoidance behavior, 232
  cognition, 172, 177
  deception, 179
  empathy, 179
  evolution of culture, 225-242
  human enculturation and, 238-242
  imitation, 179
  lack of accumulative adaptabil-
    ity, 229
  role playing, 179
  raised by humans, 239-242
  self-consciousness, 179
  shame, 179
  signaling, 77
  social transmission of learning,
    229
Apprenticeship
  assessment, 187
Arithmetic ability
  see Prehistory and cognitive
    development